# PHYSICAL SECURITY:

## Practices and Technology

Charles Schnabolk

**BUTTERWORTHS**
Boston • London
Sydney • Wellington • Durban • Toronto

**Library of Congress Cataloging in Publication Data**
Schnabolk, Charles, 1931-
Physical security.
Includes bibliographical references and index.
1. Burglary protection. I. Title.
TH9705.S36   1983      658.4′73      82-14700
ISBN 0-409-95067-X

Published by Butterworth Publishers
10 Tower Office Park
Woburn, MA  01801

10  9  8  7  6  5  4  3  2  1

*Printed in the United States of America*

# About the Author

Charles Schnabolk is a nationally recognized expert in the field of security technology and training. He has been a consulting engineer since 1970 and was a director of a government surveillance research laboratory for ten years prior to entering his own practice. Among his unique assignments were security studies for such diverse buildings as the World Trade Center, the Newark School System, various museums, retail stores, banks, and commercial buildings. Some of the customized systems he helped develop are in use today at institutions such as The Library of Congress and the Baseball Hall of Fame. He has also introduced and taught security courses at Rutgers University and Jersey City State College as well as developed a program used by the New Jersey Department of Education for the training of school guards throughout the state. He is co-founder of the National Council for School Security Administrators and is Executive Director of The Institute for Security Design and Training. He has participated in various standard writing associations and has received research grants from the National Endowment for the Arts and Law Enforcement Assistance Administration. He is a graduate of Stevens Institute of Technology with a Masters degree from New York University and is a registered Professional Engineer. Mr. Schnabolk has lectured before many of the professional organizations involved in security and has written extensively for many professional and national journals.

# Contents

# Preface

The private security industry has developed into a major market controlling almost 10% of the GNP, and yet, it is often treated as the private domain of the alarm salesmen, the central station operator, and the ubiquitous manufacturer. It is an industry clouded in mystery and one that has grown without standards and with little public scrutiny. This book was written for the purpose of removing some of the mystery behind the technology, and the subjects selected cover every conceivable aspect of the private security profession and industry. The book is intended to be used as a text for college courses in physical security and as a reference for professionals. The style of writing and type of illustrations were selected so that the reader would understand the practices and peculiarities of security and the technology of the devices used in the industry. Hopefully, this book will clarify and expose some of the myths that have grown around an industry that has for, far too long, avoided public questioning.

I have attempted to write a useful introduction to physical security practices and technology. The bulk of the book describes the equipment commonly found within the security industry (i.e. electromechanical alarm devices, volumetric intrusion detection systems, locks, access controls, the polygraph), and discusses their applications. In Chapter 4 I make a special effort to apply security methods and the technology to a variety of specific situations usually addressed by the security industry. Bank buildings, public schools and retail stores all demand different approaches to security. In order to make proper use of the available security equipment, the professional needs to understand the environment in which it is to be used.

In Chapter 3 I digress, perhaps, from the main topic of the book to treat the subject of security and the law. The legal aspects affect the security professional's job at every level no matter what his or her position or title might be. This is an important subject long neglected in almost every security book, and I feel it is necessary that we now tackle this complex issue.

Throughout the text the reader will come across material contained in 'boxes.' I have included this device to focus attention on information, data, and examples which I find particularly interesting and which are closely related to the immediate discussion.

While the text was conceived and written by myself, much of the information and a great deal of the editing was provided by nationally recognized experts.

Robert McCrie, editor of Security Letter, was of particular help and provided most of the material and data on security standards, the various protective services, and salary levels in Chapters 2 and 5. David Steeno, Professor at Western Illinois University, developed all the legal concepts presented in Chapter 3, and Gene Fuss, Honeywell Corporation, edited and made suggestions on all the technical chapters, a contribution that was extremely important because of controversies that usually surround literature on the technical aspects of security. J. Kirk Barefoot of Cluett, Peabody prepared the section on the polygraph used in Chapter 2, and Richard Greer, the author of HISTORY OF ALARMS, was kind enough to write a condensation of his book specifically for inclusion in Chapter 1. Kevin D. Murray submitted the section on "Electronic Surveillance and Eavesdropping," and Bruce Sedley, President of Corkey Control Systems, allowed us to reprint the table illustrating the historic development of access control equipment. Pamela James, Managing Editor for SECURITY MANAGE-MENT magazine, gave up some of her free time to edit portions of my manuscript. And, of course, special mention must be made to John LoPresti who translated the technical transcript into easy to understand illustrations.

Lastly, Miss Marie Fosello, Dean at Jersey City State College, edited the entire 10 chapters, and her continued encouragement was the main reason this book was published.

Charles Schnabolk

# Chapter 1
# The Development of Private Security

According to statistics, approximately 2 percent of all the people now reading this book stole it from a bookstore, library, or a fellow classmate.

Crime has become a major business in the United States. Each year over 5 percent of the gross national product is stolen, and more than a million people are actively engaged in an occupation either detecting criminal activity or preventing crime.

Recent statistics from the U.S. Department of Labor indicate that the third fastest growing occupation in the United States today is security guard (public employees are first and hospital workers second). It is estimated that revenues from guard and investigative services should top $5.7 billion annually by 1985 — an increase of 113 percent over 1978's base-year income of $2.7 billion.[1]

The security industry currently employs one and a half times the number of employees as public law enforcement. These figures indicate that crime prevention, in economic terms, has become at least as critical a problem as public law enforcement.

Police are trained to discourage crime, but their primary function is to apprehend the criminal after the crime has been committed. Private security, however, attempts to protect person and property by preventing the crime in the first place.

The major difference between private security and public law enforcement is that the former is primarily concerned with specialized protective responsibilities in a specific location, whereas the latter has general duties in many varied locations. It should be understood that when the term "private" is attached to the word "security," it refers to the specific nature of the task and work location, and not to the status of the employer. "Private" security does not necessarily mean the performance of security tasks for a private as opposed to a public employer. The federal government is a major employer of private security personnel in public museums, hospitals, offices, military bases, parks, and many other specialized locations.

Historically, private security is older than public law enforcement by at least 1500 years. As is demonstrated in the next section, however, there were many periods in which the development of these parallel professions overlapped, as man strove to develop new forms of self-protection for himself and his possessions.

## SECURITY IN ANCIENT TIMES

Prostitution may be the world's oldest profession, but the history of the private security field is as long and as varied. From the day Neanderthal man rolled a rock in front of his cave to protect himself and his possessions from enemy attack, man began devising ways and means to develop and refine security protection systems. Even the pyramids were equipped with booby traps and other elaborate devices to protect the burial havens of ancient kings from evil spirits, as well as the not-so-spiritual crimes of pilferage, theft, and vandalism.

Archeologists have uncovered evidence that early civilizations lived in protected tribal communities where crimes against persons and property were punishable by such techniques as flaying, impalation, exposure to wild beasts, burning, slavery, and crucifixion. Criminals were often identified by branding, mutilation, or both.[2]

The first recorded body of laws was the Code of Hammurabi established in approximately 1700 B.C. This code regulated trade, commerce, agriculture, and the professions.

Early Greek city-states were the first to establish a professional security force to protect life and property. The earliest centralized security force — the Praetorian Guard — was established by Caesar Augustus, Emperor of Rome at the time of Christ. The guard was responsible for protecting the life and property of the emperor and the palace. From this group evolved the urban cohorts whose duty it was to maintain the security of the city and the vigiles (vigilantes), a secret police agency established to protect state security.[3]

## THE DEVELOPMENT OF SECURITY IN ENGLAND

When the Roman Empire fell, many groups emigrated to the British Isles where a feudal system of government was in effect. People settled there in widely scattered small localities known as *tuns* (later called towns), and the laws of each tun were enforced separately by groups of community members banded together for this purpose. This is said to have been the origin of municipal police departments.

Under English Common Law, every able-bodied man was obliged to join in the communal pursuit of offenders. The word "cop" is said to have originated from the acronym "civilian on patrol." This was the origin of citizen's arrest, which remains to this day the only authority of arrest vested in private security personnel.

Feudal England was divided into fifty-five separate areas called *shires*. Each shire was headed by a *shire-reeve* (evolved to sheriff) who was in charge of overseeing the activities of its members as well as ensuring their safety.

There was no death penalty in feudal England, and prisons did not exist. Since crime was regarded as an injustice against the individual, criminals were typically punished by being placed in servitude to the individual or family whom they had harmed by their crime.

The conquest of England by William, duke of Normandy, in 1066 brought about a major reform in law and law enforcement techniques. During the Norman period, the concept of crime was transformed from being an offense against the individual to an offense against the state.

The Norman period saw the beginning of the circuit judge system; King William decided that cases would no longer be tried by sheriffs but instead by judges who would travel to the various shires.

Another important event of the Norman period was the enactment of the Laws of Henry in 1116 A.D. Under these laws, the distinction between a felony and a misdemeanor was clearly defined and the grand jury system was established.

In 1215 A.D. the Magna Carta was signed, establishing the due process system to protect the rights of the individual. This was followed by the Westminster period (1285–1500), during which the following laws were enacted:

1. *Statutes of 1285* — Established a curfew as well as a night watch for guarding the gates of the city from sunset to sunrise.
2. *Statutes of Treason* (1352) — Established the death penalty for acts of treason and counterfeiting.
3. *Justice of the Peace* (1361) — Established three or four positions in

every county, largely because of the inefficiency of the sheriffs.
4. *Local Government* (1370) — Allowed cities to establish their own ordinances.
5. *Star Chamber* (1478) — Special court established by the king to try those accused of crimes against the state. This court was given the power to force testimony and that power was not repealed until the enactment of the Bill of Rights in 1688.

During the Renaissance period, commerce and trade expanded and a prosperous merchant class emerged. As trade increased and caravans were needed to transport merchandise to all parts of the known world, the need for security increased.

Beginning in 1500, a number of different types of police agencies were formed in an attempt to alleviate the crime problem. These included: (1) the *merchant police* — a private security force hired to guard buildings, shops, and stores; (2) the *parochial police* — hired to protect people and property within a parish (religious division within a city); (3) *watches and wards* — a system of civilian patrol; (4) *Bow Street Runners* — special investigators; (5) Thames River police; (6) special constables; and, (7) special detectives.

The onset of the Industrial Revolution prompted the birth of slums and an accompanying increase in crime. Laws were rewritten, making punishments for crime more severe; however, this method was found ineffective in reducing the crime rate. As an alternative, a reward system was established, fixing monetary rewards for individuals who assisted the police in apprehending criminals.

During this period, the concept that "every man's home is his castle" emerged, and individuals exercised their right to bear arms to protect themselves and their property. Popular security devices at this time were wolf traps placed inside doors and windows to prevent break-ins.

In 1822, Sir Robert Peel was appointed Britain's home secretary. Peel is responsible for a major revision of the British police system. His recommendations are often referred to as the "Peelian Reform." Peel pointed out that the existing security forces were segmented and ineffectively utilized. He felt that a competent security operation must be nonmilitary, professional, trained, and ethical. He reorganized the many existing police agencies into one centralized unit — the Metropolitan Police. To this day, police officers in England are referred to as "Bobbies," in honor of Sir Robert Peel.

## THE DEVELOPMENT OF SECURITY IN THE UNITED STATES

Settlers who migrated to Colonial America from England soon learned that the New World had not been spared the security problems of their motherland. Westward expansion created small, widely scattered towns and settlements that prompted crimes such as highway robbery, rape, assault, and murder. There were no police departments, and the few existing cities employed a variety of paid and unpaid peacekeeping personnel, such as night watchmen, constables, sheriffs, jailkeepers, and justices of the peace.

Boston was the first city to establish a night watch in 1636. The city of New York followed suit with the establishment of a night watch in 1658, and in Philadelphia one was instituted in 1700.

The first public police force was established in 1844 in New York City, and by 1856, police departments had been set up in Detroit, Cincinnati, Chicago, San Francisco, Los Angeles, Philadelphia, and Dallas.

Industrialization had a profound effect upon American lifestyles and mores. As individuals migrated from outlying rural areas to bulging urban centers, the crime rate in cities continued to grow. The population was attracted to the cities because of the ever-expanding supply of jobs that could be found there. The growth of so many newly created industries resulted in resentment on the part of many small handicraft businessmen and one-cottage manufacturers, and soon many new kinds of crime, including sabotage and arson, began to appear.

The scope of crime in the cities forced public law enforcement and private security to move in different directions. Public law enforcement had all it could do to respond to the chief problems posed by rapid population increases: control of vice, gambling, crime, and public disorder. Factories found they needed more than a couple of watchmen; they now had to employ a security force to protect both their employees and their property (machines, buildings, stocks, grounds, etc.). When inadequate lighting created new problems in large factories, companies began to explore mechanical alarm systems to replace the human watchmen or "cryers" who had been relied on for centuries.

As urban industry and commerce grew, producers of raw materials as well as of finished products employed larger and larger numbers of workers. Many of the workers were immigrants, who were under tremendous social, psychological, and economic pressures to adjust to a new homeland. Frequently working conditions were bad, and labor laws and unions to protect the rights of workers had not yet been developed. Large security forces were created to prevent fights among employees and between employees and managers, and to deal with the mounting problem of pilferage.

By the mid-nineteenth century, large retail establishments — the forerunners of modern department stores — emerged nationwide. A new security device was developed at this time to assist in controlling employee theft. It was called a cash register.

As the nation grew and commerce and industry expanded at a rapid rate, increasingly complex methods were introduced to control cash and inventory losses. These methods included use of tools, machines, and construction materials, as well as bookkeeping and auditing techniques, and the use of security personnel.

As industrialization developed, the competition for business became intense. This situation resulted in more money available to spend on products and services. The availability of an immense population of workers, who would work long hours at low pay and under frightful conditions, and the plentiful supply of capital to invest (especially where there was little risk) contributed to a highly energized, fierce climate for manufacturing and selling. A factory that produced a tested product frequently could not keep up with the demand. One result of this business climate was that patent theft became widespread beginning in the 1840s and continuing to the end of the century.

Patent infringement spurred the development of private security. One of the most notable examples is the sewing machine. The first practical sewing machine, developed by Elias Howe in the 1840s, was of considerable interest to small shops. Since there were no aspects of the invention that could be protected in a vault, competitors copied the design and sold instruments directly to shopkeepers, or they added a minor innovation and established their own patent.

In mid-century Isaac Singer, combining and refining the ideas of others, came up with a machine that could be mass produced and sold on a worldwide scale to individual housewives. The patents protecting his highly accessible machines became subject to repeated — virtually uncontrollable — theft. The courts were flooded with lawsuits by people suing over a wide variety of infringements leading back to the Singer design. Many suits dragged on for 10 to 20 years, and there was no year during the period 1870–1900 when some sewing machine case was not in the courts.

A parallel situation existed in the motion picture industry, where the greatest risk to filmmakers was not the "theft" of talent by one studio from another, but the theft of the patent for a projection lens, a novel sprocket for a camera, or an improved lighting device that might reduce the hazard of fire. Although many studios maintained security agents to watch over the precious patented devices and processes, the secrets could not be guarded for long. The tremendous wealth of people in the industry, matched with an intense competitive drive, made bribery inevitable with the result that patents were often compromised. Some movie-producing companies linked by common investors found isolation and, for awhile, a genuine protection in a desert-like region of southern California known as — Hollywood.

Over time, similar threats plagued other new technologies, such as the telegraph, telephone, radio, and electronics industries. In a competitive environment it became necessary to protect ideas, devices, and products from the early stages of development, through all the steps of production, to the application of the idea, device, or process.

## Alarm Security Monitoring

In 1853 a Massachusetts inventor, Augustus Pope, patented the first automatic burglary sensor. It consisted of electromagnetic contacts, which were attached to doors and windows. The contacts acted like on-off switches, not too different from modern designs. The opening of a window, for instance, turned the switch "on," an event that connected a battery to a vibrating bell.

A Boston entrepreneur named Edwin Holmes bought Pope's patent in 1858 and set up the first electric burglar alarm business. In his marketing endeavors, he embellished the methods for both detecting and reporting burglaries. His refinements were so revolutionary that today Holmes is regarded as the pioneer of modern electric protection. The range of burglar alarm services Holmes had developed by the late 1800s is still used a century later.

Holmes's achievements did not come easily at first. Homeowners who barely understood electricity were skeptical of an electric alarm system that set a bell ringing in the master bedroom when an intruder entered through the basement window. But Holmes proved to be an able salesman. By the mid-1860s, many wealthy homeowners in Boston and New York City had retained his services on a lease basis (the preferred method of obtaining alarm security to this day). As his enterprise grew, Holmes improved his alarm services as follows:

1. A small indicator panel or annunciator with colored tabs was placed in the circuit to reveal which door or window was opened.
2. To keep servants from accidentally tripping the sensors when they entered the premises, a clock was added to shut the alarm off in the morning.
3. With the advent of the electric lightbulb in the 1880s, a switch was added to illuminate the premises when a sensor was triggered.

These concepts of Holmes are still employed today, though in some cases for slightly different purposes. Annunciators are used, not only to identify where intruders enter, but also to isolate system failures. Timing mechanisms are used widely in business establishments to shut off alarms at opening time and to reactivate them at closing time.

Holmes's greatest contribution to alarm security lay in his central station system. It provided a way to monitor sensors installed on numerous premises from a single location, and therefore expedite police response to crimes in progress.

It was primarily for his business subscribers that Holmes had his engineers design this system in 1872. The jewelers, bankers, furriers, and merchants retailing other precious items needed something more effective than a bell to scare intruders away at night. For these high-risk establishments, Holmes developed an automatic alarm signaling system around the *galvanometer*, a device commonly used to detect changes in current levels on electric circuits. The galvanometer served Holmes's needs perfectly. Not only could it indicate when a sensor was tripped, but it could also detect efforts by more enterprising burglars who dared to circumvent alarm systems by tampering with the circuitry.

At his offices in Boston and New York, Holmes erected monitoring panels consisting of galvanometers stacked in a modular fashion. He assigned a galvanometer to each central station subscriber and strung cables to each business that desired the protection.

When the system was in place, Holmes had operators watch the panels around the clock. When the needle on any meter moved, the operators immediately sent word to the police telling them the location of the crime. By the late 1870s, Holmes had retained his own force of patrolmen who were dispatched to the scene as well — a practice widely used by central station companies today.

Holmes made one more refinement to his sensor apparatus that deserves mention. His engineers designed the first electric vault protection system in 1872. Holmes first had carpenters fashion elegant cabinets to encase safes. His engineers then wired the cabinets with contacts discreetly attached to the hinges and latches. Moreover, Holmes introduced metallic foil to the protection science, lining the wooden panels with the paper-thin strips. Accordingly, any attempt to open the cabinet or break through its panels would affect the circuit and cause the needle in the galvanometer at the central station to jump.

By about 1880, the Holmes Protection Company was monitoring almost every high-risk establishment in Boston, New York, and Philadelphia. The company was so highly regarded in security circles that the name "Holmes" became synonymous with electric protection.

Other enterprises spread alarm security to cities in the South, Midwest, and West. These entrepreneurs developed a different mode of alarm signaling, based on the callbox concept, which brought the price of electric protection within the range of the less affluent.

The genius behind this service was E. A. Calahan, whose inventions included the stock market ticker and reporting system. In 1871, Calahan formed the American District Telegraph Company to provide a range of dispatch services involving messengers and patrolmen. He introduced the business in New York City, where he erected a network of callboxes divided into districts. Each district was served by a central station where attendants received the signals and dispatched the appropriate personnel.

Central stations were so located that when a subscriber used a street callbox to summon either a messenger or a policeman, it took only three minutes for a fleet-footed messenger to travel the distance between the central service station and the callbox. The signal was received on a paper tape in the form of a series of dashes. A bell rang after the transmission to alert the attendant. By referring to a master list, he could identify the source of the signal and the nature of the service required.

In 1872 the American District Telegraph Company opened seven central stations. The service was well received, for by 1874 it had opened twelve more stations. As the demand for the service grew, the firm diversified. Subscribers were soon running messenger boys on all kinds of errands, from delivering flowers and escorting ladies, to passing out advertising literature. In 1875 this service hand-delivered two-thirds of the stock sold on Wall Street, and employed over 500 people.

It did not take long for the idea of alarm protection to spread to most major U.S. cities. Some of these district telegraph companies shared facilities with Western Union, although none had any corporate relationship to the telegraph giant. By the late 1880s as many as twenty companies offered district protection and messenger services across the nation.

Up until the mid-1870s the district companies rendered protection only during daylight hours. As the story goes, however, one of the telegraph operators had an elderly father working as a night watchman in a plant whose owner subscribed to the messenger service. The telegrapher worried about his father's health and well-being. One night he instructed his father to use the messenger call switch once an hour, on the hour, throughout the night. The signal coming in on time to the telegraph office would indicate that his father was safe. The absence of hourly transmission would mean help was needed. This was the first use of the delinquency signal concept, which is still in use today.

As a method of alarm security, the district telegraph callbox service could hardly compete with Holmes's galvanometers and automatic sensors. In a few locales during the 1870s the companies attempted to monitor burglar sensors, but records indicate they made few inroads. Even if they wanted to use galvanometers, they couldn't — for Holmes owned the patent.

Before the turn of the century the burglar alarm business was affected fundamentally by the invention of the telephone. The story begins as an historical footnote, but it unfolded into a relationship that many alarm industry leaders regret today.

The telephone emerged immediately as a natural service for central station companies to use. It expedited communications with police, firefighters, and subscribers needing various services. Nevertheless, that service from the telephone company soon became secondary to a more basic service. Weary of stringing and maintaining alarm circuits, Holmes contracted to lease his transmission facilities from the telephone companies. By paying the companies installation costs and a monthly fee, Holmes obtained sub-voice grade circuits designed to transmit direct current (d.c.), as opposed to the alternating current (a.c.) necessary for voice communication.

The district telegraph companies followed Holmes's lead after they merged in 1901 under the ownership of Western Union, forming the modern-day American District Telegraph Company (ADT). In particular, ADT began leasing d.c. circuits from the telephone industry after AT&T (formed in 1900) bought a controlling interest in Western Union in 1909. AT&T had already bought out Holmes's operation through its New York Telephone subsidiary in 1905.

Although antitrust complaints forced AT&T to divest itself of Western Union (and ADT) in 1914, ADT and others continued to rely on the phone company for alarm circuits. As AT&T expanded its monopoly to 95 percent of the nation's market, every central station came to rely almost exclusively on its operating companies for alarm transmission facilities.

The negative consequences of such total reliance didn't appear until the 1970s. Well into the twentieth century, this service relationship served Holmes and ADT well. It was likewise a boon for a central station fire alarm company formed in the 1870s, Automatic Fire Alarm (AFA). But for most other businessmen aspiring to enter the alarm trade, the need to obtain circuits from AT&T was a major obstacle.[4]

## The Express Companies

The opening of the western part of the United States to settlers had a tremendous impact on the development of private security. Discovery of gold in California and other natural resources throughout the West resulted in the hiring of armed guards and watchmen.

Although the first companies founded to transport money and valuables in a secure manner emerged in the eastern United States, their greatest growth occurred in the West. These firms, known as express companies, actually began in the 1830s. Several of these companies, under the leadership of Henry Wells and William Fargo, joined together as the *American Express Company*. The two men then started a new organization to operate in the West and called it *Wells Fargo and Company*. The objective was to get some of the business that almost exclusively fell to Adams Express, a firm that enjoyed success bringing gold to the East.

The development of express companies, along with the advent of the railroad, created a number of security problems. With their rich cargos, these companies quite naturally attracted thieves. Great distances were involved, and law enforcement was spotty. In addition, the political jurisdictions effectively limited the authority of sheriffs and other law enforcement officers. This latter point in particular led to a most significant development in security — the private detective.

### The Pinkertons

While not the first private detective in the world (Eugene Vidocq of France probably holds that honor), Allan Pinkerton, through a combination of good timing, luck, superior investigatory techniques, and a flair for publicity, became the most famous real-life private detective in history. The detective agency he established — the Pinkerton Agency — still flourishes today.

Allan Pinkerton was born in Scotland in 1819. At the age of 23 he emigrated to Canada, but along the way he changed his destination and settled in Chicago. At first, Pinkerton worked as a "cooper," the trade he had learned in Scotland. While engaged in this business, he stumbled across some counterfeiters in a town near Chicago. He contacted the local sheriff and the bank that was being victimized. Pinkerton offered his services and helped capture the crooks. As a reward he was appointed deputy sheriff. Not long after that Pinkerton became a deputy sheriff in Chicago. Then, in 1849, he was appointed the city's first detective.

Pinkerton saw the potential in detective work, and a year later he resigned his position in the city of Chicago to found his own private detective agency. By 1853, he had five full-time detectives working for him, one of whom, incidentally, was a woman.

As the years went by, Pinkerton hired more associates and specialized in protecting railroads. One of his contracts was with the Pennsylvania Railroad. When President-elect Abraham Lincoln was on his way to Washington for his inaugural in March 1861, rumors surfaced concerning a plot to assassinate the new president. Pinkerton investigators were able to uncover details of the plans and spirited Lincoln through Philadelphia and Baltimore without alerting the conspirators.

Prior to the Civil War, Allan Pinkerton became a good friend of George McClellan, who was then an official of the Illinois Central Railroad. In the early days of the war, McClellan was Commander-in-Chief of the Union Army. He made Pinkerton head of intelligence. After McClellan was relieved of his duties as army chief in 1863, Pinkerton left the army and returned to his private business.

Following the war, the business of the Pinkerton Detective Agency expanded rapidly; with headquarters in Chicago, offices were opened in Philadelphia and New York City. Adams Express Company, operating in New England, lost $700,000 in cash, bonds, and other valuables. Pinkerton was called in, and his investigators wasted little time in recovering almost all of the stolen money and securities. The size of the robbery, combined with the swift action of the Pinkertons, resulted in a considerable amount of favorable publicity.

Allan Pinkerton died in 1884. During his later years, he became less active in the daily affairs of his agency and spent more time writing books and retelling stories detailing affairs of the firm. This publicity helped promote his detective business and eventually made his name synonymous with the phrase "private detective."

**Homestead.**    In the latter part of the nineteenth century, the union movement began to develop. Many fledgling labor groups began by organizing miners. To help protect their land and facilities, a number of mining companies employed the Pinkerton Agency.

One of Pinkerton's operatives infiltrated a particularly violent underground labor group known as the Molly Maguires. After a short-but-bloody period of activity, the leaders of the Molly Maguires were arrested. This agent testified against them and his testimony was so damaging that it almost totally destroyed the effectiveness of the organization.

One of the most notorious episodes in union–management relations centered on the Homestead, Pennsylvania, works of the Carnegie Steel Company, and eventually involved the Pinkerton Agency.

Skilled workers at the Homestead plant, near Pittsburgh, were represented by the Amalgamated Association of Iron and Steel Workers. They had an agreement with the company that was to expire at the end of July 1892. Negotiations on a new contract broke off during June, and Carnegie hired 300 Pinkerton agents to protect its interests.

On July 1 the workers, augmented by many who were not in the union, seized the plant. Sheriff's deputies and Pinkerton personnel were barred from the town by the workers. Since the mayor of Homestead was a member of the union, company and law enforcement officials could not get any support from the town.

Armed with Winchester rifles and other weapons, the force of 300

Pinkertons sailed down the Monongahela River on a barge in the dark of night. The workers found out about the plan somehow, and as many as 10,000 of them were waiting at the dock when the barge arrived. The battle that followed was bloody, leaving three Pinkertons and five workers dead. The Pinkertons, badly outnumbered, surrendered. Four days later the plant was occupied by troops called out by the governor.

As a result of the battle, the Pinkerton Agency declared it would no longer involve itself in labor disputes. Actually, the company did become involved in industrial espionage involving union activities during the 1920s and early 1930s. This activity ended following censure by the U.S. Senate in 1935.

The Homestead situation was investigated by Congress. No illegality was found in the use of Pinkerton agents by Carnegie; however, Congress did indicate that the execution of laws should not be delegated to private individuals employed by corporations.

In 1893 a law was passed barring the employment of Pinkerton and other detective agencies by the government. Because it was the direct result of the Homestead dispute, it was popularly known as the Pinkerton Law; it is still on the books today.

## Brinks Armored Truck Service

In 1859 Washington Perry Brink formed a truck and package delivery service in Chicago. He transported his first payroll in 1891, thereby initiating armored car and courier service. Although not a direct competitor, Brink's firm built upon and extended the activities of Pinkerton. The firm's major objective was to provide protection for its clients as well as their valuables and facilities. Eventually, the company's business evolved to the point where it was exclusively related to the protection of valuables being transported from one place to another. Today, it is the largest armored truck service in the world.

A more direct competitor at the time — as it is today — was the William J. Burns, Inc., Detective Agency, founded in 1909 by a former agent of the U.S. Secret Service. Not long after the Burns operation began, it replaced Pinkerton as the investigative agency for the American Bankers Association. The ABA, during those days, provided assistance to member banks in solving a variety of bank crimes.

Until the establishment of the Federal Bureau of Investigation in 1924, Pinkerton and Burns were the only nationwide organizations that provided protection and investigated crime. The Secret Service was then relatively small, and only became involved in certain types of crimes.

### Railway Police

In the latter half of the nineteenth century, the great era of railroad development coincided with westward expansion in the United States. Long distances could be covered in reasonable time only by railroads that bridged the spaces between widely scattered population centers in the West. Here, as in the rest of the country, railroads were the lifeline of commerce. They were also prime targets for all kinds of bandits.

A major problem was the fact that railroads crossed many state boundaries, making it difficult for local law enforcers to go after such legends as Butch Cassidy and Black Jack Ketchum. Moreover, the Secret Service had insufficient numbers of federal agents to cope with the problem.

As a result, most of the states passed some form of railway policing act. While they were different to a degree, each law authorized railroads to hire security personnel to protect equipment, property, and people.[5] It wasn't long before the "railroad dick" became the symbol of authority, particularly in the broad expanses of the western states.

By 1914 the railroads employed approximately 12,000 police.[6] During World War I, most railroad lawmen were deputized by the federal government to help combat sabotage. Although the number of railroad security personnel has diminished over the years, most railroad companies still maintain their own police units.

### Between the Wars

As a result of World War I, almost overnight the United States grew more sensitive to security needs. The crime problem worsened during the prohibition era brought about by the Volsted Act of 1919. During this same period, insurance companies began to give premium discounts to subscribers who obtained certain types of alarm protection, particularly those certified by Underwriters' Laboratories (UL).

Insurance companies had established UL in 1894, primarily to test fire protection equipment. In 1921, UL's charge was extended to test and certify burglar alarm systems and services. The standards set by UL granted a better rating for some types of protection than others, which was determined by the level of security provided. Accordingly, central station alarm services received a higher rating than local alarm services, and central station subscribers were granted larger discounts in their property insurance premiums.

Corporate organizations continued to expand their use of private security forces after World War I. Some firms, in fact, began to rely more heavily on their own security devices because the police were increasingly occupied trying to control abuses of the prohibition law. In addition, particularly after the war, the public became concerned with the possibility that municipal police forces might not always be available to help investigate crime. This feeling was nurtured by the 1919 strike of the Boston police, who were trying to form a union — something rare in those days. The strike was broken by Massachusetts Governor, Calvin Coolidge, who called in the National Guard.

## Ford Motor Company and the Union

During the 1930s, private security activities at the Ford Motor Company were under the direction of Harry Bennett, who was a close associate of Henry Ford, and probably in line to succeed Ford as head of the company. Security personnel were assigned to a unit called the Ford Company Service Department.

Security personnel acted as bodyguards for officials of the company, and even for members of the Ford family. They investigated lawsuits that arose and guarded facilities from espionage. This was a time when the auto firms vied with one another to attract the limited business available, bringing out new technological advances and style changes each year.

Ford was the last and largest auto firm to be unionized. At first, the relatively high pay offered by the company kept the workers satisfied. But gradually all the automobile manufacturers offered comparable wages. Then, during the Depression, unions became more active in trying to organize companies and protect jobs. One by one the auto companies were unionized, until only Ford was left.

The unions, and specifically the United Auto Workers, were anxious to organize Ford. Henry Ford was strongly antiunion and vowed to keep the unions out. While the other auto companies had fought the unions, during which there were periods of violence, nothing compared to what became known as the "Bridge Fight" at Ford's River Rouge plant in 1937.

There was a bridge leading into a section of the factory. Two union officers — one was Walter Reuther who later was president of the UAW — positioned themselves on the bridge where they could observe the workers going in. Company guards told the two union men to leave. Before they could respond, the guards attacked and brutally beat them. Several news reporters and photographers who took pictures of the incident were also beaten by the Ford guards and many cameras were smashed. Not all the pictures were destroyed, however, and newspapers and radio stations reported the story across the country. The publicity was devastating to Ford, resulting in even lower sales.

The company changed its position and finally recognized the union.

Mr. Bennett fell from favor and never became president of Ford. In addition, the company drastically curbed the activities of its security forces.

## World War II to the Present

The advent of World War II and the changeover of production facilities to meet war needs resulted in mobilization and expansion of private security forces. There were enemies across both oceans, and danger of sabotage was real. Any and all facilities involved with production for the war effort — even remotely — had some security personnel assigned. Local law enforcement agencies were charged with the responsibility of training these people. By the end of the war, approximately 200,000 men and women were actively involved in private security activities.

As crime continued to increase during World War II and the post war years, a few small security alarm firms began to gain a foothold in the market. Central to their emergence was the creation of the National Burglar and Fire Alarm Association (NBFAA).

About a dozen independent companies formed the trade group in 1948. In doing so, they endeavored to overcome a shortage of alarm components (bells, contacts, copperwire, etc.), as well as a lack of alarm suppliers willing to fill small orders from single firms scattered across the country. NBFAA invited manufacturers to exhibit their systems at trade shows and meet with numerous potential buyers under one roof. This arrangement offered the alarm service companies an education in alarm technology available nowhere else.

**The 1950s.** After the war, the use of private security began expanding to all segments of public and private life. Because of the greatly increased role of private security in government and the military during the war, industry became more aware of the need to protect its assets by utilizing private security.

By the 1950s the "Cold War" had begun, accompanied by a widespread concern about the spread of Communism. Senator Joseph McCarthy and the House Un-American Activities Committee fanned those fears with their investigations of industry practices and probes into the lives of private citizens. During the Korean hostilities, security requirements in business were tightened.

The Department of Defense formalized the security requirements of defense contractors. It established the Industrial Defense Program in 1952, which is still in use today and monitored by Department of Defense industry security representatives.

It was in this decade that the Wackenhut Corporation was organized. Today, Wackenhut is one of the largest contract guard and investigative agencies in the country.

**The 1960s.**   The 1960s were years of affluence, growing expectations, and accomplishments as varied as the Civil Rights Act and the Apollo moon landing. For many segments of American society, however, they were years of turbulence and social upheaval. Black Americans organized and protested to win their civil rights. The war in Vietnam spawned controversy and animosity among many, alienating many draft-age young men.

According to the FBI Uniform Crime Reports for those years, the national crime rate showed a significant rise. This increase was especially evident in the nation's large cities. A pattern of increased heroin traffic and drug-related crime, along with the politically inspired urban unrest such as the Watts riots, were contributing factors to what many newspapers of the day called a "crime wave."

In addition to this crime wave, many lost confidence in law enforcement and criminal justice institutions. The three political assassinations of the decade — John and Robert Kennedy and Martin Luther King, Jr. — stunned many and raised doubts about the effectiveness of the police. The New York City Police Department, for one, was shaken to its foundations by the Serpico scandal, which was ultimately investigated by the Knapp Commission.

It was in this climate that growing numbers of private businesses and corporations turned for protection to the private security industry. Vietnam veterans and an influx of relatively young retirees from police departments helped meet the accelerating demand for security guards and personnel.

Congress responded to the law enforcement problems of the 1960s with two pieces of legislation that have significantly affected private security activities.

*The Bank Protection Act of 1968.*   Increased robberies, check kiting, embezzlement, and other crimes led to passage of the Bank Protection Act of 1968. The law required the various federal bank supervisory agencies to "promulgate rules establishing minimum standards with which each bank or savings and loan association must comply."

Those rules were issued and became effective in 1969. They covered the installation, maintenance, and operation of security procedures and devices. The objective of the law and the regulations was to discourage robberies and other criminal acts against banks, as well as the apprehension of those committing such acts. The legislation also required each bank, regardless of size, to designate an officer to be responsible for the development and operation of a written security program.

*Law Enforcement Assistance Administration (LEAA).*   An Office of Law Enforcement Assistance (OLEA) was created in 1965 to distribute funds to states, localities, and private organizations to improve "methods of law enforcement, court administration, and prison operation." Then the Omnibus Crime Control and Safe Street Act went into effect in 1968. It replaced OLEA with the Law Enforcement Assistance Administration (LEAA).

In addition to allocating funds for the improvement of law enforcement procedures, LEAA also provides funds for the collection and dissemination of crime statistics. About $1 billion is appropriated each year, most of which goes to crime reduction programs. Since its establishment, little LEAA money goes to private industry. There is hope by some in the private security sector that this condition will change in the years ahead.

**The 1970s.**   As the crime rate continued to skyrocket, the law enforcement and private security agencies of the nation continued their struggle to prevent and reduce crime. A U.S. Department of Commerce report indicated that in 1975 ordinary crimes cost business more than $23.6 billion, while another survey claimed that $6 billion was expended that year to employ more than 1 million private security personnel and purchase alarm equipment.

In 1975, the National Advisory Committee on Criminal Justice Standards and Goals established the *Task Force on Private Security* to study and propose standards and goals for the private security field. The task force was comprised of a cross section of experts and leading practitioners in the fields of criminal justice and private security.

Owing to the small amount of formal literature in the field, the research of the committee was limited, adding to the significance of the final report. *The Report of the Task Force on Private Security* remains today as one of the most highly regarded documents in the field.[7]

**The National School Resource Center.**   In response to the growing problems of violence and vandalism in the nation's schools, the National School Resource Center was established in 1978 under a grant from LEAA. Its purpose was to serve as an information and retrieval network for the accumulation and dissemination of information regarding incidents of school crime, disorder, and violence as well as proposed solutions to these problems.

During the brief, three-year life span of the School Resource Center, over $4 million was expended on a project whose results were short lived. The National School Resource Center was a well-intentioned project whose accomplishments fell far short of its goals and the anticipated needs of the nation's schools.

## CONCLUSION

The rising rate of crime in this country has placed a tremendous burden on both public and private agencies for the protection of the public. The simple fact that private security forces outnumber the public law enforcement sector by a ratio of two to one mandates that the private security industry assume a more professional role in the decade of the eighties.

With over a million people employed in private protection, more federal government control of this activity is needed. There are distinct signs that the government is about to subsidize certain areas in the private sector, as it did for the public sector only 15 years ago. Hopefully, the direction this control takes will not be wasteful and will not be influenced by the traditional limitations that the private security industry has followed. The Private Security Task Force Report has pointed out the shortcomings in the field of private security. It is hoped that the recommendations made in this report will be implemented by the federal, state, and local governments. That report may well be the most important document ever to be published on the subject of private security. Many of the findings in that report were used as resource material in the preparation of this textbook. A copy of that report should be on the desk of every security professional in the country.

Guard services have been the most rapidly growing segment of the private security industry in recent years. There has been a dramatic increase in the number of guards hired by individual companies and by the contract guard services, but both groups share a common lack of adequate training and supervision. A remarkable document was published in 1972, referred to as the *Rand Report*. This comprehensive study outlines the critical shortcomings of the uniformed guard and the guard service industry as a whole. The report was quoted widely, resulting in some federal activity in the area of licensing and training. In the ten years since the document was published, however, there has been little improvement, and the guard-for-hire industry remains little changed from the days when Pinkerton built his empire over 100 years ago. Some of the immediate problems associated with the private guard industry will be covered in later chapters.

According to many sources the greatest impact on the security industry will be in the area of electronic technology, rather than on guards or other human services. Very few professionals in the field are equipped by education or training to understand the differences among various alarm devices. Consequently, the alarm sector has been permitted to experiment and install equipment that has produced an unacceptable rate of false alarms.

While the technical advances in electronics are now influencing the alarm industry, some of the devices being installed do not appear to be very different from the units installed by Mr. Holmes in the mid-nineteenth century. Security alarms have proven highly effective if selected intelligently. The second half of this text is devoted to explanations of every conceivable device currently on the market. The technology chapters deal with the subject in a manner that attempts to bring the technical operation into clear language so the nonengineer can determine the operating-theory that separates one device from another. Included in these chapters is a description of the various methods available for transmitting signals from one point to another — a subject that for a long time has been left to the sole discretion of a salesman. This is one way to present the subject of private security without dealing with the technical concepts, since the trend in today's society is to replace a guard with an alarm device, if at all possible.

There is an urgent need for the private security sector to set its own standards or face the alternative of being controlled by state or federal regulations. Only with proper regulations and a workable set of standards and goals will the industry attain the level of professionalism found in public law enforcement.

## NOTES

1. Kingwell, Robert G., "What Lies Ahead? A Look Into the Future of the Guard Service Industry," *Security Management*, September 1981, p. 19.
2. Ursic, Henry S. and Pagano, Leroy, *Security Management Systems* (Springfield, Ill.: Charles C. Thomas, 1974), p. 5.
3. Post, Richard S. and Kingsbury, Arthur, *Security Administration: An Introduction* (Springfield, Ill.: Charles C. Thomas, 1973), p. 9.
4. The information on alarm security was excerpted from *A History of Alarm Security*, published by the NBFAA, Washington, D.C., and with the assistance of William Greer.
5. Green, Gion and Parker, Raymond C., *Introduction to Security: Principles and Practice* (Los Angeles: Security World Publishers, 1975), p. 27.
6. Post and Kingsbury, p. 33.
7. National Advisory Committee on Criminal Justice Standards and Goals, *Report of the Task Force on Private Security* (Washington, D.C.: U.S. Government Printing Office, 1977), pp. i–x.

## UNDERWRITERS LABORATORY (UL)

### Product Testing

Underwriters Laboratories began its association with the burglar industry in the 1920s when a group of insurance companies requested the assistance of UL in the establishment of a rating system for alarm installations and for the few existing security products available then. The result of this request was the development of a definition of different levels of alarm protection and the establishment of priorities of vulnerability and grades of alarm protection, a reference that was totally lacking until this time.

The creation of the Burglar Protection and Signaling department brought the number of engineering departments at UL to six, the others being: Casualty and Chemical Hazards; Electrical; Fire Protection; Heating, Air Conditioning, and Refrigeration; and Marine. These departments list products from the standpoint of electrical shock, fire hazards, and casualty.

UL safety standards are developed according to a procedure that provides for participation and comment from the affected public as well as from industry. The procedure takes into consideration a survey of interests concerned with the subject matter of the standards. Consequently, input is provided from manufacturers, consumers, individuals associated with consumer-oriented organizations, academicians, government officials, industrial and commercial users, inspection authorities, insurance interests, and others. This information is used by UL in the formulation of standards for safety, keeping them consonant with social and technological advances. Sometimes, though, UL is slow to react to a changing technology.

Published lists are available with the names of manufacturers that have had their products examined, tested, and accepted. All listed products can be identified by a UL listing mark (almost two billion listings are issued by UL each year).[1]

The manufacturer pays a fee to have the unit tested against the related standard. If the device is eventually listed, there may also be a fee for the label affixed to each unit. Since the establishment of standards is time consuming, some devices are in use for years before an appropriate standard can be developed and approved. It is possible that industry members who contribute to the formulation of standards may be manufacturers of products that could conceivably become obsolete under the terms of the new standards. This situation could appear to create a conflict of interest. While it is important that manufacturers be involved in establishing standards, the process should not be limited to only one or two alarm manufacturers as it was up until the mid-1960s.

Users of UL Standards should also be aware that requirements do change as dictated by engineering principles, research, records of tests, and field experience.[1] Standards are dynamic in principle; for example, UL 611, the standard for Central Station Burglar Alarm units, was in its eleventh edition in 1981, specifying changes to be incorporated by May 1982.

Vendors sometimes obfuscate the status of their UL listing. Revisions from one edition of a standard to another may not be significant. However, conscientious and reliable vendors appreciate and respect customers who understand the nuances of standards. It is worth the effort to know what the *latest* standards are for a particular security product or system. Additionally, it is desirable to judge such a product or system in its entire context, including state of the art, reliability, flexibility, service, and UL Standards listing.

### Certification Service

While shortcomings may exist in the UL listing system for products, the second category of UL involvement in the alarm industry is more noteworthy and probably more worthwhile. This category deals with UL's certification service for alarm-installing companies and central stations. The leading companies in central station service as determined by UL are listed in Table 2-1. This certificate is simply a serially numbered printed form furnished by UL for each installing company to record the following information: name and address of subscriber, information on the listed equipment used, extent of protection, classification of system, and issue period of service contract. The UL designation, which is intended primarily for insurance purposes, implies that the central station company providing the alarm monitoring has met the following requirements:

- A fire-resistant building with its own standby power.
- A security-controlled entrance to the structure and equipment that conforms to UL certification standards.
- All functions, from equipment operations to paperwork, conforming to UL rules.
- Instructions on file describing the special handling of alarm signals for each account.
- A supervisor and attendants at the signal receiving board on premises at all times.
- Runners to respond to alarms within the maximum time allotment for UL certified systems and adequate service personnel to assure continuing function of all alarm systems.

**Table 2-1. The UL Central Station Leaders**

| Company | Central Stations Meeting UL 611[a] | Central Stations Meeting NFPA 71[b] | Total Central Stations in U.S. |
|---|---|---|---|
| ADT Security Systems New York City | 119 | 141 | 143 |
| Honeywell Protection Services, Minneapolis | 35 | 40 | 40 |
| Wells Fargo Alarm Services, King of Prussia, Pennsylvania | 33 | 32 | 36 |
| Electro-Protective Corporation, Parsippany, New Jersey | 9 | 9 | 9 |
| Alarmex, Division of Vangas, Inc., Fresno, California | 7 | 9 | 9 |
| Holmes Protection, Inc., New York City | 8 | 8 | 8 |
| American Protection Industries Los Angeles | 5 | 5 | 5 |
| Smith Alarm Systems Dallas | 3 | 3 | 3 |
| Crime Control, Inc. Indiana | 3 | 2 | 3 |
| Subtotal | 225 | 253 | 260 |
| Others | 122 | 199 | 200* |
| **Total** | **347** | **452** | **460*** |

Source: Underwriters Laboratories, 1981 listings.

[a]A central station listed under Underwriters Laboratories standard No. 611 is constructed to resist fires and sabotage attempts. In the event of electrical failure, the central station can supply backup power for at least 48 hours. The alarm monitoring systems are installed and operated according to many specifications. The station must be staffed with guards and technicians who, if the subscriber's service requires it, can respond to alarm calls immediately after they come in.

[b]UL lists these central stations as protective signaling services. They meet many of the requirements in UL 611, which appear in the National Fire Protection Assn. standard No. 71; although, the monitoring centers need not provide guard response on a timely basis.

*These numbers are approximations.

Underwriters Laboratories uses four categories in describing burglar alarms:

1. Grade of central station response
2. Extent of alarm protection
3. Type of system
4. Class of system

## Grade of Central Station Response

*Grade A.*  Indicates a response of 15 minutes from receipt of an alarm or unauthorized opening to the time a guard arrives at the premises.

*Grade AA.*  The same response time as above, plus an approved line security feature that is able to detect compromise attempts of the connecting line between the central station and the protected premises. Under a standard published in 1980, the circuit cannot be defeated by:

- Substitution of resistance or voltage
- Tape record and playback
- Synthesized signals
- Substitution of equipment of like manufacturer

*Grade B.*  Refers to a response time of 20 minutes.

*Grade BB.*  Refers to a response time of 20 minutes, plus the line security feature.

*Grade C.*  Refers to a response time of 30 minutes.

*Grade CC.*  Refers to a response time of 30 minutes, plus the line security feature. (The line security feature usually means that line security equipment has been added to the subscriber's telephone line to prevent, or make it extremely difficult to circumvent, the telephone lines, thereby compromising the system.)

**Extent of Alarm Protection.**  The extent of alarm protection at mercantile premises is classified as No. 1, 2, or 3, in accordance with the following specifications.

*Installation 3.*  The minimum and, therefore, the most common installation. It may be completed according to different methods. The *oldest method* requires completely protecting all accessible openings such as windows, doors, skylights, etc., leading from the premises.

The *second method* is to contact all moveable, accessible openings leading from the premises, and providing one or more invisible channels of radiation equivalent to the longest dimension of the area, so as to detect movement through the channel (or beam) within four steps at a rate of one step per second.

The *third method* is to contact only all doors leading from the premises, and provide volumetric, invisible radiation to all sections of the enclosed area in order to detect movement within four steps.

The *fourth* and last alternative is the use of sound. A sound detection system is used around the perimeter of the area with additional microphones located near fixed and moveable floor and ceiling areas.

*Installation 2.*    Follows the same basic protection patterns as required in Installation 3, but the openings are more fully protected.

*Installation 1.*    Represents the highest classification. It is used primarily to protect small stockrooms where an unusually high concentration of valuables justifies a complete protection pattern on all six sides of the structure.

---

*Example 1. A-3 Central Station Mercantile*
Indicates the central station will respond in 15 minutes to a signal from premises wired within Installation 3.

*Example 2. BB-1 Central Station Mercantile*
Indicates a central station will respond within 20 minutes, and the phone line is supervised with the premises protected on all six sides.

---

## Type of System

*Local Alarms.*    Premises may still fulfill the UL certification requirement without actually having a direct connection to a central station. They are clearly designated as "local alarms," and may be classified as Grade A or Grade B. Essentially, the difference between the grades relates to the resistance to attack on the bell housing and control unit (Grade A being the better protected system). The alarm annunciator is mounted locally on the premises, specifically in an enclosed, tamper-protected device attached to an outside wall of a building. The alarm will emit a loud sound until stopped by key control inside the premises or by exhaustion of the standby battery supply.

*Police Station Connected Systems.*    Police station connected systems are a relatively new category, established to overcome the objections of many police departments who want to respond and catch thieves, rather than have a bell scare them away. The alarm signal, initiated at the protected premises, is also annunciated at the constantly attended receiver at police headquarters. All the requirements for local burglar alarm systems apply, except that the bell at the protected premises may have a delay of up to 5 minutes so that the police may respond before the bell rings. These systems must be maintained and inspected at least once a year by the installing company.

*Proprietary Systems.*    Proprietary systems are those in which central control and power equipment (generally equivalent to that employed in a central station) is provided at the protected premises. In this system, all equipment is supervised and operated by the premises owner. UL has issued standards covering these systems.

**Class of System.**    The UL certificate classification chart in Table 2-2 specifies UL requirements for each system classification.

**Approved UL Listed Companies.**    The issuance of a UL certificate for a burglar alarm system assures that certain minimum requirements have been met. Equal or superior alarm service can still be obtained without a certificate, but most insurance companies use UL as a standard because their own staff usually is unable to judge the different levels of security.

  The majority of central stations are not listed with UL (there are about 350 listings). Furthermore, most companies listed with UL can install only local alarm systems, and are not listed for central station service (almost all listed central stations are also approved to install local alarm systems). Separate approval listings exist for both local and protective signaling installing companies.

  To become a listed central service operator is much more difficult than to be listed as a local alarm company. UL representatives investigate a central station over a four-month period to determine compliance with building construction, security arrangements, and night service tests. Four premises are visited to demonstrate compliance with the installation requirements. Listing as a local alarm company involves a one-day visit for purposes of reviewing four typical alarm installations, as well as the company service and maintenance facilities.

  Local installers are not restricted by any area boundaries as long as they meet the requirements of UL Standard 609, paragraph 34,4:

> Trouble calls received before 12:00 noon should be responded to the same day, and troubles thereafter shall be responded to as soon as possible and in no case later than the business day following.

UL's Burglar Protection and Signaling Department, Melville, New York, issues a completely revised list three times a year of approved central station, local bank, and local mercantile installing companies.[2]

## OTHER STANDARD WRITING ORGANIZATIONS

### National Fire Protection Association (NFPA)

The United States has a long history in publishing standards relating to fire protection equipment. Both UL and the NFPA use the consensus method to establish standards; however, the NFPA does not actually test the equipment. This organization was established in 1898 by insurance executives and a leading manufacturer of automatic sprinklers. Their initial efforts led to the development of a set of "sprinkler rules," which were soon followed by rules to regulate hydrants, fire hoses, wire glass, and fire doors. These NFPA rules, or standards, now number over 230 in the fire protection field. These codes (after being adopted by municipal authorities) have had a significant effect on building design. The NFPA remains the organization responsible for many of the advances in the fire protection area.

Problems do arise where certain codes recommended by fire code writing groups conflict with the interests of groups dealing with burglary alarm standards. A good example of this conflict concerns fire exit doors. Because of the fire codes in almost all municipalities, most exit doors in public buildings are furnished with panic hardware to permit individuals to evacuate a burning building simply by depressing the bar mounted across the interior of the door. In recent years (where unauthorized intrusion has created a security problem), these easy-to-open exit doors have compromised the security of the building. For example, individuals can open the door for accomplices or leave with stolen merchandise. From a security standpoint, these secondary exits should be locked from both sides. Since fire regulations obviously prevent locking the door from the inside, a security device was perfected that is mounted on the upper, inner edge of the door. This "electromagnetic" lock holds the door shut even if the panic bar is depressed. The power for the lock is funnelled through the fire alarm control panel, which releases the power to the door when a fire signal is detected. Once the power is removed from the lock (due to fire or power failure), the panic bar then functions normally. This concept protects the interests of both the fire insurance group and the security insurance group. Very few cities recognize the need to integrate both security and fire protection techniques. This electromagnetic lock is approved in only a relatively few cities. It is difficult to change old procedures, especially when the technology is misunderstood by the committees writing the codes and standards.

**Table 2-2. UL Certificate Classification Chart (March 26, 1979)**

| Type of Alarm | Certi-fication | Extent of Protection | Bell Required | Police | Listed Central Station | Guard Response | Line Security Certificate Available |
|---|---|---|---|---|---|---|---|
| Local Mercantile (outside bell) Premises, Safe or Vault | A,B | Premises 2, 3 safe and vault complete or partial | Yes | Optional | Optional | No | No** |
| Local Mercantile (inside bell) Premises, Safe or Vault | A, B | Premises 2, 3 safe and vault complete or partial | Yes | Either Police or listed central station (fire or burglary) | | No | No** |
| Police Connected Mercantile Premises, Safe or Vault | AA, A BB, B | Premises 2, 3 safe and vault complete or partial | Yes | Either police or listed central station (fire or burglary) | | No | AA, BB |
| Local Bank Safe or Vault | A, B | Complete or partial | Yes | Optional # | Optional # | No | No** |
| Police connected Bank Safe or Vault | AA, A BB, B | Complete or partial | Yes | Either police or listed central station (fire or burglary) | | No | AA, BB |
| Central Station Direct Wire Premises, Safe or Vault | AA, A BB, B CC, C | Premises 1, 2, 3 safe and vault complete or partial | No | No | Yes @ | 15 min* (A, AA) 20 min (B, BB) 30 min (C, CC) | AA, BB, CC |

| System | Grade | Protection | | | | Response times | |
|---|---|---|---|---|---|---|---|
| Transmitter Systems (circuit alarm) Premises, Safe or Vault | BB, B<br>CC, C | Premises 1, 2, 3 safe and vault complete or partial | No | No | Yes @ | 20 min (B, BB)<br>30 min (C, CC) | BB, CC<br>*** |
| Combination Central Station and Local Alarm Premises, Safe or Vault | AA, A<br>BB, B<br>CC, C | Premises 1, 2, 3 safe and vault complete or partial | Yes | No | Yes @ | 20 min* (A, AA)<br>20 min (B, BB)<br>30 min (C, CC) | AA, BB, CC<br>*** |
| Central Station Multiplex Alarms Premises, Safe or Vault | AA, A<br>BB, B<br>CC, C | Premises 1, 2, 3 safe and vault complete or partial | ## | No | Yes @ | 15 min* (A, AA)<br>20 min (B, BB)<br>30 min (C, CC) | AA, BB, CC |
| Central Station Digital Communication Premises, Safe or Vault | B, C | Premises 1, 2, 3 safe and vault complete or partial | Grade B Yes<br>Grade C No | No | Yes @ | 20 min* (B)<br>30 min (C) | No |

* Response times are maximum times.

** Line security is an option but can not be shown on the Certificate.

*** Line security is available but on a limited basis.

# If bell is inside, remote connection required.

## May or may not be required depending upon equipment used.

@ RECORDING OF OPENING AND CLOSING SIGNALS IS MANDATORY.

THE ABOVE INFORMATION IS TAKEN FROM UL 365, 609, 611, 681 and UL 681 APPENDIX A.

1 Party Control          2 Party Control

### American Society for Testing and Materials (ASTM)

In the mid-1970s, the American Society for Testing & Materials created a committee (F-12) that brought together individuals from the lock industry, the fire protection field, and the security sector to develop voluntary performance standards. They also cooperated with the National Bureau of Standards so that practical testing methods could be developed based on consensus standards. The object was to progress further than UL had gone so that one device could be compared to another. Most of the initial standards that were issued by this group dealt with locking hardware and door protection. They barely touched on electronic intrusion detection — a subject that needed much attention. By 1982, the activity of this committee was limited. They did, however, publish a technical book in cooperation with the National Bureau of Standards, entitled *Building Security*.[3]

Aside from this publication, the ASTM has had little effect on the security industry. Owing to funding limitations after 1980, the Law Enforcement Laboratory (the division within the Bureau of Standards that has dealt in security device testing) ceased to contribute to this field. However, a new F-12 subcommittee of ASTM is exploring the need for new vault and financial building security.

### The National Endowment for the Arts

The National Endowment for the Arts provided funds for upgrading security systems in museums during the late 1970s, but the size of the project did not have much effect on the problem.

### Additional Governmental and Organizational Involvement in Standards

During the mid- to late-1970s, the government entered the area of standards by funding some testing and by passing legislation dealing with the subject of security. The Department of Energy, under a contract with Sandia Laboratories, sponsors tests on security devices to determine the most effective system for sensitive areas such as nuclear plants. While these test results are available to the public, very little useful information has been disseminated.

Standards are informally created by organizations that set minimum standards products must meet. This occurs for products or systems not within the current scope of standard-setting organizations. An example is the U.S. Navy Physical Security Laboratory, which is part of the Naval Civil

Engineering Laboratory, Port Hueneme, California. This laboratory has established minimum requirements for high-security military hardware, which in turn may serve as guidelines for facilities associated with the military.

In the law enforcement sector, the Technology Assessment Program Information Center (TAPIC) scrutinizes supplies, products, and equipment used by police. The guidelines of TAPIC, which is operated by the International Association of Chiefs of Police, Gathersburg, Maryland, influence the purchase decisions of security directors and others outside of law enforcement.

## THE OCCUPATIONAL SAFETY AND HEALTH ACT (OSHA)

Prior to the twentieth century, there were few public laws directed toward promoting safety in the workplace. In 1908 the federal government passed a compensation law for certain civil employees; in 1911 the first state compensation laws were passed. Although workmen's compensation laws were much needed and valued, they were designed to treat the effects rather than the causes of the problem. As a result, hazardous conditions in factories and other workplaces remained uncorrected, and injuries and occupationally related illnesses continued.

In 1910 the U.S. Public Health Service and the U.S. Bureau of Mines conducted studies of occupationally related diseases in the mining and steel industries. In 1913 the first state industrial hygiene programs were established by the New York Department of Labor and the Ohio Department of Health. By 1943 federal employee health service was offered by the Army, Navy, Air Force, and Atomic Energy Commission, and by 1948 compensation laws had been enacted in all forty-eight states.

The Metal and Non-Metallic Mine Safety Act of 1966 provided for mandatory reporting of all accidents, injuries, and diseases of the mines. In addition, training programs for personnel regarding the avoidance and prevention of accidents or unsafe or unhealthful working conditions were required.

The Federal Coal Mine Health and Safety Act of 1969 further delineated mandatory health standards and provided for an advisory committee to study mine problems.

Although the regulations of the 1960s were forerunners in the field of industrial safety legislation, they were directed toward specialized fields and were not applicable to the majority of employers or employees. With the rising incidence of job-related accidents, the public and a vast majority of labor unions began to seek federal guidance in the area of occupational safety and health. After years of political debate and numerous compromises, the *Occupational Safety and Health Act (OSHA)* was signed on December 29, 1970. It is regarded by many as a landmark piece of federal legislation.

The Occupational Safety and Health Act was created " . . . to assure so far as possible every working man and woman in the nation safe and healthful working conditions."

The act and the standards issued by OSHA apply to every employer with one or more employees — a total of five million employees. The act regulates workplaces in all the states, the District of Columbia, Puerto Rico, the Canal Zone, and all other territories under federal government jurisdiction.

---

*Checklist of Employer Responsibilities and Rights Under OSHA*

Responsibilities
As an employer, you must:

- Meet your general duty responsibility to provide a workplace free from recognized hazards that are causing or are likely to cause death or serious physical harm to employees.
- Be familiar with mandatory OSHA standards and make copies available to employees upon request.
- Inform all employees about OSHA.
- Examine workplace conditions to make sure they conform to applicable standards.
- Minimize or reduce hazards.
- Make sure employees have and use safe tools and equipment and that such equipment is properly maintained.
- Use color codes, posters, labels, or signs to warn employees of potential hazards.
- Establish or update operating procedures and communicate them so that employees follow safety and health requirements.
- Provide medical examinations when required by OSHA standards.
- Report to the nearest OSHA office any fatal accident or one which results in the hospitalization of five or more employees.
- Keep OSHA-required records of work-related injuries and illnesses, and post a copy of the totals from the last page of OSHA No. 200 during the entire month of February each year.
- Post, at a prominent location within the workplace, the OSHA poster (OSHA 2203) informing employees of their rights and responsibilities.
- Pay employees for any time spent taking part in an OSHA inspection.

- Provide employees, former employees, and their representatives access to the Log and Summary of Occupational Injuries and Illnesses (OSHA No. 200) at a reasonable time and in a reasonable manner.
- Cooperate with the OSHA compliance officer by furnishing names of authorized employee representatives who may be asked to accompany the compliance officer during an inspection.
- Not discriminate against employees who properly exercise their rights under the act.
- Post OSHA citations at or near the worksite involved. Each citation must remain posted until the violation has been abated, or for three working days, whichever is longer.
- Abate cited violations within the prescribed period.

Rights

As an employer, you have the right to:

- Seek advice and off-site consultation as needed by writing, calling, or visiting the nearest OSHA office.
- Be active in your industry association's involvement in job safety and health.
- Request and receive proper identification of the OSHA compliance officer prior to inspection.
- Be advised by the compliance officer of the reason for an inspection.
- Have an opening and closing conference with the compliance officer.
- File a Notice of Contest with the OSHA area director within 15 working days of receipt of a notice of citation and proposed penalty.
- Apply to OSHA for a temporary variance from a standard if unable to comply because of the unavailability of materials, equipment, or personnel needed to make necessary changes within the required time.
- Take an active role in developing safety and health standards through participation in OSHA Standards Advisory Committees, through nationally recognized standards-setting organizations, and through evidence and views presented in writing or at hearings.
- Avail yourself, if you are a small business employer, of long-term loans through the Small Business Administration to help bring your establishment into compliance, either before or after, an OSHA inspection.

- Be assured of the confidentiality of any trade secrets observed by an OSHA compliance officer during an inspection.

*Checklist of Employee Responsibilities and Rights Under OSHA*

Responsibilities
As an employee, you should:

- Read the OSHA poster at the jobsite.
- Comply with all applicable OSHA standards.
- Follow all employer safety and health rules and regulations, and wear or use prescribed protective equipment while engaged in work.
- Report hazardous conditions to the supervisor.
- Report any job-related injury or illness to the employer, and seek treatment promptly.
- Cooperate with the OSHA compliance officer conducting an inspection if he or she inquires about safety and health conditions in your workplace.
- Exercise your rights under the act in a responsible manner.
- Have your authorized employee representative accompany the OSHA compliance officer during the inspection tour.
- Respond to questions from the OSHA compliance officer, particularly if there is no authorized employee representative accompanying the compliance officer.
- Be paid for any time you spend on OSHA inspection activity.
- Observe any monitoring or measuring of hazardous materials and have the right to see these records, as specified under the act.
- Have your authorized representative, or yourself, review the Log and Summary of Occupational Injuries (OSHA No. 200) at a reasonable time and in a reasonable manner.
- Request a closing discussion with the compliance officer following an inspection.
- Submit a written request to NIOSH for information on whether any substance in your workplace has potential toxic effects in the concentrations being used, and have your name withheld from your employer if you so request.
- Object to the abatement period set in the citation issued to your employer by writing to the OSHA area director within 15 working days of issuance of citation.

Rights
As an employee, you have the right to:

- Demand safety and health on the job without fear of punishment.
- Complain to an employer, union, OSHA, or any other government agency about job safety and health hazards.
- File safety or health grievances.
- Participate on workplace safety and health committees or in union activities concerning job safety and health.
- Participate in OSHA inspections, conferences, hearings, or other OSHA-related activities.
- Review copies of appropriate OSHA standards, rules, regulations, and requirements that the employer should have available at the workplace.
- Request information from your employer on safety and health hazards in the area, on precautions that may be taken, and on procedures to be followed if an employee is involved in an accident or is exposed to toxic substances.
- Request the OSHA area director to conduct an inspection if you believe hazardous conditions or violations of standards exist in your workplace.
- Have your name withheld from your employer, upon request to OSHA, if you file a written and signed complaint.
- Be advised of OSHA actions regarding your complaint and have an informal review, if requested, of any decision not to inspect or issue a citation.

Excluded from the act's coverage are (1) self-employed persons, (2) farms at which only immediate members of the farm employer's family are employed, and (3) workplaces already protected by other federal agencies under federal safety and health statutes.

The primary purposes of the act are as follows:

- To encourage employers and employees to reduce workplace hazards and to implement new or improved safety and health programs.
- To establish "separate but dependent responsibilities and rights" for employers and employees for the achievement of better safety and health conditions.

- To maintain a reporting and recordkeeping system to monitor job-related injuries and illnesses.
- To develop mandatory job safety and health standards and enforce them effectively.
- To provide for the development, analysis, evaluation, and approval of state occupational safety and health programs.

Under the act, employers are responsible for providing their employees with a workplace free from recognized hazards to safety and health. OSHA issues standards and rules for safe and healthful working conditions, tools, equipment, facilities and processes, and conducts workplace inspections to assure that the standards are being followed. When hazards are discovered, employers may be issued citations listing alleged violations, and penalties and abatement periods may be proposed.

OSHA provides a free consultation service in every state for employers who desire help in reorganizing and correcting safety and health hazards in their workplaces. This service may be requested by telephone or letter. The consultation visit will consist of an opening conference, a walk-through tour, and a closing conference at which problems, solutions, and abatement periods may be discussed.

Small Business Administration (SBA) loans are available to small businesses that are likely to suffer financially in making the necessary additions or alterations to their facilities in order to become compliant with OSHA regulations.

## THE TASK FORCE ON PRIVATE SECURITY

Crime prevention is now regarded as a joint venture between the public and private sectors in the United States. Until the advent of studies supported by the Law Enforcement Assistance Administration (LEAA), however, little qualitative information about private security was available. LEAA grants provided the impetus for the Task Force on Private Security to provide research, analysis, and recommendations on the security industry. This comprehensive report, which was issued in 1976 through the National Advisory Committee on Criminal Justice Standards and Goals, establishes goals and proposed standards for the private security industry.

These goals and standards are not meant to be the "law of the land," but they do serve as guidelines for local communities, counties, and states in preparing their own regulations and in understanding what the trends are concerning private security. What the Task Force on Private Security recommended in many cases will become public policy, or already is, in many parts of the country.

The Private Security Task Force Report emphasizes the fact that the public sector should take closer note of the strengths and weaknesses of private security. Private security probably will support the responsibilities of law enforcement more in the future than it has in the past. Private security increasingly may provide services that relate directly to the protection, detection, and prosecution functions of public law enforcement. In a few communities private security companies provide security officers, on a test basis, replacing or supporting law enforcement officers.

Many security directors have learned that a case must be presented on "a silver platter" to the prosecuting attorney in order for it to be accepted. As a result, security directors are beginning to learn what prosecutors need and are taking steps to provide it.

Some of the goals and standards of the task force report are particularly important in that they reflect the weaknesses of the security industry today, making predictions as to where changes are likely to occur (see Table 2-3 for a state-by-state summary of security regulations and procedures). Standards are specific objectives to be recognized by public policy and goals relate to the general objectives to improve security and help make the standards work. Following are some of the more important standards identified by the task force:

**Goal 1.1: Selection of Qualified Personnel.** Primary emphasis in the screening process should be placed on selecting qualified personnel who will perform efficiently and preferably will make a career in private security. Currently, most security personnel are not in, and do not remain in, security work by choice, but rather by necessity.

**Goal 1.2: Commensurate Salaries.** In an effort to reduce the attrition rate of the industry, salaries for private security personnel should be commensurate with experience, training and/or education, job responsibilities, and other criteria related to the job performed.

In an annual study of security/patrol guard compensations published in *Security Letter*, among all positions (except for material handler) the security guard received the lowest hourly pay among approximately 20 to 60 different positions. In fact, the security guard's compensation is significantly lower than that for cleaning personnel, the next lowest paying position.

**Standard 1.3: Preemployment Screening.** In order to determine whether prospective personnel are trustworthy and capable, preemployment screening should be initiated. Preemployment screening should include a screening interview, honesty test, background investigation, and other appropriate job-related tests. The security industry attracts at least the same

**Table 2-3. Private Security Task Force To The National Advisory Committee on Criminal Justice Standards and Goals**

| State | Armored car | Central station alarm | Counter-intelligence service | Couriers | Detection-of-deception examiner | Guards and patrol | Guard-dog service | Private detective or investigator | License for revenue only | No regulation | Written exam | Residency required | Citizenship: U.S. | Resident Alien | Min. age 18 | 20 | 21 | 25 | Exp. req. 1 | 2 | 3 | 4 | 5 | general |
|---|---|---|---|---|---|---|---|---|---|---|---|---|---|---|---|---|---|---|---|---|---|---|---|---|
| Alabama | | | | | | | | | × | × | | | | | | | | | | | | | | |
| Alaska | | | | | | | | | × | × | | | | | | | | | | | | | | |
| Arizona | | | | | | × | | × | | | × | × | × | | × | | | | | 2 | | | | |
| Arkansas | | | | | | × | × | × | | | × | | × | | × | | | | | | | | | |
| California | | | | | | × | × | | | | × | × | | | | | × | | 1 | | | | | |
| Colorado | | | | | | | | | | × | | | | | | | | | | | | | | |
| Connecticut | | | | | | × | | × | | | | | | | × | | | | | | | | | |
| Delaware | | | | | | × | | × | | | | | | | × | | | | | | | 4 | | |
| Florida | 1 | | | | × | × | × | × | | | × | | × | × | × | | | | | | | 4 | | |
| Georgia | | | | | | × | × | × | | | × | | × | | × | | | | | | | | | |
| Hawaii | | | | | | × | × | × | | | × | | × | | | | | | | | | | | |
| Idaho | | | | | | | | | | × | | | | | | | | | | | | | | |
| Illinois | | | | | × | × | | × | | | × | | × | | × | | | | | | | | | |
| Indiana | | | | | | × | | × | | | × | | × | | | | | | | | | | | |
| Iowa | | | | | × | × | | × | | | × | | × | | × | | | | | | | | | |
| Kansas | | | | | | × | × | × | | | × | | × | | × | | | | | | | | | |
| Kentucky | | | | | | | | | | × | | | | | | | | | | | | | | |
| Louisiana | | | | | | | | | | × | | | | | | | | × | | | | | | |
| Maine | | | | | | × | | × | | | | | | | | | × | | | | | | 5 | |
| Maryland | | | | | | × | | × | | | | | × | × | × | | | | | | | | 5 | |
| Massachusetts | | | | | | × | | × | | | | | × | × | | | | | | | | | | |
| Michigan | × | × | | × | × | × | | × | | | | × | × | | × | | | | | | | | | |
| Minnesota | | | | | | × | | × | | | | | × | | × | | | | | | | | | |
| Mississippi | | | | | | | | | | × | | | | | | | | | | | | | | |
| Missouri | | | | | | | | | | × | | | | | | | | | | | | | | |
| Montana | | | | | | × | | × | | | × | × | × | | × | | | | | | | | | |
| Nebraska | | | | | × | × | | × | | | × | × | × | | × | | | | | | | | | |
| Nevada | | | | | | × | × | × | | | × | × | × | | × | × | × | | | | | | | |
| New Hampshire | | | | | | | | × | | | | | | × | | | | | | | | | | |
| New Jersey | | | | | × | × | | × | | | × | | × | | × | | | | | | | | | |
| New Mexico | | | | | | × | × | × | | | × | | × | | × | | | | | 6 | 7 | | | |
| New York | | | | | × | × | | × | | | × | | × | | | | | | | 6 | 7 | | | |
| North Carolina | × | × | × | × | × | × | × | × | | | × | | × | | × | | | | | | | | | |
| North Dakota | | | | | | × | × | × | | | × | | × | | × | | | | | | | | | |
| Ohio | | | | | | × | × | × | | | × | | | | | | | | | | | | | |
| Oklahoma | | | | | | | | | × | × | | | | | | | | | | | | | | |
| Oregon | | | | | | | | | × | × | | | | | | | | | | | | | | |
| Pennsylvania | | | | | | × | | × | | | × | | × | | | | × | | | | | | | |
| Rhode Island | | | | | | | | | | × | | | | | | | | | | | | | | |
| South Carolina | | | | | | × | | × | | | × | | × | | × | | | | | | | | | |
| South Dakota | | | | | | | | | | × | | | | | | | | | | | | | | |
| Tennessee | | | | | | × | | | × | | | | | | | | | | | | | | | 8 |
| Texas | × | × | | × | | × | × | × | | | × | | × | | × | | | | 1 | | | | | |
| Utah | | × | | | | × | × | × | | | × | × | × | | × | | | | | | | | | |
| Vermont | | | | | | × | | × | | | × | | × | | × | | | | | | | | | |
| Virginia | | | | | | | | | × | × | | | | | | | | | | | | | | |
| Washington | | | | | | | | | × | × | | | | | | | | | | | | | | |
| West Virginia | | | | | | × | | × | | | × | | × | | × | | | | | 2 | | | | |
| Wisconsin | | | | | | × | | × | | | × | | | | | | | | 1 | | | | | |
| Wyoming | | | | | | | | | | × | × | | | | | | | | 1 | | | | | |

| | |
|---|---|
| **Education:** High school | |
| No felony conviction | |
| Good character | |
| **Licensing Period** | |
| One year | |
| Two years | |
| Five years | |
| **Application Procedures** | |
| Photo and fingerprints | |
| Address of applicant | |
| References | |
| Employment record | |
| Age, date, and place of birth | |
| Business name | |
| Name and residence of partners, officers, directors | |
| Experience qualifications | |
| Nature of business | |
| Previous residences | |
| Criminal record | |
| Statement of classification seeking | |
| Address of principal place of business | |
| Branch offices | |
| Info deemed necessary | |
| Letter from sheriff and police | |
| Physical description | |
| **Grounds for Denial** | |
| Previous refusal or revocation | |
| Dishonesty or fraud | |
| Bad character | |
| Convicted of: | |
| felony | |
| moral turpitude | |

**Table 2-3.** (continued)

| State | Weapon violation | Burglars instruments | Stolen property | Unlawful entry | Aiding escape | Drugs | Picking pockets | Lewdness | False statement in application | Committed act which is grounds for revocation | Doing an act which requires license | Officer of agency whose license refused or revoked | Hold employment agency license | Negligent in debt payment | Vested with police powers | Failure to provide info | Violate provision of Act | Fingerprint check (Background Investigation) | State | FBI | Grounds for Suspension or Revocation | Violate provision of Act |
|---|---|---|---|---|---|---|---|---|---|---|---|---|---|---|---|---|---|---|---|---|---|---|
| Alabama | | | | | | | | | × | × | | | | | | | | | | | | |
| Alaska | | | | | | | | | | | | | | | | | | | | | | |
| Arizona | | | | | | | | | × | × | | | | | | × | × | | | | × | × |
| Arkansas | | | | | | | | | | | | | | | | | | | | | | |
| California | × | | | | | | | | × | × | × | × | | | | | | | | | | |
| Colorado | | | | | | | | | | | | | | | | | | | | | | |
| Connecticut | | | | | | | | | | | | | | | × | | | | | | | |
| Delaware | | | | | | | | | | | | | | | | | | × | × | × | | × |
| Florida | | | | | | | | | × | × | × | | | | | | | | × | | | |
| Georgia | | | | | | | | | | | | | | | | | | | | × | | |
| Hawaii | | | | | | | | | | | | | | | | | | | | | | |
| Idaho | | | | | | | | | | | | | | | | | | | | | | |
| Illinois | | | | | | | | | | × | | | | | | | | | | | × | × |
| Indiana | | | | | | | | | | | × | | | | | | | | | | | × |
| Iowa | | | | | | | | | × | × | | | | | | × | | | | | | × |
| Kansas | × | | | | | | | | × | × | × | × | | | × | | | | | | | |
| Kentucky | | | | | | | | | | | | | | | | | | | | | | |
| Louisiana | | | | | | | | | | | | | | | | | | | | | | |
| Maine | | | | | | | | | | | | | | | | | | | | | | |
| Maryland | | | | | | | | | × | | × | | | | | | | | | | | |
| Massachusetts | | | | | | | | | | | | | | | | | | | | | | |
| Michigan | | | | | | | | | | | | | | | | | | | | | × | × |
| Minnesota | × | × | × | × | × | | | | × | | | | | | | | | | × | | | × |
| Mississippi | | | | | | | | | | | | | | | | | | | | | | |
| Missouri | | | | | | | | | | | | | | | | | | | | | | |
| Montana | | | | | | | | | | | | | | | | | | × | | | | × |
| Nebraska | | | | | | | | | | | | | | | | | | | | | | × |
| Nevada | × | | | | | | | | × | × | × | × | | | | | | | | | | × |
| New Hampshire | | | | | | | | | | | | | | | | × | | | | | | |
| New Jersey | | | | | | | | | × | | | × | | | | | | | | | | |
| New Mexico | × | | | | | | | | × | × | × | × | | | | | | | × | × | | × |
| New York | × | × | × | × | × | × | | | × | × | | | × | | × | × | | | | | | × |
| North Carolina | × | | | | | | | | × | × | | | | × | | | | | | | | × |
| North Dakota | | | | | | | | | | | | | | | | | | | | | | × |
| Ohio | | | | | | | | | | | | | | | | | | × | | | | × |
| Oklahoma | | | | | | | | | | | | | | | | | | | | | | |
| Oregon | | | | | | | | | | | | | | | | | | | | | | |
| Pennsylvania | × | × | × | × | × | × | × | × | | | | | × | | | | | | × | | | × |
| Rhode Island | | | | | | | | | | | | | | | | | | | | | | × |
| South Carolina | | | | | | | | | | | | | | | | | | | | | | × |
| South Dakota | | | | | | | | | | | | | | | | | | | | | | |
| Tennessee | | | | | | | | | | | | | | | | | | | | | | |
| Texas | × | | | | | | | | × | × | × | × | | | | | | | | | | × |
| Utah | | | | | | | | | | | | | | | | × | | | | | | |
| Vermont | | | | | | | | | | | | | | | | × | | | | | | |
| Virginia | | | | | | | | | | | | | | | | | | | | | | |
| Washington | | | | | | | | | | | | | | | | | | | | | | |
| West Virginia | × | × | × | × | × | × | | | × | | × | | | | | | | | | | | × |
| Wisconsin | | | | | | | | | | | | | | | | | | | | | | × |
| Wyoming | | | | | | | | | | | | | | | | | | | | | | |

Conviction of:
- felony
- moral turpitude
- weapons offense
- assault and battery

False statement in application

Impersonate officer

Failure to render services

Violate court order

Operate without license

Solicit for attorney

Dishonesty fraud

Reveal confidential info

Give legal advice

Mentally incompetent

Insolvency of surety

False advertising

Falsely stating someone employed
  by you

Employees

Licensee responsible

May employ any number

Employee statement

Employer must maintain record

Temporary need not register

Registration required

Application procedure:
- Name and address
- Aliases, former names
- Date and place of birth
- Citizenship
- Employment: 5 year
-   3 year
-   general

**Table 2-3.  (continued)**

| State | Education: 8th | Experience in position | Position duties | Criminal record | Physical description | Fingerprints | Photograph | Never refused a license or revoked | No criminal record | felony | moral turpitude offense | weapon violation | burglars instruments | aiding escape | drugs | Good character | Identification cards | Badge restrictions | Uniform restrictions | Confidentiality of info | Local regulation allowed | Advertising regulated | Surety required |
|---|---|---|---|---|---|---|---|---|---|---|---|---|---|---|---|---|---|---|---|---|---|---|---|
| Wyoming | | | | | | | | | | | | | | | | | | | | | | | |
| Wisconsin | | | | | × | × | × | | × | | | | | | | | × | × | | | | | |
| West Virginia | | | | | | | | × | × | | | | | | | × | × | × | | | | | × |
| Washington | | | | | | | | | | | | | | | | | | | | | | | |
| Virginia | | | | | | | | | | | | | | | | | | | | | | | |
| Vermont | | | | | | | | | | | × | × | | | | | × | | | × | | | |
| Utah | | | | | | | | | | | | | | | | | | | | | | | |
| Texas | | | × | | | × | × | × | | × | × | × | | | | × | × | × | | × | | × | |
| Tennessee | | | | | | | | | | | | | | | | | | | | | | | |
| South Dakota | | | | | | | | | | | | | | | | | | | | | | | |
| South Carolina | | | | × | | × | × | × | | × | × | | | | | × | × | × | × | | | | |
| Rhode Island | | | | | | | | | | | | | | | | | | | | | | | |
| Pennsylvania | | | | × | | × | | × | | | | × | × | × | × | × | × | × | | × | | | |
| Oregon | | | | | | | | | | | | | | | | | | | | | | | |
| Oklahoma | | | | | | | | | | | | | | | | | | | | | | | |
| Ohio | | | | | × | × | × | × | | | | | | | | | × | × | × | × | | | |
| North Dakota | | | | | | | | | | | | | | | | | × | | | | | | |
| North Carolina | | | | × | | × | × | | | | | | | | | | | | | × | | × | |
| New York | | | | | | | | | × | × | × | | | | | | × | × | | | | × | × |
| New Mexico | | | × | | | × | × | | | × | × | | | | | | × | × | × | × | × | × | |
| New Jersey | | | | | | | | × | × | × | × | | × | × | × | | × | × | × | | | | |
| New Hampshire | | | | | | | | | | | | | | | | × | × | × | | | | | |
| Nevada | | | | | | × | | × | | | | | | | | | × | × | × | × | × | | |
| Nebraska | | | | | | | | | | | | | | | | | | | | | | | |
| Montana | | | | | | | | | | × | | | | | | | | | | × | | | |
| Missouri | | | | | | | | | | | | | | | | | | | | | | | |
| Mississippi | | | | | | | | | | | | | | | | | | | | | | | |
| Minnesota | | | | | | | | | | | | | | | | | × | × | × | × | | | |
| Michigan | | × | | | | × | | | | × | × | | | | | | × | × | × | × | × | | |
| Massachusetts | | | | | | | | | | | | | | | | | × | × | × | | | | |
| Maryland | | | | | | × | | | | | | | | | | | × | × | | × | | | |
| Maine | | | | | | | | × | | × | × | | | | | | | | | × | | | |
| Louisiana | | | | | | | | | | | | | | | | | | | | | | | |
| Kentucky | | | | | | | | | | | | | | | | | | | | | | | |
| Kansas | | | | | | | | | | | | | | | | | × | × | × | × | × | | |
| Iowa | | | | | | | | | | | | | | | | | × | × | × | | | | |
| Indiana | | | | | × | | × | | | | | | | | | | × | × | | × | | | |
| Illinois | | | | | | × | × | × | | × | × | | | | | | × | | | × | | | |
| Idaho | | | | | | | | | | | | | | | | | | | | | | | |
| Hawaii | | × | | | | | × | | | × | × | | | | | | | | | | | | |
| Georgia | | | × | × | | × | × | × | | × | × | | | | | | | | | | | | |
| Florida | | | | | | | | | | | | | × | × | | | | | | | | | |
| Delaware | | | | × | | × | × | × | | × | × | × | | × | × | | | | | | | | |
| Connecticut | | × | | × | | × | × | × | | × | × | | | | | | | | | | | | |
| Colorado | | | | | | | | | | | | | | | | | | | | | | | |
| California | | × | | | | × | × | × | | | | | | | | × | | | | | | | |
| Arkansas | | | | | | | | | | × | × | | | | | | | | | | | | |
| Arizona | | | × | | | × | × | × | | × | | × | | | | × | × | × | × | × | | | |
| Alaska | | | | | | | | | | | | | | | | | | | | | | | |
| Alabama | × | | | | | | | | | | | | | | | | | | | | | | |

| | 11 | 12 | 13 | 14 | 15 | 16 | 17 | 18 |
|---|---|---|---|---|---|---|---|---|
| $25,000 | | | | | | | | |
| $10,000 | x | x | x | x | | x | x | x |
| $ 5,000 | x | x | x | x | x | | | x |
| $ 3,000 | x | | x | x | | | | |
| $ 2,500 | | | | x | | | | |
| $ 2,000 | | x | | x | | | | x |
| Liability insurance required | x | | x | | | x | | x |
| Firearms | | | | | | | | |
| Must possess state weapons permit | x | x | x | x | | x | | x |
| Authorized to carry firearms when on duty | | | | x | | | | |
| Training required before authorization | x | | | | x | | | |
| Training for Unarmed Personnel | | | | | | | | |

number of emotionally disturbed persons as does any other industry. Yet because of the potential liability from irrational acts that a security guard may make, the need to assure the emotional strength of the individual is great.

The security industry has been slow to date in applying insights from the behavioral sciences. Only one firm among the larger security companies — Guardsmark — routinely conducts psychological screening of prospective employees. Guardsmark administers the well-established MMPI test (Minnesota Multiphasic Personality Inventory). This multiple choice test, which is actuarially based, permits identification of psychopathic signs among those who take it.

**Standard 1.4: Employer Exchange Information.** Employers should cooperate in exchanging information on previous work performance and other data relating to selective criteria. Since 10 to 15 percent of security guards have previously worked as a security guard, this simple background check can be valuable.

**Standard 1.5: Equal Employment Opportunity.** Employers should comply with equal employment opportunity guidelines and other federal, state, or local guidelines that preclude discrimination based on sex, race, or age. In fact, women and minority group persons have good opportunities in private security. In its 1978 annual report Pinkerton's noted that it had increased minority employees in the United States from 21.3 to 22 percent of the total 1978 employee population over the previous year. The number of women employees rose from 10.7 to 14 percent. Women have been used in large numbers in airport preboarding screening and in crowd control assignments. Since that time other gains have been made.

**Standard 1.7: Availability of Criminal History Records.** Criminal history records for offenses that are specified by statute or other authority as grounds for denying employment should be made available to employers to assist them in the screening of private security personnel. Since January 1, 1978, each state has had the right to access private security industry conviction data. Furthermore, criminal history record information, including arrest data, that relates to an individual currently being processed through the criminal justice system may be made available to employers. This information must be made available as a matter of state policy, however.

The very nature of security work itself seems to attract certain people who are ineligible for security employment because of their criminal records. Yet privacy legislation has made criminal conviction records unavailable to security employers in many areas. Consequently, undesirable workers have been employed by security companies with the result that some of their actions have created liability for the security companies and their clients. States should make this information available to security employers to assure that persons with criminal records are not hired for security positions. Meanwhile, employers should screen applicants for security-related employment carefully.

**Goal 2.1: Training in Private Security.**  Private security personnel require training for the type of responsibilities they assume in the protection of persons and property. Training should be instituted at all levels to insure that personnel are fully prepared to exercise their responsibilities effectively and efficiently.

The lack of training of any real quality or duration has been a barrier in the past to the professionalism of security personnel. In recent years, however, college-level programs and courses, police academy training, private seminars and courses, and textbooks have provided resources. Nevertheless, at the operations level a great need exists for greater and better training for security personnel.

**Goal 2.2: Professional Certification Programs.**  Professional associations should study the feasibility of developing voluntary certification programs for private security managerial personnel.

The American Society for Industrial Security currently offers training through its institute and certification examinations that lead to a certificate of Certified Protection Professional (CPP). Some security people who have passed this examination place these initials after their names on stationery and on correspondence relating to security activities.

**Standard 2.5. Preassignment and Basic Training.**  Any person employed or assigned for employment as an investigator or detective, guard or watchman, armored car personnel or armed courier, alarm system installer or servicer, or alarm respondent, including part-time personnel, should successfully:

1. Complete a minimum of 8 hours formal preassignment training.
2. Complete a basic training course of a minimum of 32 hours within 3 months of assignment. A maximum of 16 hours can be supervised on-the-job training.

**Standard 2.6: Arms Training.**  All private security personnel, including part-time personnel, should:

1. Be required to complete successfully a 24-hour firearms course that includes legal and policy requirements (or submission of

evidence of competence and efficiency) prior to assignment to a job that requires a firearm.

2.  Be required to requalify at least once every 12 months with the firearms they carry while performing private security duties (the requalification phase should cover legal and policy requirements).

**Standard 2.7: Ongoing Training.**   Private security employers should insure that private security personnel are given ongoing training by using roll call training, training bulletins, and other training methods.

**Standard 2.8: Training of Supervisors and Managers.**   Private security employers should provide effective job-related training for supervisory and managerial employees. Appropriate prior training or educational or professional certification should be accepted to meet this requirement.

**Standard 2.9: State Authority and Responsibility for Training.**   A state government regulatory agency should have the authority and responsibility to accredit training schools, approve training curriculums, and certify instructors for the private security industry.

Commercial schools have sometimes charged disadvantaged young people, as well as those with limited financial resources, large sums of money for security training programs. While some of these programs may be worthwhile, others have been of little value relative to their cost. Minimum standards would help raise the significance and value of all types of security training programs.

**Standard 2.10: State Boards to Coordinate Training Efforts.**   Appropriate state boards and agencies should coordinate efforts to provide training opportunities for private security personnel and persons interested in preparing for security employment, through utilization of physical and personnel resources of area vocational schools and colleges and universities.

**Goal 3.1: Code of Ethics.**   A code of ethics should be adopted and enforced for private security personnel and employers.

The proposed codes of ethics for private security management and for private security personnel are as follows:

### Code of Ethics for Private Security Management

As managers for private security functions and employees, we pledge:

I. To recognize that our principal responsibilities are, in the service of our organizations and clients, to protect life and property as well as to prevent and reduce crime against our business, industry, or other organizations and institutions; and, in the public interest, to uphold the law, and to respect the constitutional rights of all persons.

II. To be guided by a sense of integrity, honor, justice, and morality in the conduct of business; in all personnel matters; in relationships with government agencies, clients, and employers; and in responsibilities to the general public.

III. To strive faithfully to render security services of the highest quality and to work continuously to improve our knowledge and skills, and, thereby, improve the overall effectiveness of private security.

IV. To uphold the trust of our employers, our clients, and the public by performing our functions within the law, not ordering or condoning violations of law, and ensuring that our security personnel conduct their assigned duties lawfully and with proper regard for the rights of others.

V. To respect the reputation and practice of others in private security, but to expose to the proper authorities any conduct that is unethical or unlawful.

VI. To apply uniform and equitable standards of employment in recruiting and selecting personnel, regardless of race, creed, color, sex, or age, and in providing salaries commensurate with job responsibilities and with training, education, and experience.

VII. To cooperate with recognized and responsible law enforcement and other criminal justice agencies; and to comply with security licensing and registration laws and other statutory requirements that pertain to our business.

VIII. To respect and protect the confidential and privileged information of employers and clients beyond the term of our employment, except where their interests are contrary to law or to this Code of Ethics.

IX. To maintain a professional posture in all business relationships with employers and clients, with others in the private security field, and with members of other professions; and to insist that our personnel adhere to the highest standards of professional conduct.

X. To encourage the professional advancement of our personnel by assisting them to acquire appropriate security knowledge, education, and training.

## Code of Ethics for Private Security Employees

In recognition of the significant contribution of private security to crime prevention and reduction, as a private security employee, I pledge:

I. To accept the responsibilities and fulfill the obligations of my role: protecting life and property; preventing and reducing crimes against my employer's business, or other organizations and institutions to which I am assigned; upholding the law; and respecting the constitutional rights of all persons.

II. To conduct myself with honesty and integrity, and to adhere to the highest moral principles in the performance of my security duties.

III.  To be faithful, diligent, and dependable in discharging my duties, and to
      uphold, at all times, the laws, policies, and procedures that protect the
      rights of others.
IV.   To observe the precepts of truth, accuracy, and prudence, without allow-
      ing personal feelings, prejudices, animosities, or friendships to influ-
      ence my judgments.
V.    To report to my superiors, without hesitation, any violation of the law or
      of my employer's or client's regulations.
VI.   To respect and protect the confidential and privileged information of
      my employer or client beyond the term of my employment, except
      where their interests are contrary to law or to this Code of Ethics.
VII.  To cooperate with all recognized and responsible law enforcement and
      government agencies in matters within their jurisdiction.
VIII. To accept no compensation, commission, gratuity, or other advantage
      without the knowledge and consent of my employer.
IX.   To conduct myself professionally at all times, and to perform my duties
      in a manner that reflects credit upon myself, my employer, and private
      security.
X.    To strive continually to improve my performance by seeking training
      and educational opportunities that will better prepare me for my private
      security duties.

Source: The Law Enforcement and Private Security Relationship Committee
of the Private Security Advisory Council.

**Standard 3.2: Conduct of Private Security Personnel.**   Private security personnel should perform their security functions within generally recognized guidelines for the protection of individual rights.

Private security officers do not have to provide persons arrested and
detained for law enforcement with the *Miranda* warning. This warning
informs the detainee of his or her rights: to remain silent; that anything he
or she says may be used in court against the person; that a lawyer may be
present during questioning; and that a lawyer will be provided if one is not
available.

The fact that this warning does not have to be given by private security
personnel to those they arrest often greatly aids private security in obtaining confessions or in obtaining information that can help lead to a conviction. Nonetheless, private security has a responsibility to protect individual rights, while simultaneously recognizing the basic responsibility of
private security to protect private property.

**Standard 3.3: Reporting of Criminal Violations.**   All felonies and serious
misdemeanors discovered by private security personnel should be reported to the appropriate criminal justice agencies. Private security personnel should cooperate with these agencies in all subsequent actions
relating to the crimes.

A SUMMARY OF PRIVATE SECURITY LEGISLATION

Key to Numbers Used in Summary of Private Security Legislation

1.  Except if regulated by public service commission.
2.  Require 1 year as guard or 3 years as policeman.
3.  Investigator must have 2 years related experience. Guard or watchman must have 1 year related experience.
4.  1 year of the 3 year requirement must be met in Florida.
5.  Require 3 years as Police Investigator, 5 years as full-time licensed Investigator, or 10 years as a Police Officer.
6.  Require 2 years experience for Investigator license. Require 1 year experience for Private Patrol Operator license.
7.  Investigator must have 3 years related experience. Security Patrol Operator must have 2 years experience.
8.  Licensee must have 2 years experience in security or 3 years experience as Policeman.
9.  Require photograph only.
10. Require fingerprints only.
11. Require a maximum of 10 hours.
12. Armed security guards employed in a police capacity shall receive not less than 16 hours.
13. Require 30 hours.
14. Require 16 hours beyond the 97 hours required for security commission.
15. Hours deemed necessary by the Board.
16. Require minimum of 16 hours.
17. Unarmed guard — 4 hours. In-house investigators — 28 hours. Private detective — 45 hours.
18. A person employed by and compensated by a private organization for the purpose of enforcing the ordinance and laws they are empowered to enforce, to secure the premises of their employer and to enforce their rules must complete a 118 hour training program.

Source: Prepared by the Private Security Task Force to the National Advisory Committee on Criminal Justice Standards and Goals (1976).

**Standard 3.4: Employer Responsibilities.** Employers should provide a working environment, including adequate and serviceable equipment, conducive to the efficient performance of the security functions assigned.

**Standard 3.5: Maintaining Data on Criminal Activities.** The private security industry has a responsibility to maintain internal data on criminal activities to develop, improve, and assess effectiveness of crime reduction programs.

### SUMMARY

The private security industry today is in need of direction and some form of regulation. Before the private security sector can become an accepted part of the criminal justice system, it must establish standards that are meaningful both to the industry and the public.

Alarm manufacturers in their competitive haste to produce a marketable device often neglect to establish and follow standardized testing procedures. As a result, devices are often left to be "tested" on the customer's wall. When a device is found to be defective, it is not recalled (as in the automobile industry) but instead is declared obsolete and replaced by a "newer and better" model the following year. Of course, the customer is required to pay twice for this innovation.

Attempts to upgrade the industry by its own membership have proven futile, and often disastrous. The American Society of Testing and Materials (ASTM) tried to establish standards for alarm manufacturers, but the voting members of the various standard-writing committees were manufacturers who were unwilling to establish standards that made their own devices obsolete. The few standards issued by this society after efforts of many months dealt with nonchallenging topics, such as "the thickness of door jambs," completely avoiding the subject of electronic alarms. Additional standards may yet come from ASTM in the future.

The National Bureau of Standards tried to become an objective influence on the industry by creating the Law Enforcement Standard Lab (LESL) under a Department of Justice grant. The standards produced by this small, short-lived group were so esoteric that they were, and still are, largely ignored by the industry.

The only testing organization commanding the respect of both the public and the industry is Underwriters Laboratories (UL). Although UL standards are extremely valuable and have done much to advance the level of workmanship in the burglary and fire alarm field, it must be realized that these standards deal basically with safety factors (fire and shock hazards) and the equipment's resistance to defeat. Although insurance companies rely heavily on UL designations, there is no assurance that an installation with the UL designation is better protected than premises without it.

Private security is a growing, but misguided, industry. Indications are that public policy is beginning to force, or at least guide, the industry into a more professional status. The Private Security Task Force Report has taken the first major step toward establishing standards and goals for upgrading the industry. In addition, Congress has issued laws governing bank security and, through the Occupational Safety and Health Act (OSHA), workplace safety requirements.

The primary effect of OSHA on the security profession has been to expand the duties traditionally assigned to the security function. In many cases this has provided security directors with increasing authority and salaries, and it has upgraded their status within the firm's hierarchal structure. Most large firms already have a security force standing ready to provide the manpower necessary to identify potential sources of hazards and unsafe working conditions. This security force is capable of applying its investigative skills that are a necessary component of so many security positions to this task. As the industry continues to develop means for complying with OSHA regulations, a growing need will exist for a body of professionals skilled in both safety and security operations.

The goals and standards established by the Task Force on Private Security serve as guidelines for local communities, counties, and states in preparing their own regulations and understanding the trends concerning private security. Arthur J. Bilek, Task Force Chairman and a former vice-president of Pinkerton's, emphasized that law enforcement has much to gain from cooperation with private security, which he terms:

> . . . one massive resource filled with significant numbers of personnel, armed with a wide array of technology and directed by professionals who have spent their adult lifetime learning how to prevent and reduce crime. . . .[4]

Today, criminal justice practitioners are beginning to perceive private security professionals as allies in their struggle with crime. There remains, however, a continuing need to upgrade existing standards in this industry, raising them to the level of other phases of the criminal justice system. Until this is accomplished, it will be difficult to elicit the cooperation necessary for the combined resources of the public and private law enforcement sectors to combat crime facing society in the 1980s.

A start has been made toward the establishment of nationally accepted standards and goals for the private security industry. In addition, as already mentioned, the government is beginning to become involved in this area. An issue that will undoubtedly be argued from both sides in the years ahead is how much, or how little, government intervention there should be and whether it should come primarily from the state, local, or federal government.

## NOTES

1. The *Catalog: Standard for Safety* is issued periodically by UL free of charge. It lists all standards, including the latest revisions. The catalog and other information are available from UL, Publication Stock, 333 Pfingsten Rd., Northbrook, IL 60062.

2. To receive the latest copy of the list, write Underwriters Laboratories, Inc., Burglar Protection and Signaling Dept., 1285 Walt Whitman Road, Melville, NY 11747.

3. *Building Security*, edited by John Strolk, ASTM Special Technical Publication 729, available from ASTM, 1916 Race St., Philadelphia, PA 19103.

4. Bilek, A. J., *Private Security: Report of the Task Force on Private Security*, National Advisory Committee on Criminal Justice Standards and Goals, 1976, Superintendent of Documents, U.S. Government Printing Office, Washington, D.C. #052–003–00225–6. This report was also printed as *Private Security: Standards and Goals — From the Official Private Security Task Force Report*, 1977 (Cincinnati, Ohio: Anderson Publishing Co.).

# Chapter 3
# Legal Considerations in Private Security

Private security developed because of the need to provide protection and security in excess of that provided by public law enforcement. Patrol and investigative services similar to the services provided by local police, but which local police could not or would not perform, became available from private sources.

Private security personnel perform functions similar to public law enforcement officers and often wear uniforms and badges and carry weapons, all of which suggest they are carrying out "official" duties. Their legal authority differs in many significant respects from that of public officers, however.

In general, private security personnel have no more formal authority than does the average citizen in the United States. A private security officer or investigator possesses only that authority which the person or company that hired him possesses — no more and no less. Because the security officer acts in the place of the entity that hires or employs him, the employer's basic right to protect persons and property is transferred to the security officer.

There are situations, however, in which the security officer's authority differs from the authority possessed by his employer. When security officers have gone through a special commissioning process, they are given authority and responsibilities similar to public police officers. The difficulty in discussing rules of conduct for security officers revolves around the different types of people who perform security related duties. As a minimum, three categories of personnel currently perform security tasks in the United States: (1) the private citizen, (2) the commissioned citizen, and (3) the public law enforcement officer who works in an off-duty security job. The authority of these security personnel often changes when the individuals leave their employer's premises. Most security personnel today fall into the first category, and for this reason the discussion in this chapter concentrates on the private citizen as security officer.

The material in this chapter is divided into three sections. The first section examines the sources of authority for private security personnel. The second section explores the authority of private individuals to arrest, search, seize evidence, interrogate others, and use force. The third section describes some of the criminal and civil sanctions that can be taken against security officers who abuse their authority.

## SOURCE OF AUTHORITY

There is no single source of authority for the private security officer. The authority of private security personnel is derived indirectly from various sources of law — the substantive areas of tort, contract, and criminal law as well as constitutional law and administrative law. Each area must be considered when determining the legal basis for a security officer's actions.

### Tort Law

Tort law is the primary source for the authority of security personnel.[1] The law of torts is found in statutes and common law as it has been developed by judges. Tort law regulates civil relationships between people. It allows a person who has been injured or damaged by another to sue that person in civil court to obtain compensation for the injury inflicted.

The word "tort" is derived from the Latin word "tortus," which roughly translates as "wrong." A tort is a civil wrong arising out of conduct that affects some legally protected interest and causes damage.

Tort law differs from criminal law in that it involves a private party seeking individual relief for an injury. A crime is a wrong against the public as a whole for which the state seeks redress. A tort is commenced and maintained by the injured party (the plaintiff) in order to obtain compensation for the wrong done by the tortfeasor (the defendant).

Tort law is a source of private security authority in a negative way. The law restricts rather than authorizes activity of security personnel because of the threat of a lawsuit against a security officer for some act or failure to act that might cause injury. Tort law sets limits on the activity of security personnel by defining, through case precedent, the boundaries of reasonable conduct.

Tort liability may be imposed for an intentional or a negligent act. In some circumstances liability for a tort can be imposed even though an individual is without fault. Imposing liability without fault is called strict liability and generally does not apply to the actions of security personnel. Tort law is discussed further in the third section, "Sanctions for the Misuse of Authority."

### Criminal Law

A crime is any act or failure to act that injures the public at large and that is prohibited and punishable by law. In the case of crime, the state brings the action in the form of a criminal prosecution to protect the interests of society.[2] The perpetrator is answerable to society and not to an individual.

An action by an individual can result in both criminal and civil liability. For example, assault, battery, criminal defamation, and criminal damage to property are torts as well as crimes. The injured party can bring a civil suit against the wrongdoer and the state can bring a separate criminal prosecution against the same offender.

Criminal law, like tort law, acts only as a deterrent to improper conduct and sets forth parameters within which the security officer functions. Other aspects of criminal law are discussed in the third section.

### Contract Law

A contract is an agreement between two or more competent persons and consists of a promise or set of promises, which the law will enforce, or the performance of which the law recognizes as a duty.[3] Under the agreement, each party promises to perform some act or to refrain from performing some act in reliance upon, and in consideration of, the other party's promise to perform or to refrain from performing some act.

A contract may be express or implied, oral or written. An express contract is one in which the agreement between the parties has been indicated in words, oral or written. However, if the promises of the parties are inferred from their conduct or acts alone, without spoken or written words, the contract is said to be an implied contract. The law implies an agreement because the facts and circumstances demonstrate an intent to agree even though the parties failed to formally state their mutual assent.

A contract is breached where, without legal excuse, a party either fails to perform or performs in a manner not in accord with the terms of the agreement. A court can remedy the breach by requiring the breaching party to perform or by awarding money damages to the innocent party.

Contractual arrangements can limit the authority of the security officer. In contracts between a business enterprise and a contract guard service, the business could create standards of conduct for agency guards more restrictive than those permitted by law. For example, the business enterprise could indicate in the contract that guards are to be unarmed even though according to local law the guards could carry weapons.

Guard service contracts typically determine the respective liabilities of the business entities should someone be injured by an action of the guard.[4] Such agreements cannot prevent an entity from being sued by a third party, but they can determine which entity will ultimately bear the burden of assuming the cost of any judgment awarded against them.

Labor contracts may restrict the type of action security personnel may take against union employees. For example, collective bargaining contracts might limit inspections of employees' packages or restrict the conditions under which interrogations are conducted.[5]

## Constitutional Law

The U.S. Constitution sets forth the basic rights of all individuals. In so doing, it places limitations on the conduct of the government and its officers. Government officers include police officers; security officers who have been commissioned by a government agency and thereby given similar authority to the public police officer, and anyone who is acting for, or in conjunction with, either the police officer or the commissioned security officer.

With the notable exception of private security officers in California,[6] constitutional restrictions apply only to government officers and not to private citizens.[7] However, the courts are beginning to look closely at the purpose of noncommissioned private security officers. If their activities are similar to those of the public police and are performed with the same ultimate purpose (e.g., prosecution of the offender), constitutional restrictions could be applied to them.

The mere licensing of private security personnel by a state regulatory agency is not "state action" and does not bring the acts of a noncommissioned security officer within the scope of the U.S. Constitution.[8] State licensing laws are generally intended to regulate some form of business and, with few exceptions, do not confer any type of police authority on the person licensed.

The U.S. Constitution is applicable to the activities of security personnel if they have been commissioned as some type of special officer. In these cases, the parts of the Constitution most applicable are the Fourth

Amendment's prohibition against unreasonable searches and seizures, the Fifth Amendment's guarantee against compelled testimony, the Sixth Amendment's right to legal assistance in criminal proceedings, and the Fourteenth Amendment's guarantee of due process.[9]

In 1914 the U.S. Supreme Court provided a remedy for the violation of an individual's constitutional rights by government officers. In the case of *Weeks v. United States*[10] the Court adopted an exclusionary evidence rule. The Court held that evidence obtained by federal officers through unconstitutional methods rendered the evidence inadmissible in a federal criminal prosecution. This "exclusionary rule" was made applicable to state court criminal proceedings in 1961 in the case of *Mapp v. Ohio.*[11]

The primary purpose of the exclusionary rule was, and is, to deter unlawful conduct by public law enforcement officers. A public officer will be discouraged from engaging in unlawful activities — illegal arrests, unreasonable searches — if he is forewarned that any evidence obtained through such improprieties will be rendered inadmissible in a criminal prosecution.

Shortly after the *Weeks* decision the Court formulated an equally important corollary in holding that any indirect product of an illegal search was also inadmissible in a criminal proceeding.[12] This was clarified by the Court years later when it used the "fruits of the poisonous tree" metaphor in holding that any tangible evidence gathered as a result of illegally obtained information was subject to exclusion.[13]

Constitutional restrictions and the exclusionary rule do not apply to private persons as a general rule. However, as with most rules of law, there are exceptions. Two recent cases concerning the exclusion of evidence are of significance.

The first case is *People v. Zelinski*[14] which concerns an arrest by store detectives in a retail store in the state of California. In the course of a search by private security personnel, a vial containing heroin was discovered. The police later took custody of the vial and the defendant was charged with unlawful possession of heroin. The California Supreme Court concluded that the narcotics evidence was obtained illegally by the store detectives and excluded the evidence from the criminal trial. The State supreme court quoted from an earlier California case, which had held that a citizen effecting an arrest was only authorized to take from the arrestee offensive weapons, not to conduct a search for contraband incidental to the arrest or to seize such contraband.

The court in *Zelinski* noted that the rationale for the rule limiting searches by private persons is that, without statutory authorization, private citizens are not permitted to take property from other private citizens. Private citizens are permitted to retrieve only those items in plain view. The state supreme court applied the California State Constitution, Article I, Section 13, which provides in part that "The right of the people to be secure in their persons, houses, papers and effects against unreasonable seizures and searches may not be violated. . . ."

The evidence was excluded on the basis of the state of California, not the United States, Constitution. The court said: "[I]n any case where private security personnel assert the power of the state to make an arrest or to detain another person for transfer to custody of the state, the state involvement is sufficient for the court to enforce the proper exercise of that power by excluding the fruits of illegal abuse thereof. We hold that exclusion of the illegally seized evidence is required by Article I, Section 13, of the California Constitution."

Shortly after the Zelinski decision, a District of Columbia trial court suppressed evidence in United States v. Lima.[15] The judge ruled that a private store detective had illegally obtained evidence and he excluded that evidence. The language of the trial court suppression order was similar to that in the Zelinski decision and resulted in some commentators predicting that the exclusionary rule would soon be applied to security officers across the United States.[16]

The Lima case began with the filing of an information for petit larceny that resulted from a shoplifting incident in the District of Columbia. The trial court granted a defense motion to exclude the evidence on the basis of an illegal search by the licensed store detective. The trial judge determined that those who are regularly employed as retail store security guards are subject to the Fourth Amendment prohibition against unreasonable searches and seizures.

Eventually, the full court of appeals heard the government's appeal of the trial court suppression order and reversed the trial court's decision.[17] The decision is an excellent case for researching other jurisdictions that have considered the question of whether evidence illegally obtained by private persons should be excluded from a criminal trial.

In reversing the trial court, the court of appeals in Lima said that searches and seizures by private security employees traditionally have been viewed as those of private citizens and therefore not within constitutional proscriptions. However, where a security officer has powers akin to a regular police officer and is appointed by a government official, these "trappings" of state authority are sufficient to trigger Fourth Amendment restrictions. What is sufficient government involvement to trigger application of the Fourth Amendment is decided on a case by case basis. The Court said:

> We reject the contention that application of the Fourth Amendment can be resolved by looking at the nature of the activities performed by security employees.***Private businesses have a right to protect their property from damage and loss. But they enjoy no special public trust, nor do they have any special powers in protecting their property. Application of the Fourth

Amendment is not determined by the behavior of the security employee or the mistaken belief by others in his powers.[18]

The Court of Appeals in *Lima*, then, reaffirmed the general principles that the federal Constitution does not apply to actions of private citizens, and the licensing of a security officer does not automatically transform that person into an agent of the state. In general, evidence obtained illegally by private security personnel is admissible in court, although in isolated instances courts have excluded evidence because of some peculiar circumstances involved in the case.[19]

*Zelinski* also illustrates a key concept about constitutional law. Even though the United States Supreme Court may rule that the federal Constitution does not require some action, a state court may apply the provisions of its state constitution to require the same action. Security personnel in that state, then, are obliged to comply with that state decision.

### Administrative Law

Administrative law is the area of civil law that deals with the creation and activities of federal and state independent agencies and executive departments.[20]

The business of private security is frequently regulated by state and local statutes, ordinances, rules, and regulations that are concerned with the qualifications and hiring and training of security personnel. These statutes generally do not confer any special authority on the personnel who are licensed.[21] In some jurisdictions special police powers are given to licensed security personnel under certain, specified circumstances. The method by which a private citizen becomes vested with special police powers is called "deputization" and includes individuals designated by such terms as "special police officer," "auxiliary police officer," "special officer," and "special deputy sheriff." A commission does not confer upon the private citizen all of the public peace officer's powers, but it does subject the commissioned security officer to the constitutional obligations and limitations placed upon the public officer.

## AUTHORITY OF SECURITY PERSONNEL

Having examined the sources of authority of private security personnel, we now turn to the specific law enforcement functions security officers perform. The following material concerns the authority of private individuals to arrest, conduct searches and seizures, interrogate suspects, and use force. The discussion focuses on the security officer who is neither a commissioned officer nor a public law enforcement officer "moonlighting" in a security position because personnel in these categories are governed by a different set of rules. The discussion concerns the typical private security officer in the United States — the security officer who possesses only those powers possessed by the average citizen.

### Arrest

A citizen can arrest another citizen validly when, with lawful authority, he deprives the other of his liberty. Whenever practicable, an arrest warrant should be obtained. However, because most citizen arrests are made in situations where it is not possible to obtain a warrant, the discussion in this section deals with the warrantless arrest.

The power of a private individual to arrest someone is derived from the common law and has been maintained in every state by statute or court pronouncement. In general, every citizen enjoys some privilege to arrest someone who is committing or has committed an offense, for the purpose of turning him over to government authorities.[22] The extent of the privilege to arrest varies greatly among jurisdictions and depends upon the type of crime involved (felony or misdemeanor), the status of the person making the arrest (private citizen or commissioned officer), and whether the crime was committed within the presence of the arrestor.

Crimes are usually classified as either felonies or misdemeanors. A felony is a crime punishable by death or by imprisonment in a penal institution for a period of one year or more. A misdemeanor is a minor offense punishable by a fine and/or incarceration, usually in a local correctional facility, for a period of less than one year.

A minority of states follow the common law approach to warrantless citizen arrest. A private citizen may arrest someone for a felony actually committed where the arrestor has reasonable grounds for believing the person arrested committed a crime. An arrest for a misdemeanor is permitted if the offense constitutes a breach of the peace and occurs in the arrestor's presence. A "breach of the peace" is an offense involving violence or one causing or likely to cause an immediate disturbance of public order.

The majority of states have modified the common law approach to warrantless arrests by private citizens. With few exceptions, most states permit an arrest for a felony where the felony was in fact committed and where reasonable grounds exist for believing the person arrested committed it. Reasonable grounds exist where an ordinary, reasonable person of average experience and in like circumstances would have perceived the facts as the arrestor and would have reached the same conclusion.[23] A few states permit a felony arrest without reasonable grounds as long as a felony was in fact committed. Although a few states do not permit a private citizen to arrest for misdemeanors, most permit arrests for misdemeanors committed in the arrestor's presence (see Table 3-1).

The law of citizen arrest has traditionally allowed little room for error. In contrast to the public officer, who is protected from civil liability for false arrest where the officer had probable cause to believe a crime was committed, the private citizen is liable if a crime was not in fact committed — regardless of the reasonableness of his belief. Because the citizen's authority to arrest depends upon the fact that a crime was committed, where the person arrested is not guilty of a crime the arrestor has acted without lawful authority and incurs liability for his wrongful conduct. The importance of this distinction in arrest authority between the private citizen and the public officer is demonstrated by the case of *Cervantez v. J. C. Penney Company.*[24]

*Cervantez* involved an off-duty police officer working as a store detective in a retail store in California. He arrested two individuals who were subsequently released for lack of evidence. The plaintiff then sued the store and the officer for false arrest and imprisonment, malicious prosecution, assault and battery, intentional infliction of emotional distress, and negligence in the selection of the employee by the employer. The case was typical of tort cases in the use of multiple theories of tort liability against multiple defendants. The decision was not typical, however.

The key issue in *Cervantez* concerned the availability of the defense of probable cause. The resolution of the issue depended on whether the suspects were arrested by a private citizen in California or by a law enforcement officer. The case involved a warrantless arrest for a misdemeanor.

In California a private person may arrest upon probable cause for felonies actually committed and for misdemeanors committed in one's presence. A peace officer may arrest for misdemeanors when there is reasonable cause to believe an offense was committed. The store and its employee argued that the employee was an off-duty peace officer and since peace officers can arrest on the basis of probable cause, they had the probable cause defense available. The plaintiff contended that the store's employee should be governed by the rules of arrest applicable to private citizens because the employee was not working as a peace officer at the time of the incident.

The California Supreme Court held that the standard for arrest is dependent upon whom the officer is working for at the time of the arrest. If operating as a private citizen at the time of arrest, the off-duty officer's arrest powers are those of a private citizen, not those of a police officer. The court held that the off-duty officer working as a retail store detective was acting as a private citizen at the time of the arrest. Therefore probable cause could not be used as a defense to the civil suit. (In reference to the following

**Table 3-1. Statutory Arrest Authority of Private Citizen.**

| | Minor Offense | | | | | | | | | | | Major Offense | | | | | | | | | | | | | | Certainty of Correct Arrest | |
| | Type of Minor Offense | | | | | | | Type of Knowledge Required | | | | Type of Major Offense | | | | | | Type of Knowledge Required | | | | | | | | | |
| | Crime | Misdemeanor amounting to a breach of the peace | Breach of the peace | Public offense | Offense | Offense other than an ordinance | Indictable offense | Presence | Immediate Knowledge | View | Upon reasonable grounds that is being committed | Felony | Larceny | Petit Larceny | Crime involving physical injury to another | Crime | Crime involving theft or destruction of property | Committed in presence | Information a felony has been committed | View | Reasonable grounds to believe being committed | That felony has been committed in fact | In escaping or attempting | Summoned by peace officer to assist in arrest | Is in the act of committing | Reasonable grounds to believe person arrested committed | Probable cause |
|---|---|---|---|---|---|---|---|---|---|---|---|---|---|---|---|---|---|---|---|---|---|---|---|---|---|---|---|
| Alabama | x | | | x | | | | x | | | | x | | | | | | | | | | x | | | | x | |
| Alaska | | x | | | | | | x | | | | x | | | | | | | | | | x | | | | x | |
| Arizona | | | | x | | | | x | | | | x | | | | | | | | | | x | | | | x | |
| Arkansas | | | | | | | | x | | | | x | | | | | | | | | | x | | | | x | |
| California | | | | | | | | x | x | | | x | | | | | | | | | x | | | | | x | |
| Colorado | x | | | | | | | x | | | | x | | | | x | x | x | | | | | | | | | |
| Georgia | | | | | x | | | x | | | | | | | | x | x | x | | | | | x | | | x | |
| Hawaii | x | | | | | | | x | | | | | | | | | | | | | | | | | x | | |

| State | | | | | | | | | | | | |
|---|---|---|---|---|---|---|---|---|---|---|---|---|
| Idaho | × | | | | | × | | | | × | | × |
| Illinois | × | | | | | | | | × | | | |
| Iowa | × | | | | | × | | | | × | × | × |
| Kentucky | × | | | | | | | | × | | | |
| Louisiana | × | | | | | | | | × | | | |
| Michigan | × | | | | × | | | | × | × | | |
| Minnesota | × | | | × | | × | | | × | | × | |
| Mississippi | × | × | | | | × | | | × | | × | |
| Montana | × | | × | | | × | | | × | | × | |
| Nebraska | × | | | × | | | | | × | | × | |
| Nevada | × | | | | | × | | | × | | × | |
| New York | × | × | | | | × | | | × | | × | |
| N. Carolina* | × | | | | × | | | | × | × | | × |
| N. Dakota | × | | | | | × | | | × | | × | |
| Ohio | × | | | | | × | | × | × | | × | |
| Oklahoma | × | | | | | × | | | × | | × | |
| Oregon | × × | × | | | | | × | | | | | × |
| S. Carolina | × | | | | | × | | × | × | | × | |
| S. Dakota | × | | | | | × | | × | × | | × | |
| Tennessee | × | | | | | × | | × | | | × | |
| Texas | × | | × | | | × | | × | × | | × | × |
| Utah | × | | | | | × | | | × | | × | |
| Wyoming | × | × | | | | × | | | × | | × | |

*Statute eliminates use of word arrest and replaces with detention.

discussion regarding shoplifting detention statutes, it should be noted that the mercantile privilege to use probable cause as a defense applied only to detentions, not to arrests as was the situation in *Cervantez*.)

A few statutes have extended the probable cause defense to private citizens. The most frequently adopted statute in this regard is the shoplifting detention statute. These statutes permit a private person (a merchant, his employee, or agent) to detain in a reasonable manner another person believed to have stolen merchandise in order to recover the merchandise or to have an arrest made by a law enforcement officer. A few states have extended this authorization to the employees of libraries, museums, or archival institutions to allow them to detain individuals suspected of damaging property, as well as of theft.[25]

Shoplifting detention statutes state the conditions under which such detention is authorized. They may include:

1. *Cause for detention* — reasonable cause to believe; probable cause to believe; suspected belief.
2. *Manner of detention* — detain in a reasonable manner; detain without using undue restraint; detain in the establishment or vicinity thereof.
3. *Length of detention* — reasonable period of time; detention cannot be longer than a specific period of time.
4. *Purpose of detention* — arrest by peace officer; search; recovery of property taken; investigation.
5. *Other restrictions* — no search without consent of person; minimum age for person making detention.

The security officer employed by a merchant will have the same authority as the merchant. The merchant's authority is specifically extended to employees and agents in most statutes. An in-house security officer is an employee of the merchant, while an agent is a security officer who is employed by a security agency, which in turn was hired by the merchant.

These detention statutes relieve the merchant from some forms of civil liability where a detention was based on reasonable grounds for believing an individual committed the theft and the person was detained in a reasonable manner for a reasonable length of time. The extent of the protection afforded from civil liability depends upon the language of the statute. Some statutes protect against liability for false arrest, false imprisonment, and defamation. Other statutes offer protection only against false imprisonment, but not against false arrest or other forms of liability. Protection against a wrongful search is rarely afforded.

### Search and Seizure

A search is an examination of a person, his house, or his premises for the purpose of discovering evidence of his guilt in relation to some offense. The observation of articles in the open or "plain view" is not considered a search as long as the observer was at a place where he was legally entitled to be at the time of the observation. This may include public or private property normally open to the public (e.g., a shopping center and its surrounding parking lot, or the lobby of a hotel or hospital) and areas of public or private property normally accessible to the public such as streets and sidewalks.

A seizure means to take possession forcibly, to grasp, to snatch, or otherwise put in possession.

The parameters for a lawful search by law enforcement officers and commissioned private security officers are established by the Fourth Amendment to the U.S. Constitution and its interpretation by the courts. Violations are sanctioned primarily through the exclusionary rule. In addition, the fact that public officers can be held criminally and civilly liable for an unlawful search establishes parameters of conduct.

Common law authority for private persons to search is sparse and inconclusive. Private persons were recognized as having the authority to repossess their goods that had been wrongfully taken as long as they were in fresh pursuit of the goods. However, this "right" came about as a defense to the tort of trespass.

Searches by private citizens have been upheld where there was consent by the person searched and where searches were made incident to a valid citizen's arrest.

Like the situation with arrest warrants, a private person should obtain a search warrant whenever practicable. The U.S. Supreme Court has continually indicated that in the ordinary case a search of private property must be reasonable and performed pursuant to a properly issued search warrant.[26] A search warrant must be issued by a neutral magistrate and must be based on probable cause, supported by oath or affirmation, and must particularly describe the place to be searched and the things to be seized.

The search warrant is generally issued to a law enforcement officer commanding him to search the place described in the warrant. Search warrants must be executed within a specified period of time. Reasonable force may be used in executing the warrant.

If the private security officer is unable to obtain a search warrant for some reason, a search may still be possible on the basis of consent or incident to an arrest.

**Consent Searches.**    A person may voluntarily waive his legal protections. A waiver of one's rights may be accomplished orally, in writing, or in some circumstances by conduct. If a guard asks a woman to allow him to look inside her purse and she voluntarily opens the purse and shows its contents to the guard, her conduct demonstrates her assent to the guard's request.

In a consent search, it is important to define clearly the scope of the permissible search. Consent to search a purse does not authorize the search of a package the woman may have been carrying.

The consent must be given voluntarily and without any coercion. Courts will examine all the facts under which the consent was given in determining the voluntariness of the consent. Voluntariness is more easily demonstrated by written consent. Therefore it is preferable to obtain consent in writing in order to indicate the scope of the consent and that the consent was freely given (see Figure 3-1).

Consent must be given by a person authorized to give such consent. Only a person who is legally in possession of the property can give valid consent to the search. Possession of the property, not ownership, is the factor a court will use in determining whether one could validly consent to the search.

Consent searches of employee lockers, work areas, packages, and so forth, are frequently based on a preemployment agreement to abide by company security rules and procedures, or as part of a collective bargaining contract. However, because consent may be revoked at any time, a security officer confronted by an employee objecting to a search should carefully consider his subsequent action. To continue the search after revocation of consent will expose the officer to liability for battery, invasion of privacy, and other charges. The officer could arrest the individual if the facts would support such action, or he could permit the individual to leave without conducting a search and handle the case administratively through company disciplinary channels.

One solution to the company search problem has been for the company to maintain control over lockers, desks, and other equipment used by employees and to make periodic health and safety inspections. By maintaining such control over the employer's property, the theory is that the employee does not have a reasonable expectation of privacy in the property and cannot object to a search.

**Search Incident to a Valid Arrest/Detention.**    Where a valid arrest has been made by a security officer there is case precedent that justifies a contemporaneous search of the arrestee and the area within his immediate control, which is defined as the area within which one could lunge and reach a weapon or destructible evidence. Reasonable force may be used to conduct the search.

CONSENT TO SEARCH

I, _____ , age _____ , admit that merchandise stolen from

_____ is presently stored at _____

_____
(Description and Location)

I hereby consent to take _____
(Names of persons making search)

_____

to _____ and agree to return all of such stolen
(Description and Location)

merchandise to the above named individuals, after identifying the stolen items by placing my initials thereon.

I certify that the above consent has been freely and voluntarily given by me and that no threats or promises have been made to me.

I further agree that the above named individuals may enter the above described premises to assist me in locating the stolen merchandise, and that I shall make no claim whatsoever against the above named persons, (Company Name), its officers and employees, in connection with the entry and search of the above premises and the return of the stolen merchandise.

Date: _____

Witnesses:                          Signature: _____

_____

_____

Consent of Spouse, or Co-Owner, or Proprietor of Premises:

I, _____ , hereby
(Name of person and relationship to employee or premises)

consent to the entry of the above described premises by the above named individuals.

Date: _____

Witnesses:                          Signature: _____

_____

_____                    APA - 1973 SAMPLE

Figure 3-1.   Consent to search form.

It is unclear whether most courts approve of private searches incident to arrest. California expressly disapproved of such searches in *People v. Zelinski*,[27] although the California Supreme Court left the door open to protective searches for weapons by private persons. In contrast, the New York courts appear to permit searches incident to private arrests, believing the rationale for such searches by public officers applies with equal force to searches by private citizens.[28] In jurisdictions where the law is not clear regarding searches incident to an arrest by private citizens, the security officer who does not fear that an arrestee is armed should probably await the arrival of local law enforcement officials and have them perform the search.

Prior to conducting a search based on a mercantile shoplifting statute, the statutory language should be examined to determine whether such searches are permitted. Some mercantile statutes permit detentions for "investigation" but not for "searches." Indiana permits detentions to determine whether the person detained has unpurchased merchandise in his possession. Illinois permits a detention "to make reasonable inquiry as to whether such person has in his possession unpurchased merchandise." Oklahoma sepcifically states in its statute that the purpose of the detention is the performance of "a reasonable search of the detained person and his belongings."[29] California and Minnesota forbid searches of detained individuals although California permits searches of objects carried by the suspected shoplifter.[30] Items in plain view may be seized under such detention statutes and the courts have generally permitted a protective frisk or search for weapons under a self-defense theory where the security officer feared for his safety.[31]

As was noted previously, an illegal search by a police officer or commissioned private security officer will result in the exclusion of the evidence in a criminal trial. However, when a private person performs an illegal search, the fruits of such searches are generally admissible in both civil and criminal cases. The United States Supreme Court decided the issue in *Burdeau v. McDowell*[32] in 1921. The Court said, "It is manifest that there was no invasion of the security afforded by the Fourth Amendment against unreasonable searches and seizures, as whatever wrong was done was the act of individuals in taking the property of another."

If evidence resulting from an illegal search by a private person is admissible in court, why should the private security officer concern himself with the law surrounding searches? Why should he obtain search warrants when the Fourth Amendment does not apply to private conduct? The answer is that even though the evidence is generally admissible, the security officer and probably his employer will be civilly liable because of his unauthorized action. An illegal search is not privileged under the law. Therefore, when the officer touched the person to perform the search he engaged in unprivileged, unconsented, and offensive conduct, which is battery. The civil and criminal liability of security personnel in such situations is discussed in the next section.

Before leaving the area of searches, there remains an area of special concern. Electronic surveillance has been held to constitute a search in decisions of the U.S. Supreme Court. Various statutes have been enacted to regulate private conduct in performing wiretaps and other forms of electronic surveillance.

The U.S. Congress enacted the Omnibus Crime Control and Safe Streets Act of 1968[33] to, among other purposes, forbid the interception of oral or wire communications by the use of electronic or mechanical devices. Title III of the act provides civil and criminal penalties for violations. It authorizes a civil suit for damages by anyone injured by illegal electronic surveillance and permits the confiscation of devices and equipment used to conduct an illegal electronic surveillance.

Title III controls electronic surveillance of private communications by law enforcement officers and by private citizens. The section applies only to nonconsensual interceptions. It recognizes the need to protect an individual's right to privacy in his private conversations by forbidding the use of electronic devices to overhear such conversation without the consent of one of the parties.

Congress, recognizing that the interception of oral communications to obtain evidence of crime would be an indispensable aid to law enforcement and the administration of justice, enacted an exception to the law. The exception allows the issuance of a warrant to law enforcement officers (but not to private citizens) to permit electronic surveillance. The requirements that must be met before this type of warrant will be issued are so stringent, however, that the warrant has taken on the name "exceptional warrant."

Although the Omnibus Crime Control and Safe Streets Act allows private persons to intercept communications with the consent of one party, Title III sets forth the restriction that the interception not be done for the purpose of committing a criminal or tortious act. This qualification was added to punish monitoring for purposes such as blackmail and the theft of business secrets.

Title III permits interceptions where a party consents because there is no justifiable expectation that another party to the communication will keep the communication private. Some states have rejected this rationale and have enacted their own electronic surveillance laws. As was the case in other areas of the law (e.g., searches in California), the citizens of a state may be afforded greater protections under state law than they are given under federal law.

Florida has an electronic surveillance statute that permits eavesdropping with the consent of one party to the conversation.[34] The Florida Supreme Court held the statute unconstitutional in State v. Sarmiento[35] to the extent that it authorizes a warrantless interception of private conversations within the home. The case involved an undercover police officer equipped with a "body bug" who purchased drugs from the defendant. No warrant had been obtained because neither the state statute nor the federal statute required a warrant under the situation where one party (the wired agent) consents to the interception.

The Florida Supreme Court ruled that the Florida Constitution requires a warrant to eavesdrop under such conditions because one has a reasonable expectation of privacy when he is engaged in conversation in his own home.

Illinois has enacted legislation that prohibits eavesdropping by any citizen — even where one of the parties consents. A private person cannot "eavesdrop" unless all the parties consent. Illinois law enforcement officers investigating a felony may eavesdrop if they obtain consent of one party plus a judicially approved search warrant.[36] Other states have similar restrictions.[37]

### Interrogation

Nothing prohibits a private person or law enforcement officer from engaging in a conversation with a willing participant. However, if the "conversation" is really an "interrogation" for the purpose of illiciting information about the individual's activities, the results of the interrogation may be inadmissible in a subsequent criminal prosecution.

The traditional and principal test to determine the admissibility of a confession is that of voluntariness. In order for a confession to be admissible in evidence it must have been freely and voluntarily made. Admissions and/or confessions are admissible only if they have been made without duress, coercion, fear, or compulsion. If a statement is not voluntary it is not trustworthy and is therefore inadmissible.

The voluntariness requirement applies to all interrogations regardless of whether the interrogation was conducted by a peace officer or private citizen.[38] A security officer may not obtain a confession from an employee by threatening the employee with physical harm or loss of his job. Such intimidation affects the reliability of any statement made and renders it inadmissible under principles of evidentiary law. Evidentiary law focuses on the trustworthiness of evidence presented during a trial. Additionally, such threats can subject the interrogator to civil and criminal liability.[39]

The voluntariness test was supplemented by the U.S. Supreme Court decision in *Miranda v. Arizona.*[40] The principal thrust of *Miranda* was to dispel the compulsion inherent in custodial surroundings. The Court noted that custodial interrogation by public law enforcement officers contains pressures that undermine the suspect's will to resist and compel him to speak when he would not otherwise do so.

In *Miranda* the Court ruled that as a prerequisite to the admissibility of any statement, the police must demonstrate that the suspect was advised prior to questioning that he need not make any statement, that any statement made could be used against him, that he had the right to counsel, and that if he could not afford counsel the state would provide him with counsel prior to questioning.

The warnings are not required unless the person is in custody or otherwise deprived of his freedom of action in any significant way and is to be questioned by a law enforcement officer or a government agent. Therefore, private persons are generally not required to inform a suspect of any *Miranda* rights prior to interrogation because they are not public officials.[41]

A few jurisdictions require private persons to advise suspects that they have the right to remain silent, that anything said can be used in court, and that they have the right to have an attorney present during questioning. The exact form of the warning is unclear, especially with regard to providing counsel. Jurisdictions which require some type of warning by private security officers do so on the basis of local custom and constitutional interpretation rather than on any specific ruling by the United States Supreme Court. Absent special circumstances such as deputized citizens, interrogation by private security guards does not constitute governmental action and advisement of rights is not required in the overwhelming majority of jurisdictions.

The California Supreme Court in the case of *In re Deborah C.*[42] recently reaffirmed the principle that a suspect's statements are admissible even though a private security officer fails to advise the suspect of *Miranda* rights. The court said that the rationale for the *Miranda* decision (overbearing, third-degree tactics) are not a problem in the retail environment. Store security officers lack the psychological advantage which the police officers have in the compelling atmosphere of the police station.

Most shoplifting codes authorize a temporary detention by a merchant for reasonable questioning or investigation. However, a few states prohibit questioning under such statutes. For example, the Wisconsin shoplifting detention statute provides in part that: "The detained person must be promptly informed of the purpose of the detention and be permitted to make phone calls, but shall not be interrogated or searched against his will before the arrival of a peace officer who may conduct a lawful interrogation of the accused person."[43]

## Use of Force

There are occasions when security personnel may have to resort to the use of force to accomplish their purpose. Force may be used to effect an arrest, to protect oneself or others, to defend property, and to prevent the commission of a crime. The use of force is limited to the amount of force that is reasonable under the circumstances. Reasonable force is the minimum amount of force needed under the situation. Deadly or fatal force is force likely to cause death or serious bodily injury.

If a person's use of force is unwarranted, that is, if it is excessive or unreasonable under the circumstances, the person faces potential liability under criminal and civil law. Depending on what happens to the victim, the person who used excessive force could be criminally liable for crimes ranging from assault and battery to homicide.

**Self-Defense and Defense of Others.**   A person may use reasonable force to protect himself against someone who threatens him with physical injury. The amount of force a person may use must be commensurate with the amount of force he is attempting to repel. This rule precludes the person from using force likely to result in serious bodily harm unless he is defending himself against an equivalent danger. Deadly force may be resorted to when a person is threatened with great bodily harm. Some states require the defender to retreat by any reasonable means prior to using deadly force in defense of self (except where the defender is in his own dwelling and is not the original aggressor). In the majority of states, one may stand his own ground and meet force with force as long as the defender was not the original aggressor.

This right to protect oneself extends to the protection of another. There are two major approaches to the use of force to protect others. The more restrictive approach states that one may use reasonable force in defense of another as long as the person defended would have been justified in using force. Under this approach, the defender "stands in the shoes" of the one defended. If he defended the "wrong" person (e.g., the aggressor in the situation), the defender is liable regardless of the reasonableness of his action. The other approach to defense of others allows the defender to use force when he reasonably believes such force is necessary under the circumstances. Under this second approach, which is designed to encourage citizen intervention, the defender would be protected from liability for his actions as long as they were reasonable under the particular facts involved.

**Defense of Property.**   Reasonable force may be used to protect property from interference. The privilege to use deadly force in defense of one's property is recognized only in those cases involving a felonious threat to property with the additional requirement that there be a threat to life. For instance, one may use deadly force to protect a home against an arsonist but the use of deadly force against a mere trespasser would not be permitted.

The security officer who is employed to protect another's property may use that amount of force which his employer could have used under the circumstances. In other words, if the owner of the property could use reasonable force to remove a trespasser, the employee can also use reasonable force to remove the trespasser.

**Arrest and Detention.** Whether it be a private citizen, security officer, or public police officer, any person making a lawful arrest or detention of another has the authority to use reasonable force to bring that person within their control.

At common law, deadly force could be resorted to only in felony situations, and then only after all other means had failed in attempting to make the arrest. The purpose of allowing the use of deadly force was not to punish the fleeing felon but to bring the fleeing felon within the arrestor's control. All felonies were punishable by death at common law. As one court put it, "It made little difference if the suspected felon was killed in the process of capture since, in the eyes of the law, he had already forfeited his life by committing the felony."[44] Deadly force could not be used against a fleeing misdemeanant. "[T]o permit the life of one charged with a mere misdemeanor to be taken when fleeing from the officer would, aside from its inhumanity, be productive of more abuse than good. ***The security of person and property is not endangered by a petty offender being at large. . . ."[45]

Although many states still follow the common law relative to the use of deadly force, others have narrowed its application to individuals who have committed violent felonies and are in immediate flight. The common law rule was modified to reflect the changes in punishment authorized for felonies. Today most felonies are punishable by imprisonment; very few are punishable by death. Many felonies do not involve force or violence (e.g., embezzlement, fraud, or tax violations), and to permit the use of deadly force against such offenders seems to many, if not "cruel and unusual," at least unduly severe.

**Prevention of Crimes.** The common law recognized the right of an individual to use force to prevent a crime from being committed. The theory was that one need not wait for the commission of an unlawful act before being authorized to do something.

The right to use force was limited to situations where the threatened act would have constituted a felony or breach of the peace. The threatened commission of a nonviolent misdemeanor, such as petty theft, provided no basis for the use of preventive force.

The use of deadly force was limited to those cases involving potential harm to persons. Rather than narrowing this concept, some states have broadened it to permit the use of deadly force to prevent any felony. Therefore in some jurisdictions a security officer may be justified in using deadly force to prevent a theft from property he is protecting, even though the attempted crime involved no personal danger to the officer.[46]

In determining the reasonableness of the force used by a private person, a reviewing court will look at the circumstances in light of the force used, the seriousness of the crime prevented, and the possibility of preventing the crime by other means.

**Use of Firearms.**   An issue closely related to the use of force is the carrying and use of firearms by private security personnel. Although subject to intense debate, many citizens believe their right to bear arms for self-defense is guaranteed by the Second Amendment to the U.S. Constitution.[47] The debate focuses on whether the Second Amendment was intended to grant each state the right to arm a militia to ensure law and order, or whether it was intended to grant each citizen the right to possess a gun free from government oppression. The constitutions of many states have attempted to resolve this debate by specifically stating that their citizens have the right to bear arms for their defense.[48]

Most states regulate the carrying of firearms in one way or another. With few exceptions, all states prohibit carrying a concealed weapon. Approximately half of the states prohibit carrying an exposed handgun. States with such regulations usually exclude police officers from coverage. Some extend this exclusion to security officers.[49]

Many states that prohibit the carrying of handguns have provisions for obtaining a permit or license to do so. Unless the security officer is authorized by statute to carry a firearm, his authority to do so will be governed by the law as it applies to private citizens. That is, of course, unless the security officer has gone through some type of commissioning process, in which case his authority to carry a firearm will be the same as a police officer's.


## SANCTIONS FOR THE MISUSE OF AUTHORITY

Two of the sources of authority for private security personnel, which were mentioned at the beginning of this chapter, are tort law and criminal law. Both of them act primarily as negative sources of authority because the security officer who acts outside the boundary of permissible activity faces the possibility of civil and criminal sanctions.

In this section some of the possible civil and criminal liabilities of security personnel are surveyed. Although the discussion examines civil and criminal areas separately, they are not mutually exclusive concepts and the same action could result in both criminal and civil liability.

### Civil Liability

There has been a significant increase within the past few years in judicial and legislative sanctions against the security industry.[50] The increase is due in part to the exceptional growth of the industry, as well as to the rising expectations of the public with regard to the quality of security services; the increase in the number of new laws and lawyers, the availability of liability insurance, the developing legal sophistication of the public, who has become aware of its rights, the willingness of juries to award substantial judgments, and evolving theories of liability that have improved a plaintiff's chances of obtaining a recovery in a civil suit.[51]

The basic civil liability for the security industry is the area of tort law. A tort is a civil wrong and results from a violation of a duty owed to another that causes a compensable injury. In some instances the tort may result in a court issuing an injunction to prohibit the continuation of some kind of tortious activity.

The individual who commits the tort is called the tortfeasor. The tortfeasor is the defendant in a civil suit and has liability for damages because he acted with an unreasonable intention or because he failed to exercise reasonable care.[52] A tortfeasor may be a person, a corporation, an association, or some other entity. The person who was injured by the action of the tortfeasor is called the plaintiff.

Torts are classified as intentional, negligent, or strict liability.

A plaintiff may recover general and special damages in a negligence action to compensate him for the injury resulting from the defendant's failure to exercise reasonable care. General damages are awarded on the basis of the "enlightened consciences" of the jurors and cover the plaintiff's pain and suffering, loss of limbs, disfigurement, and mental grief. Special damages are those ascertainable as to amount and include present and future medical expenses and loss of income.

Punitive damages (also called exemplary damages in some jurisdictions) are designed to deter and punish the tortfeasor for his intent to injure. Since negligence does not involve such an intention, punitive damages are generally not awarded in negligence cases. However, punitive damages are sometimes awarded for gross (as distinguished from "simple") negligence because of the defendant's outrageous conduct. In gross negligence cases the defendant acted in such total disregard for the safety of others and for the consequences of his actions that the punishment is the same as that for intentional acts.

Two evolutionary theories of liability are having an impact on the security industry.

The first area concerns the willingness of courts to impose a legal duty of protection, which has not existed to the same extent in the past. A duty of protection has been extended to motel/hotel owners and landlords, which renders them liable for a failure to protect their guests and tenants adequately from foreseeable criminal activity.

Historically, a landlord's responsibility to his tenant was primarily to keep the areas under his control in a reasonably safe condition by maintaining and repairing the areas. The landlord had no duty to police the areas under his control.

Recently an issue has been raised as to whether a landlord owes a duty to those persons legally on his premises to protect them from foreseeable criminal activity. Liability was not generally extended to the landlord for criminal attacks on his tenants because of the causation requirement of tort liability. It was accepted tort theory that a crime was an intentional act of a third party. Intentional acts are usually considered to be unforeseeable events because one cannot predict what another person will do in any particular circumstance. However, in some circumstances a landlord may be held civilly liable for injuries occurring to his tenants that result from an intentional act of another.

In *Klein v. 1500 Massachusetts Avenue Apartment Corporation*,[53] a tenant was criminally assaulted in a common hallway of an apartment house. The landlord had notice of prior criminal activity against his tenants and their property. He was also aware of conditions that created a likelihood that further criminal attacks would occur. Despite such information, the landlord decreased the amount of security provided in the apartment complex. In the *Klein* case the court held that the landlord's failure to provide adequate security in light of the knowledge he possessed made him liable for the resulting injuries to the tenant.

Some jurisdictions are resisting efforts to extend liability to the landlord in such situations.[54] However, for a number of different reasons, the concept of landlord liability for a failure to protect tenants is gaining acceptance. New Jersey, for example, has imposed liability on the theory that a landlord's implied warranty of habitability obliges him to furnish reasonable safeguards to protect tenants from foreseeable criminal activity on the premises.

Note that under any approach to landlord liability the acts of the criminal must be reasonably foreseeable based upon the landlord's actual or constructive knowledge of prior crimes occurring on the premises.

A similar duty of protection has been extended to innkeepers. The case against a Howard Johnson's motel brought by singer Connie Francis after she was raped in her motel room gained notoriety and was of great interest because of the theory of the case. Her civil suit alleged that the attack against her was due to the motel's failure to provide adequate locks on the doors — in her particular case, the lock on the sliding door leading to her room. The jury decision awarding her over a million dollars raised the consciousness of the hotel/motel industry to their exposure in this type of case. Although intentional acts of third parties have traditionally absolved one of liability because such acts were considered unforeseeable, such acts may not relieve liability where the act of the third party was reasonably foreseeable under circumstances within the defendant's knowledge.

The second evolutionary theory, and one somewhat related to the area just discussed, is the concept of a nondelegable duty. Previously, one could avoid liability in certain instances by delegating a duty to another. A frequently invoked method of delegation was to hire an independent contractor.

Under principles of agency law,[55] the independent contractor relationship relieves the one who hired the independent contractor of liability because there is no control exercised over the activities of the contractor. Thus, for example, a motel owner could employ a security agency to provide protection for the motel. If an incident occurred that resulted in an injury, the motel owner would claim he was not responsible for the injury because the duty to provide protection had been given to the guard service. Under the concept of a nondelegable duty, the motel owner remains liable regardless of his attempt to relieve himself of liability by contract.

Some duties rightfully belong to certain individuals, according to the courts, and the law will not permit these individuals to escape liability for a failure to perform the duty by delegating it to someone else. The law will allow a delegation of authority, but not of responsibility, for the performance of a legal duty.[56] Contract provisions that attempt to delegate such duties to others are not enforced by the courts and have not relieved individuals of civil liability.

**Negligence.**    Negligence is the absence of due care or due diligence. It is the failure to act as a reasonable and prudent person would have acted under the same or similar circumstances. One who is negligent has failed to conduct himself with due regard for the safety and rights of others.

In a negligence case the plaintiff is responsible for demonstrating by a preponderance (more than 50 percent) of the evidence that there was:

1.   An act or failure to act (an omission) by the defendant
2.   A legal duty owed to the plaintiff by the defendant
3.   A breach of duty by the defendant
4.   A foreseeable injury to plaintiff and/or
5.   Damages

Where the law has imposed a legal obligation or duty upon the defendant, the jury must determine if the defendant's conduct was reasonable under the circumstances and, if the defendant breached his duty, the amount of damages necessary to compensate the plaintiff.

Security personnel have been held liable for negligence in failing to exercise due care in the use of firearms, motor vehicles, and force. Any time a security officer fails to use reasonable care in fulfilling his duty of protection, and his breach causes damage, he is exposed to liability for his negligence. His negligent act, or failure to act, will also expose his employer to civil liability.

Supervisors are especially vulnerable to three areas of civil exposure: (1) negligent supervision of personnel, (2) negligent training, and (3) negligent supervision. The supervisor is liable when his negligence was a substantial factor in bringing about the plaintiff's injury. The Restatement of Torts, Second, Section 307, states that, "[I]t is negligence to use an instrumentatility, whether a human being or a thing, which the actor knows, or should know, to be incompetent, inappropriate or defective and that its use involves an unreasonable risk of harm to others."

**Intentional Torts.**   Intentional torts occur when a person acts in a manner designed to bring about an intended result. That is, the tortfeasor intended the consequences of his act or at least intended to perform the act that caused damage to the plaintiff.

Because the tortfeasor has committed a willful wrong, the law may seek to punish the wrongdoer through the imposition of punitive damages over and above the compensatory damages available in a negligence action.

The following list of intentional torts, though not exhaustive, defines the intentional torts of most concern to the security professional.

*Assault.*   This is an unauthorized act that results in a reasonable apprehension of imminent harmful or offensive contact. There is no physical contact, but the actor does intend to place the plaintiff in fear of immediate touching. The plaintiff must have become apprehensive as a result of the defendant's gesture. In most cases, words alone are not sufficient to create a reasonable apprehension of harm.

*Battery.*   This is a harmful or offensive contact with the person of the plaintiff. The defendant intended either to touch the plaintiff physically or some object immediately associated with the plaintiff, such as a cane used by the plaintiff for walking. Such contact must be nonconsensual and not privileged. For example, a merchant has a common law privilege to recover his property reasonably and this privilege would be a defense to an action for battery. However, if the merchant's action was unreasonable, the privilege would not be available and would subject the merchant to civil liability for battery. Any illegal search by a security officer will probably constitute a battery. If the plaintiff consented to the search, however, there would not be a battery.

*False Imprisonment or False Arrest.*   This is considered an unlawful detention: confinement of the plaintiff within fixed boundaries. Any unauthorized restraint will give rise to a cause of action for false imprisonment.
Such restraint can be imposed by physical contact or by intimidation that
suggests to the plaintiff that physical force will be used if an escape is
attempted. A false imprisonment is a wrongful detention for a private
purpose, with no intention to bring the detainee before a court. A false
arrest is a wrongful detention by reason of an asserted legal authority to
enforce the processes of the law. It is essential for recovery that the restraint
be against the plaintiff's will. If the plaintiff agrees of his own choice to
surrender his freedom of motion, as by voluntarily accompanying the
defendant to clear himself of an accusation, there is no imprisonment.
Consent on the basis of force, duress, or fraud is not a valid consent.

Because an action for false imprisonment is one of the torts most
frequently brought against security personnel (along with malicious prosecution, defamation, and assault), a few cases will be discussed to illustrate
the tort.

In the first case a store employee suspected a customer of having
hidden a can of flea spray on his person. The employee stopped the
customer in the middle of an aisle and loudly demanded to know what had
happened to the can. Eventually the employee called the customer a thief in
front of about thirty customers, who watched as the employee searched the
customer and then grabbed the customer and marched him to the manager's office at the front of the store — where other customers observed the
commotion.

No can of flea spray was ever found on the customer's person. The
customer sued the store for assault and battery, slander, and false imprisonment and recovered $10,000 in compensatory damages and $30,000 in
punitive damages.[57]

A second case involved an employee interrogation. A corporate employee was called into the manager's office and accused of theft. She was
told she could not leave until she signed a confession. After additional
threats and a five-hour period of forcible detention, she signed a statement
admitting the theft. The court held this to be a false imprisonment. Although one is sometimes permitted to detain another upon the belief that a
theft is being committed, one cannot do so if the offense occurred at a prior
time and the detention was not for investigation but to obtain a
confession.[58]

Another employee detention case involved a bank's investigation of a
suspected theft of money a bank customer claimed to have deposited. Bank
officials forcibly detained the employee for more than two hours. After
threats of prosecution and offers to drop the matter, the employee agreed
to write a confession. The employee later refused to execute a confession,

and later the customer discovered her failure to make the deposit. The bank employee recovered $30,000 in damages from the bank for false imprisonment.[59]

In addition to illustrating the tort of false imprisonment, these employee cases illustrate that the tort can occur even where an employee is interviewed at his or her place of employment while "on company time." The test is not whether an employee was being paid (although payment helps to demonstrate the voluntariness of the interview situation), but rather whether the employee was free to leave the site of the interview. If the employer's actions or words demonstrate that the individual's liberty was restricted, the imprisonment situation exists.[60]

Additionally, although the advising of *Miranda* rights is not required prior to an interview by an employer,[61] in a union environment the employee has the right, upon his request, to have a union representative present during an investigatory interview. The employer cannot deny the collective bargaining unit member's request to have union representation during any interview the employee reasonably believes could result in disciplinary action against him. A failure to honor such a request "interferes with, restrains and coerces the individual right of the employee to engage in concerted activities for mutual aid or protection."[62]

The interviewer does not have to offer union representation, but is required only to honor such requests if they are made. The employer has the option to continue or terminate the interview if union representation is requested, and he may point out his option to the employee. Finally, if a union representative is present during the interview, the representative's role is to assist the employee by clarifying facts or by suggesting names of others who could help. The representative is not to assume the role of a legal advisor, nor is the representative supposed to answer questions for the employee.

*Defamation.* This is any form of unconsented, unprivileged communication to a third party that injures the reputation of the plaintiff in the eyes of the community. Slander is the oral defamation of another (other than over the radio or television), and libel is defamation by the written word. The defendant may have a defense to the tort where the statements made were true, privileged, or consented to by the plaintiff. Punitive damages are awarded when the communication was made (called "publication") because of malice or when the words are slander per se. Imputing the commission of a criminal offense to another is slander per se, and it is not necessary that the plaintiff demonstrate actual damages in such a case. For example, a security officer who yells, "Stop thief!" across a crowded room while pointing to a particular person has incurred potential liability for defamation if a third person witnessed the incident.

Certain communications are absolutely or partially privileged. A former employer has a qualified privilege to respond to requests for information about former employees from a prospective employer. If such requests are answered in "good faith" (e.g., having reasonable grounds for the response), the employer is protected from liability even if the communication later turns out to be incorrect. However, because of the threat of litigation, many employers have become reluctant to "test" their qualified privilege in court by responding to requests for employment information. Therefore many former employers refuse to provide information about the work record of a former employee.

Although it is generally true that "truth is an absolute defense" to defamation actions, the statement must be qualified by adding, "provided that it is published with good motives and for justifiable ends."[63] Truth is not a defense to criminal defamation,[64] nor is it an absolute defense to the civil tort in every jurisdiction. Some states have statutes that render one liable for a true statement published for malicious motives.[65] Even where such statutes have been ruled unconstitutional as violative of the First Amendment's provision regarding freedom of the press,[66] liability has been extended for the publication of true statements under theories of invasion of privacy or intentional interference with a beneficial employment contract.[67]

*Malicious Prosecution.* To constitute the tort of malicious prosecution, the defendant must have instituted criminal proceedings, the proceedings must have been terminated in a manner that indicates the innocence of the plaintiff and there must be lack of probable cause for the proceeding and malice. Malice is defined as instituting or continuing the criminal proceeding for a primary purpose other than to bring the offender to justice. Examples of malice include prosecutions brought by defendants to extort money, collect debts, or force performance of contracts.

Although probable cause is not a defense to false imprisonment in most jurisdictions, it is a defense to the tort of malicious prosecution.

One may be liable for either instigating or continuing a criminal prosecution. One is not liable unless he takes an active part in instigating or encouraging the prosecution. There is no liability for merely reporting the facts to police officials and permitting them to exercise their discretionary charging function. But if the criminal prosecution resulted from the defendant's persuasion, or his incomplete or biased statement of the facts, there may be liability where such statements were the determining factor in inducing the decision to prosecute.[68]

*Invasion of Privacy.* This is an unjustified intrusion into another's reasonable expectations of privacy. The tort encompasses four distinct causes of action: (a) the misappropriation of plaintiff's name or picture for commercial advantage, (b) the placing of another in a false light, (c) the public disclosure of private facts, and (d) an intrusion into the seclusion of another. Typically, this tort is committed where a security officer engages in an illegal search, such as an unauthorized inspection of employees' packages. The tort may also occur where there is electronic surveillance or visual surveillance of individuals. Visual observation of individuals trying on clothes in fitting rooms has given rise to a number of cases alleging an invasion of privacy. However, there have been other cases that indicate if signs posted outside the fitting rooms give sufficient notice that the rooms are subject to surveillance, a person would not have a justifiable expectation of privacy and reasonable observations could be made without incurring liability for invasion of privacy.

Overzealous surveillance by private detectives may lead to invasion of privacy charges.[69] In one case a woman brought an action against an insurance carrier and a private detective agency because of constant shadowing by detectives after she had filed a personal injury action against the insurer. Generally, the filing of a civil suit implicitly waives the right of privacy because a defendant (the insurance carrier in the case) has a right to investigate by reasonably unobtrusive methods. However, in this case the court held that the methods used violated the plaintiff's right to privacy. The court said:

> After finally discovering the identity of the defendants on August 13, her attorney contacted the attorneys for the defendants and informed them of her condition and that their conduct had almost made her lose her mind, and defendant's attorney stated he would request his client to discontinue these activities; nevertheless, the surveillance continued in as aggravated a form as before, and plaintiff was forced to undergo electroconvulsive shock treatment from August through November. The conduct of the defendants in shadowing, snooping, spying and eavesdropping upon plaintiff was done in a vicious and malicious manner not reasonably limited and designed to obtain information needed for the defense of plaintiff's lawsuit against Bell but deliberately in way calculated to frighten and torment her. Plaintiff's neighbors also noticed the espionage and thereby gained the impression that she was engaged in some wrongful activity and began to discontinue any association with her. The shock and injury to her nervous system is permanent.[70]

Of increasing concern to security personnel are actions that involve possible tort liability for invasion of privacy, including reference checks, background investigations, and the use of truth detection devices.[71]

*Trespass and Conversion.* An unauthorized, intentional, physical invasion of plaintiff's real property is a trespass, as is remaining on land after permission has been rescinded. The wrongful taking of a plaintiff's personal property is called a conversion and subjects the tortfeasor to civil liability where there has been an intentional interference with the plaintiff's use or right of possession of a chattel.

*Intentional Infliction of Mental Distress.* This is where defendant intentionally causes physical injury or mental suffering by highly aggravating words or conduct. Early tort cases refused to recognize a remedy for a mental injury because it was thought that such an injury was too difficult to prove and damages too difficult to determine. However, cases of extreme misconduct eventually resulted in a gradual recognition of a remedy for intentional conduct that was calculated to cause, and that did cause, serious mental distress.

One of the leading cases in this area is the English case of *Janvier v. Sweeney* 2 K.B. 316 (1919) in which a private detective, representing himself as a police officer, threatened to charge a plaintiff with espionage unless she surrendered some private papers. Recent cases against abuses by collection agencies have been based on this theory of liability.

Just as tort law protects against certain interferences with another's life, property, or reputation, it also provides privileges and immunities with which one can defend tort actions.

Consent of the plaintiff or the existence of a privilege in the defendant will absolve the defendant from liability for an act that might otherwise be a tort. Consent may be express or implied. The following are privileges that can exonerate a defendant: self-defense, defense of others, defense of property, recovery of property, and necessity. For example, a lawsuit alleging a battery is subject to the defense that the defendant was privileged under the circumstances to use reasonable force to effect an arrest.

**Vicarious Liability.** Security officers who engage in tortious conduct are individually liable for the damages caused by their action. Because the security officer usually is employed by an entity more solvent than he is, the plaintiff typically will sue the employer as well as the employee and attempt to establish liability under the doctrine of "respondeat superior," which is also called vicarious or imputed liability.

Respondeat superior is a doctrine based on principles of agency law. Agency law deals with the situation where two persons agree that one is to act for the benefit of the other according to the latter's directions. An agency arises where one individual, called the principal, has the right to control the action of the other individual, who is called his agent.

The term "principal" includes in its meaning the term "master." A "servant" is a species of "agent" and is normally one who gives personal service as a member of a business or domestic household, subject to the control of the master.

"Respondeat superior" is the phrase used to indicate the situation where a master (employer) is liable for the torts of the servant (employee) that are connected with the service of the master. In other words, an employer is legally responsible for the employee's actions when the action occurs in the scope of employment. The employer is liable for the negligence of his employee even though the employer did nothing to cause the plaintiff's injury. The employee's negligence is "imputed" to the employer whose liability rests upon the master–servant relationship.

Numerous justifications have been advanced by legal scholars to explain the imposition of liability under such circumstances. Some have argued that the employer is liable because he controls the employee or because the employer set the events in motion by selecting the particular individual as his employee. The justification may be that vicarious liability is a policy decision that attempts to allocate risk by allowing an injured person to sue the party most financially capable of compensating him — the business employer.

Early decisions refused to hold an employer vicariously liable for the intentional acts of an employee because it was difficult to infer that the employer approved of such conduct. Today, "[I]t may be said, in general, that the master is held liable for any intentional tort committed by the servant where its purpose, however misguided, is wholly or in part to further the master's business."[72] Employers may be liable for punitive as well as compensatory damages where the employer ratified, participated in, or authorized the employee's intentional act.[73]

In cases where an employee acts for strictly personal reasons and not in furtherance of his employment, an employer may still have liability, though not under the vicarious liability rationale, where the employer's negligence was a substantial factor in causing the plaintiff's injury. For example, assume that a guard was provided with a weapon by his employer. While at home and off-duty, the guard used the weapon to injure a neighbor. The neighbor might be able to bring an action against not only the guard for the guard's intentional act, but also against the employer under theories of negligent entrustment of a dangerous instrumentality or negligence in the selection of an individual with known dangerous propensities.[74]

Because vicarious liability is dependent upon an employer-employee relationship, the doctrine does not apply to situations where one hires an independent contractor. The general rule does not extend liability to the independent contractor situation because the "employer" has no right to control the way an independent contractor performs the work. However, the rule that one is not responsible for the acts of an independent contractor has so many exceptions that the exceptions are the rule. For example, one who hires an independent contractor may be liable because of the negligent selection of the contractor, because of the "inherent danger-ousness" of the work, or because he owed a nondelegable duty to the injured party.[75]

In the case of *Brien v. 18925 Collins Avenue Corp.*,[76] the plaintiff brought an action against a motel owner to recover damages for the death of her husband who had been killed by a security guard at the motel. The guard was an employee of an independent contractor hired by the motel owner to provide protection for the motel. The plaintiff sued the guard, the guard agency, and the motel owner. Although the contract guard service and the guard were liable (the service was vicariously liable for the negligence of the guard/employee, and the guard was liable for his own negligence), the motel owner was dismissed from the case by the trial court. The Florida appellate court affirmed the dismissal on the basis of the general rule that an "owner is not ordinarily liable for the negligence of an independent contractor employed by the owner." The court rejected the plaintiff's contention that the owner was liable because the work of an armed security guard is inherently dangerous.

The *Brien* court noted that the owner might have had liability if the plaintiff had alleged that the owner had actual or constructive notice of the dangerous propensities of the guard. Thus the defendant could have been liable on a negligence theory, even though vicarious liability was not applicable under the facts.

The case also illustrates the point that a plaintiff in a civil case will use as many theories of liability as are possible under the facts of the case and will bring into the suit as many individuals with potential liability as possible. Most cases, therefore, involve multiple theories (counts) of liability and multiple defendants. The torts and defenses discussed in this chapter should not be considered in isolation, but rather as interacting components of a single liability system.

**Strict Liability.** Liability without "fault" is sometimes imposed where persons are engaged in ultra-hazardous or abnormally dangerous activities. Examples of ultra-hazardous activities are dynamite blasting and oil drilling. An abnormally dangerous activity might involve ownership of a vicious animal such as a lion. Strict liability is imposed on the theory that, because of the danger involved in such activities and the difficulty of protecting against the risks involved, liability should attach to those who engage in such activities.

Strict liability is seldom applied to activities of security personnel. Perhaps such liability might attach in situations involving a "vicious" guard dog. However, cases involving vicious dogs have not applied strict liability against the owner where the dog attacked trespassers or tortfeasors — the most likely victims of a guard dog attack.

Strict liability appears to attach to security agencies as a result of statutory enactments that make holders of certificates of authority liable for the torts of agency employees committed while on the job.[77]

## Criminal Liability

Many of the aspects of criminal liability are similar to the concepts of tort liability. Therefore much of the above discussion regarding tort law applies to the criminal sanctions against security officers. One exception is that an employer is not vicariously liable for the criminal acts of his employees. However, there are circumstances where an employer will be held liable for an employee's violation of a "regulatory offense." In most jurisdictions, before liability is imposed the prosecution must prove that the employer knowingly and intentionally aided, advised, or encouraged the employee's criminal conduct.[78]

As with the tort law, criminal law is concerned with the enforcement of legal duties to act, not moral duties to act. A legal duty may arise as the result of a contract (e.g., a lifeguard obligates himself to attempt to rescue the drowning swimmer); by virtue of a special relationship (e.g., a parent has a duty to provide for the welfare of his child); by statute (e.g., a hospital has a duty to provide emergency care); or by common law (e.g., where one places another in peril, there is a duty to make reasonable attempts to assist the one endangered).

Elements of criminal liability are (1) a voluntary act or omission (actus reus or "guilty act"), (2) a mental state (mens rea or "guilty mind"), and (3) causation of the crime charged. As previously noted, certain regulatory offenses impose liability by deleting the requirement of mens rea — the fact that the "regulatory offense" was committed is sufficient for criminal liability regardless of the intention of the actor.

Corporations as well as individuals can commit crimes. In contrast to the situation where an employer is generally not responsible for the criminal acts of his employees, corporations may be liable for criminal offenses even where a mens rea is required for the crime. A corporation can act only through its agents. Thus the mental state (mens rea) is supplied by the corporate officer when he acts in behalf of the corporation. A corporate officer who commits theft for a corporate purpose within the scope of employment can make the corporation criminally liable.[79] The corporation is punished by the imposition of financial penalties and forfeitures. It is also punished by the stigma that attaches to the reputation of a corporation convicted of a criminal offense. In extreme cases of corporate officer criminality, corporations may have their corporate charter revoked — a form of capital punishment for the corporation.

Corporations must be aware of the following areas of business crime: securities fraud, Foreign Corrupt Practices Act, criminal antitrust, bank fraud, commercial bribery, tax fraud, commercial espionage, Hobbs Act, Travel Act, Racketeer Influenced and Corrupt Organizations Act (RICO), labor law violations, Occupational Health and Safety Act (OSHA), food and drug violations, environmental law, mail and wire fraud, as well as the "traditional" areas of criminal liability.[80]

Criminal liability is most frequently imposed on private security personnel in situations involving the use of force against another — assault, battery, manslaughter, and murder. Actions by security officers may also result in criminal liability for burglary, trespass, criminal defamation, false arrest, unlawful use of weapons, disorderly conduct, extortion, eavesdropping, theft, perjury, and kidnapping, among others.

An individual charged with a crime has various defenses available. The security officer might defend himself by demonstrating that he was privileged to use force in self-defense or that he made a reasonable mistake of fact negating criminal intent.[81] Other defenses include entrapment, compulsion or necessity, consent, intoxication, and insanity.

In general, a private citizen has no legal duty to report crime or to prevent it. Under the common law, citizens were liable for a failure to report felonies and could be charged with misprision of a felony. Early common law required the citizen to act affirmatively when a felony was committed within his presence. Some jurisdictions have retained the concept of misprision of felony:

> Whoever, having knowledge of the actual commission of a felony cognizable by a court of the United States, conceals and does not as soon as possible make known the same to some judge or other person in civil or military authority under the United States, shall be fined not more than $500 or imprisoned not more than three years, or both. (18 U.S.C. 4)

The federal statute quoted above and most state "misprision" statutes have been interpreted to require the purposeful concealment of a major offense. The term "purposeful" requires some affirmative action on the part of an individual rather than simply a failure to report a crime about which one has knowledge. There is, however, some case precedent for applying criminal liability for a mere failure to report a felony or to take obvious steps in prevention of violence. The rule in England, for instance, is that if one knows a felony has been committed and fails to report it he is guilty of misprision of felony. In England and Australia concealment need not involve a positive act and a mere omission is sufficient for criminal liability.[82]

In the U.S. federal system and most state systems, to be guilty of misprision the prosecution must prove beyond a reasonable doubt: (1) that the principal had committed and completed the felony alleged; (2) that the defendant had full knowledge of that fact; (3) that the defendant failed to notify the authorities; and (4) that the defendant took affirmative steps to conceal the crime of the principal.[83]

Although the security officer who fails to report a crime occurring in his presence on property he has agreed by contract to protect may not be guilty of misprision, there may be liability as a result of his failure to perform a duty he was physically capable of performing. For instance, assume a guard has been employed to protect tenants in an apartment building. As he is making his rounds, he comes upon an apartment with smoke pouring out the window and a tenant inside screaming for help. If the guard fails to act in this situation, the case law suggests that he could be criminally liable for his omission to perform a duty arising out of his contract.[84] The law of criminal liability in this area is unclear, however. Certainly the guard would have tort liability and liability for breach of contract. Whether he would also be criminally liable cannot be stated with any degree of certainty. As a minimum one would have to show a duty, that the guard's action was a gross violation of his duty, and that his breach of duty was the cause of the resulting injury.

An offense similar to misprision because it relates to the hindering of criminal prosecution is the compounding of a felony. Illinois law states:

> A person compounds a crime when he receives or offers to another any consideration for a promise not to prosecute or aid in the prosecution of an offender. Ill. Rev. Stat. chp. 38 § 32-1[85]

The common law defined compounding a crime as "the making by one directly injured by the commission of a crime of an agreement not to inform against or prosecute the offender in return for a reward, bribe or reparation for the injury."[86] The elements of the crime are (1) knowledge of the commission of the original crime, (2) an agreement not to report or prosecute that crime, and (3) the receipt of consideration.

Compounding a crime is an unlawful agreement to accept something of value (consideration) in exchange for a promise to curtail criminal prosecution. Because prosecutors have a discretionary charging function, a prosecutorial agreement to drop charges in exchange for a release from liability for the arrest is considered a lawful agreement that does not give rise to the compounding offense.[87] But where a security officer, for example, agrees to let an individual he apprehended go in exchange for money or some other form of compensation to which he is not legally entitled, he has compounded a crime and is subject to criminal prosecution. Depending on the exact circumstances of the case, he may be guilty of theft, extortion, or blackmail as well.

A problem faced by private security officers, especially those involved in undercover investigations, is the allegation that they solicited a crime by encouraging another to commit a crime. The criminal offense of solicitation is committed when one requests, commands, entices, or induces another to commit a crime with the intent that the other person engage in the criminal conduct.[88] The security officer acting without such an intent has not committed solicitation nor has he committed the offense of conspiracy, which is a combination of two or more people for the purpose of committing a criminal act.[89]

Where the security officer intends that a crime be committed, he could be charged with solicitation or conspiracy. Whereas public law enforcement officers are usually protected by statute for "crimes" they commit in the performance of their official duties,[90] private persons are not similarly protected. Therefore intent of the private person may become an important jury question upon which the person's liability will depend.

An issue related to the preceding discussion involves the matter of entrapment. Entrapment is an affirmative defense that completely exonerates a criminal defendant if his crime was incited or induced by a public officer or agent.

The defense of entrapment is not constitutionally required, but it is a judicially[91] or statutorily[92] created defense. Entrapment is applied in many jurisdictions when a private person works in concert with public officials.

In general, entrapment does not apply to private conduct. Particular factual situations and local law can cloud the otherwise clear "rule" that entrapment does not apply to private citizens. Consider the following case of *United States v. Maddox*,[93] which is frequently cited for the proposition that the entrapment defense does not extend to inducement by private citizens.

In *Maddox*, Alatex, Incorporated, a shirt manufacturer, was experiencing severe inventory shortages and, suspecting theft, obtained the investigative services of its parent corporation, Cluett-Peabody, Incorporated. Investigation by these private officers eventually led to the arrest of the defendants in Atlanta, Georgia. The case was tried in federal court and the defendants raised the entrapment defense. The trial judge submitted the entrapment issue to the jury, which found against the defendants who appealed the conviction to the U.S. Court of Appeals for the Fifth Circuit. The court of appeals affirmed the conviction and said:

> The defendants argue that the company's deep involvement in the conspiracy, to the extent of suggesting and arranging for the transportation, amounts to complicity and precludes their conviction because of entrapment as a matter of law. The argument overlooks the fact that private investigators, rather than governmental agents, participated in the arrangements. The en-

trapment defense does not extend to inducement by private citizens. Moreover, the defendants received the benefit of the defense when the District Court submitted the issue of entrapment to the jury for factual determination. The jury found against the defendants. In any event, the conduct of the private investigators merely afforded opportunities and facilities for the commission of the offense, a continuing illegal enterprise, without initiating the criminal design in the defendants' minds.[94]

The specific rationale for the *Maddox* decision is unclear. In the paragraph quoted above the appellate court indicated: (1) the entrapment defense does not apply; (2) the defense might apply but the jury decided the issue against the defendants as a matter of fact; and even if entrapment applies, the investigators did not put the criminal design in the mind of any defendant and therefore there is no entrapment as a matter of law.[95] Because the court covered all the bases in its decision, there is no single rationale for the decision. The case provides scant authority for an unequivocal statement that entrapment does not apply to private citizens. Furthermore, the *Maddox* court applied the federal rule of entrapment. Some states have extended their state entrapment rule to private persons acting in concert or support of the police. One draft of the proposed Federal Code would apply entrapment to persons acting in expectation of reward, pecuniary or otherwise, for assisting public officials.

The law is far from settled on the entrapment question and various state approaches will have to be examined in the future — particularly the developing security law in California. Even where the law is clear that entrapment does not apply to the conduct of private citizens, local prosecutors, judges, and juries may individually apply the entrapment defense "unofficially" because they do not agree with an investigative technique used by private personnel in a particular case.

Security officers employing undercover operatives who are also on the payroll of local police, security officers involved in a situation where they are coordinating a "private" investigation with local police, or security personnel working in a jurisdiction that applies an ad hoc entrapment rule to private citizens must be aware of the entrapment issue and use investigative techniques that can successfully avoid the defense.

### Civil Rights Act

Actions by private citizens are not regulated by the Civil Rights Act. However, security officers who have been commissioned and are therefore acting "under color of state law" are potentially liable under the Civil Rights Act when they deprive another of a right, privilege, or immunity secured by the Constitution.[96] An off-duty police officer working as a private security guard has been held to be acting under color of law for jurisdictional purposes under the Civil Rights Act.[97] However, other cases have held that off-duty officers are not acting under color of law when they perform private duties.[98]

The U.S. Supreme Court held in *Williams v. United States*[99] that the Federal Civil Rights Act applied to the actions of a commissioned private detective. Because of his commission by the city of Miami, the private detective had special police powers that created the necessary nexus to government action that subjected him to liability under the federal statute.

To come within the provisions of the Civil Rights Act the plaintiff must show: (1) that his constitutional rights were violated, and (2) that the violation was accomplished under color of a statute, ordinance, regulation, custom, or usage of a state or territory.

One of the few cases to date where a private party has been found to come within the language of the Civil Rights Act is *Smith v. Brookshire Brothers, Inc.*[100] In this case two store managers detained two shoppers, and a police officer summoned by the managers arrested a shopper and took her to the police station. The police officer's action was pursuant to an agreement with the store management. The law enforcement officer did not independently investigate the incident. Subsequently, the charges were dismissed, but the Civil Rights action commenced in federal court, which found jurisdiction on the basis of a customary plan by which store officials could have persons detained merely by telephoning local officials and designating the subject to be arrested.

As a general rule, noncommissioned security officers, even if acting pursuant to a state licensing law or mercantile shoplifting law, are not liable for actions under the Civil Rights Act. As the court said in *Weyandt v. Mason Stores, Inc.*, "[T]he fallacy of plaintiff's argument appears to be in equating acting under license of state law with acting under authority of state law."[101]

## SUMMARY

Although there are many similarities in function and dress between public law enforcement officers and private security personnel, the legal authority of each group differs in many significant respects. Generally, private security personnel possess no more authority than the average private citizen. Exceptions to this general rule occur when the security officer is specially commissioned or when he is a public law enforcement officer working in an off-duty security position. The private citizen as private security officer is the focus of this chapter, however.

The security officer derives his authority from tort, contract, criminal, constitutional, and administrative law.

A tort is a civil wrong arising out of conduct that affects some legally protected interest and causes damage. Tort law is the primary source for the authority of security personnel. Rather than authorizing their activity, however, it sets limits on their conduct.

A crime is any act or failure to act that injures the public at large and that is prohibited and punishable by law. Like tort law, criminal law restricts the activity of the security officer.

A contract is an agreement between two or more competent persons and consists of a promise or set of promises the law will enforce, or the performance of which the law recognizes as a duty.

The U.S. Constitution establishes the basic rights of all individuals and sets limits on the conduct of government officers. In general, these limitations do not apply to private persons.

Administrative law is the area of civil law that deals with the creation and activities of federal and state independent agencies and executive departments. Private security is frequently regulated by state and local laws. Commissioning of private security officers does not confer the authority of the public law enforcement officer, but does subject the commissioned security officer to the constitutional restrictions and obligations placed on the public officer.

Private security personnel have the authority to arrest, perform limited searches and seizures, interrogate, and use force.

A citizen has arrested another when, with lawful authority, he has deprived another of personal liberty. In general, a private person may make a warrantless arrest where a felony has actually been committed and there is reasonable cause to suspect that the person committed the crime. A private citizen may make a warrantless misdemeanor arrest only where the misdemeanor was committed in the arrestor's presence.

At common law, there was a limited right for a person to arrest and detain but the arrestor acted at his peril. Probable cause to believe another had committed a crime was not sufficient if the arrestor was mistaken. This is still the rule with regard to private citizens in the overwhelming majority of states. The rule has been modified by some state courts and statutes to allow a merchant to arrest and detain on the basis of probable cause in order to protect his merchandise. The acts of the merchant or his agent must be reasonable. Furthermore, the shoplifting statutes provide protection only for certain types of liability.

Private searches have been judicially approved on the basis of search incident to a valid arrest and pursuant to consent of the party searched.

Where possible, private security personnel should obtain a search warrant to be executed by a public official.

A private citizen acting under citizen's arrest authority is not required to inform a suspect of his constitutional rights. However, some jurisdictions by local custom require private security personnel to give *Miranda* warnings. Statements must be voluntarily made to be admissible in court.

Citizens are privileged to use reasonable force in defense of self or others, to protect property, to arrest, and to prevent crime. Excessive or unreasonable force will result in criminal and civil liability.

Persons are liable for the tort of negligence when they fail to act as a reasonably prudent individual would have acted under the same or similar circumstances and this failure caused injury to a person to whom they owed a duty. A plaintiff injured as a result of another's negligence will be awarded compensatory damages and may be awarded punitive damages in some states for a defendant's gross negligence.

Intentional torts occur when one acts in a manner designed to bring about a certain result. Intentional torts include assault, battery, false arrest, defamation, malicious prosecution, invasion of privacy, trespass, and infliction of mental distress.

Punitive damages can be obtained for intentional torts and are designed to punish and deter the tortfeasor.

Employers are vicariously liable for the negligence of an employee occurring within the scope of employment. An employer may also be liable for an employee's intentional act if it can be shown that the employer's negligence was a substantial factor in bringing about the harm, or where the employer ratified, authorized, or approved the employee's intentional act.

Criminal liability is based on a voluntary act or failure to act, performed with a culpable mental state, that results in conduct proscribed by society.

A security officer most frequently incurs criminal liability as a result of the use of force. However, criminal charges of compounding a crime, theft, extortion, solicitation, and conspiracy, among others, may arise from his conduct. As a general rule, the Civil Rights Act and the entrapment defense do not apply to private security personnel.

The law as it applies to security personnel is in a period of transition and development. Some issues raised in this chapter have not been addressed by the courts or legislatures in many jurisdictions. Thus there is no single body of law to which the private officer can turn at present. In order to determine the legal limits of a security officer's authority in a particular jurisdiction, a local prosecutor or private counsel should be consulted.

## NOTES

1.  Bird, W. J., Kakalik, J. S., and Wildhorn, S., et. al., *The Law and the Private Police*, The Rand Corporation (Santa Monica, California, December 1971), Vol. IV, p. 7.

2.  Prosser, W. L., *Handbook of the Law of Torts*, fourth edition (St. Paul, Minn.: West Publishing Company, 1971), p. 7.

3.  Calamari, J. D. and Perillo, J. M., *The Law of Contracts* (St. Paul, Minn.: West Publishing Company, 1970), p. 1.

4.  See Annotation, "Liability of One Contracting for Private Police or Security Services for Acts of Personnel Supplied," 38 ALR 3d 1332 (1971).

5.  For a further discussion of this area, see Bilek, A. J., Klotter, J. C., and Federal, R. K., *Legal Aspects of Private Security* (Cincinnati: Anderson Publishing Company, 1981), pp. 169–173.

6.  In *People v. Zelinski*, 594 P. 2d 1000 (1979) the California Supreme Court applied the State of California Constitution to a private search which had been performed pursuant to a statutorily-authorized citizen arrest. The Montana Supreme Court applied the Montana Constitution to illegal searches by private citizens in *State v. Helfrich* 600 P. 2d 816 (1979) and *State v. Hyem* 29 CrL 2038 (June 4, 1981) and excluded the evidence illegally obtained.

7.  *Burdeau v. McDowell*, 256 U.S. 456 (1921).

8.  *Weyandt v. Mason's Store, Inc.*, 279 F. Supp. 283 (W.D. Pa. 1968).

9.  *Fourth Amendment:* "The right of the people to be secure in their persons, houses, papers, and effects, against unreasonable searches and seizures, shall not be violated, and no Warrants shall issue, but upon probable cause, supported by Oath or affirmation, and particularly describing the place to be searched, and the persons or things to be seized."

    *Fifth Amendment:* "No person shall be held to answer for a capital, or otherwise infamous crime, unless on a presentment or indictment of a Grand Jury, except in cases arising in the land or naval forces, or in the Militia, when in actual service in time of War or public danger; nor shall any person be subject for the same offence to be twice put in jeopardy of life or limb; nor shall be compelled in any criminal case to be a witness against himself, nor be deprived of life, liberty, or property, without due process of law; nor shall private property be taken for public use, without just compensation."

    *Sixth Amendment:* "In all criminal prosecutions, the accused shall enjoy the right to a speedy and public trial, by an impartial jury of the State and district wherein the crime shall have been committed, which district shall have been previously ascertained by law, and to be informed of the nature and cause of the accusation; to be confronted with the witnesses against him; to have compulsory process for obtaining Witnesses in his favor, and to have the Assistance of Counsel for his defence."

    *Fourteenth Amendment*, Section 1: "All persons born or naturalized in the United States and subject to the jurisdiction thereof, are citizens of the United States and of the State wherein they reside. No State shall make or enforce any law which shall abridge the privileges or immunities of citizens of the United States; nor shall any State deprive any person of life, liberty, or property, without due process of law; nor deny to any person within its jurisdiction the equal protection of the laws."

10.  232 U.S. 383 (1914).

11.  367 U.S. 643 (1961).

12. *Silverthorne Lumber Co. v. United States*, 251 U.S. 385 (1920).
13. *Nardone v. United States*, 302 U.S. 379 (1937); 308 U.S. 338 (1939).
14. Note 6.
15. *U.S. v. Lima*, D.C. Superior Court, 47 LW 2696 (April 16, 1979).
16. Euller, S., "Private Security in the Courtroom: the Exclusionary Rule Applies," *Security Management*, Vol. 24, No. 3, March 1980, pp. 38–42.
17. *U.S. v. Lima*, D.C. Court of Appeals, 48 LW 2668 (March 12, 1980).
18. Ibid.
19. Montana applied exclusion to actions of private citizens in the case of *State v. Helfrich* 600 P. 2d 816 (1979). The rule was reaffirmed in *State v. Hyem* 29 CrL 2308 (June 4, 1981).
20. See Walsh, T. J., and Healy, R. J., *Protection of Assets Manual* (Santa Monica, Calif.: The Merritt Company, 1979), Part III, Administrative Law, pp. 21–45.
21. See *Private Police*, Report of the Task Force on Private Security, National Advisory Committee on Criminal Justice Standards and Goals, Washington, D.C., 1976, pp. 381–387.
22. "Law of Citizen's Arrest," 65 *Columbia Law Review*, 494 (1965); "Private Police Powers: Legal Powers and Limitations," 38 *University of Chicago Law Review*, 567 (1971).
23. Bassiouni, M. C., *Citizen's Arrest* (Springfield, Ill.: Charles C. Thomas, 1977), p. 36.
24. 156 Cal. Rptr. 198 (1979). The *Cervantez* decision presents problems for the "moonlighting" police officer who is uncertain of his status and powers while working as a security officer. Traditional doctrine has been that a police officer retained his police powers within his jurisdiction on a 24-hour a day, seven-day-a-week basis. *Cervantez* and subsequent attorney general opinions in a few states indicate that his authority depends upon his employer at the time he takes action. For a discussion of some of the liability considerations regarding off-duty police officers while working as private security officers see commentary letter by D. Steeno appearing in *Security Industry and Product News*, November 1980, p. 11.
25. In response to the *Cervantez* decision, the California legislature enacted changes in California Penal Code 490.5 to broaden the authority of merchants and library employees in California to detain and search. The amended section remedies the *Cervantez* decision by providing that probable cause to believe that the person detained had stolen or attempted to steal merchandise is a defense to any civil action brought by any person as a result of a detention or arrest by a merchant or library employee who acted reasonably under all the circumstances.
26. *Arkansas v. Sanders*, 442 U.S. 753 (1979).
27. Notes 6 and 14.
28. Compare *People v. Santiago*, 378 N.Y.S. 2d 260 (1967) with *People v. Alberta*, 237 N.Y.S. 2d 51 (1962).
29. Indiana Statutes Annotated, Section 35–3–2–1; Illinois Revised Statutes, Chapter 38, Section 16A-5; Oklahoma Statutes Annotated, Chapter 22, Section 1343.
30. California Penal Code, Section 490.5; Minnesota Statutes Annotated, Section 629.366. The amended California statute permits merchants and library employees to detain individuals upon probable cause to believe the person detained was attempting to unlawfully take or did take any item from the premises. Those empowered to act under the statute may request the person de-

tained to voluntarily surrender the item taken. If the person refuses to surrender the item, a limited and reasonable search may be conducted of packages, shopping bags, handbags or other property in the immediate possession of the person detained. A search of the clothing worn by the person detained is not authorized.

31. "Scope of Legal Authority of Private Security Personnel," A Report Prepared by the Private Security Advisory Council to the Law Enforcement Assistance Administration, United States Department of Justice, 1976, p. 14.

32. Note 7.

33. 18 U.S.C. 2510 et. seq.

34. Florida Statutes, Section 934.03(2)(c).

35. 397 So. 2d 643 (1981).

36. Illinois Revised Statutes, Chapter 38, Section 14-1.

37. Massachusetts General Laws, Chapter 272, Section 99.

38. *Peak v. State*, 342 So. 2d 98 (Fla. App. 1977).

39. Illinois Revised Statutes, Chapter 38, Section 12-7 states that one commits a felony under the following circumstances: "A person who, with intent to obtain a confession, statement or information regarding any offense, inflicts or threatens to inflict physical harm upon the person threatened or upon any other person commits the offense of compelling a confession or information by force or threat" (Class 4 felony).

40. 384 U.S. 436 (1966).

41. *People v. Raitano*, 401 N.E. 2d 278 (Illinois 1980); *United States v. Antonelli*, 434 F. 2d 335 (CA 2, 1970); *Owens v. State*, 266 N.E. 2d 612 (Indiana 1971); *U.S. v. Bolden*, 461 F. 2d 998 (CA 8, 1972).

42. 635 P. 2d 446 (1981).

43. Wisconsin Statutes Annotated, Section 943.50.

44. *Petrie v. Cartwright*, 70 S.W. 297 (1902).

45. *Head v. Martin*, 3 S.W. 622 (1887).

46. *People v. Silver*, 108 P. 2d 4 (1940).

47. *Second Amendment:* "A well regulated Militia, being necessary to the security of a free state, the right of the people to keep and bear Arms, shall not be infringed."

48. See "The Impact of State Constitutional Right to Bear Arms Provision on State Gun Control Legislation," 38 *Chicago Law Review* 185 (1970).

49. See *Business and Industrial Security Practical Legal Problems — 2d.*, Practising Law Institute, New York, 1972.

50. Barry, R. L., "Loss Prevention for the Loss Preventors," *Security Management*, Vol. 23, No. 3, March 1979, p. 22.

51. Steeno, D. L., "Be Sure Your Security Is Legally Secure," *Security World*, Vol. 18, No. 6, June 1981, p. 35.

52. Ibid.

53. *Kline v. 1500 Massachusetts Avenue Apartment Corporation*, 439 F. 2d 477 (1970).

54. Compare Stalmack, J. M. "The Illinois Landlord's Obligation To Protect Persons On His Premises Against the Criminal Activities Of Third Persons," *Illinois Bar Journal*, June 1980, pp. 668–675, with *Holley v. Mt. Zion Terrace Apartments, Inc.*, 382 So. 2d 98 (Fla. App. 1980) where the Florida Court of Appeals upheld the theory of liability for failure to protect tenants against foreseeable criminal activity.

55. Principles of agency are discussed in the material dealing with respondeat superior.

56. Prosser, op. cit., p. 470.
57. *Great Atlantic and Pacific Tea Co. v. Paul,* 261 A. 2d 731 (Md. 1970).
58. *Moffatt v. Buffums' Inc.,* 69 P. 2d 424 (Calif. 1937).
59. *Parrott v. Bank of America Nat. Trust and Sav. Assoc.,* 217 P. 2d 89 (Calif. 1950). Annotation, 35 ALR 2d 263.
60. For an excellent discussion of generally accepted techniques of employee theft investigation, see Barefoot, J. L., *Employee Theft Investigation* (Los Angeles: Security World Publishing Company, 1979).
61. Caveat: Some jurisdictions by "local custom" and not by case or statutory law require the advisement of warnings by private security personnel prior to interrogation. Local officials in a few jurisdictions may refuse to handle a private case where private security personnel failed to comply with local "law." Thus it behooves the security officer to contact local prosecutors, police officials, and judges to determine the local custom.
62. *NLRB v. Weingarten, Inc.,* 420 U.S. 251 (1975) and *International Ladies' Garment Workers' Union v. Quality Manufacturing Company et. al.,* 420 U.S. 276 (1975).
63. Prosser, op. cit., p. 797.
64. For example, Illinois Revised Statutes, Chapter 38, Section 27–1 provides: "A person commits criminal defamation when, with intent to defame another, living or dead, he communicates by any means to any person matter which tends to provoke a breach of the peace." Section 27–2 states: "In all prosecutions for criminal defamation, the truth, when communicated with good motives, and for justifiable ends, shall be an affirmative defense."
65. Prosser, ibid.
66. *Farnsworth v. Tribune Co.,* 253 N.E. 2d 408 (Ill. 1969).
67. Prosser, op. cit., p. 802–818; 927–949.
68. *Smith v. Allied Supermarkets,* 524 S.W. 2d 848 (Mo. 1975).
69. *Nader v. General Motors Corp.,* 255 N.E. 2d 765 (1970).
70. *Pinkerton National Detective Agency, Inc. v. Stevens,* 132 S.E. 2d 119 (Ga. 1963).
71. Belair, R. R., "Awareness of Privacy Rules Is Crucial for Security Pros," *Security Management,* Vol. 23, No. 3, March 1979, p. 14.
72. Prosser, op. cit., p. 464.
73. *Dart Drug v. Linthicum,* 300 A. 2d 442 (D.C. 1973).
74. See "Negligent Entrustment Revisited: Developments 1966–1976," 30 *Arkansas Law Review* 288 (1976) and *Bonsignore v. City of New York,* U.S. District Court, S.D.N.Y., reported in 24 ATLA L. Rep. 262, Vol. 24, No. 6, August 1981, where jury awarded $425,000 in compensatory and punitive damages against the city of New York for negligent entrustment of firearm to a policeman who shot his wife.
75. Prosser, op. cit., 468–475.
76. 233 So. 2d 847 (Fla. App. 1970).
77. Illinois Revised Statutes, Chapter 111, Section 2622(10) states: "The holder of a certificate of authority who employs persons to assist him in the work of private detective and in the conduct of such business shall at all times during such employment be legally responsible for the good conduct in the business of each and every person so employed."
78. *Commonwealth v. Koczwara,* 155 A. 2d 825 (Pa. 1950). But contrast with *Ex parte Marley* 175 P. 2d 832 (Calif. 1946) where the court imposed liability on an employer even though he did not know about, or authorize the employee's violation.

79.  See W. T. Grant Co. v. Superior Court, 23 Cal. App. 3d 284 (1972); New York Central and Hudson Railroad v. United States, 212 U.S. 481 (1908); and People v. Canadian Fur Trappers Corp., 161 N.E. 455 (NY 1928).

80.  Business crime has become an area of such concern that corporate counsel can now purchase a multi-volume series called Business Crime: Criminal Liability of the Business Community (New York: Mathew Bender, Business, Legal and Tax Publishers).

81.  Bassiouni, op. cit., p. 64.

82.  See Sykes v. Director of Public Prosecution, 3 All. Eng. L. R. 33 (1961) discussed in Inbau, F. E., Thompson, J. R., and Moenssens, A. A., Criminal Law, second edition (Mineola, N.Y.: The Foundation Press, 1979), p. 642.

83.  United States v. Stuard, 566 F. 2d 1 (CA 6, 1977) quoting Neal v. United States, 102 F. 2d 643 (CA 8, 1939).

84.  See Guthrie, C. N., and Bridgman, B. C. Security Guard Powers to Arrest (Gardena, Calif.: Harcourt Brace Jovanovich Legal and Professional Publications, Inc., distributed by Law Distributors, 1978), pp. 3–4, discussing Perrine v. Pacific Gas and Electric Company, 186 Cal. App. 2d 442; and Powell v. U.S., 2 F. 2d 47 (CA 4, 1924) discussed in Bilek et al., op. cit., p. 153.

85.  See also California Penal Code, Section 153, and the Nevada Revised Statutes, Sections 178.564, 178.566, and 178.568, as well as the Comment, "Compounding Crimes: Time for Enforcement," 27 Hastings Law Journal, 175 (1975).

86.  15A Am. Jur. 2d, Compounding Crimes, Section 1, p. 767.

87.  Hoines v. Barney's Club Inc., California Supreme Court, 80 Daily Journal D.A.R. 3337 (1981), overruling 166 Cal. Rptr. 577.

88.  People v. Lubor, 272 N.E. 2d 331 (NY 1971).

89.  Sigler, J., Understanding Criminal Law (Boston: Little, Brown and Company, 1981), p. 253.

90.  See Iowa Code Annotated, Section 704.11 Police Activity: "A peace officer or person employed by any police agency who joins in the participation of a crime by another person solely for the purpose of gathering evidence leading to the prosecution of such other person shall not be guilty of that crime, provided that all of the following are true: 1. He or she is not the instigator of the criminal activity. 2. He or she does not intentionally injure a nonparticipant in the crime. 3. He or she acts with the consent of his or her superiors or the necessity of immediate action precludes his or her obtaining such consent. 4. His or her actions are reasonable under the circumstances."

91.  The United States Supreme Court recognized and applied entrapment in Sorrells v. United States, 287 U.S. 435 (1932). See a discussion of entrapment in federal cases in Jones, D. A., The Law of Criminal Procedure (Boston: Little, Brown and Company, 1981), pp. 111–113.

92.  Illinois Revised Statutes, Chapter 38, Section 7-12 states: "A person is not guilty of an offense if his conduct is incited or induced by a public officer or employee, or agent of either, for the purpose of obtaining evidence for the prosecution of such person. However, this Section is inapplicable if a public officer of employee, or agent of either, merely affords to such person the opportunity or facility for committing an offense in furtherance of a criminal purpose which such person has originated."

93.  492 F. 2d 104 (CA 5, 1974).

94.  Ibid.

95.  The federal courts and the majority of states use the subjective approach to entrapment which concentrates on the predisposition of the defendant to

commit the crime. A minority of states use an objective approach to determine if entrapment exists, focusing on the conduct of the governmental officials.

96.   Federal Civil Rights law, Section 1983 of Title 42 of the United States Code is based on the Civil Rights Acts of 1871 and states: "Every person who, under color of any statute, ordinance, regulation, custom, or usage, of any State or Territory, subjects, or causes to be subjected, any citizen of the United States or other person within the jurisdiction thereof to the deprivation of any rights, privileges, or immunities secured by the Constitution and laws, shall be liable to the party injured in an action at law, suit in equity, or other proper proceeding for redress." 42 U.S.C. § 1983.

The major federal civil rights laws of a criminal nature which remain on the federal statute books are Sections 241 and 242 of Title 18 of the United States Code. Section 242, Title 18, of the United States Code states: "Whoever, under color of any law, statute, ordinance, regulation, or custom willfully subjects any inhabitant of any State, Territory, or District to the deprivation of any rights, privileges, or immunities secured or protected by the Constitution or laws of the United States, or to different punishments, pains, or penalties, on account of such inhabitant being an alien, or by reason of his color, or race, than are prescribed for the punishment of citizens, shall be fined not more than $1,000 or imprisoned not more than one year, or both." 18 U.S.C. § 242.

Section 241, Title 18, United States Code is a conspiracy statute and states: "If two or more persons conspire to injure, oppress, threaten, or intimidate any citizen in the free exercise or enjoyment of any right or privilege secured to him by the Constitution or laws of the United States, or because of his having so exercised the same; or if two or more persons go in disguise on the highway, or on the premises of another, with intent to prevent or hinder his free exercise or enjoyment of any right or privilege so secured, they shall be fined not more than $5,000 or imprisoned not more than ten years, or both." 18 U.S.C. § 241.

97.   *Davis v. Murphy*, 559 F. 2d 1098 (CA 7, 1977) later appealed 587 F. 2d 362 (1978).

98.   Vroman, J. A., "The Potential Liability of Private Police Under Section 1983 of the Civil Rights Act," 4 *Law Forum*, 1185 (1976).

99.   341 U.S. 97 (1951).

100.   519 F. 2d 93 (CA 5, 1975).

101.   Note 8.

# Chapter 4
# Physical Security Applications

This chapter explores the security characteristics of various familiar institutions and organizations. It attempts to delineate unique and special considerations separating one security situation from another.

It might seem as if a prison would require more security devices than a school, and yet in actuality many schools possess far more sophisticated alarms than those contained in prisons. This is simply because surveillance in a jail is constantly maintained by guards, whereas schools, which are typically left unoccupied during the night, have to rely on electronic surveillance for detection.

To further illustrate the point, a special teacher alarm was installed in a number of U.S. schools. The device was a small handheld transmitter that could summon help from the principal's office. This device, which was developed for an educational environment, was subsequently copied for use in prisons to protect patrolling guards from prisoner attack. It seems that although most security situations are unique, there are characteristics that are universally shared by many industries.

Some security concepts have undergone revolutionary changes in the last 10 to 15 years, and some concepts will continue to be altered as new and different security problem areas arise. Security is now an important element in such traditional establishments as museums, hotels, universities, and hospitals. Budgets for security controls in some establishments have risen from nothing to more than 20 percent of the total operating budget in the last 20 years. Some of today's most critical areas (e.g., computer security and nuclear power plants) did not even exist 10 to 20 years ago.

In addition to nuclear plants, other situations are considered targets of crime today that only 10 years ago were not considered a security risk. People are now routinely searched at airports, some universities and secondary schools have become prone to violence, and prisons have experienced increasing violence. In many instances, traditional methods are no longer effective in protecting property. Private security is becoming a customized industry, designed to meet different conditions in different areas of commerce. Although this chapter cannot explore and evaluate all security situations, it does define some major areas of concern and offers information that indicates unique characteristic differences between one situation and another.

## AIRPORTS AND AIRLINES

The problems confronting private security continue to change with the social and political climate of the nation. These changes almost always result in a need for differently trained security personnel and alarm devices. These "new" situations cannot be predicted nor can they usually be handled with conventional programs and procedures. Thus they require new concepts and different approaches to protection. One of the most dramatic changes occurred in the airport–airline industry. The earliest known act of air piracy occurred in 1930 when hijackers took over a Peruvian aircraft, but this type of criminal action was a rarity until the 1970s. Between 1963 and 1967, there were only four attempted sky jackings of U.S. registered aircraft. During the period 1970–1979, however, there were 149 hijacking attempts on U.S. scheduled and general aviation aircraft. Congress set up in the mid 70s the Office of Civilian Aviation Security under the FAA that reports twice a year to Congress on the various problems occurring in commercial aviation and the actions being taken to protect civilians. Since the period that skyjacking data have been kept, there have been a total of 209 incidents with about 53 percent of them successful. These data do not include bomb threats, weapons detected, or other offenses related to screening. The success rate has been lowered significantly since 1979, but the cost of security at airports has risen tremendously.

The 1976 Official Private Security Task Force Report indicates that mentally deranged persons, inebriates, and practical jokers are frequently the perpetrators of bomb threats and skyjackings.[1] Terrorists are also principals in this growing crime.

Skyjacking 1971

According to published newspaper accounts, a man wearing a top coat over a dark suit and tie boarded Northwest Orient Flight 305 at Portland. It was the day before Thanksgiving (November 24, 1971) and there were only 36 passengers on board. As the plane was taxiing for takeoff, the man (listed as Dan Cooper) handed a note to the stewardess, instructing her to "read it now!" The note said: "I have a bomb in my briefcase." As the plane headed toward Seattle, Mr. Cooper announced that he would blow up the plane unless he was given $200,000 and four parachutes. At Seattle, he was given the money and parachutes. He then *allowed all the passengers* and two of the stewards to deplane.

The pilot took off again, flying at low altitudes and minimum cruising speed, with flaps down and ventral stairs extended. The crew was instructed to stay in the front cabin with the curtain drawn. When the plane landed at Reno, Mr. Cooper was not aboard.

Mr. Cooper's feat helped to create a new industry and a new field of criminal activity. Government and civilian agencies changed procedures at airports and, in effect, ushered in a new eve of airport security. The use of skyjacking to gain either financing or political ends has resulted in extortion demands exceeding $8 million, of which about $5 million was actually paid.[2] All of the money has been recovered except for the $200,000 paid to the mysterious man on Flight 305. (Some of the bills were recovered in February 1980, but the money, and Mr. Cooper, is still unaccounted for.)

## Preventive Measures

The increasing frequency of skyjacking and bomb threats since 1972 has promoted the development of improved security measures and procedures at airports. In December 1972, the Federal Aviation Authority initiated compulsory screening of persons and carry-on luggage entering the departure area of an airport. In that same year, federal legislation was adopted that provided specific criminal penalties for criminal actions against aircraft. Since the implementation of tighter security measures, there have been few successful skyjackings of common carrier aircraft in the United States. In 1969, the President of the United States directed the FAA to research all aspects of aircraft hijacking.

**Sky Marshals.**  "Sky marshals" were assigned to accompany commercial aircraft. While this program enjoyed some success, it had its weaknesses. This was clearly demonstrated when one flight was hijacked while two marshals were on board. The program was under constant criticism from the airlines who considered the coverage too sparse, and who were deeply concerned about the possibility and consequences of a shoot-out at high altitudes. The program fell into disuse in the mid-1970s when better search procedures were instituted.

**Other Suggestions.**  Other suggestions to deter skyjacking involved arming in-flight attendants, training stewardesses in karate and judo, and fingerprinting or photographing passengers. These last two techniques were ruled out since less than 10 percent of skyjackers had remained unidentified and such a procedure would, it was decided, not have deterred future hijackings. One carrier proposed to the FAA that photo-identification cards be issued to a select group of "safe" individuals, but the idea was rejected as discriminatory. It was totally discarded when in 1972 a respected employee of the Department of Commerce tried to hijack a plane.

Some of the suggestions included the installation in each passenger seat of a hypodermic needle filled with a drug that would render the passenger unconscious. By pressing the proper seat button in the cockpit, the pilot could inject the hijacker. Still another idea was to lock the passenger to his seat with manacles and leg irons. Another suggestion required each passenger to strip completely in dressing rooms and don overalls for the flight. The Airline Pilots Association came out in favor of "inaccessible cockpits," with no voice communication from the cabin to the cockpit, and which could not be entered from the cabin side. In an emergency, a cabin attendant could push an alarm button, and the pilot could land at the nearest airport without further communication.

### Legal Aspects

When the airlines and airports selected the screening process as the solution to hijacking, they overlooked the Fourth Amendment to the Constitution, which declares that without a "probable cause" (and a warrant) search and seizure is a violation of the rights of the people. When air carrier personnel suspect that a suitcase or a piece of freight may contain explosives, they must call in the law enforcement organization with the requisite expertise to handle such risks.

Legal problems arise when these searches for explosives turn up narcotics or stolen goods. Air carrier employees are "private persons," and as such, have only the legal authority of private persons in regard to search. Airport searches are conducted under the instructions of a federal agency (FAA) that imposes upon the air carriers the requirement to "adopt and put into use a screening system that is designed to prevent or deter the carriage aboard its aircraft of any explosives or incendiary device or weapon in carry-on baggage, etc." Since the search is in reference to exigent national circumstances and the invasion of privacy is minimal, the courts have maintained that no violation of the Fourth Amendment exists. Furthermore, the courts state that the Constitution does not forbid searches and seizures — it only forbids searches that are unreasonable. The use of a magnetometer at airports to detect the presence of metal on individuals boarding an aircraft is not considered an unnecessary intrusion of privacy, and such a search is deemed reasonable in that it is a compelling necessity to protect essential air commerce and the lives of passengers.

### X-Ray Metal Detection

X-ray units used at U.S. carry-on luggage stations are low-dosage type. Characteristics that must be considered in the selection of an X-ray unit include: speed of inspection (twelve items per minute is average), mobility, maintenance, picture quality, training required, and relative cost. Initially, the introduction of X-ray baggage inspection caused concern to airline companies. The assumption that these units developed the same dosage as medical and dental X-ray machines prompted the federal government to issue a set of safety standards that limited the power and operation of units so that the X-rays could not contaminate the public. While there is still some concern about the dangers of X-ray beams, it remains the most feasible system available to search baggage without actually opening the baggage for a visual inspection.

Metal detectors must meet standards set by the FAA. These test standards specify a metal of specific size, weight, and metallic content used to calibrate the detector. Until this test mechanism was provided, the carriers were in a rather untenable position. A carrier could be liable for a possible violation if a detector was not up to the standard specified, and yet there was no way in which the unit could be tested. Up until this time, the typical testing mechanism usually consisted of having the law enforcement officer at the screening point walk through the detector with and without his gun. The FAA now has developed a standardized test block. Each station receives one of these units for regular calibration and adjustments to the equipment.

## Air Cargo

The first commercial business of U.S. airlines was the carriage of mail in 1918 — eight years before the introduction of commercial passenger traffic. Cargo carriage did not grow at the same rate as air mail, and it wasn't until 1956 that air freight passed air mail as a source of revenue for the airlines. The growth rate in recent years has been dramatic. Air cargo has a greater proportion of high-value shipments than any other method of freight carriage, which makes it more attractive to theft. The FAA and the Department of Transportation estimate that about 0.32 percent of the total cargo revenue is stolen and results in theft-related claims. This is equivalent to a loss of about $6 million based on a $2.153 billion revenue in 1978. By contrast, the theft component for truck transport is 0.69 percent, representing a value of about 25 percent of this industry's profit. (Losses of luggage are not reported by airlines, but are obviously substantial.)

In efforts to deter thefts of air cargo, careful consideration is given to the following factors:

1.  *Exterior areas* — require proper fencing and lighting. Employee parking should be isolated from the terminal area.
2.  *General conditions* — must be addressed in developing a security system. These include hours of operation, past period of thefts, sharing a facility with another tenant, etc.
3.  *Receiving and storing procedures* — must be evaluated. Access by truckers, locking methods, inventory controls, identification and recording of vehicles.
4.  *Law enforcement liaison* — must be established. Relevant agencies include FAA, FBI, and U.S. Customs.

Since the greatest portion of the loss in air cargo theft results from employee theft, most security controls have been concentrated in internal procedures. In addition to these measures, careful consideration should be given to the use of high fences, package seals, and restricted parking areas.

According to a Department of Transportation study, approximately 10 percent of cargo theft of all kinds can be attributed to hijacking, 5 percent to burglary, and 85 percent to "opportunity" (i.e., goods leaving the premises during working hours in the hands of persons authorized to be there).

Historically, air carriers derive approximately 90 percent of their revenue from passenger traffic and 10 percent from the carriage of cargo (including mail). Logically enough, security attention has been divided between passenger security and cargo security in much the same proportion. With the growing frequency of cargo theft, and the large dollar amounts being stolen, it is reasonable to assume that considerably more than 10 percent of a carrier's security effort must be expanded in the cargo area if losses are to be further contained.

## COLLEGES AND UNIVERSITIES

Until the 1950s and early 1960s, security at institutions of higher learning was an administrative function carried out by the physical plant or buildings and grounds staff. Night watchmen or guards were used for fire detection and to control parking.

It was not until the late 1960s that the need for organized, well-trained security personnel at colleges was demonstrated. Laboratory buildings were blown up; students went on strike and in some instances forcefully occupied administration buildings. Some schools closed their doors because of the lack of preparation by school administrators to deal with the problem. Most school administrators had no training or experience in dealing with this type of student disorder, and some resorted to local and state law enforcement agencies to control the situation. In some cases the police tended to overreact. For the most part the intervention of law enforcement agents on campus only complicated matters, and it was viewed by many students, faculty, and administrators as unwarranted.

An outgrowth of the demonstrations of the 1960s was the establishment of academic departments in criminal justice science at colleges across the United States. These programs attracted thousands of police officers who received federal grant monies to attend college. Since the police now had a vested interest in the college community, these programs helped to establish a better rapport between the university and the police, and a more understanding, effective approach to campus uprisings. There were probably fewer than 20 criminal justice departments in existence before 1965. Today, there are over 150 such programs, with several granting degrees in security administration.

More recently, violent crime and property theft have increased on some campuses. While the situation is worse in urban centers, even the sprawling, rural campuses have experienced a dangerous growth in campus crime. Although attacks against property are apparent, the safety of individuals has become the major priority of campus security departments. There has been a dramatic increase in the last half of the 1970s in the number of robberies, assaults, muggings, and rapes at college campuses across the country. On some campuses the students have organized rape crisis centers to provide counseling and assistance to rape victims. On other campuses male students have formed protective night escort services for female students.

New problems have been created in recent years by the creation of high-rise dormitory buildings. In such a large complex it becomes virtually impossible for students to be familiar with all the other residents of the dormitory. This creates a setting in which it is easy for an intruder to assume the identity of a student. To alleviate this problem, many colleges have installed extensive locking and access-control systems in an effort to restrict access to residential areas.

Theft of college property far outweighs that of student property on most campuses. Commonly stolen items include audiovisual and laboratory equipment, typewriters, calculators, books, art objects, and examinations.

### Preventive Measures

In an effort to prevent armed robberies, many colleges have installed closed-circuit television and alarm systems in areas such as the bursar's or comptroller's office, which serve as collection points for tuition payments and cash receipts from campus facilities.

Theft of library books has been dealt with on some college campuses by the installation of electronic sensor devices in libraries. Although the installation of this device has significantly reduced the number of books stolen, it has not totally eliminated the problem. Since only main exits are alarmed, students can, for example, toss books out of windows or exit via fire doors.

In recent years many colleges have established proprietary security forces and appointed security directors. Most proprietary forces on publicly funded campuses have some power of arrest or police authority. In fact, approximately forty states have legislation providing police authority for proprietary security personnel on campus. Most of these states restrict such police powers to public institutions of higher education, but some states, such as Massachusetts and New Jersey, extend these powers to private institutions.

There has been a movement on college campuses to involve students more actively in campus security. Students are used on some campuses to assist in crowd control and traffic direction at college events. Other colleges maintain student patrols or student marshall programs. Some carry two-way radios and wear arm patches identifying them as "student security services." One campus has an entire security department made up of students. In this program, the security personnel must have undergraduate degrees and be pursuing a graduate degree in criminal justice.

### SHOPPING CENTERS

The migration of city residents to the suburbs has created a new commercial entity — the shopping mall. The problems that are involved in maintaining a safe and secure shopping center are complex and different from those designed for other commercial establishments.

Management of shopping centers has become a specialized field, but despite widespread use of uniformed guards, most shopping centers do not employ a security director. A study by a leading contract guard firm[3] of 263 malls revealed that only three out of ten malls have full-time security directors, whereas two out of ten malls have operations managers who spend more than half their time on protection matters. This leaves seven out of ten centers without a security program of merit.

The primary security concerns of shopping centers focus on maintaining order, controlling traffic, and handling medical emergencies. Tenants generally provide their own security for their particular establishment. Shopping centers typically utilize various combinations of local law enforcement personnel and proprietary and/or contractual guard forces. Local law enforcement officers are sometimes employed in larger shopping centers. Some security personnel in shopping centers are given limited police powers by local ordinances. According to the survey mentioned, more than half of the centers employ in-house guards; almost four in ten use contract security services; and three out of ten hire off-duty police. Eight in ten have both full- and part-time guards, and more than eight in ten prefer conventional uniforms to the "soft look" blazers.

Shoplifting is by far the most common security concern of the shopping center. Other problems include loitering, public intoxication, vandalism, parking lot thefts, too few parking spaces, and unqualified guards. In an effort to alleviate the shoplifting problem, some stores have instituted an incentive program in which store detectives (or employees) are financially rewarded for catching shoplifters. This technique has proven successful, but when extended to other areas it can be detrimental to employee morale. For example, one large chain added a second incentive to the bonus program, giving a greater reward to store detectives for catching an employee stealing merchandise (the higher the rank of the employee, the larger the amount of the reward). As a result, store detectives changed their habits and concentrated their efforts on top management. This technique sometimes resulted in managers requesting transfers and the rate of customer shoplifting sharply rising.

Supermarkets can be considered a specialized category falling within the subject of shopping malls. The problems associated with supermarkets are enormous and almost impossible to control. Shoplifting by visitors is only one aspect of the problem because internal theft may pose a bigger threat to management than shoplifting. Cashiers sometimes purposely misregister the items at the takeout counter and the stocking of the merchandise often leads to temptations that are hard to overcome by a low-paid staff.

A manufacturer of antishopping devices published the results of a study conducted in 1980–1981 that listed the items most frequently stolen from supermarkets. The study recorded the number of apprehended shoplifters and items stolen from a cross section of full-service supermarkets in middle-income neighborhoods. The results were as follows:

1. Men's, women's, and children's socks
2. Women's perfume
3. Steaks
4. Ham
5. Pens
6. Pork and lamb chops
7. Lipstick
8. Men's, women's, and children's underwear
9. Gloves
10. Vitamins
11. Tylenol, cough syrup
12. Candles, silverware, film, chocolate bars
13. Peanuts, batteries[4]

Like any other security situation, the shopping mall/supermarket is unique and of growing importance to the security community.

## OFFICE BUILDINGS

Recent statistics indicate there has been a marked increase in the last few years in crimes committed in the central business districts of major cities. From 1973 to 1977, New York City's Wall Street District experienced a 50-percent rise in grand larcenies (thefts of $250 or more) and a 35-percent increase in robberies (thefts that involve physical force or intimidation). Both these increases exceeded citywide statistics for the same period. In Chicago thefts from downtown office buildings jumped 57 percent between 1973 and 1977, and in Cleveland robberies in the downtown section rose 19 percent in 1977 alone.[5]

Office buildings are particularly vulnerable to crime because of their need to create an "open" atmosphere for visitors and employees. No workable system has been found that can be used to screen visitors. As a result, losses from tenant spaces have become a growing problem. At one time most high-rise structures employed an elevator operator, but now practically all elevators are automatic and anyone can walk in and out of them without notice. Most office offenses take place during the daylight hours when it is easy for the well-dressed thief to blend into the crowd and slip away.

Millions of dollars worth of office equipment (particularly electric typewriters) are stolen from high-rise office buildings every day. A popular guise used is for thieves to pose as repairmen, wheeling away typewriters, copying machines, and other office equipment while the secretary assists by holding the door.

Only a few years ago, very few items were locked to a desk, and pencils and stamps were the most common items stolen. Today, the average office typewriter is valued at approximately $1000 and can be "fenced" for around $400. This has created a new industry for both the thief and the manufacturer. The business of office equipment locks seems to have grown up overnight. This is another example of how the security industry adapts itself to the kind of criminal activity encountered. Even though some manufacturers furnish a lock with their product, the general burden of securing office equipment rests with the tenant.

Most high-rise buildings are constructed and owned by a private developer who usually assumes the responsibility of providing security for the building and the tenants or assigning this task to the prime tenant of a particular building. This security sometimes consists of a cleaning staff whose function doubles as a quasi-security force during nighttime hours. The major security problems encountered in office buildings during night hours include burglaries; theft by another tenant's employees; theft by custodial staff; and assaults, rapes, and other crimes against persons. By far the most recurring crime is the theft of office equipment.

Tenant space is generally protected by a master keying system. In many large complexes, control of the key is difficult to maintain. The police have discovered syndicates that "rent" master keys for specific periods to certain famous buildings. In larger buildings, it is almost impossible to eliminate master keying because of the large number of keys that the custodial staff would have to carry with them in order to carry out their duties. It is often members of the custodial staff who are most suspect in nighttime theft. Tenants cannot very easily keep custodians out of their offices, and yet this creates a situation in which offices are open 24 hours a day to individuals even while the building is seemingly protected from outside intrusion. It also makes effective security of a large office building complex almost impossible. Most tenants lock up their valuables and bolt down office equipment to secure these items from the thieves who have keys.

There are special situations that require tenants to take additional precautionary measures. Oil companies, foreign embassies, and other organizations have been forced to provide their own internal security because of threats by extortionists, bombings, and incidents of arson. In these buildings, elevator doors open only on floors occupied by a security officer; visitors are carefully screened; and staircase fire doors open outward from the occupied area only.

> In Rockefeller Center, one of the nation's largest office complexes (housing 19 buildings and inhabited by 60,000 workers), tight security is the rule. Washrooms are kept locked at all times, and stairwells can be entered only on the upper floors, with exits available only at ground level.

This type of controlled environment is expensive to maintain. As a result, most buildings are relatively unprotected, and losses from theft are treated as part of the cost of doing business in the inner city. Of course, some residential high-rise buildings have better security than some commercial structures because residential buildings can, to a certain degree, control the flow of traffic through the front door. This comparison is mentioned because there is a new type of building appearing in the United States that combines a residential and commercial function in one structure. For example, a 60-story building may have offices on the first 30 floors and apartments on the top 30 floors. Maintaining security in this type of structure takes a great deal of ingenuity. The security professional has to organize a set of procedures that are open to certain visitors and yet restrictive to other visitors. These structures are so new that the problem areas are still unknown.

## INDUSTRIAL AND MANUFACTURING COMPANIES

Industrial and manufacturing security has its beginnings during World War I when concerns over sabotage and espionage prompted the large-scale hiring of guards to protect plants and factories. This practice was continued during World War II when more than 200,000 plant guards were given the status of military police because their primary responsibilities included the protection of war goods and products, supplies, equipment, and personnel.

Manufacturing security, or "plant protection" as it is commonly called, comprises the functions of crime prevention and detection, fire prevention, monitoring of electrical and utility systems, and inspections for OSHA (Occupational Safety and Health Act) violations. Larger manufacturers have continued to maintain proprietary forces for these functions, but recently there has been a shift toward contractual security guards. In some industrial concerns, both contractual guards and guards employed by the company have been replaced by burglar and fire alarm systems.

A U.S. government study conducted in 1978 showed that the 24-hour staffing of a single security post requires the equivalent of 4.3 guards (three shifts including weekends and holidays) at an annual cost of $100,000, which includes benefits.[6] In comparison, if an alarm system were purchased and installed, this replacement for a single guard post could conceivably cost far less than $100,000.

A fourth of the total labor force in the U.S. is employed by the manufacturing industry, with twice as much money being committed to security by the manufacturing sector than the retail industry. It can be estimated that industrial and manufacturing losses exceed $5 billion each year (this figure is based on the U.S. Department of Commerce estimate of $3.2 billion made in 1975 and adjusted for inflation).

The majority of industrial and manufacturing losses take the form of employee theft and pilferage. Goods taken usually consist of small items, but the number of items stolen a year often adds up to an enormous figure.

The problem of creating a secure factory or warehouse is not primarily concerned with the theft of small, inexpensive items by employees, but rather with the disappearance of cargos of furnished products, appliances, raw material in usable form, and other items that are stolen on a regular

---

In 1980 an estimated $2 billion will be spent on guard and investigative services, $550 million on central station services, $430 million on armored car services, and $750 million on fire-extinguishing systems and devices for the industrial, commercial, and business sector.[7]

| Guard and Investigator Services | | Locks Barriers Lighting |
|---|---|---|
| 50% | | 25% |
| ($1 billion) | | ($½ billion) |
| Fire Control Systems | Proprietary Systems | Central Service Systems |
| 18% | 4% | 7% |
| ($360 million) | ($85 million) | ($55 million) |

basis by individuals who are authorized to handle these goods. The Office of Transportation Security, U.S. Department of Transportation, has conducted studies that demonstrate that most cargo thefts occur in and around loading docks, shipping and receiving areas, and distribution centers.

The security priorities of the manufacturing industry are as varied as the types of products manufactured. The drug industry, for example, is obviously concerned with the protection of chemical substances used in the production of drugs and the prevention of theft or loss of narcotics and dangerous drugs as well as their diversion into illegal distribution channels. In contrast, the chemical industry places heavy security and safety emphasis on preventing fires and explosions.

A major sector of the manufacturing industry deals with government contracts. These firms not only have the task of protecting their assets by means of "normal" procedures, but they also have to adhere to the specific regulations mandated by the Department of Defense (DOD) if they are involved with classified information and material. These plants are subject to inspections by the Office of Industrial Security, U.S. Defense Supply Agency. Such inspections typically focus on visitor control, document flow, guard assignments and responsibilities, classified material destruction, records of accountability, and so on.

Another security problem that will continue to challenge security professionals is the area of "trade secrets." Such subjects as production processes, chemical formulas, and advertising budgets can be "stolen" simply by observing a blueprint or formula.

---

Manufacturing and Industrial Security Priorities

The security and fire protection problems of a manufacturing plant are so varied that security controls have to be carefully matched to the particular environment. Some problem areas are common to all industries and can be given a priority ranking in accordance to their importance in the overall security:

1. Access control
2. Internal pilferage
3. Outdoor storage
4. Crime in employee parking lot
5. Warehouse storage
6. Tool cribs
7. Emergency evacuation of personnel
8. Computer centers
9. Watch supervision
10. Arson

## HOSPITALS AND HEALTH CARE FACILITIES

The establishment of security controls in hospitals, nursing homes, or health care facilities is a difficult task. A hospital, unlike other institutions, cannot close at 5:00 P.M. or lock its entrances at midnight. A facility that is open 24 hours a day must guard against large inventory losses. The opportunity to steal food, linen, medical equipment, and personal valuables is always present. Added to the usual theft problem is the fact that, occasionally, patients are assaulted by other patients, and visitors may roam freely through the building.

Hospital losses from theft run into millions of dollars each year and all of these losses cannot be blamed on the housekeeping staff: some doctors have been known to "borrow" expensive medical equipment to furnish their new offices; some orderlies and other employees steal narcotics. Added to these conditions is the theft by some patients and visitors of other patients' valuables.

By far the greatest losses are suffered from the theft of hospital property (including drugs). This problem has been magnified by the shift to smaller, disposable items. The opportunity to steal a calculator is greater now that it fits into a pocket; the wheelchair today is lightweight and collapsible and can fit into a passenger car; the microscope is becoming smaller, and so on.

The size and nature of the typical hospital work force creates still another security problem. The total number of individuals employed in hospitals in the United States exceeds 3.2 million. To control the movement of this number of people is an almost impossible task, especially with over 150 different job titles being involved, with a turnover rate as high as 50 percent.

### Preventive Measures

There is, of course, no security system that can remedy these problems overnight, but as the economic impact of hospital crime continues to rise, some hospital administrators are becoming more aware of the problem. The present level of hospital security is generally considered to be substandard. Considering the amount of money spent on health care, the qualifications of staff involved, and the value of equipment used in hospitals, the number of people employed to protect over three million beds seems disproportionately small. In 1950, there were fewer than 1000 people employed in medical facilities as security specialists. In 1960, the figure grew to about 7000, and during the late 1970s the number probably reached less than 35,000 individuals.[8] This is equivalent to 3.24 employees per patient at an average hospital. This is quite high when compared to a hotel, which employs an average of 1 staff member per 6 hotel guests.

Many security problems common to hospitals are caused by poor design and architectural indifference from a security standpoint. Structural weaknesses include too many hidden doors, elevators that open into areas concealed from nursing stations, hidden corridors, and the typical remote locations of incoming patient areas, pharmacies, and cashier offices.

Some security professionals maintain that there are architectural provisions that would benefit hospital security. For example, wiring for security devices and surveillance cameras should be installed during construction of the building. Not all these devices are for the purpose of preventing theft, however. They are also needed in many cases to prevent the unauthorized departure of patients. This is a particularly serious problem confronting mental hospitals, where patients wander off hospital grounds. Patients must be restricted subtly, however, since the hospital has no legal right to forcibly contain a patient who was admitted voluntarily. Legally, the patient can leave at almost any time, but if he is injured or dies because of the negligence of staff, the hospital is liable to legal suit.

Hospitals spend very little on electronic surveillance equipment or security hardware. Key control is almost nonexistent because of the difficulty in getting doctors to cooperate with a security program. Almost the entire security budget is spent on manpower to guard facilities. In view of the technology available, some security experts feel that these expenditures should be more evenly spread between hardware and manpower.

Computerized inventory controls are usually instituted before a security program can be designed. Some hospital administrators have not only placed billings on computers, but also can, through telephone links, monitor the patient's medical history. With this advancement in medicine, a new security vulnerability emerges — that of guarding the computer that stores this vital information, and which is sometimes located miles away from the hospital.

Hospitals possess many of the security vulnerabilities present in other large structures (e.g., assaults, thefts of employee property and patient property, homicides, armed robbery, and natural disasters). It would be difficult to solve the security problem in a large hospital using conventional techniques, for an innovative approach is needed. The development of hospital security is one area with potential for significant growth in the coming years.

## PRISONS, JAILS, AND CORRECTIONAL FACILITIES

A prison is generally defined as a correctional facility utilizing long-term rehabilitation techniques. An inmate serves a period of time in prison commensurate with the type of crime committed. The population in the 43 federal prisons and 1000 state institutions is approximately 349,118 inmates. About half of these in-state prisons house fewer than 25 inmates, and consist of workhouses and farms. Usually there are one or two major state-run penal institutions in each state housing as many as 2000 inmates. (The prison in Jackson, Michigan, for example, houses over 5000 inmates.)

A *jail* may be defined as a holding or detention facility where a person is held awaiting trial. Jails are also used to house people for short-term minor offences. There are more than 3300 city, county, and local jails. Sometimes county and city institutions are combined into a single building. Most cities with a population larger than 25,000 usually provide some form of a jail even if it is a cell in the rear of the police station. Seventy-five percent of these jails include farms, camps, workhouses, and correctional institutions. These types of institutions typically have been adopted by larger municipalities or by states as short-term confinement facilities (the term "jail" characteristically refers to the county level of government).

Future trends for U.S. detention systems are highly controversial. Organizations such as the American Correction Association urge the federal government to continue funding the construction and renovation of small institutions (less than 100 cells) and community based detention facilities at the state and local levels. Other respected organizations have recommended that no new major facility be built unless a comprehensive study indicates that no other alternative is possible.

Security in prisons is obviously very strict and closely controlled. It generally relies more on the physical presence of a guard than on electronic alarms or electronic surveillance. The largest expense in security hardware is for locks and door construction (the total market for security hardware is about $80 million — keeping pace with the 20 percent increase in purchases each year). One lock manufacturer has almost 20 percent of the prison and jail market with the remaining business distributed over a dozen or so smaller companies. These limited resources for hardware indicate a specialized type of market and a lack of interest in innovation.

### Problems and Solutions

The basic function of any correctional institution is to protect the public by detaining people judged to be a threat to society. This concept has been a prime factor in the design of the physical structure of jails and prisons and the internal programs and operational procedures. The disturbances and riots of the last decade have emphasized the need to reassess ritualistic and "fixed" concepts. Traditionally, security has been a function of the custodial staff of the jail or prison. Whenever an administrator required consulting services, he usually relied on the custodial staff of other institutions for recommendations. This narrow outlook has perpetuated security procedures and, to a degree, has discouraged innovation.

Prison or jail security may be approached by separating the design into two concepts: (1) perimeter security and (2) internal security. Most efforts in the past have concentrated on perimeter security. This involved the erection of insurmountable and expensive barriers, such as stone or granite walls, completely restricting visibility beyond the facility. Nowadays, these kinds of walls are rarely built, primarily because of the expense involved. Chain link fencing and barbed wire are more frequently used instead because of their increased visibility as well as their relatively low cost. Even more recent is the practice of using double chain-lock fencing, in which each fence is set 10 to 20 feet apart with high-intensity lighting in between the fences. Rolls of barbed wire between the two fences help to slow down a potential escapee. In some cases attack dogs are placed inside the confines of the two fences.

In recent years modern security systems (such as closed-circuit TV, radar, photoelectric or microwave beams, buried sensors, or fence disturbance sensors) are being used in correction facilities. These expensive and sophisticated devices, while still a rarity, are employed in an attempt by architects and planners to conserve internal security techniques.

Internal security relates to the ability to control or influence behavior within interior areas, such as residential, work, mess, and leisure facilities. This includes: (1) the protection of prisoners from each other; (2) the protection of staff from inmates; and (3) the control and prevention of riots and disturbances.

In an effort to economize, many large institutions house the maximum number of inmates in the minimum amount of space at minimum cost. This approach is usually followed by smaller institutions as well. High density means a smaller security staff is needed. The use of perimeter security techniques in internal security situations, however, has resulted in the overutilization of hardware (e.g., individual cell construction to control and isolate individuals). As a result, costs have increased, thus defeating the original intent to economize.

According to some law enforcement experts, the major effort in the 1980s will be toward creating facilities that house small groups of inmates rather than high-density populations. This is likely to bring about an increase in automated surveillance equipment instead of increased guard forces.

Many correctional facilities divide the building complex into six optional areas. These are (1) personal or housing, (2) activity, (3) movement, (4) administrative, (5) control points, and (6) perimeter. Each basic area tends to have subareas such as cells, rooms, bathrooms, segregation areas, and high security cell blocks. Some of these subareas require protective devices whereas others do not. Some of the protective equipment in certain areas may require "hardening" to prevent it from being destroyed by the more violent inmate population.

Two examples of "hardening" equipment are as follows:

- Smoke detectors should have some type of enclosure to protect them from vandalism.
- Magnetic door contacts, if they are accessible in any way, must be recessed or otherwise protected against physical abuse.

One device that is particularly adaptable to correctional institutions is the card reader system described in Chapter 5. This device can be employed when a guard tour is required. The special features of this device serve to prevent inmates from vandalizing the card slot required for conventional card reader systems. In addition, the proximity system utilizes a completely hidden (behind the wall) antenna that reads the card held by the guard.

Another innovative device is the small cigar-shaped transmitter originally designed for use by classroom teachers. This device can be carried unobtrusively on the guard's belt. When activated, it can transmit a signal to receivers in strategically located areas. By adding a small mercury switch, the transmitter could be programmed to transmit a signal automatically if it remains in a horizontal position for more than three seconds (i.e., it would react automatically if a guard were knocked unconscious, shot, etc.).

Correctional facilities constitute a unique security situation that is likely to benefit from the adaptation of existing security systems. However, new security technology may make an important contribution to the design and operation of future prisons.

## BANKING INSTITUTIONS

Banking institutions have been targets of robbery attempts for over 150 years (because "that's where the money is").

Today, banks are being robbed more frequently than ever before. FBI statistics indicate that in the late 1960s, the total number of bank robberies nationwide was about 450 annually. The number of robberies in 1979 exceeded 6000 annually, of which 600 occurred in New York City alone (in July 1979, New York City experienced a record of 125 robberies).

Banks are "self-insured" against losses under $1 million and carry insurance protecting them against additional losses. Since most robbers take less than $2000, the bank is, in effect, absorbing all losses. Federal law requires banks to carry a blanket bond as protection against robbery, burglary, in-transit theft, and embezzlement. These bonds (premiums can cost $1 million) have a deductible amount (much like auto insurance). The deductible amount can be as high as $2 million.

Banks must adopt a policy that avoids jeopardizing the lives of tellers and customers, while at the same time the payout to the robber is kept as low as possible by limiting the amount of cash at each teller's area. The resulting security program seems to have the goal of getting the robber out with a minimum amount of trouble.

## The Federal Bank Protection Act of 1968

The Federal Bank Protection Act, adopted in 1968, is one of the few pieces of government legislation attempting to mandate security controls and procedures in nongovernment agencies. The act was passed by Congress in an effort to stem the growing incidence of crime against financial institutions. It covers the banking offices of insured state banks and offices of national banks. The Board of Governors of the Federal Reserve System and the Federal Home Loan Bank Board have issued similar regulations for their respective institutions. Under the law, standards are established with respect to the installation, maintenance, and operation of security devices and procedures to discourage robberies (holdups), burglaries, and larcenies, and to assist in the identification and apprehension of persons who commit such acts.

Some of the provisions of the act are as follows:

*Surveillance Devices*

- Must be reasonably silent in operation
- Must be readily serviceable
- Must be capable of reproducing images (by photographic enlargement producing a one-inch head size) of sufficient clarity to facilitate the identification and apprehension of robbers or other suspicious persons
- Must possess a minimum rate of exposure of one picture (frame) for every two seconds with capability of running for 3 minutes. If film is used, it must be at least 16 MM in size.
- Devices at walk-up and drive-in teller stations must be located so as to reproduce identifiable images of persons at each station. If stations are protected by bullet-resistant barriers, surveillance devices may be omitted.

- Devices located at locations other than teller's stations should be located so as to reproduce identifiable images of persons at the point of transacting business or when leaving the banking office.

## Advice

- One provision of the act is to suggest that the bank security officer seek advice of the local law enforcement agency.

## Security Officer

- The act mandates that each bank must designate a security officer who is responsible for the installation, maintenance, and operation of security devices and the development program.
- In large urban banks the person in charge of security may very well be an ex-FBI agent or police official. Smaller banks, however, may retrain an employee from another department to assume the security function. This may hamper the effectiveness of the security program.

While many people consider the idea of a protection act commendable, they feel that some of the stipulations of the 1968 act are somewhat vague. For example, the act attests to the need for a burglar alarm system, but neglects to explain the difference between one device and another. It avoids specifying precise guidelines in architectural design. The only technical definition provided is the description of vault doors, which was taken verbatim out of standards set by the Insurance Realty Board.

In view of the rising number of bank robberies and potential losses predicted from the Electronic Fund Transfer program, some have suggested that the Federal Bank Protection Act of 1968 be updated. One area in which modification is actively needed is in architectural design.

---

### Some Innovative Approaches to Bank Security

A major U.S. bank installed a large neon sign outside its lobby (facing the street). The sign is programmed to light up the words, "Robbery in Progress," whenever a teller activates the silent alarm signal.

Rather than concentrating on preventing armed robbery, one large banking facility has installed a numbering system as part of the lobby exit signs. Whenever a teller becomes suspicious of someone, he or she presses a switch that lights up within the exit sign a number corresponding to the teller's window location. At the same time, a buzzer is activated on the receiver unit carried by the lobby guards. This sound alerts the guard to look up at the exit sign where he sees the number "8" lighted up, for example. This indicates that he should go to the aid of the number "8" teller — not necessarily to capture a robber, but possibly to discourage someone from passing a bad check simply by his standing near the teller's cage. This is a simple, inexpensive system that produces effective results.

A bank in a Spanish-speaking neighborhood employed tellers who were fluent in Spanish but who spoke only minimal English. The farsighted security director was concerned about the confusion that might ensue if any of the tellers were given robbery instructions (verbal or written) in English. In an attempt to overcome this problem, he posted the following sign at the entrance to the bank:

ATTENTION WOULD-BE BANK ROBBERS

THIS IS A SPANISH-SPEAKING BANK, IF YOU
INTEND TO ROB US, PLEASE BE PATIENT FOR
WE MIGHT NEED AN INTERPRETER.

THANK YOU,
THE MANAGEMENT

## COMPUTER SECURITY (Electronic Data Processing — EDP)

The nation's growing reliance on computer information storage facilities has given birth to a new kind of criminal activity that even the court system has found difficult to categorize. The actual amount of money stolen through computer manipulation is impossible to tabulate or even estimate. Some conservative sources set the amount at $1.2 billion a year, but even this figure is suspect since most companies either refuse to divulge the amount stolen or are unaware of the theft. And it is only in recent years that industry is even admitting that the problem is potentially critical.[9]

When computer terminals were first introduced into the industrial and commercial market, they quickly became a showcase for any firm purchasing the "machine." The computer complex was usually placed in a conspicuous section of the building, in a room completely paneled in glass. Today, however, most of these "glass palaces" are hidden in remote areas of the building guarded with sophisticated access control devices. This dramatic change was brought about by the sudden realization that more assets can be stolen through the computer network than through armed robbery. Relying on the use of standard alarm devices and locking hardware has become practically useless against the theft of information and new security control measures have to be developed to deal with this new threat.

Significant amounts of assets (including, but not limited to, money) are now stored on tape cartridges and round discs, and these assets are moved from one computer terminal to another through the highly vulnerable commercial telephone line. The few criminals who are brought to justice tend to be employees caught removing or altering data of insignificant magnitude. Rarely are the courts involved in the million-dollar, computer-based embezzlements performed by computer experts. Protecting the computer against manipulation is a new task and challenge facing private security today and probably for the next two decades. (Protecting funds stored in a computer bank is far more difficult than protecting money stored in a vault.)

The rapid advance of computer technology and the tremendous growth in its use by industry and the consumer have made all traditional concepts of security obsolete. The use of computers to transfer funds through a computer network has, for example, revolutionized the banking industry. This technique is better known as electronic fund transfer (EFT) and is one form of electronic data processing (EDP). Adding auditory functions to guard against computer abuse has not proven very successful because most auditors do not understand the complex computer language involved. They have to rely on the honesty of the computer programmer, a relationship that is counter to basic security practices.

The problems relating to computer safeguards are not limited to preventing unauthorized individuals from entering the equipment room. Often, the potential computer thief is a trusted, long-time employee or even the person who actually wrote the program from which he is now stealing. Guarding against theft by these people is not only difficult, but also probably impossible. Many techniques have been tried, but surprisingly few of them have proven successful against the so-called programming expert. Computer security is still a new challenge to the security professional as the traditional methods of security do not seem to have a significant effect. The method of requiring more than one person to create the program is a step forward, but the possibility of collusion is still real. Using code words to control the computer terminal is very popular, but if someone steals the computer storage discs, the code can be deciphered (or the code book could be stolen). Even if the thief is captured, the crime is difficult to define and the penalties are light compared to the amount of assets stolen, removed, or altered.

## Computer Related Crime and the Law

There are now about forty federal statutes that the government can use to combat computer-related crime. Computer thefts are not always economic thefts. The information stolen could, for example, involve missile deployment or trade secrets. Moreover, the crime may be executed so subtly that it may never be detected. Many of the convictions for computer crime were obtained under statutes that were originally written to counter other abuses. Federal prosecutors have been handicapped in bringing computer thieves to justice, because until 1980 there was no law against computer crime per se in most states. The Federal Computer System Protection Act became law in 1980, and it is the first such law enacted by Congress for directly controlling crime by computer.[10]

"Electronic money" has become a viable and negotiable asset even though all these funds are in the form of electronic pulses and magnetic patterns that are stored in a machine. Altering these "pulses" can sometimes be accomplished by high school students whose only goal is to prove that the data can be decoded and removed with little possibility of being detected. The potential for compromising the EDP system is frightening. Even the individual consumer is becoming involved in the desire to store and transfer data with the introduction of automated teller machines and point-of-sale computer terminals. Protecting these exposed terminals with door locks and alarm devices is futile since conventional techniques of protection are valid only when applied to protecting money stored in safes or stuffed under the mattress. This kind of protection has little effect when the money is in the form of a few digits printed on a tape or disc sent as a digit over a phone line.

Computer technology clearly represents an achievement with many benefits for society, but it must be protected against potential criminal exploitation. Advances in computer security, however, have not kept pace with advances in computer technology. The people involved in developing computer concepts and programs are usually engineers and scientists. These technologists generally feel that the computer function is noble and socially beneficial for all mankind. They are not concerned with the possibility that data stored in a computer could be altered for personal profit. The opportunity for fraud, theft, and embezzlement is enormous whereas the safeguards to protect against computer theft are practically nonexistent. Furthermore, the court system is trying to catch up with this new criminal activity. After all, this "theft" of information often is in the form of a $5.00 roll of tape or round plastic disc. However, the theft could very easily result in a million-dollar loss to the using organization — but is the action a $1 million crime or is it a $5.00 case of petty theft involving about $5.00 worth of plastic discs? How does the court system establish the level of loss when the material stolen is non-negotiable and worthless to everyone except the company using the disc?

## Cases in Computer Related Crime

*Case #1.*  An engineering student stole more than $1 million of equipment from a large California telephone company, simply by using the telephone and the computer's secret entry code. He placed orders to the computer through the phone, requesting that equipment be delivered to a designated location. He was finally caught, not because of a security check or police investigation, but because an associate notified the authorities of the crime. The courts found him guilty of grand theft, sentencing him (a man who stole over $1 million) to a few days in jail and three years probation. The student realized the error of his ways; he is now self-employed as a private consultant advising businesses on techniques for preventing a theft like his.

*Case #2.*  Bookies active in the New York City area in the summer of 1979 will remember for a long time the effects of computer technology on the numbers racket. The "numbers" game is based, supposedly, on chance. Its objective is for participants to predict successfully the three-digit number of the day. This number is usually taken from the last three digits of the daily sum taken in by the local racetrack. For example, if the daily intake were $18,376,427.00, the winning number would be 427. During the summer of 1979, a New York City computer programmer toyed with the input from the local racetrack, manipulating the tabulations so that the last three digits would come out as he specified. Since the track expected some errors in a tabulation of this magnitude, a mistake of a few hundred dollars is not only tolerated, but also ignored. The "mistake" by this individual resulted in millions of dollars of payouts by local bookies. The question still remains as to what actual crime was committed.

The computer programmer did not steal anything. He made a simple mathematic manipulation of the computer key board. Furthermore, the people who lost money and those who "got rich" on the "mistake" were playing an illegal game anyway.

*Case #3.*  The most common method used in computer-related crime involves changing data before or during their input to computers, such as forging or counterfeiting documents or exchanging valid computer tapes or discs (this technique is called data diddling). Instructions to the computer that will perform unauthorized functions but still allow the program to perform its intended purposes are placed into the system.

In the so-called Salami technique small amounts of assets from a large number of sources are removed without noticeably reducing the entire amount. When used in a bank, it involves the random reduction of a few hundred accounts by 10 cents and placing the funds into a favored account where the funds can be legitimately withdrawn through normal methods. This "rearranging" of accounts is difficult to detect because each checking account customer loses so little that it is of little consequence and never reported as missing.

These examples are just a few of the methods used to obtain or alter data stored in a computer that constitute a criminal activity. Anyone with a technical knowledge of computer programming can conceivably discover a method of getting into and out of the computer without being detected. Hopefully, in the next decade more effort will be placed on designing safeguards than has been expended in the last 20 years. During this explosive period of computer application the colleges have concentrated on filling the demand for programmers. There are practically no courses directed toward securing data stored in computer software. Unless more effort is directed toward controlling the vulnerability of computer terminals, the amount of money stolen through computer manipulation will certainly surpass all other criminal activities of this nature.

### MUSEUMS

Before World War II most valuable pieces of art were owned by museums or a few art collectors. After the war, however, art collection began to attract more people, as well as private corporations, all of whom began competing with museums for works of art. As a result, the value of museum pieces began to rise at a faster rate than inflation.

Along with this increase in value came an increase in art theft. The break-in at the Montreal Museum of Fine Arts in 1972 which resulted in the loss of eighteen paintings (including a Rembrandt) caused museums to treat security with more respect (the theft is still unsolved). Yet, little was done to significantly improve security until the theft of three Cezannes by an employee at the Chicago Art Institute in 1978. Today, museums employ better trained guards, use closed-circuit TV and ultrasonic devices, and display certain priceless exhibits in shatter-resistant containers. Despite these precautions, 75 percent of all the museums in this country have at least one major theft each year.

While museums were experiencing an enormous increase in theft, galleries and private collections were not immune to the problem. An osteopathic surgeon in Philadelphia was caught in 1982 with over 170 pieces of art, valued at over $1,000,000, displayed in his apartment. He had simply been shoplifting from galleries throughout the country over a ten-year period. Since the objects were difficult to identify, he openly displayed them in his apartment and even went so far as to loan them to two museums for special exhibits.

Until the mid-1970s thefts from the nation's art museums and galleries were generally committed by the professional and well-educated thief (or by an employee of the institution). This stereotype of the "high-class" thief disappeared when the value of paintings started to double every 3 or 4 years. It became easier and more profitable to remove a painting from its frame and walk out of a museum than to rob a bank.

In 1979 there were 45,000 art thefts, with 13,000 of them occurring in the United States alone. Thefts are rising annually at a rate that could be as high as 30 to 40 percent. At one time most museums were reluctant to report actual figures for fear of jeopardizing their security image which is an important factor in obtaining loans of valuable art pieces from private collections or other museums.

In the 1980s museums began to be more open about reporting theft when they realized that the problem was common to all museums and the proven fact that publicity often aided in recovering the stolen art objects. The major museums in the nation now report the theft not only to the FBI but also to such private organizations such as the International Foundation for Art Research which publishes a monthly newsletter, "Stolen Art Alert."

Many museums are appropriating 10 or 20 percent of their operating budget for protection of their collection (this amount was unheard of only ten years ago). Large, well-financed museums usually have a full-time security director and a well-trained security staff, but most museums are too small to support such an expensive payroll. Sometimes museums hire retired senior citizens at minimum wage to patrol galleries and collections. Few museums train guards because the area of security is relatively new to this type of establishment. Inventories are sometimes unreliable, and curators do not always maintain accurate records. Record keeping is very important, particularly in an age that is witnessing $50-million thefts from the nation's museums each year. Sometimes pieces of art sold at public auction are traced to museums who never knew the work of art was missing from their storage area.[12]

### Alarming Works of Art

Alarms in museums, as in other public buildings, vary. Some museums can afford a proprietary system at night, but most of them rely on a direct wire to a central station monitoring service. One of the most popular devices is a space alarm such as an ultrasonic, infrared, or audio detector. One unique device, created specifically for painting and exhibit protection, utilizes a small, cigar-shaped, ultrasonic transmitter that is activated if the painting is moved. The "noise" is picked up by a wall-mounted receiver and an alarm signal is then sent to a control or annunciator panel. Only one receiver is needed in each gallery, with portable transmitters mounted on each painting. There is some concern that the sound waves utilized in ultrasonic equipment may damage sensitive paintings, but there has been no reliable research or definitive proof that this is so.

The majority of museums in the early 1970s were fairly well alarmed and guarded at night, but they were not secure during the visiting hours. And it was during these periods that most of the artwork was leaving the premises illegally. The solution, obviously, was to protect the paintings without making visitors uncomfortable. Too many alarms and too many guards can scare away the visiting public. Security had to be subtle, but it had to operate 24 hours a day — not just at night. Adding guards to the daytime staff was ineffective and too expensive. *The most logical approach was to protect the "object" rather than the environment.* The devices that suddenly appeared on the market typified the attitude of the security industry, and while each item added a certain amount of security, none of them offered the perfect solution. But at least these innovative ideas encouraged museum administrators to use novel approaches to a unique problem rather than rely on the commercial equipment available.

The first system used to protect paintings was the simple magnetic contact switch. The switch was mounted on the wall, directly behind the painting, which rested against a metal tab that was attached to the rear of the frame. When the painting was moved away from the wall, the switch would react in the same manner as the contact switch on the door. Each switch was required to be wired to the main console panel, which proved expensive and unflexible in an institution that constantly changed its exhibits. Furthermore, the system did not protect against someone cutting the canvas out of the frame and rolling it up under his coat (without moving the frame in any direction).

Other methods included using a mercury switch instead of a contact switch, which proved to be more reliable in detecting tilting movements of the frame, but still it was not sensitive to all movements of the canvas.

The most elaborate system was to install a wire mesh behind the frame and attach a capacitance detector (like those used in safes and metal cabinets). When someone tried to touch the painting, the system would record this action as a change in the electrical field and the alarm signal would be sent over the wire, linking the mesh to a console. This is a very difficult system to install and extremely expensive. It also went off too often because an innocent visitor would stand too close to the canvas. (Moving people further away from the exhibits was self-defeating.)

Still another technique was to install light beams parallel to the wall but a few inches away from the painting surface. The idea was that anyone trying to remove the painting would inadvertently break the beam and set off the alarm. It soon became apparent to the would-be thief that if he could determine the beam path he could reach over or under it to steal the painting. The way to determine the path was to practice, apologizing to the guard each time the alarm went off. After three or four apologies, the painting would be gone.

The most feasible technique is to attach a shock sensor to the rear of the frame and connect it to a wireless transmitter that is also installed behind the frame. The obvious advantages of this approach are that it requires no wiring and it is able to detect the slightest shock (attempting the cutting of canvas, touching of the frame, etc.). Therefore, any movement is detected by the sensor and transmitted to a receiver many feet away. The attempted theft is annunciated on a panel and a guard is sent to investigate (see Figure 4-1).

While all these devices have some drawbacks, they still fulfill a need that is not addressed by commercially available equipment, a situation that is all too prevalent in the security industry. The ideal system is not always available from the alarm salesman, and maybe it doesn't even exist.

### Recovery of Stolen Works of Art

Recovery of stolen art works can be a difficult task, particularly when law enforcement officials have only a written description of a painting to go on. Imagine trying to identify a Jackson Pollack painting from the following description: "a forceful arrangement of lines overlapped with blotches of paint with multidirected lines running through the scene."

For this reason, it is recommended that photographs or video tapes or both be taken of all important art objects. Also of assistance in recovery are the numerous international and national organizations that act as clearing-houses for recovering art works. These organizations publish and distribute descriptions of stolen art, and some try to act as an intermediary between the thief and the insurance company.

There are no easy solutions to the problem of museum security. Artworks have become a very marketable commodity desired by both collectors and the public at large. Finding means for appropriately displaying priceless works of art while at the same time protecting them from harm is a primary challenge of modern museum security.

## HOTELS AND MOTELS

The growing number of motels and hotels in the United States has created a new challenge for the security professional. No matter what the size of the

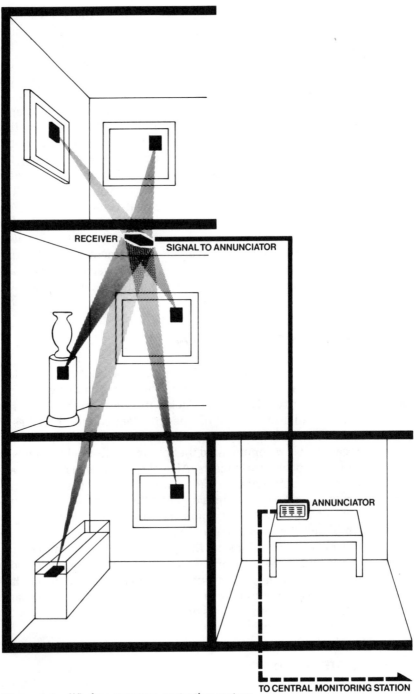

Figure 4-1.   Wireless museum protection system.

establishment, hotels and motels are vulnerable to various crimes. Violence, along with new and sophisticated ways of stealing from hotels and their guests, has caused innkeepers to reevaluate their priorities, placing more emphasis on security.

Few hotels fail to post notices indicating their limited liability in the case of theft of guest property left in rooms. These notices remove the responsibility for protecting private items from the hotel, unless they are checked at the front desk.

The responsibility for providing security in a hotel or motel lies with the owner of the property. He must abide by civil law, in addition to some laws pertaining only to hotels and motels.

Both the rate and severity of criminal activity committed against hotels and motels have steadily risen in the 1970s. The incidence of rape, murder, arson, and armed robbery has increased in some hotels. This situation has caused insurance costs to rise and has made hotel liability insurance more difficult to obtain. It has, in some cases, resulted in the replacement of the house detective by a well-trained security force (adding better security controls and guards has become a financial necessity for hotels because insurance rates are often based on the type of security maintained).

Key control is perhaps the single most difficult security problem confronting the hotel and motel industry. In many large motels and resort hotels, the same key (in one year's time) may be held by hundreds of different individuals — some of whom never return it. Some hotels are reported to have 15,000 new room keys made per year to replace keys that are not returned by guests. Added to this is the number of master keys held by the cleaning staff (a group of employees known for their high turnover rate). Some burglars pay up to $1000 for a master key. Since hotels and motels change locks so infrequently, a master key may be used for as long as ten years in certain hotels.

At one time, hotels were not held liable if a pass key was used to enter a room. The test of negligence was whether or not there was a forced entry into the room. If forced entry could not be proven, the innkeeper could not be held liable. As a result, the door locks on hotel rooms were rarely changed. This is no longer a common practice because today the courts contend that when a lock is inadequate or easily compromised, the owner of the hotel may be held liable. This decision was influenced by the famous lawsuit brought by Connie Francis against a motel chain after an intruder entered her room in 1974 and raped her. A lock must provide security against unauthorized entry — forced or otherwise. This new attitude has caused hotels and motels to use more sophisticated locking systems and procedures.

Among new key concepts now in use is a plastic card that is issued to each guest in place of a metal key. A computer programs the card to be accepted by the room lock for a particular guest, only for his or her period of stay, however. After the guest leaves, a new card is created for the room and (reprogrammed) for the next guest.

This concept indicates the constantly changing philosophy affecting security in all areas including the motel and hotel industry.

## ELEMENTARY AND SECONDARY SCHOOLS

School crime is a problem of major concern to parents, educators, and, most important, to students themselves. In some schools its effects have debilitated the educational process to the point where teachers are very much involved in discipline.

The $2.4-million dollar Safe School Study, sponsored by the U.S. Department of Health, Education, and Welfare points out that within a given month, the average secondary school student has one chance in nine of having something stolen and one chance in 80 of being attacked. Similarly, the typical secondary school teacher has approximately one chance in eight of having something stolen and one chance in 200 of being attacked.

Disruptive behavior in schools is a problem reaching beyond individual districts and is by no means confined to a few urban centers. It is a contagion affecting some school districts regardless of their geographic location or per capita income.

Serious losses suffered by schools also result from the actions of otherwise honest teachers, disgruntled employees, vendors, intruders, and even parents. The very openness of schools is a factor contributing to reckless and irresponsible conduct.

The school building is the most frequent target of vandalism, and in some school districts window breakage accounts for 100 percent of the problem. The second most frequently cited school-related crime is theft or burglary. Property damage is another big expense. The gamut of areas ravaged ranges from playground equipment and furniture to trees, toilet fixtures, and thermostats. Arson can be the single most expensive school crime suffered, with costs ranging from several hundred dollars to a million dollars per incident.

### Preventive Measures: Alarms and Guard Services

The almost 17,000 school districts in the United States expend over $200 million on alarm devices and salaries for school guards each year.[13] This enormous exercise has not produced the desired results simply because schools use conventional devices that do not always function effectively. The school building is a unique structure requiring a customized approach to security protection.

The task of selecting the protection device for a security system usually falls upon the school business administrator who typically has little background in the technological aspects of security protection.

One large school district on the East Coast hired an engineering firm to draw up a set of alarm system specifications to protect 68 of its 100 schools. The system was installed by an electrical contractor. After four turbulent years of error, testing, redesign, accusations, frustrations, and despair, the school system became the owner of $500,000 worth of nonfunctioning electronic equipment. Many months of negotiations and a grand jury investigation showed that the system appeared to fulfill all the requirements of the specifications except for one detail — it did not work.

The designer said it was a phone line problem; the manufacturer blamed the installer; and the installer said it was due to mismatched combination of equipment. Meanwhile, 68 schools remained unprotected.[14]

The security professional must be made aware of the special needs of schools and the importance of selecting a security system that is difficult to vandalize, easy to maintain, and able to distinguish a false signal from an actual intrusion.

A recent security development in the last seven or eight years has been the addition of guards as school personnel. Sometimes their mere presence in the school achieves an increase in order and discipline. In addition to daytime surveillance, some guards are used in lieu of an alarm system at night to protect the school building from vandalism.

School guards rarely receive sufficient training; in addition, there is some confusion as to their proper role and scope of their authority. In some districts they receive training from the local police. As a rule, however, they have no police powers. Legally, they have no more authority to search or restrain a student than a teacher or principal. They can be an effective force if they are properly motivated and trained by specialists in the field as well as supervised by a principal who understands the function and duties of a school security officer. Without proper training, however, school guards may create additional problems.

Limiting access to the schools through close surveillance of exits and entrances has had an immediate effect in preventing criminal acts from taking place within the school building. There are many other physical changes that can be made to improve school security. The simple expedience of removing outside door knobs from secondary exits has discouraged unauthorized entry to a significant extent. Many physical aspects could have been built into the original architectural design if school officials had realized the importance of security in developing an educational atmosphere.

Some security experts apply a "fortress" mentality in designing a school security system. This may cut down the vandalism costs, but it also alienates the school building from the very neighborhood it was built to serve. The solution to restoring a safe atmosphere to the nation's schools will prove difficult, but it is a challenge that should be met by private security professionals.

## SUMMARY

This chapter has attempted to demonstrate that the need for private security in various situations has grown in proportion to mounting increases in crime in the community. Security is now an essential part of traditional establishments, such as museums and banks, and it is important to some organizations in which it was unheard of twenty years ago, such as computer facilities and nuclear power plants.

The public's acceptance of private security is not the result of an upgrading in the industry, but possibly because of crime statistics. Statistics clearly indicate that when electronic alarms and uniformed guards are properly utilized, the crime rate can be significantly lowered. This phenomenon has caused a growth in the number of uniformed guards and an increase in the purchase of alarm systems. Successful actions taken by the private security sector to prevent and reduce crime against property decrease the number of crimes to which public law enforcement agencies must respond. Thus these valuable public law enforcement resources are freed for other important activities. There are types of crime beyond the scope of the protective measures that public law enforcement can provide (e.g., corporate theft, embezzlement, retail trade, etc.).

Private security is clearly an important and viable force that has proven its value in the fight against criminal activity.

## NOTES

1.  Bilek, Arthur, ed., *Private Security Standards and Goals — From the Official Private Security Task Force Report*, Law Enforcement Assistance Administration, Washington, D.C., p. 41.

2.  The FAA and FBI do not keep data on how much is rewarded or paid and whether the acts are political or apolitical. These estimates were extracted from the "Semiannual Report to Congress on the Effectiveness of the Civil Aviation Security Program," Office of Civil Aviation, FAA, U.S. Department of Transportation.

3.  Burns Security Institute, Burns International Security Service, Inc., Briarcliff Manor, N.Y.

4.  Compiled by Checkpoint Systems, Inc., Thorofare, New Jersey, 1981.

5.  Klein, Frederick C., "Inside Jobs: Urban Office Buildings Become Prime Locales for Thefts & Assaults," Wall Street Journal, December 5, 1978.

6.  Government Accounting Office audit.

7.  "Growing Markets for Security Monitors and Alarm Services," Business Communication Co., Inc., Stanford, Ct. 06906.

8.  "Hospital Statistics," published by the American Hospital Association, 810 N. Lake Shore Dr., Chicago, Ill.

9.  Porter, Thomas W. Jr., "Computer Raped by Telephone," New York Times Magazine, September 8, 1974, p. 33.

10. Ribicoff, Senator Abraham, "A New Era — for Technology and for Crime," Security Management Magazine, November 1979, p. 18.

11. Rutledge, Renata, "Strengthening Museum Security," Security World Magazine, October 1979, pp. 20–26.

12. "Museum Curators Meet to Talk Security," New York Times, February 16, 1979, p. C16.

13. "Alarm Systems Rarely Work in School Buildings," School Business Affairs, October 1979, p. 12.

14. Frazier, Osborne, "Salvaging a School Alarm System," American School and University, October 1979, p. 64.

# Chapter 5
# An Assessment of Private Security

Crime in America is big business, and from all the information and statistics available, this business is booming! The FBI Uniform Crime Reports indicate that, as we enter the mid-1980s, crime against people and property is at its highest point in this century. It is certainly at the highest point since the FBI began releasing crime reports two generations ago. A crime is committed every two seconds, and a burglary occurs every 8 seconds,[1] affecting an estimated 4 million homes and businesses each year.

Private security has continued to expand each year, growing at a rate faster than any other phase of the criminal justice system. Well over a million uniformed guards work in the field today, and the National Burglary and Fire Alarm Association reports that over 6000 alarm companies have installed an estimated 45 million fire detectors and millions of burglar alarms. Yearly, security firms help police capture 30,000 burglars and vandals, and probably scare off millions more.

The security industry has come a long way from the era of Messrs. Holmes and Pinkerton, and the future will witness consistent, perhaps even spectacular, growth. The industry is clearly showing signs of becoming an adult, if not mature, and is, in many ways, contributing to the public good, as are the other groups that constitute the criminal justice system.

The long-range decline in law enforcement resources has had a devastating effect on the ability of the existing law enforcement agencies to counteract crime. While it is difficult to explain why the criminal justice system is controlling crime so inadequately, several factors have been identified as probable explanations of this phenomenon. A long-term decline in the ability of society to support public services (e.g., police and fire departments) has resulted because of the demands of other services and expenses (e.g., welfare payments, debt servicing, programs for the aging and disadvantaged, among others). In addition, the decline of the sense of community in all geographic areas has led to a predisposition to crime. Finally, the hard reality exists for tens of thousands of people: crime pays — and it can pay very well for an indeterminate period of time. But if in the 1980s bigger opportunities exist than ever for a career in crime, even greater opportunities can be found in careers fighting crimes and protecting assets.

Security, by definition, is the protection of assets from loss and, where possible, the recovery of lost assets. It is a concern of private industry and commerce, public institutions and organizations, and every facet of government.

Security work may be described by many different titles. Table 5-1 itemizes common titles for both the public and private sectors.

The security industry may be divided into five subindustries. They are (1) guard and investigative services, (2) central alarm stations, (3) armored car and courier services, (4) manufacturers and distributors of security hardware and systems, and (5) specialized services, including polygraphists, repossessors, and consultants. The characteristics of each of these subindustries and a description of the various occupational categories within each field follow.

## GUARD AND INVESTIGATIVE SERVICES

### The Security Guard

Guards or security officers compose the largest percentage of all persons employed in private security. Seventy percent of them are "in-house" guards (employed by the firm they are guarding), while the remaining 30 percent are employed by contract guard agencies.

A *guard* may be defined as any person who is paid a fee, wage, or salary to perform one or more of the following duties:

1.  Prevent and/or detect intrusion, unauthorized entry or activity, vandalism, or tresspassing on private property.
2.  Prevent and/or detect theft, loss, embezzlement, misappropriation or concealment of merchandise, money, bonds, stocks, notes, or other valuable documents or papers.
3.  Control, regulate, or direct the flow or movements of the public,

**Table 5-1.  Occupational Titles for Security People**

---

*Private Sector*

---

| | | |
|---|---|---|
| Agent | Key Carrier | Special Investigator |
| Alarm Investigator | Manager | Special Police Officer |
| Armed Guard | Merchant Patrolperson | Store Detective |
| Attendant | Messenger | Timber Watchman |
| Bodyguard | Operative | Truck Guard |
| Bouncer | Patrol Officer | Undercover Agent/ |
| Collector | Plant Protection Guard | Operative |
| Credit Investigator | Polygraphist | Watchman |
| Doorshaker | Private Detective | Woods Warden |
| Fact Finder | Private Police | |
| Floorperson | Private Investigator | |
| Floorwalker | Private Watchman | |
| Gate Officer | Railroad Detective/Officer | |
| Guard | Receptionist | |
| House Detective | Roundsman | |
| Intelligence Officer | Salvage Corps Man | |
| Interviewer | Security Guard/Officer | |
| Investigator | Shipkeeper | |

---

*Public Sector*

---

| | | |
|---|---|---|
| Agent/Special Agent | Inspector | Security Police |
| Alarm Operator | Installer of Alarms | Sheriff |
| Attendant | Investigator | Special Officer |
| Baliff | Jail/Prison Guard | Tipstaff |
| Central Station Operator | Law Enforcement Officer | Trooper |
| Convict Guard | Marshall | Underground Agent |
| Correction Officer | Matron | Watchman/Watcher |
| Cottage Master/Supervisor | Mounted Police | |
| Criminal Investigator | Narcotics Agent/Investigator | |
| Deputy | Officer | |
| Design Engineer | Park Guard/Officer | |
| Detective | Patrol Officer | |
| Gang Pusher | Police Officer | |
| Government Card | Process Server | |
| Hall Tender | Range Rider | |
| Harbor Patrol Officer | Ranger | |
| Homicide Investigator | Reformatory Attendant | |
| Houseparent | Roundsman | |

---

whether by vehicle or otherwise, to assure the protection of property.

4. Protect individuals from bodily harm.
5. Enforce rules, regulations, and policies related to crime reduction.

Data collected by the Private Security Task Force indicate that the typical security guard is an aging white male and poorly educated, trained, and paid. Usually the guard has had little education beyond the ninth grade, has few job-related skills, earns a marginal income with few fringe benefits, and may have to take additional employment in order to make ends meet. Related to this is the fact that job turnover among guards may approach or exceed 300 percent in contract guard firms, or one-tenth of that figure in private positions.

**Training.**   The typical prework training period (including on-the-job training) for most security officers is less than two working days. Many guards, including some who are armed, receive less than two hours of training. Most guard personnel do not know their legal powers or authority. And, while some contract guard companies provide a brief orientation for new security personnel, many do not. The new security officer is put into the field, hopefully under the eyes of an experienced supervisor, and learns the job by trial and error, if at all.

A growing number of companies and schools are providing excellent training in this area. The problem is that, since there is no regulatory agency established to oversee security programs, the good exists alongside the bad, and there is no readily accessible means for judging a training program's worth.

One salutary development has been the establishment of the Academy of Security Educators and Trainers (ASET). This group, numbering over 400, supports elevated standards of security training and conducts regular programs for security educators leading to a certificate.

Demands upon security guards are increasing. One reason for this is the growing number of states requiring minimum training standards. Table 5-2 outlines the general orders proposed for use by security firms. These orders constitute the general rules under which a security guard may operate.

Perhaps the most important reason of all for the improvement of security training relates to potential legal liability. In the event of a false arrest action or a suit instituted for negligence, the plaintiff may claim that the arrest or loss was because the security officers were not trained properly. The defendant should expect the security director or some other organizational manager to be asked to testify exactly how security officers are selected, trained, and supervised. If the training procedures are not substantive, the defendant's case likely will be weakened.

**Proprietary vs. Contract Guard Services.**   The growth of security guard services in the past generation can be traced to several factors already mentioned in this and other chapters. Much of this growth has come from

**Table 5-2. General Orders for Security Guards**

---

1. Intoxicants of any kind are prohibited to be consumed while on duty or while wearing the uniform, or slacks, or blazers. Security officers reporting on duty with the smell of intoxicants on their breath, regardless of their apparent sobriety, will not be permitted to assume their assigned posts.

2. The security officer will maintain an alert attitude and observe everything that takes place within sight or hearing.

3. The security officer will report all violations witnessed or informed of and enforce all orders, rules, and regulations as instructed in the special orders or verbally received from the client, or from his superiors.

4. The security officer will not leave his post unless properly relieved, or is required to do so in the proper performance of his duty, or if specified in the post special orders.

5. The security officer will obey and pass on to his relief all orders received on his tour of duty, whether received verbally or in writing.

6. The security officer will speak to no one unless in the line of duty. Unnecessary conversation between security officers will not be condoned and conversation with the public or employees will be restricted to business matters only.

7. In an emergency not covered by any instructions, the security officer will call the client or his superior if he needs guidance, and if time permits. Otherwise, he will act in the best interest of the client and his employer, and exercise his best judgment and common sense in initiating the action he feels is required.

8. The security officer will carry out all instructions which are given him by his superiors or by an authorized client representative. If a security officer receives instructions from a client representative other than the designated representative, he should inform this individual that he has received the instructions but will not carry them out until he has either checked with the authorized representative or his superior.

9. Security officers will use the telephone only for business calls and personal calls are never authorized. Any personal long-distance calls that are made and proved to be made by a specific security officer will be paid for by that security officer and is punishable by suspension from duty without pay up to and including termination, depending upon the severity of the violations.

10. Any security officer who issues false information or makes false statements concerning matters that pertain to his work, to his fellow security officers, or to his superiors, will be subject to immediate dismissal after review of the allegations by the vice president for operations.

11. Security officers are prohibited from accepting tips or gratuities from anyone for any purpose whatsoever, unless approved by the vice president for operations and as indicated by company policy as stated.

12. Security officers will not remove material of any type, regardless of the value, or any equipment from the premises to which they are assigned unless specifically authorized to do so by the authorized client representative, and then only after notification of a superior next in the chain of command.

13. Security officers will use discretion in questioning employees whenever an irregularity exists. Under no circumstances should a suspected party be threatened,

**Table 5-2.   (continued)**

---

manhandled, or coerced. No individual will be apprehended or placed under arrest unless that security officer is commissioned with the authority to make an arrest. All security officers not otherwise commissioned or deputized must do so as a private citizen and not as a representative of his employer, or the management of the facility to which he is assigned.

14.   All security officers are expressly prohibited from having the following articles at their posts: radios, television sets, reading materials of any kind other than company-issued material, or coffee-making devices unless this type of equipment is furnished by the client and is being used in conjunction with the duties he must carry out.

15.   The seasonal uniform, as prescribed by company management, must be worn at all times while on duty. This means that if the posts require that head gear be worn it will be worn at all times while on duty, regardless of whether the post is inside or outside the building.

Source: Reprinted with permission from: "The Contract Security Service Company Policy and Procedure Manual," © 1978 by Walter M. Strobl, published by Walter M. Strobl, P.O. Box 694, South Houston, Texas 77587.

---

organizations themselves hiring independent contractors rather than using in-staff personnel for security patrol activities. The independence of the guards from regular employees of the organization is an important factor in assets protection management.

Most contract guard services (large and small) hire from the same labor pool. Chances are that no matter which guard service wins the contract, the same group of individuals will show up at the client's premises. When a guard service receives $4.50 per hour from the client, the guard will receive, at the maximum, only 65 to 70 percent of this amount, and often far less. In simple terms, a $3.50-per-hour salary will not produce a guard that resembles Robert Redford, nor will he function as enthusiastically as a William H. Webster.

Salaries may vary slightly in different parts of the country, but the rate below shows a typical range. The guards assigned under Category I are adequate for situations where simply having a person in uniform will act as a deterrent, such as standing at the entrance of small retail stores, fire watch patrols, and minor messenger duties. Problems arise when a person with minimum training and ability is assigned to critical situations where a Category IV guard should be assigned.

| Category | Guard Service Fee |
|----------|-------------------|
| I | $4.25 per hour |
| II | $4.90 per hour |
| III | $5.50 per hour |
| IV | $7.00 per hour |

Balancing the advantages and disadvantages of contract guard services is a decision that must take into consideration the individual needs and circumstances of the client. As a general rule, if fewer than twenty guards are involved, it is economically better to use in-house guards; when more than twenty individuals are required, however, the cost of contract guards becomes substantially lower. Unless carefully selected, motivated, and trained, the guards employed by either means are likely to prove inefficient. The guard assigned by a contract service should prove that he or she has undergone a minimum amount of training, and the hiring firm should reserve the right to an interview before any assignments are made.

The trend in security guard utilization is toward greater use of contract guard services relative to in-house staff. This change has been promoted because of the rising wage rates and compensation packages of staff guards who may become unionized.[2] (In-house security personnel generally belong to a different union from the union to which a majority of the organization's employees belong.) If the compensation packages of unionized employees were stabilized or decreased, the use of in-house security personnel might also increase.[2]

See Table 5-3 for a comparison of the advantages and disadvantages of contract versus proprietary guard services.

### Investigative Services

Besides providing guard services, some security patrol organizations provide investigative personnel. In addition, specialized firms exist that conduct investigations and offer managerial consultations related to investigators' findings.

Investigators are involved in such work as retail store shopping, preemployment screening, interrogations in loss situations, estimating the true financial status of debtors, determining the true value of proposed mergers, tracing the evidence trail in losses, following up on information provided by undercover agents, collecting data in a competitive information system, and in many other types of inquiries.

Investigators are trained to be impartial and factual in their information-gathering processes. Investigators may not invade the personal privacy of the people they are investigating, and they must not take actions that would subject the employer (or client) to possible litigation for invasion of privacy. During the interrogation of persons suspected of stealing from the organization, the investigator, who is not in law enforcement, may be more effective than someone who is. This is because an investigator who is employed outside of law enforcement and who interrogates without the presence of a law enforcement officer does not have to give the person

**Table 5-3.  Proprietary vs. Contract Guards**

| Advantages of Contract Guards | Disadvantages of Contract Guards |
|---|---|
| 1. *Selectivity.* Employer retains only those persons personally approved. | 1. *Turnover.* Extremely high, industrywide. |
| 2. *Flexibility.* More or fewer personnel supplied, as required. | 2. *Divided Loyalties.* Serving two masters. |
| 3. *Absenteeism.* Replacement of absentees on short notice. | 3. *Moonlighting.* Low-paying salaries tend to force guards into secondary jobs. |
| 4. *Objectivity.* Judgment not clouded by personalities. | 4. *Reassignment.* Some agencies send in their best men at inception of contract; then replace them with others as new contracts open. |
| 5. *Training.* Supplied at no cost to client; may be superior to in-house program. | 5. *Screening Standards.* May be inadequate. |
| 6. *Supervision.* Supplied at no cost to client. | 6. *Insurance.* Determining liability and ensuring that individual guards are bonded and insured. |
| 7. *Cost.* 20% less than in-house (not counting administrative savings, e.g., insurance, Social Security, and retirement pension). | |
| 8. *Quality.* May be of higher caliber than an in-house guard. | |
| 9. *Administration and Budgeting.* Brunt borne by guard company. | |
| 10. *Unions.* Very little problem because contract guards are rarely unionized. | |
| 11. *Variety of Services and Equipment.* Guard company may specialize in various criminal justice skills. | |
| 12. *Hiring and Screening Costs.* Borne by guard company. | |
| 13. *Better Local Law Enforcement Contacts.* May know more law enforcement personnel. | |
| 14. *Sharing Expertise and Knowledge.* As a result of varied jobs, may have developed security skills that can be shared with client. | |

being interviewed the *Miranda* warning. This warning informs the person being questioned of his or her constitutional rights. Additionally, the investigator must not be guilty of entrapment of the person being questioned; otherwise, evidence obtained in such an investigation may not be used in prosecution.

**Table 5-3.** (continued)

| Advantages of Proprietary Guards | Disadvantages of Proprietary Guards |
|---|---|
| 1. *Loyalty.* A positive quality. | 1. *Unions.* May go on strike with the company union, refuse to cross picket lines, etc. |
| 2. *Incentive.* Promotion possibilities within the entire company structure. | |
| 3. *Knowledge.* Of operation, products, personnel, etc. | 2. *Familiarity.* May become too familiar with personnel to be effective on the job. |
| 4. *Tenure.* Lower turnover rate than contract guards. | |
| 5. *Control.* Stays inside company structure. | 3. *Cost.* Expensive (salary, benefits, Workmen's Compensation, Social Security, liability insurance, work space, equipment, and training). |
| 6. *Supervision.* Stays inside company structure. | |
| 7. *Company Image.* May become a status symbol. | 4. *Flexibility.* Difficult to replace absent personnel. |
| 8. *Morale.* A hoped-for state maintained by security manager. | 5. *Administrative Burdens.* Must develop an upper-level staff to handle these problems. |
| 9. *Training.* Can be specifically geared to the job performed. | |
| 10. *Courtesy.* Can render courtesies to VIPs because of familiarity with company personnel. | |
| 11. *Better Law Enforcement Liaison.* Security manager can informally develop law enforcement liaison with less conflict. | |
| 12. *Selection.* Company selection procedures used. | |
| 13. *Better Communication.* More direct. | |

The security guard and investigative business is highly competitive. Good and excellent services are offered by large and small companies. All security companies, regardless of size, that have been in business for any length of time have had their share of problems. The following companies are briefly profiled because of their size, significance, and history. Mention here does not constitute a recommendation.

**The Pinkerton Agency.** Pinkerton's Inc. is the oldest and largest security guard and investigative company. Founded by Robert Pinkerton in 1850, the company's voting stock is still controlled by a trust for the benefit of Robert Pinkerton's descendants. Robert Pinkerton was, for a time, the bodyguard of Abraham Lincoln during his presidency. Later, the company's trademark — an unblinking eye — was to become synonomous with the moniker for detective, "private eye."

Of approximately 22,000 full-time employees, about 20,200 of them are guard personnel. They are supplemented by a substantial number of part-time guard personnel. In 1981 the company had sales of $294 million, with a net income of $13.4 million (4.5 percent of sales). Pinkerton's maintains about thirty offices in the United States, Canada, and England.

**Burns International Security Services, Inc.**   This company was founded in 1909 by William J. Burns who had developed a national reputation as an investigator, particularly in connection with counterfeit investigations. In 1982 Burns was acquired by Borg-Warner, a Chicago-based conglomerate that had also acquired Baker Industries (Wells Fargo) in late 1977. When Wells Fargo and Burns are combined, which is expected to occur gradually on a market-by-market basis, the new combination will be the largest security guard company.

In 1981 Burns's sales were $260 million, with a net income of $951,000 (0.4 percent of sales). The company employs 36,000 people, including part-timers, in offices in the United States, Canada, Spain, the United Kingdom, the Bahamas, and South America.

**The Wackenhut Corporation.**   This corporation was founded in 1954 as a partnership by George R. Wackenhut and three associates. Originally, the company was formed to conduct investigative work, but as the possibilities for providing guard services became available, the company rapidly expanded into that field. The company earned important contracts from the government in its early years, providing security services for NASA installations in the 1960s. The company received the largest single security contract ever awarded at that time (in 1974) to provide partial security services in connection with the construction of the Alaska pipeline. About 17,000 employees work in about 78 domestic offices.

The company has attempted increasingly to integrate security technology with guard service patrol responsibilities. The company has pioneered in providing nuclear material security. George Wackenhut, his wife, and his son control a majority of the outstanding common stock.

**Other Leading Security Guard and Investigative Companies.**   Some other leading companies include Wells Fargo, a subsidiary of Borg-Warner; Globe Security and its affiliated companies, which are owned by Kidde, Inc.; Stanley Smith Security, an operating company within the Loomis Corporation; Allied Security, California Plant Protection; Advance Industrial Security owned by Figgie Intl.; Bell Security; and Per-Mar Security.

## CENTRAL ALARM STATIONS

Alarm systems and products are a fundamental part of protection of assets from loss. Alarms can receive messages through many different sensing capacities: touch, movement, heat, light, sound, taste, unique physical characteristics, and so on, or a combination of any of these capacities. The message from the sensor then goes to the control function (multiplexor — if it is a computer system) where the quality of the message is interpreted.

Next is the action phase. This may be a ringing of a bell, or a silent alarm may be signaled to a law enforcement or private police monitor who, in turn, may call the police or investigate the alarm themselves. The action may also cause certain doors or windows to lock or open, activating a closed-circuit TV camera or an audio-recording system, or any one of numerous other responses. The objectives of alarms and their systems are (1) to deter persons from entering the alarmed premises in the first place, (2) to capture the interlopers or criminals, (3) to recover the stolen property, and (4) to lower insurance premiums by the presence of such devices and services.

Private security companies that provide alarm services may be concerned with more than antiburglary protection. Panic or holdup alarms, medical emergencies, fire protection, humidity and environmental control, energy management, utility meter reading, and process engineering malfunction may all be followed by the same electronic system. Microprocessor-controlled systems are the basis of the technology that monitors all of these functions separately, reporting "alarm systems" to the appropriate offices as needed.

Most central service stations, however, are concerned primarily with basic antiburglary, antiintrusion, or antirobbery signals, which they receive and respond to or for which they create the system and turn it over to the customer for monitoring.

Generally, this portion of the security industry can be divided into two types of organizations. The first type, which comprises a large group of companies, supplies burglar alarms and also installs and maintains them. The second type, which consists of a smaller group of companies, may also supply alarms, but primarily is in the central station monitoring business. These companies monitor the signals received from sensors at distant locations and respond appropriately when messages are received.

The central service station burglar and sprinkler alarm business is dominated by three companies, although there are more than several hundred companies with approved UL central stations in existence. A brief sketch of each of the three leaders follows.

APPENDIX — A

Standard form contracts of the Central Station Industry
Summary of Clauses

1.  The Title Retention Clause: All firms in the industry insist, in their contract forms, that they retain title to the equipment installed on the subscribers' premises.
2.  The Two-Part Tariff Clause: The Subscribers are required to pay a flat fee upon installation of the equipment, and to pay, additionally, an annual or monthly service charge thereafter.
3.  The Equipment Removal Clause: In the event the subscribers fail to perform under any of the contractual stipulations, this clause ensures the right of the protection firms to enter the premises of the subscribers and remove the equipment installed. Removal of the equipment does not constitute a waiver to collect up to 100 percent of the accrued or remaining charges owed.
4.  The Price Flexibility Clause: This clause secures the right of the firms to increase or decrease the service charge, subject to the approval of such changes by the subscriber.
5.  The Damage-Facilitated Exit Clause: In the event the alarm system is destroyed or irreparably damaged, the protection firms have the right to cancel the agreement. However, the subscribers could cancel the agreement in the event their plant was destroyed or irreparably damaged. No damages have to be paid.
6.  The Duration Clause: The life of most contracts is commonly specified as five years. Furthermore, the contracts contain an automatic extention clause, according to which, the contracts are to be renewed automatically after the official expiration date, unless one of the parties invokes its cancellation rights.
7.  The Liability Clause*: Payments are based only on the value of the protective services performed, and the protection firms,

according to the clause, are not to be thought of as insurers. Damages resulting from system failures or any failures on the part of the protective firms to fulfill any of their contractual obligations are limited to a fixed percentage of the annual service charge.

8. The Liability-Voiding Factors Clause: The protection firms are not responsible for failure to fulfill their contractual obligations because of strikes, riots, acts of Providence, *etc.*

9. The Non-Transferability Clause: The Subscriber is not allowed to assign the contract without the written consent of the protection firm.

10. The Validation Clause: The contract has to be approved by a representative of the protection firm. The statements of the sales personnel are not binding.

11. The Exclusiveness Clause: The protection firms do not recognize any verbal or other agreements that modify the terms of the contract.

12. The Sales Tax Clause: All sales taxes are to be borne by the subscribers.

13. The Default Clause: The protection firms may terminate the service upon written notice in the event the subscriber defaults under the provision of any of the stipulated clauses.

14. The Damages Clause: If the right to cancel the agreement should be exercised by the protection firm (because of failure on the part of the subscriber to fulfill any of the contractual stipulations) the subscriber is required to pay a specified amount of damages to the protection firm.

15. The Inability to Transmit Exit Clause: The agreement may be cancelled by the protection firm in the event the necessary connections cannot be made through the network of the Telephone Company.

*Source:* Security Letter, Inc., New York.

*Liquidated damages clauses have been upheld by the courts. See *Rest Foods vs. A.D.T.* (40 Cal 2d. 179, 253 p.2d 10 (1963).

## American District Telegraph Company (ADT)

American District Telegraph Company, founded in 1874, is the dominant force in central station protection today. According to a Predicasts industry study, released in 1982, ADT in 1980 represented about 35.7 percent of the entire central alarm company market of $770 million. Increasingly, the company is selling proprietary systems to large customers who will operate their own systems.

ADT is composed of two divisions; the larger is ADT Security Systems, which markets and manufactures its systems and which provides control alarm station service. The other division is the ARI Group, which manufactures and sells small detectors and other products.

ADT is now an international business with 160,000 customers in the United States, Canada, and several European countries.

## Other Large Central Station Companies

Other large burglary and fire central station companies include AFA Protective Systems, Electro-Protective Corporation of America (a subsidiary of the Hawley Group), Holmes Protection, Honeywell, and Wells Fargo Alarm Services (a subsidiary of Borg-Warner Corp.). Many security guard companies that formerly owned and operated control alarm stations have divested themselves of such operations. Some examples of companies that have sold central alarm stations are Burns International Security Services, Purolator, and Wackenhut.

## ARMORED CAR AND COURIER SERVICES

A specialized type of guard is employed by armored car companies. These personnel usually transport monies between district or federal reserve banks and retail banking establishments or between retail banks and their customers. More generally, they move valuable commodities between two locations. Armored car personnel may distribute a payroll directly to a customer's employees or deliver it to a paymaster who will handle the distribution.

Armored car services do business under a variety of operating authorities, including the Interstate Commerce Commission, the Department of Transportation, and individual state regulations. Probably the biggest regulators of all (in effect) are the insurance companies that insure armored car companies and their customers against loss from theft and other casualties. In return for providing insurance, insurers require armored car companies to follow certain prescribed standards. They include the size and construction of the vehicle to be insured, the number of guards per vehicle, the procedures to be followed at the customer's facility, and the steps to be taken in the event of a loss.

An armored car company is responsible for assets entrusted to it the moment the guard signs for and receives the assets; the company is relieved of liability the moment a party at the other end signs for and receives the assets. This distinction has importance in law. Several armored car carriers have received and signed for bags of money within the secured areas of banks or other facilities and have been robbed only moments later on bank property. The armored car company and their insurers were responsible for the total amount of the loss.

Four companies dominate this segment of the protection field: Brinks (a subsidiary of Pittston), Wells Fargo armored service and Pony Express courier (a subsidiary of Baker Industries of Borg-Warner), Purolator Armored, and Loomis (a subsidiary of Wormald Intl.). These four companies account for an estimated two-thirds of the armored carrier business. The remaining volume is shared among about 125 other companies, some with substantial growing routes, while others have only one or two vehicles.

Armored cars are highly visible, and therefore they must give the impression (not necessarily justified) of being impenetrable. Not surprisingly, most attacks on armored cars occur when the guards are stopping somewhere for a coffee break, or are stopped while transporting money, either on foot or between a customer's premises and the armored vehicle.

Because of their vulnerability to attack, almost all armored car guards are armed. While insurance regulations vary, generally a carrier must have three persons traveling with the vehicle: a driver who remains in the cab during the transfer of money and who usually is the senior employee, and two or more guards who transport the money to or from the customer's cash location.

Armored car companies generally try to retain satisfactory employees for long periods of time. But the armored car carrier business is so competitive that operators are unable to pay personnel considerably above, if at all above, the prevailing average industrial wage. Hence, turnover is a problem for managers of these facilities, although less than it is for conventional contract guard operations.

Managers of armored car establishments are highly concerned with scheduling. Bearing the costs of several security personnel, high fuel costs, expensive vehicle construction and maintenance costs, and, increasingly, higher liability insurance rates, the armored carrier company must sustain a considerable volume of activity to succeed. Yet the schedule must be randomized so that potential robbers, either casing or planning a theft, will not be able to anticipate the carrier's timing. Recent security measures for the protection of armored car personnel include the use of bullet-resistant vests, the carrying of pocket transmitters, and the strengthening of the vehicles themselves.

## MANUFACTURERS AND DISTRIBUTORS OF SECURITY HARDWARE AND SYSTEMS

Supported by products and technology created for aeronautical and space explorations and for use in the Vietnam conflict, the security systems and hardware industry has benefited by making available to customers a wide variety of these new products. Microcircuits, minicomputers, and miniaturization of products and their components have made possible an array of security devices unimagined only a decade ago. Furthermore, the cost of sophisticated computer security programs has been reduced relentlessly in the past decade. As technological products continue to be classified by the military, many newer, better, and less expensive products can be anticipated in the years ahead.

It is not necessary to discuss the full range of security products in this book. Indeed, the full range of security hardware and systems is difficult to analyze qualitatively and economically. Construction materials, communications equipment, transportation vehicles, office equipment, and other industries make their own important contribution to security, without these industries normally being classified as part of security. Table 5-4 lists categories of security and security-related products used widely in organizations today. Chances are the list will be even longer tomorrow. The effectiveness of a security system will be primarily dependent on the ingenuity applied to put it together, rather than on the newness of the products used.

## SPECIALIZED SERVICES

In terms of annual expenditures, specialized security services represent the smallest division of the security industry, but one with considerable interest. Security has developed a number of specialized services and consultants who offer particular skills and resources for specific needs. Many consulting-type services are provided, not only by private service group, but also by others outside the security industry proper.

An investigation, for example, may be conducted by trained investigators working for a large security guard company, or the investigators may work for an organization that specializes in this type of work. An

**Table 5-4.   Security Products and Systems**

Alarm Control Devices
   Electronic and mechanical personnel
   ID systems; area passage and remote
      entrance control equipment

Alarm Intrusion Devices and Systems
   Alarm panels and monitoring systems
   Central receiving systems
   Evacuation and emergency services
   Contraband detectors
   Annunciators
   Pressure mats
   Vehicle and portable

Alcohol Detection Devices

Ammunition and Ammo Components

Amplifiers

Apparel (including fire retardant and
   fluorescent)

Armor (vest, vehicles)

Audio Dection and Sound Monitoring

Auto Theft (preventive devices)

Batteries and Battery Chargers

Binoculars

Bomb Security Devices
   Detection devices
   Disposal blankets
   Disposal equipment

Cameras
   Identification systems
   Closed-circuit television (CCTV)
   Security and still
   Surveillance
   Night Vision

Check and Document and Credit Card
      Protection
   Credit card verification systems
   Check and document verification
      systems

Communication Systems
   CCTV
   Computer and data systems
   Facsimile
   Microwave
   Paging systems
   Playback repeaters
   Radio
   Scramblers
   Security systems
   Speech compression or expander
   Telephone
   Teleprinters
   Transceivers and transmitters

Electronic Crime Countermeasures

Emergency and Disaster Equipment
   Power supplies
   Emergency battery systems
   Emergency lighting
   Rescue equipment

Evidence Identification and Marketing
   Systems

Film

Fire Protection and Emergency
      Equipment
   Sprinkler systems
   Extinguisher systems
   Fire exit systems
   Smoke detectors

First Aid and Safety Equipment

Glass and Glazing
   Safety and bullet-resistant

Guard Patrol Equipment

Helmets and Face Shields

Identification Systems

Insurance

Intelligence and Surveillance Equipment

**Table 5-4.   (continued)**

| | |
|---|---|
| Investigative Devices | Seals (locking and marking devices) |
| Laminating Equipment | Secured Storage Facilities |
| Lights | Shooting Ranges and Targets |
|   Black, ultraviolet, flashers, halogen, oscillating, search, strobe, etc. | Shoplifting Deterrents |
| Locks | Signs |
| Metal Detectors | Systems |
| Mirrors |   Access control |
|   Convex, wide-angle, surveillance, etc. |   Alarm |
| Motion Detectors |   Automated data |
| Narcotics Detection Equipment |   Computer dispatching |
| Night Vision Equipment |   Countermeasure |
| Patrol Cars |   Document retrieval |
| Photoelectric Controls |   Microfilm recording |
| Photography |   Outdoor security |
| Polygraph Equipment and Stress Detection Devices |   Vehicle identification |
| Premises Protection | Tape Recorders |
|   Perimeter barriers (fences, screens, grilles, etc.) | Telephone Recorders and Analyzers |
|   Lock timing devices | Television (see also Cameras) |
| Public Address Systems | Time and Date Stampers |
| Recorders | Traffic Signs and Signals |
| Restraining Equipment | Training Systems and Programs |
| Resuscitators | Ultrasonic Devices |
| Safes and Vaults | Voice Identification Devices |
| Scramblers and Encoders | Weapons |
| |   Firearms and accessories |
| |   Chemical |
| |   Nonlethal |
| | Wire Cable and Components |
| | X-ray Equipment |

investigation also may be conducted by an internal audit group, outside auditors, or others competent to perform investigative work.

The purpose of this section is to describe and list many of the specialized services currently available. Certainly, other new services will be created to meet challenges in the years ahead.

## Undercover Operatives

Organizations sometimes have an interest or need in determining operational information outside of traditional methods. This is particularly so if a loss has recently occurred, or if a high-value loss potential exists. Undercover agents are one way in which informal information that can reduce vulnerabilities or aid in the recovery of losses can be obtained. Employees who perform covert assignments work within the organization in a normal capacity.

Earlier in this century, undercover agents were primarily "spies" who provided management with information on union activity. Today, however, undercover agents are largely concerned with loss investigations and high-risk exposure analysis. Undercover operatives are in a position to detect thefts, falsification of work records, vouchers, receipts, and other records, sabotage, subversive activities, and collusion with competitors. They may later be called upon to give depositions or testify in court against thieves. Principally, their findings should be employed to enhance management checks and controls.

Unlike the previously cited vocations, a person cannot normally apply for a position as an undercover operative. Security managers generally find that persons recruited without experience in security or law enforcement make the best operatives. They are hired primarily for their ability to perform a particular job well, which will enable them to work in a position where they can observe information critical to the loss investigation. Some consulting firms make a speciality of providing undercover operatives for management. Two such firms, both based in New York City, are Norman Jaspan Associates and Management Safeguards.

Undercover agents, sometimes called fact finders, perform very important security services. This experience can often be valuable in a security career, but it probably is not vital to the careers of security people.

## Lie Detection: Polygraphs and Voice Stress Analyzers

**Polygraphists.**  For many years, scientists have known that approximately twenty physiological indices in the human body could theoretically be used to measure emotional stress during lie detection or truth verification tests. Included are such exotic or remote indices as pupillary reflexes of the eye, brain waves, the acid content of the stomach, changes in the activity of the salivary glands, and blood volume.

Most commonly used, however, are the indices that lend themselves more easily to economy and simplicity in monitoring, such as blood pressure, pulse rate, respiration pattern, and body response to electricity, commonly referred to as galvanic skin response (G.S.R.). All of these features are commonly incorporated and utilized in the modern-day polygraph instrument. "Poly" means "more than one" or "many," and more than one physiological tracing is produced on a polygraph chart or polygram.

In recent years an additional physiological parameter has been presented in an effort to broaden this field — voice stress analysis. This is generally utilized as a single parameter in an instrument that can be generically described as a voice stress analyzer.

At the risk of oversimplification, it can be stated that a detection of deception examination, using either the polygraph or the voice stress analyzer, is concerned with detecting deviations from an emotional norm. Regardless of how nervous or emotionally upset or distraught a person may be at the time of such an examination, he or she has an emotional state that can be considered a norm for that person at that time. The polygraphist is concerned with detecting the deviations from that norm at that time. Persons who utilize the polygraph are referred to as voice stress analysts.

The concept behind lie detection by instrument is that persons who are lying will normally show more stress or emotional disturbance than when they are telling the truth. This refers to the above-mentioned deviations from the norm.

These emotional disturbances or stresses are often enhanced by the fear of detection and its consequences (e.g., if the examinee is detected lying, he could ultimately go to jail, lose a job, or fail to get a job for which he had applied). The so-called fear of detection goes hand in hand with the subject's belief in the general infallibility of the technique and his confidence in the professional ability of the examiner. This belief in the technique's infallibility or the professional competence of the examiner is not essential, however, to the success of the procedure. It only enhances the responses that are obtained and increases the "batting average" of the examiner from about 75 percent to around 90 to 95 percent accuracy. In other words, even without believing in the technique or having any fear of repercussions if the technique is successful, three out of every four persons in the general adult population can be successfully examined by the polygraph or voice stress analyzer.

*History and Development.*    The history of civilization is filled with attempts to detect lies and to verify the truth. Ancient methods of detection included the ordeal of the red-hot iron, the ordeal of boiling water, the ordeal of the red-hot stones, and the ordeal of the sacred ass. Often, methods that were employed appeared to be based on pure chance. For instance, truth or the lack of it might be determined by the throw of a knife, or the pattern assumed by a handful of tossed pebbles. Though some ancient tests reflected a shrewd understanding of psychology or physiology, they were hardly reliable or scientific.

The earliest scientific approach was developed by the Italian criminologist Cesare Lombroso, who, in 1895, conducted experiments in the detection of deception by attempting to record, with a device called "Lombroso's Glove," changes in the subject's blood pressure. Unfortunately, Lombroso's principal interest was in the area of criminal identification through physical characteristics; therefore he never followed through on his experiments. Mosso, another Italian scientist, conducted further investigations of blood-volume changes during deception tests by using a crude device known as "Mosso's Cradle."

Around the beginning of World War I, a third Italian, Vittorio Benussi, conducted experiments in lie detection with a device that measured and recorded the rate and depth of the subject's respiration. These experiments convinced Benussi that distinct changes in the respiratory pattern occur during attempts to deceive. A Russian, A. R. Luria, also made significant contributions to the theories that underlie present-day lie detection. Although he did not use an instrumental approach, many of his theories of the psychology of deception are embodied in polygraph procedure.

The first American to become directly involved in the field of lie detection was Dr. William M. Marston, a psychologist. He was commissioned by the U.S. government to devise a method for the interrogation of prisoners of war during World War I. Using a sphygmomanometer, the device physicians use to take the patient's blood pressure, Marson conducted experiments by taking intermittent readings of blood pressure during interrogation periods.

In 1921, inspired by the success of Marston's endeavors with prisoners of war, Chief August Vollmer of the Berkeley, California, Police Department, encouraged Dr. John A. Larson, a psychiatrist, to develop what became the forerunner of the modern-day polygraph. Although large and cumbersome, Larson's instrument made the first continuous, permanent record of three phenomena: blood pressure, pulse, and respiration. This original polygraph was used for many years by the Berkeley Police Department and enabled Larson to identify many hundreds of criminals, as well as thousands of innocent persons who had been suspected of crimes.

Because of the amazing record built up by Larson and his original polygraph, a young psychologist, Leonarde Keeler, became interested in the technique and developed his own apparatus. His instrument had the added feature of measuring changes in the skin's resistance to electricity, commonly known as galvanic skin response. It is Keeler who is generally recognized as the true pioneer in the field of modern-day polygraph. He not only refined the technique in its application to police work, but also pioneered its use in wartime and was responsible for its introduction into business and industrial security.

*Validity.* To give some idea of the effectiveness of the polygraph technique, a few statistics are necessary. High validity was reported by Lykken in two experiments in 1959[3] and 1960,[4] in which accuracies of 89 percent and 94 percent, respectively, were obtained. Marston, employing a mock crime, reported 94 percent correct judgments of the actor-subjects.[5] The vast majority of other investigations have yielded similar figures: Elson, 73 percent;[6] Baesen et al., 86 percent;[7] Thackray and Orne, 86 percent;[8] Kubis, 97 percent;[9] and Ruckmick, 83 percent.[10] Only in relatively rare instances has low accuracy been reported in the literature; for instance, by Landis and Wiley, who obtained only 50 percent correct judgments in a study they did in 1926.[11]

While the accuracy obtained in experimental situations is most impressive, it is not as high as that reported by polygraphists for real-life situations. Virtually all polygraph examiners quote validity statistics of about 90 percent. This is understandable, given the differences between laboratory and field research. A number of theories exist that explain why the polygraph is effective, of which the theory of the fear of punishment is perhaps the best. It is hypothesized that the greater the consequences of being detected, the greater is the fear of detection. The increased fear, in turn, triggers greater physiological changes, thereby creating a greater likelihood of detection. It is, therefore, not so much the lying or guilt feelings that alter the subject's physiological responses, but rather the fear of punishment. A volunteer subject in a laboratory experiment, in contrast to a criminal suspect, has very little punishment to fear; without the drastic fear and stress, the physiological changes associated with lying are reduced, resulting in lowered accuracy levels. This has been substantiated by Gustafson and Orne,[12] who found that the more motivation there was to deceive, the more readily the deception was detected. Larson reported that once a confession had been obtained, the physiological changes in response to critical questions were not so great as before.[13]

Opponents of the polygraph are quick to point out that no polygraphist or polygraph agency is able to "prove" claims of 90 to 95 percent accuracy. The reader must recognize the difficulty of obtaining meaningful statistics in real-life situations. The principal problem is getting verification of the polygraph examination administered; this can only be done when a confession is obtained. In a case where there are ten suspects and the tenth confesses, then an accuracy rate of 100 percent can be claimed for all ten. On the other hand, if only nine are tested and the tenth is not examined and cannot be proved guilty, then there is no way to verify the findings on the first nine. Consequently, they cannot be included in any statistical analysis. Moreover, if the tenth suspect were available for testing but made no admission of guilt, then all ten would have to be discarded for statistical purposes. In actual practice, far more innocent than guilty persons are tested by the polygraphist, and in many cases the guilty person is never discovered. Thus there is no way to verify the findings on the innocent persons.

*The Profession.*    As we have seen, the polygraph technique had its beginnings in law enforcement in the Berkeley Police Department in 1921. Since then its use as an aid in official investigations has spread throughout the country, not only to large police departments, but to medium-sized and small departments as well. Police officials agree that tremendous savings in manpower and money have resulted from the use of the polygraph technique to pinpoint criminal suspects and to clear innocent persons. The biggest beneficiary of the polygraph has probably been the average citizen. Most police departments, placing great faith in the technique, will not press forward with the prosecution of a suspect who, though a prime candidate because of circumstantial evidence, has been cleared by the polygraph. It cannot be emphasized too strongly that thousands and thousands of Americans have been released from police custody and spared public prosecution because their innocence had been verified by the polygraph. Moreover, not a single case has been found in which an innocent person was convicted because of polygraph error.

The federal government entered the polygraph field in the early 1940s when Frank A. Seckler, a Secret Service agent, was dispatched to Chicago to learn the technique from Leonarde Keeler. Seckler was the forerunner of more than a thousand federal employees who were to follow. Initially, the training of government polygraphists consisted of two or three months training under the personal direction of Keeler himself. Later the training was formalized when Keeler established what is still known as the Keeler Polygraph Institute in Chicago. In the 1950s, a military polygraph school was set up at Fort Gordon, Georgia. Today, it trains the vast majority of military and government examiners, and is rated one of the top polygraph institutions in the country by the American Polygraph Association (APA).

The greatest growth in the polygraph profession during the 1960s was in private and corporate testing. Most polygraphists in this category are employed either in one-person laboratories or in larger firms that may employ upwards of thirty-five staff examiners. A few large corporations have found it economical to employ their own in-house polygraph staff, but such company examiners probably total no more than a hundred.

Some 3000 persons have been trained as polygraphists over the years; it is believed that about 2500 of them are in active practice today. Approximately 1500 are members of the American Polygraph Association. The majority of the rest belong to state associations, some of which are affiliated with the APA. The association estimated that in 1975 between 250,000 and 350,000 tests were administered (these figures include tests of all kinds, including tests by law enforcement agencies). Better than 60 percent of the persons tested were found truthful and cleared of false accusations or unjust suspicions.

Industries served by polygraphists are for the most part in the distribution, retailing, and service categories. Among them are armored car services, airlines, retail and wholesale drug companies and drug manufacturers, department and other retail stores, the trucking industry, private guard services, restaurant chains, hotels, banks and brokerage houses, automobile rental firms, wholesale and retail liquor dealers, vending machine companies, and finance companies — all businesses in which large amounts of cash or valuable merchandise may present irresistible temptations. The majority of such companies use preemployment polygraph screening; some use the polygraph technique only in investigating specific instances of theft; a few use it in periodic screening of currently employed persons. Some firms use two of the above approaches, and some use all three.

*The Test.*    In private testing for commercial firms, examinations are given either "on location" or in the polygraphist's own private polygraph suite. On-site examinations are almost always administered in a private office or conference room. The setting should be private and free from distracting influences. The normal background noises to which the employee may be accustomed, however, are not considered an unfavorable influence on the test.

When the examinations are administered at the polygraphist's own laboratory, however, extra measures are taken to insure that no distractions are present because here the examinee is in an unfamiliar environment and can more easily be distracted than on his home ground. Therefore, the person to be examined will usually encounter a scene similar to the following situation.

The polygraphist's waiting room is usually similar to the waiting room of any professional person such as a doctor, dentist, or psychologist. The decor of the waiting room is pleasant in nature and may or may not include plants, an aquarium, background music, and reading material. The reading material in some cases may be a mixture of current periodicals and descriptions of the polygraph test itself.

Normally, the person will be greeted by a receptionist upon entering the suite of offices. This receptionist may or may not be in the immediate vicinity of the waiting room, depending upon the physical layout of the suite of offices.

The examination room ordinarily is more austere than the waiting room. It is almost always devoid of pictures and paintings. It is usually soundproof, with adequate carpeting on the floor and drapes on the windows. Usually the furniture in such a room consists of the examination desk in which the polygraph instrument is recessed, the polygraphist's chair, and the examination chair, which may be of special design. The examination chair may range from an upright chair with what appears to be oversized arm rests, to a modified reclining chair, depending upon the individual preference of the polygraphist. Occasionally, the examination room may also contain a schoolroom-type chair with a writing arm, which is used by the polygraphist in conducting his face-to-face pretest interview.

In some cases, the examination room will also contain a one-way mirror opening onto an adjoining observation room, together with a sound system connected to the observation room. The purpose of the mirror and the sound is for the training of polygraph interns and is no different in purpose from similar setups found in psychological testing laboratories and medical schools. Where such an arrangement is present, the examinee is so advised in the written release he is requested to sign. In the event that the examinee should find the mirror and the sound objectionable, the polygraphist can render them inoperative.

Upon entering the examination room, the examinee is usually introduced to and greeted by the polygraphist. Normally, he will be asked to sit in the examination chair, and depending upon the preference of the examiner, the examinee may be immediately connected to the attachments of the instrument. These attachments, if connected immediately, are not activated during the pretest interview. Other polygraphists prefer to conduct the pretest interview prior to placing the attachments on the subject.

The first attachment the examinee should expect to encounter is the blood pressure cuff, which is identical to that used by physicians, and which is attached to either the upper arm, the forearm, or in some cases the wrist. During the actual examination, this cuff is inflated to a median pressure between the subject's systolic and diastolic blood pressure levels. Some persons report a mild amount of discomfort during the period of inflation, none of which is actually painful.

The second attachment consists of one or two rubber tubes that are placed around the trunk of the body. If only one tube is used, it is placed over the area of greatest movement during the respiration cycle. In some cases, two rubber tubes are used simultaneously to cover the upper and lower chest areas. The tubing is not uncomfortable in any way and simply measures and records, through the instrument, the rate and pattern of respiration.

The third attachment is usually placed on either one or two fingers, or through a dual connection with the palm of the hand. This attachment measures the changes in electrical resistance of the skin. There is absolutely no feeling of discomfort with this attachment.

*Constitutional, Personal, and Public Rights.*   Opponents of the polygraph claim the employee or job applicant should have constitutional protection against self-incrimination — that is, should be able to "take the Fifth Amendment" when a question as to his honesty arises. Of course, the question of the Fifth Amendment is moot in the employer–employee relationship. Unlike the accused criminal, who might otherwise be forced to testify and thus face criminal imprisonment, the employee or job applicant may refuse to take a polygraph test. This person is not in a court of law and therefore has a choice in the matter. It is also significant that physiological tests similar to those made by the polygraph, for instance, blood tests and alcohol tests, have always stood the test against self-incrimination.

Opponents further charge that the polygraph test violates the subject's right to privacy, including his right to conceal past criminal activities. Under common law, the right to privacy protects the individual only against unwarranted intrusions by the state. An employee or prospective employee can be given a polygraph examination only with his knowledge and consent.

The right to privacy as guaranteed by the Constitution is, indeed, sacred, and it must be guarded and respected. But in a free society, no person's right is absolute; it must give way, to a degree, to the rights of others. The right of the public to protect its business places, its job security, its hard-earned wages, and its health, safety, and welfare must be weighed against the right of the job applicant or employee to conceal undetected criminal behavior, dishonesty, and material misstatements of fact.

Reasonable people agree that the businessman has both the right *and the obligation* to inquire about the experience, skills, physical well-being, character, and honesty of job applicants. He also has not only the right, but the obligation to utilize the most effective methods available for obtaining and verifying this information. Reasonable people will also agree that the honest working person has the right to the job security and pay increases that accompany business profits, as well as security against exposure on the job to the criminally inclined. Crime on the streets is bad enough; why expose good men and women to crime on the job?

Finally, most everyone will agree that the consumer has the right to be protected against higher prices caused by the "theft tax," now estimated to cost the working public more than $4 billion each year in the form of increased costs passed on to the consumer.

An examination conducted by a competent and ethical polygraphist is both a reasonable and effective technique for protecting public rights. It should not be used for frivolous matters, and it should not be used for unethical probing into personal questions of sex, religion, or politics that have no bearing on the issue under examination. Violations of ethical considerations in the use of the polygraph should be prosecuted vigorously in the public interest. Legislation that would license and regulate the use of the polygraph, and would require prosecution for violations, would protect the rights of the public.

*The Polygraph and the Courts.* Since 1923, when a federal appellate court refused the admissability of evidence of a polygraph test, the polygraph field has traveled a very rocky legal road. The obvious limitation of space does not permit the treatment of the legal aspects of this field in a thorough manner, and therefore only some general comments can be made.

As of 1980, most state courts allow polygraph results into evidence if presented by stipulation. That is, if both sides to the dispute, whether it be a criminal or civil case, have agreed beforehand to a polygraph examination. The test can then be entered into evidence, whether it be in favor or against the interests of the defendant or plaintiff. Many civil courts will admit polygraph evidence, especially where "the door has been opened" regarding a polygraph test by the other side. Although there has been almost no movement toward admitting polygraph evidence by the criminal courts against the interests of a defendant (unless by stipulation), there has been a tendency in many judicial jurisdictions, and in some of the lower federal courts in the last ten years, to admit polygraphic evidence where it would be in favor of the defendant. It will probably be many years before the role of the polygraph in the courtroom will ultimately be established. In the meantime, the student should keep in mind that the primary purpose of the polygraph is not to gain convictions or acquittals, but rather to aid in the investigation of criminal offences and in personnel selection procedures. It is in these areas where the polygraph shows its greatest potential.

*Licensing and Restrictions.* The science of polygraph has also attempted to gain official recognition in our society through the passage of licensing laws by the state legislatures. As of this writing, twenty-three states require licensing, which generally includes a certain educational level, graduation from an approved polygraph training school, and successful completion of a comprehensive examination that usually follows a six-month internship. Most of these states have developed their approved list of schools by following the school accreditation actions of the American Polygraph Association, which maintains an accreditation committee. Table 5.5 lists the states that require licensing for polygraphists.

Conversely, approximately sixteen states have passed laws against the use of the polygraph in the employer–employee relationship. Depending on the wording of these laws, they can be classified as restrictive in

**Table 5-5. States that Require Licensing**

| | | |
|---|---|---|
| Alabama | Massachusetts | Oregon |
| Arizona | Michigan | South Carolina |
| Arkansas | Mississippi | Tennessee |
| Florida | Nevada | Texas |
| Georgia | New Mexico | Utah |
| Illinois | North Carolina | Vermont |
| Kentucky | North Dakota | Virginia |
| Maine | Oklahoma | |

nature or even outright prohibitive. These prohibitive laws are in such states as Alaska, Massachusetts, New Jersey, Delaware, and Minnesota.

Polygraph schools accredited by the American Polygraph Association generally now require, as a prerequisite, a bachelor's degree from a recognized college or university for students desiring to enter private practice. Table 5-6 lists the schools that are accredited at present for polygraphists.

**Voice Stress Analyzers.** The principal theory behind psychological stress evaluation (PSE) is that microtremors in the voice, which are controlled by the vocal chords, are suppressed when a person is under stress. (Tremors are a natural condition and when present they indicate a lack of stress.) Although these tremors cannot be detected by the human ear, there are instruments available that proponents of this system claim can produce results equal, or even superior, to the traditional polygraph. There are a number of similarities between the PSE technique and the more established polygraph. Both are limited to measuring certain physiological manifestations of psychological stress. The polygraph is capable of displaying relative stress levels and the PSE absolute stress levels. PSE processes voice characteristics and therefore does not require attached sensors. This eliminates environmental stress caused by the unnatural and sometimes painful physical constraints of polygraph attachments. The use of voice as the source of stress responses has created some of the controversy that surrounds the PSE technique of lie detection. Since the voice can be processed regardless of its final source (television, telephone, radio, etc.), it is indeed possible to do stress analysis without the subject being present and, in fact, without the subject's knowledge. On the other hand, the lack of test controls in some of these situations limits the usefulness of this approach to lie detection. *The validity of either the polygraph or the PSE technique in "truth verification" rests largely upon the training and experience of the examiner.*

**Table 5-6.   Polygraph Schools Accredited by the American Polygraph Association (January 9, 1982)**

Academy of Forensic Polygraph
1735 Virginia Avenue
Atlanta, GA 30337

Academy of Polygraph Science and
 Methodology
5701 Executive Center Drive, Suite 320
Charlotte, NC 28212

Agriculture and Technical College
Farmingdale, NY 11735

American Institute of Polygraph
Parklane Towers West, Suite 1213
Dearborn, MI 48126

Backster School of Lie Detection
861 Sixth Avenue
San Diego, CA 92101

Canadian Police College
P.O. Box (CP) 8900
Ottawa, CANADA K1G 3J2

Chicago Professional Polygraph Center
407 South Dearborn Street, Suite 1175
Chicago, IL 60605

Gormac Polygraph School
P.O. Box 424
Arcadia, CA 91006

Harrisburg Area Community College
3300 Cameron Street Road
Harrisburg, PA 17110

Israel Police Polygraph School
Police Headquarters
Jerusalem, ISRAEL

Keeler Polygraph Institute
5906 North Milwaukee
Chicago, IL 60646

Los Angeles Institute of Polygraph
4419 Van Nuys Boulevard, Suite 406
Sherman Oaks, CA 91403

Maryland Institute of Criminal Justice
517 Benfield Road, Suite 303
Severna Park, MD 21146

Michigan State Police School
714 S. Harrison Road
East Lansing, MI 48823

Munford Institute of Polygraph
1644 Tullie Circle
Suite 130
Atlanta, GA 30329

National Polygraph Institute
8515 Biscayne Boulevard
Miami, FL 33138

New York Institute of Security and
 Polygraph Sciences
82 Beaver Street, Suite 1801
New York, NY 10005

New York School of Lie Detection
165 West 46th Street, Room 415
New York, NY 10036

Reid College of Polygraph
215 North Dearborn Street
Chicago, IL 60601

Southern Polygraph Institute
734 Watterson Towers
1930 Bishops Lane
Louisville, KY 40218

Southern School of Polygraph
Suite 101, Executive Park
Augusta, GA 30907

Spokane Community College
North 1810 Greene Street
Spokane, WA 99207

Texas A&M University
Law Enforcement and Security Training
 Division
F.E. Drawer K
College Station, TX 77843

Universal Polygraph Institute
Suite 107, Dutch Square
800 Dutch Square Boulevard
Columbia, SC 29210

Table 5-6. (continued)

| | |
|---|---|
| University of Baltimore<br>Psychology Department, Polygraph<br>  Training<br>North Charles & Mt. Royal Streets<br>Baltimore, MD 21201 | Virginia School of Polygraph<br>7909 Brookfield Road<br>Norfolk, VA 23518 |
| University of Houston Downtown College<br>(Formerly Southwest School of<br>  Polygraph)<br>Polygraph Program<br>One Main Street, Room 1038-B<br>Houston, TX 77002 | Zonn Institute of Polygraph<br>Suite 212<br>1819 Peachtree Road, Northeast<br>Atlanta, GA 30309<br><br>and |
| U.S. Army Military Police School<br>Fort McClellan, AL 36205 | Suite 501<br>3050 Biscayne Boulevard<br>Miami, FL 33137 |

The PSE instrument was developed by Allen Bell, Charles McQuiston, and Wilson H. Ford and introduced to the private sector in 1971 after it was rejected by the military during that period.[14] The PSE is not a lie detector and does not detect deception. The PSE is not a voice analyzer because it does not "analyze" the voice. In a simple sense, the PSE is capable of recording the form of voice vibrations produced by the vocal muscles in the human larynx. The voice vibrations are produced by the oscillation of vibrating muscle fibers. Muscles receive their stimulation from nerves or by nerve impulses. Physiological activities of the body can be monitored by examination of nerve impulses or the consequences of such nerve impulses. The variety of voice vibrations produces different patterns, some of which have been related to stress, and research has shown that attempts to deceive create a stressful situation.

There are now three recognized units on the market utilizing the voice response as the determining factor for lie detection. All the devices are basically spectrum analyzers designed to measure selected frequencies of the human voice linked to the level of psychological stress at any given time. The PSE uses filtering and frequency discrimination circuits to produce a signal that is eventually displayed as a chart recording. There are four modes and ten different indicators of stress used on the PSE. All of them can be examined further in various ways so that, with a taped interview, thirty-two different charts can be made. As with the polygraph, the results of the PSE evaluation do not directly measure truth or deception. That kind of evaluation is made indirectly from the interpretation of physical and psychological measures by the trained examiner.

It should be noted that there are some less expensive instruments on the market, called "voice analyzers," which attempt to present their results in either a simple digital display or in a series of lights. Some of the instruments cost less than $100 and measure only the volume of the voice rather than the tremor and should not be confused by the more sophisticated and complex PSE instrument.

The Society of Stress Analysts has about 300 members, including associates, and requires graduation from one of the PSE schools (usually run by the instrument manufacturer). The PSE program offers courses totaling between 120 to 150 hours of training. About 20 percent of the full members of the international association are also qualified polygraph examiners.

There are no enforceable standards governing those now operating in field and there still remains a great deal of controversy surrounding the research conducted in the field. The polygraph society has led a well-organized campaign against the acceptance of the PSE as a valid alternative to the more established and acceptable polygraph. The PSE is still a relatively new technique that will need more time and data to achieve acceptance. (PSE results have been admitted in court in Maryland, Florida, California, Louisiana, and West Virginia but has been banned in Illinois, the home state of the American Polygraph Association.)

### General Security Consultants

Security consultants perform broad consultive and planning services for management. Such consultants tend to be independent practitioners or to perform as specialists within audit firms in general management consulting groups. Often they possess considerable experience in such fields as computer EDP security, internal controls, retail security, bank and financial institution protection, physical safeguards, museum or art gallery security, or other specialized areas.[15] In addition, other consultants outside of the usual security fields may be mentioned: insurance adjustors, fire and fire protection consultants, safety consultants and engineers, credit checking investigators, and general management consultants.

### EDUCATIONAL AND PERSONAL REQUIREMENTS FOR A SECURITY CAREER

The requirements for security personnel vary widely. At the one extreme is the security guard who gets the job simply because he fits into the available uniform. At the other end of the spectrum is the security administrator, perhaps for an international organization, whose responsibilities include a wide array of strategies and problems. This position is not easy to fill. Although requirements for a career in security vary, the following discussion specifies the essential qualifications sought in most entry-level security positions.

### Good Health

Many security companies require candidates for employment to adhere to the following health guidelines: be well proportioned as to height and weight; be in good general health without physical defects or abnormalities that would interfere with the performance of the duties; possess binocular vision correctible to 20/30; be free of color blindness; and, be capable of hearing an ordinary conversation at 15 feet, with either ear, and without benefit of a hearing aid.

### Citizenship

For security positions within the government, normally the candidate is expected to be a citizen of the United States (for a specified period of time) and to have reached a certain age. When federal contracts require it, private security contractors may also impose citizenship requirements for employment. Candidates for security positions should be prepared to produce evidence of U.S. citizenship.

### Appearance

Security personnel are expected to maintain a neat appearance. Men should be clean shaven, except for a beard or mustache, which is sometimes permissible. Hair for both men and women should be neatly trimmed. Some security employers have a requirement for guards and investigators that their hair should be brushed or combed off the forehead and not protrude beneath the band of the uniform cap. Undercover investigators may dress and wear their hair as the assignment dictates.

### Firearms Proficiency

Some security positions require proficiency in the use and safe handling of .38 service-type revolvers, which are carried during employment. In some instances, this requirement is waived if the employee makes application for a pistol permit in the jurisdiction of employment. It may be the security person's responsibility, as a requirement for continued employment, to practice using the revolver under supervised conditions, as may be required by the local jurisdiction. Regulations concerning the use of firearms differ greatly from locality to locality, and can be quite complicated. Security managers are expected to be knowledgeable about local regulations. The Federal Register publishes a national update of such legislation annually. (In private security, there is a strong tendency to resist the use of armed security personnel for routine assignments. Armored car personnel and guards who respond to burglar alarms for central service stations, however, are usually armed.)

## Lack of Criminal Record

A security person may need to be bonded or be able to obtain a federal security clearance as a requirement of employment. In either case, the candidate most likely will be asked to provide a personal, educational, and employment history to the employer, and some of this information will be verified, with the candidates's knowledge and permission. References will be checked in person by investigators or by telephone interviews. Fingerprints may be taken prior to employment.

The candidate is expected to be free of any criminal record. The candidate is also expected to be able to explain adequately any questions the employment interviewer may have related to the preemployment investigation. Credit investigations may be routinely performed.

If employed in sensitive positions, security personnel should be prepared to expect, with their knowledge and permission, postemployment security checks. In some organizations, especially in financial institutions and in positions where classified government work is involved, periodic, random credit and background investigations of otherwise satisfactory security employees may occur.

Everyone interested in security work should have a good moral character, be capable of protecting what is entrusted to them, and should be able to win the cooperation and respect of others with whom they work.

## Intelligence and Education

Anyone working in any part of the security field must possess at least average intelligence. It is essential that the security agent be able to think clearly and rationally in all situations.

At the most basic level security employers require literacy of their employees. The security employee must be able to read and to understand printed regulations, written orders, and instructions and training publications. The ability to write complete reports is also essential. Depending upon the complexity of reading and writing assignments, a high school education, or higher, will be required.

For managerial and administrative positions in the security field, specific college course training can be highly useful, especially as security work becomes more complex. The advent of college-level programs in security has enabled the person entering the field to gain a knowledge and perspective not previously available to security people. The fact that someone has been a member of a police department for 30 years does not necessarily qualify that person to perform private security work.

### Experience

An employer is likely to be interested in how the security candidate was employed in earlier jobs. Previous employment in diverse positions may indicate interest, experience, and leadership pertinent to security employment.

Experience in certain government security vocations can be highly desirable for entry into the private sector. At the risk of being categorical, many employers in private industry have developed preferences. Former FBI agents with experience in bank crime cases have found employment opportunities with financial institutions. Former agents of the Drug Enforcement Administration (DEA) or the Secret Service are believed to have superior skills for investigating loss problems and for conducting background investigations. Retired security officers from the military have found many security positions in which leadership skills and administrative capabilities are important. And police officers, particularly with investigative and crime prevention skills, may be particularly welcome in organizations in which relations with the public and the local law enforcement agency are of particular importance. These positions may be in the transportation, retailing, or entertainment industries, for example.

It should be stressed that the majority of persons in security administration fit no definite pattern in terms of prior experience. Many successful security directors have assumed their position by moving laterally from another position in the organization in response to a sudden problem or job vacancy.

### Training for Future Security Professionals

A generation ago, a security director had to be good with people and know what his specific duties and responsibilities were and how to carry them out. Although these criteria are still valid, in recent years the security professional has had to develop additional skills. Knowing one's organization thoroughly is, as ever, a highly important requirement for success. However, to accomplish the job today, and even more so in the future, a Security Director will have to know something about the following subjects:

- Law
- Finance and financial controls
- Computers
- Insurance principles relating to risk management and liability
- Electronic security systems
- Safety management
- Fire protection and fire-fighting techniques
- Undercover investigations
- Arbitration procedures
- Emergency and disaster planning
- Budgeting
- Public relations
- Executive protection
- Other related topics

It is important for a security director to be able to anticipate, as much as possible, where the growth areas in crime will be. Of particular concern is computer theft, the electronic transfer of money, and comprehensive inventory losses. The security agent who desires opportunities for advancement should seek advanced training in computer operations.

### SALARY LEVELS

At first glance, security may seem to be not only a poorly paid occupation, but actually one of the worst (see Table 5-7). According to data provided by regional offices of the Bureau of Statistics, U.S. Department of Labor, the security guard is one of the lowest paid of all hourly compensated employees in manufacturing and nonmanufacturing industries. The lowest occupational titles are janitor, porter, and cleaner, although in some cities these persons earn more than security guards.

**Table 5-7.  Guard Wages**

| Contract | Commercial | | Industrial | | Institutional | |
|---|---|---|---|---|---|---|
| | Range | Average | Range | Average | Range | Average |
| Basic Officer | $3.35–$11.25 | $5.90 | $3.25–$9.50 | $5.13 | $3.15–$15.60 | $5.22 |
| Sergeant | $3.50–$12.00 | $5.67 | $3.25–$9.02 | $5.43 | $3.55–$8.05 | $5.51 |
| Lieutenant | $4.10–$14.00 | $6.51 | $3.25–$9.00 | $5.80 | $3.65–$7.00 | $5.87 |
| Captain | $4.00–$18.00 | $7.08 | $3.25–$9.00 | $7.47 | $3.70–$5.25 | $4.40 |
| Chief Officer | $5.50–$25.00 | $10.28 | $5.00–$9.00 | $7.10 | $7.50–$9.25 | $7.85 |

| Proprietary | Commercial | | Industrial | | Institutional | |
|---|---|---|---|---|---|---|
| | Range | Average | Range | Average | Range | Average |
| Basic Officer | $2.50–$10.50 | $5.36 | $3.50–$11.50 | $6.64 | $3.50–$11.00 | $5.70 |
| Sergeant | $3.45–$10.53 | $5.91 | $4.20–$14.25 | $7.77 | $3.85–$12.50 | $6.48 |
| Lieutenant | $3.45–$14.10 | $7.07 | $4.85–$16.50 | $8.42 | $4.70–$11.25 | $7.14 |
| Captain | $3.35–$12.00 | $7.55 | $5.25–$14.50 | $8.45 | $5.00–$14.00 | $8.30 |
| Chief Officer | $4.50–$20.00 | $9.28 | $5.02–$16.65 | $10.82 | $5.30–$14.05 | $10.49 |

Source: Survey conducted by Security World Magazine and published in July 1981, p. 24.

Salary differences between guards on staff and guards employed by contract guard services are considerable. There are similar salary differences between security positions and other vocational titles. Most positions in manufacturing industries covered in the Department of Labor study pay at least 50 percent more per hour than the compensation paid to security personnel. Some workers — for example, maintenance employees, electricians, and carpenters — earn triple the hourly compensation of security guards. For a breakdown of security officer compensation in the largest U.S. metropolitan areas see Table 5-8.

Table 5-8.   Hourly Security Officer Compensation in Largest U.S. Metropolitan Areas

| Metropolitan Area | Number of Workers | (Hourly Compensation in $) Mean | Median | Middle Range | Change% Mean/Median |
|---|---|---|---|---|---|
| Albany (9/80) | 579 | 5.00 | 3.85 | 3.10– 7.49 | n.a. |
| Manufacturing | 226 | 6.61 | 7.40 | 5.46– 7.49 | |
| Nonmanufacturing | 353 | 3.97 | 3.10 | 3.10– 3.55 | |
| | | | | | |
| Anaheim (10/80) | 1,588 | 4.71 | 4.25 | 3.75– 4.90 | 11.1– 13.3 |
| Manufacturing | 248 | 7.66 | 8.42 | 5.85– 9.01 | |
| Nonmanufacturing | 1,340 | 4.17 | 4.00 | 3.60– 4.50 | |
| | | | | | |
| Atlanta (5/81) | 2,701 | 4.44 | 3.55 | 3.35– 4.30 | 23.0– 11.0 |
| Manufacturing | 359 | 8.10 | 7.45 | 5.93– 10.71 | |
| Nonmanufacturing | 2,342 | 3.88 | 3.55 | 3.38– 3.90 | |
| | | | | | |
| Baltimore (8/81) | 3,088 | 4.44 | 3.35 | 3.38– 4.25 | 19.3– 11.7 |
| Manufacturing | 381 | 8.95 | 8.95 | 7.99– 9.77 | |
| Nonmanufacturing | 2,707 | 3.81 | 3.35 | 3.35– 3.80 | |
| | | | | | |
| Boston (8/80) | 6,782 | 4.02 | 3.50 | 3.30– 3.90 | 8.6– 9.4 |
| Manufacturing | 836 | 6.32 | 6.16 | 5.89– 6.92 | |
| Nonmanufacturing | 5,946 | 3.70 | 3.40 | 3.30– 3.75 | |
| | | | | | |
| Buffalo (10/80) | 2,459 | 4.30 | 3.10 | 3.10– 4.00 | n.a. |
| Manufacturing | 457 | 8.51 | 8.70 | 7.26– 10.55 | |
| Nonmanufacturing | 2,002 | 3.34 | 3.10 | 3.10– 3.20 | |
| | | | | | |
| Chicago (5/81) | 11,251 | 5.19 | 4.09 | 3.90– 6.01 | 8.6– 9.1 |
| Manufacturing | 1,653 | 7.75 | 8.75 | 6.30– 8.75 | |
| Nonmanufacturing | 9,598 | 4.74 | 4.05 | 3.90– 5.25 | |
| | | | | | |
| Cincinnati (7/81) | 1,366 | 4.89 | 3.60 | 3.40– 5.49 | 7.7– 7.8 |
| Manufacturing | 404 | 7.72 | 8.12 | 5.55– 8.77 | |
| Nonmanufacturing | 962 | 3.70 | 3.45 | 3.35– 3.60 | |

**Table 5-8.** (continued)

| Metropolitan Area | Number of Workers | (Hourly Compensation in $) | | Middle Range | Change% Mean/Median |
|---|---|---|---|---|---|
| | | Mean | Median | | |
| Cleveland (9/80) | 3,247 | 4.64 | 3.50 | 3.20– 5.30 | 11.3– 11.1 |
| Manufacturing | 722 | 8.03 | 8.15 | 6.05– 10.05 | |
| Nonmanufacturing | 2,525 | 3.66 | 3.30 | 3.20– 3.80 | |
| | | | | | |
| Columbus (10/80) | 1,308 | 4.05 | 3.35 | 3.10– 4.50 | 10.1– 6.4 |
| Manufacturing | 136 | 7.54 | 6.46 | 5.33– 9.75 | |
| Nonmanufacturing | 1,172 | 3.64 | 3.24 | 3.10– 3.95 | |
| | | | | | |
| Dallas (12/80) | 3,812 | 4.35 | 3.75 | 3.50– 4.60 | 14.2– 15.4 |
| Manufacturing | 668 | 6.85 | 5.79 | 5.05– 9.63 | |
| Nonmanufacturing | 3,144 | 3.82 | 3.50 | 3.40– 3.90 | |
| | | | | | |
| Dayton (12/80) | 924 | 6.23 | 5.78 | 3.10– 10.56 | n.a. |
| Manufacturing | 462 | 9.11 | 10.61 | 6.79– 10.94 | |
| Nonmanufacturing | 462 | 3.35 | 3.10 | 3.10– 3.30 | |
| | | | | | |
| Denver (12/80) | 2,106 | 4.39 | 3.75 | 3.50– 4.69 | 11.4– 15.4 |
| Manufacturing | 280 | 7.21 | 7.37 | 5.61– 8.72 | |
| Nonmanufacturing | 1,826 | 3.96 | 3.55 | 3.35– 4.32 | |
| | | | | | |
| Detroit (3/81) | 5,261 | 7.19 | 6.73 | 4.46– 10.55 | 2.7–(15.9) |
| Manufacturing | 2,084 | 10.39 | 11.05 | 9.28– 11.44 | |
| Nonmanufacturing | 3,177 | 5.09 | 4.52 | 4.00– 4.80 | |
| | | | | | |
| Fort Lauderdale (4/81) | 2,533 | 3.99 | 3.55 | 3.45– 4.32 | n.a. |
| | | | | | |
| Gary Hammond (11/80) | 728 | 7.64 | 9.43 | 3.80– 9.76 | n.a. |
| Manufacturing | 493 | 9.46 | 9.60 | 9.43– 9.92 | |
| | | | | | |
| Greensboro (8/80) | 1,064 | 4.19 | 3.50 | 3.20– 4.50 | n.a. |
| Manufacturing | 374 | 5.34 | 4.76 | 3.75– 7.81 | |
| Nonmanufacturing | 690 | 3.57 | 3.30 | 3.18– 3.69 | |
| | | | | | |
| Greenville (6/81) | 1,122 | 3.65 | 3.50 | 3.35– 3.67 | n.a. |
| Manufacturing | 170 | 4.38 | 4.14 | 3.85– 5.01 | |
| Nonmanufacturing | 952 | 3.52 | 3.45 | 3.35– 3.50 | |
| | | | | | |
| Hartford (3/81) | 857 | 4.93 | 4.03 | 3.55– 6.48 | n.a. |
| Nonmanufacturing | 645 | 4.10 | 3.55 | 3.50– 4.10 | |
| | | | | | |
| Houston (5/81) | 8,877 | 4.81 | 4.50 | 4.00– 5.00 | 8.3– 9.5 |
| Manufacturing | 492 | 7.75 | 6.62 | 5.72– 10.06 | |
| Nonmanufacturing | 8,325 | 4.63 | 4.50 | 4.00– 5.00 | |

**Table 5-8.** (continued)

| Metropolitan Area | Number of Workers | (Hourly Compensation in $) | | Middle Range | Change% Mean/Median |
|---|---|---|---|---|---|
| | | Mean | Median | | |
| Indianapolis (10/80) | 1,427 | 5.13 | 3.40 | 3.10– 7.15 | 10.8– 7.9 |
| Manufacturing | 400 | 9.30 | 9.77 | 8.26– 10.78 | |
| Nonmanufacturing | 1,027 | 3.51 | 3.10 | 3.10– 3.47 | |
| | | | | | |
| Jacksonville (12/80) | 1,463 | 3.44 | 3.15 | 3.10– 3.32 | 8.2– 8.6 |
| Manufacturing | 27 | 6.01 | 5.25 | 4.93– 7.50 | |
| Nonmanufacturing | 1,436 | 3.40 | 3.12 | 3.10– 3.32 | |
| | | | | | |
| Kansas City (9/80) | 1,775 | 6.08 | 6.55 | 3.25– 7.77 | n.a. |
| Manufacturing | 465 | 8.26 | 7.78 | 7.63– 9.63 | |
| Nonmanufacturing | 1,308 | 5.31 | 5.60 | 3.20– 7.23 | |
| | | | | | |
| Los Angeles (10/80) | 13,393 | 4.62 | 3.90 | 3.40– 5.00 | 11.1– 14.7 |
| Manufacturing | 1,732 | 7.83 | 8.69 | 5.88– 9.36 | |
| Nonmanufacturing | 11,661 | 4.15 | 3.75 | 3.35– 4.40 | |
| | | | | | |
| Louisville (11/80) | 1,354 | 4.56 | 3.30 | 3.10– 5.50 | n.a. |
| Manufacturing | 305 | 8.01 | 8.16 | 7.97– 9.60 | |
| Nonmanufacturing | 1,049 | 3.56 | 3.25 | 3.10– 3.35 | |
| | | | | | |
| Memphis (11/80) | 1,236 | 3.89 | 3.25 | 3.15– 3.70 | 7.8– 6.6 |
| Manufacturing | 80 | 7.29 | 7.28 | 5.99– 9.24 | |
| Nonmanufacturing | 1,156 | 3.65 | 3.25 | 3.15– 3.45 | |
| | | | | | |
| Miami (10/80) | 1,036 | 4.11 | 3.85 | 3.52– 4.15 | 5.9– 1.0 |
| Manufacturing | 114 | 4.54 | 4.50 | 4.15– 4.80 | |
| Nonmanufacturing | 923 | 4.05 | 3.75 | 3.50– 4.13 | |
| | | | | | |
| Milwaukee (5/81) | 2,134 | 4.99 | 4.25 | 3.65– 5.45 | 15.2– 17.4 |
| Manufacturing | 324 | 7.97 | 7.91 | 6.98– 9.72 | |
| Nonmanufacturing | 1,810 | 4.46 | 4.25 | 3.55– 4.75 | |
| | | | | | |
| Minneapolis (1/81) | 2,891 | 4.68 | 4.00 | 3.45– 5.53 | 6.6– 19.0 |
| Manufacturing | 407 | 7.69 | 7.60 | 7.04– 8.44 | |
| Nonmanufacturing | 2,484 | 4.19 | 3.85 | 3.45– 4.25 | |
| | | | | | |
| Nashville (6/81) | 490 | 4.97 | 4.76 | 3.50– 4.98 | n.a. |
| | | | | | |
| Nassau (6/81) | 2,909 | 4.58 | 3.50 | 3.35– 5.26 | 10.1– 9.4 |
| Manufacturing | 304 | 6.53 | 6.30 | 5.60– 7.86 | |
| Nonmanufacturing | 2,605 | 4.35 | 3.45 | 3.35– 4.42 | |

**Table 5-8.** **(continued)**

| Metropolitan Area | Number of Workers | (Hourly Compensation in $) Mean | (Hourly Compensation in $) Median | Middle Range | Change% Mean/Median |
|---|---|---|---|---|---|
| Newark (1/81) | 3,813 | 4.24 | 3.60 | 3.35– 4.35 | 6.8– 3.7 |
| Manufacturing | 361 | 7.37 | 7.47 | 5.03– 9.84 | |
| Nonmanufacturing | 3,452 | 3.92 | 3.50 | 3.35– 4.17 | |
| | | | | | |
| New Orleans (10/80) | 2,669 | 3.43 | 3.20 | 3.10– 3.35 | 3.6– 3.9 |
| Manufacturing | 133 | 5.79 | 5.29 | 4.50– 5.64 | |
| Nonmanufacturing | 2,536 | 3.31 | 3.20 | 3.10– 3.30 | |
| | | | | | |
| New York (5/81) | 21,607 | 4.71 | 3.75 | 3.50– 6.05 | 11.3– 13.6 |
| Manufacturing | 656 | 7.28 | 7.37 | 5.75– 8.59 | |
| Nonmanufacturing | 20,951 | 4.63 | 3.70 | 3.50– 5.75 | |
| | | | | | |
| Norfolk (5/81) | 566 | 3.80 | 3.45 | 3.35– 3.72 | n.a. |
| Manufacturing | 91 | 4.86 | 5.21 | 3.96– 5.23 | |
| Nonmanufacturing | 475 | 3.60 | 3.41 | 3.35– 3.45 | |
| | | | | | |
| Oklahoma City (8/80) | 773 | 4.07 | 3.30 | 3.10– 4.15 | n.a. |
| Manufacturing | 142 | 6.66 | 5.81 | 4.50– 8.32 | |
| | | | | | |
| Omaha (10/80) | 529 | 3.73 | 3.20 | 3.10– 3.25 | n.a. |
| Manufacturing | 52 | 6.31 | 6.51 | 4.34– 8.62 | |
| Nonmanufacturing | 477 | 3.44 | 3.20 | 3.10– 3.20 | |
| | | | | | |
| Orlando (8/81) | 756 | 4.53 | 3.62 | 3.35– 5.45 | n.a. |
| | | | | | |
| Philadelphia (11/80) | 7,935 | 4.00 | 3.20 | 3.10– 3.85 | 7.8– 6.7 |
| Manufacturing | 1,022 | 7.25 | 7.44 | 5.83– 8.74 | |
| Nonmanufacturing | 6,913 | 3.52 | 3.17 | 3.10– 3.40 | |
| | | | | | |
| Phoenix (6/81) | 2,460 | 4.28 | 3.50 | 3.35– 4.25 | n.a. |
| | | | | | |
| Pittsburgh (1/81) | 3,820 | 4.37 | 3.35 | 3.35– 3.85 | 6.8– 5.7 |
| Manufacturing | 556 | 8.57 | 9.07 | 7.28– 9.89 | |
| Nonmanufacturing | 3,264 | 3.65 | 3.35 | 3.35– 3.45 | |
| | | | | | |
| Portland (6/81) | 1,093 | 4.37 | 3.85 | 3.75– 4.20 | n.a. |
| Manufacturing | 67 | 7.36 | 7.00 | 6.14– 9.30 | |
| Nonmanufacturing | 1,026 | 4.17 | 3.85 | 3.75– 4.00 | |
| | | | | | |
| Providence (6/81) | 1,431 | 3.85 | 3.50 | 3.35– 3.80 | n.a. |
| Manufacturing | 167 | 5.31 | 5.10 | 4.85– 5.80 | |
| Nonmanufacturing | 1,264 | 3.66 | 3.45 | 3.35– 3.55 | |

**Table 5-8.** (continued)

| Metropolitan Area | Number of Workers | (Hourly Compensation in $) | | Middle Range | Change% Mean/Median |
|---|---|---|---|---|---|
| | | Mean | Median | | |
| Sacramento (12/80) | 347 | 5.48 | 5.00 | 4.30– 5.87 | n.a. |
| Manufacturing | 59 | 7.72 | 7.00 | 6.95– 8.50 | |
| Nonmanufacturing | 288 | 5.02 | 4.97 | 4.08– 5.56 | |
| Salt Lake City (11/80) | 468 | 4.58 | 3.40 | 3.15– 5.50 | n.a. |
| Manufacturing | 82 | 6.96 | 5.63 | 5.00– 9.70 | |
| Nonmanufacturing | 386 | 4.07 | 3.28 | 3.15– 4.77 | |
| San Antonio (5/81) | 1,110 | 3.61 | 3.45 | 3.35– 3.60 | 8.4– 11.3 |
| Manufacturing | 74 | 4.47 | 4.58 | 4.25– 4.64 | |
| Nonmanufacturing | 1,036 | 3.55 | 3.45 | 3.35– 3.55 | |
| San Diego (11/80) | 2,641 | 4.35 | 3.55 | 3.30– 4.70 | (3.1)– 9.2 |
| Manufacturing | 283 | 6.59 | 7.14 | 5.50– 8.02 | |
| Nonmanufacturing | 2,358 | 4.08 | 3.55 | 3.30– 4.54 | |
| San Francisco (3/81) | 3,476 | 5.01 | 4.75 | 4.20– 5.35 | 10.1– 12.3 |
| Manufacturing | 264 | 7.82 | 7.34 | 6.00– 9.19 | |
| Nonmanufacturing | 3,212 | 4.77 | 4.65 | 4.00– 5.26 | |
| San Jose (3/81) | 3,632 | 5.02 | 4.63 | 4.25– 5.05 | 5.7– 8.9 |
| Manufacturing | 422 | 7.57 | 7.46 | 5.00– 9.83 | |
| Nonmanufacturing | 3,210 | 4.68 | 4.50 | 4.25– 5.00 | |
| Seattle (12/80) | 1,986 | 4.36 | 3.59 | 3.25– 4.40 | 16.0– 12.2 |
| Manufacturing | 283 | 8.11 | 9.68 | 5.11– 9.68 | |
| Nonmanufacturing | 1,703 | 3.73 | 3.50 | 3.25– 4.00 | |
| St. Louis (3/81) | 3,781 | 5.04 | 3.65 | 3.45– 5.00 | 10.0– 4.3 |
| Manufacturing | 836 | 9.14 | 9.95 | 8.02– 10.11 | |
| Nonmanufacturing | 2,945 | 3.88 | 3.65 | 3.35– 4.00 | |
| Tampa (7/81) | 2,545 | 3.63 | 3.35 | 3.35– 3.45 | n.a. |
| Toledo (6/81) | 1,713 | 4.31 | 3.50 | 3.35– 4.00 | n.a. |
| Manufacturing | 156 | 9.18 | 10.43 | 6.83– 10.46 | |
| Nonmanufacturing | 1,557 | 3.82 | 3.50 | 3.35– 3.75 | |
| Tulsa (6/81) | 647 | 5.18 | 4.50 | 3.50– 6.25 | n.a. |
| Washington (3/81) | 4,142 | 4.50 | 4.22 | 3.42– 5.26 | 23.3– 36.1 |
| Manufacturing | 61 | 5.31 | 4.50 | 4.00– 7.33 | |
| Nonmanufacturing | 4,081 | 4.49 | 4.17 | 3.42– 5.26 | |

**Table 5-8.    (continued)**

| Metropolitan Area | Number of Workers | (Hourly Compensation in $) | | Middle Range | Change% Mean/Median |
|---|---|---|---|---|---|
| | | Mean | Median | | |
| Worcester (4/81) | 214 | 4.86 | 4.40 | 3.35– 6.34 | n.a. |
| Manufacturing | 114 | 5.74 | 6.05 | 4.10– 6.81 | |

*Notes:* Mean, or average, is computed by totaling earnings of all the workers and dividing by the total number of workers. The *median* designates the wage at which half the workers earn more and half earn less than the amount stated. The *middle range* is derived from two values: a fourth of the workers receive the same or less than the lower of these two rates and a fourth earn the same or more than the higher rate. *Change % mean/median* indicates the percentage change separately for the mean and the median from the previous report, normally one year ago. (See SLX, No. 22, Pt. II.) And *n.a.* means not available or applicable.

   Hourly compensation data presented here are collected by regional offices of the U.S. Department of Labor, Bureau of Labor Statistics from selected, representative employers. Due to inflationary increases and a lag in reporting time, compensation is likely to be somewhat different since the time of the most recent report, which is indicated by the month or year stated after the metropolitan area.

*Source:* Data collected from regional offices of the U.S. Department of Labor, Bureau of Labor Statistics annual reports. Reprinted with permission from *Security Letter,* Vol. XI, No. 21 Part II (1981).

   Compensation also differs according to place of employment. For example, security guards working at utilities earned almost twice that of other guards employed in the same geographical area. Security guards who are required to be armed also earn more than their nonarmed counterparts. This pay differential is justified because of the out-of-pocket expenses associated with maintaining a gun permit, and also because the type of individual a security director wants carrying a gun on his premises apparently warrants a higher hourly compensation.

   The relatively low compensation for security guards has not, however, meant that an unacceptable quality of guard is necessarily being employed. On the contrary, the high unemployment rate over the past decade and the large number of unskilled persons seeking work have given security recruiters a large pool of talent from which to choose. While most other employees in the same organization earn more, security guards typically maintain an acceptable level of job satisfaction and morale. This may be attributed to factors such as the authority and visibility accompanying the job, wearing a uniform, personal gratification from the service-related aspect of the work, and the generally nondemanding nature of security assignments.

Most security guards employed today are not unionized. However, security personnel working for armored car companies are likely to be union members, as are some of the security personnel working for central station alarm companies. Unionized personnel earn more than their nonunionized counterparts in the majority of cases.

Investigators are compensated on a salary basis, generally beginning at $225 to $300 a week. This is based on a 40-hour work week. In addition to salary, expenses are paid.

Undercover agents receive the normal salary commensurate with the position they are occupying in business or industry. They are treated exactly as any other employee in the organization. In fact, only a very few persons may be aware of the dual role the employee plays as regular worker and undercover operative. In addition to the basic compensation, the employee receives additional compensation from the employer or security company who places and supervises him or her. This usually amounts to 20 to 50 percent of the base salary. The undercover agent is also paid expenses required in the work, such as relocation expenses and, perhaps, "socializing" money, which is required so that the agent can mingle effectively with long-established employees. Often this additional compensation is paid to the undercover employee on checks that do not reveal the source as being a security-related organization.

Polygraphists are typically self-employed, or employed by large security companies. Their names can usually be found in the classified sections of most telephone books. A few large organizations have senior security personnel with polygraph experience. These people are used, as needed, for specific internal investigations. Experienced polygraph examiners command a premium compensation, but there is no accurate information about precisely what these examiners earn.

Individual polygraph examinations for routine purposes cost $25 to $50 per test. For example, a routine examination may be a preemployment screening. In situations where large screenings of persons may be done periodically with only a few questions being asked, the charge per test may be closer to $25. In a criminal investigation when the examiner must work with investigators in planning the questioning, an examination fee per test in excess of $100 is not considered unreasonable.

Security directors are the most highly compensated people in the protection field within the organization. While compensation is somewhat lower than for other management positions, on the average the security manager's relative compensation appears to have grown in the past decade. See Table 5-9 for security management compensation figures.

*Security Letter* publishes an annual survey of management position compensation medians. In a recent survey, directors of security earned a median of $26,500 in small companies, $28,500 in medium companies, and

### Table 5-9. Corporate Management Concerned with Loss Prevention

Annual salaries are stated in medians; that is, half earn more and half less than the amount indicated, rounded off to the nearest $100. These are base salaries in effect in the first quarter of 1981. In addition managers may earn bonuses, pension contributions, profit-sharing, and other direct or indirect compensation that will be additional to the base salary.

Corporations throughout the United States contribute to this data base. Corporations are grouped to provide realistic ranges. Numbers in parentheses indicate the number of corporations that have provided information on that particular position.

| | National Compensation Medians | | |
| | Small Companies | Medium Companies | Large Companies |
| --- | --- | --- | --- |
| Chief Internal Auditor | (58) 29,700 | (63) 33,800 | (113) 41,000 |
| Corporate Insurance Manager | (26) 30,900 | (37) 33,000 | (94) 39,500 |
| Credit and Collections Executive | (56) 23,700 | (77) 26,000 | (116) 36,500 |
| Director of Safety | (147) 26,800 | (74) 30,900 | (63) 36,900 |
| Director of Security | (50) 26,500 | (79) 28,500 | (74) 35,500 |
| EDP Executive | (92) 29,100 | (110) 38,300 | (95) 49,000 |
| Employment Manager | (151) 26,200 | (90) 27,600 | (45) 34,800 |
| Labor Relations Executive | (89) 33,600 | (51) 42,100 | (45) 34,800 |
| Office Management Executive | (83) 25,300 | (70) 27,500 | (80) 34,400 |
| Personnel Manager/Director | (257) 30,300 | (56) 40,000 | (44) 42,000 |
| Personnel Assistant | (175) 17,000 | (79) 18,400 | (71) 20,300 |
| Plant/Factory Superintendent | (40) 32,600 | (154) 41,400 | (81) 51,700 |
| Plant Maintenance Exec Engineer | (75) 24,300 | (96) 28,800 | (110) 37,800 |
| Risk Management Executive | n/a | (64) 36,100 | (64) 41,300 |

Notes: Designations of small, medium, and large have been used, as appropriate, based on sales, budget of EDP facilities, value of insured assets, number of employees, or other criteria that seemed logical for grouping the companies.

Credit: © 1981 American Management Association, Executive Compensation Service.

Source: Reprinted with permission from: *Security Letter,* Vol. XI, no. 16 Part II (1981)

*Loss Related Compensation for Banks, Financial and Insurance Organizations*

Compensation listed in the first part of the table was for managers in manufacturing, processing, transportation, communications, and certain service organizations. Here are compensation medians for four selected positions in banks, financial, and insurance organizations.

**Table 5-9.  (continued)**

| Position (number reporting) | Median | 50% Salary Range | Average Staff | % With Bonus |
|---|---|---|---|---|
| Chief Internal Auditor (60) | 34,900 | 28,800– 43,700 | 6 | 18 |
| Director of Security (30) | 27,900 | 23,500– 35,000 | 21 | 21 |
| EDP Executive (65) | 44,300 | 34,100– 52,800 | 65 | 26 |
| Office Management Executive (39) | 32,500 | 26,800– 39,800 | 10 | 24 |

Notes:  50% salary range means that half of all persons covered in the study are included in the range. Bonuses range from 6 to 24% in the positions studied.

$35,500 in large companies. The median salary is defined as the point at which half the individuals earn more and half less than the stated amount. In addition to the compensation cited, bonuses, profit sharing, and other supplemental and fringe compensations may be given. Thus the actual financial package may be considerably more attractive than indicated.

In 1978, the American Society of Industrial Security (ASIS) published a compensation report that showed generally higher compensation than the compensation reported that year by *Security Letter.* The differences could be related to sampling and methodology. In the former case, the information was provided directly by the compensation department, whereas in the latter case, ASIS received the information from the respondents themselves.

## WHERE THE SECURITY CAREER OPPORTUNITIES ARE

As mentioned earlier, the need for security people is growing in response to the economic impact of crime. The number of persons employed in security is booming. (See Table 5-10, which lists the advantages and disadvantages of a career in security.) But where are the best career opportunities? The fact is that employment opportunities abound and are continually increasing. Here are some pertinent developments:

1.  Most large organizations (over $100 million in revenues) currently have a security director, or a person in administration responsible for protection. Hundreds of organizations still do not have such a position, but their number is decreasing.
2.  All national banks and most other financial institutions have a security manager on staff. The Bank Security Act of 1968 requires each institution to have someone in this position, and alsɔ man-

**Table 5-10.  Advantages and Disadvantages to a Career in Security**

*Growth of Field*

| Advantage | Disadvantage |
|---|---|
| The security field is likely to grow and support new entrants in the near future. | The growth of security electronics and systems may decrease the need for people in some areas of security and alter the nature of traditional security work. |

*Individual Advancement on the Job*

| Advantage | Disadvantage |
|---|---|
| Because of the anticipated increase in the number of security positions, the opportunity for advancement on the job within the management structure can be anticipated. | If there is a lack of expansion of the security staff, there could be limited opportunities to move up in management. |

*Equal Opportunity*

| Advantage | Disadvantage |
|---|---|
| Regardless of age, race, sex, and national origin, people find opportunities in security. The need for brute physical strength as a prerequisite for security employment is a myth. Persons with substantial physical handicaps may find employment in security. For example, some hemiplegics make excellent radio call directors (specialized education and experience always give an employment candidate an edge). Women are rapidly moving into security positions at all levels. | As a reality, many opportunities for employment may favor those with special contacts. A bank, for example, may prefer to hire an ex-FBI agent or a retail store may choose a retired local police officer over candidates without prior work experience. Other employers may overemphasize physical appearance and hire large, strong-looking persons (usually men) to achieve a security image. |

*Interesting Work*

| Advantage | Disadvantage |
|---|---|
| Security work may, by its dynamic nature, be personally interesting. | Staff-level security positions may be monotonous. |

*Job Transfer Possibilities*

| Advantage | Disadvantage |
|---|---|
| Security work often includes quite different responsibilities, making the position a challenging one. | People who perform one type of security task well might find it difficult to be transferred to another job activity because of their value in their present position. |

**Table 5-10.** (continued)

---

*Salary*

| Advantage | Disadvantage |
|---|---|
| Security people in managerial positions earn salaries comparable to those of other managerial personnel. | Most entry-level and staff positions in security do not pay well. |

*Prestige of Work*

| Advantage | Disadvantage |
|---|---|
| Security is honorable work and helps an organization to remain whole, viable, and efficient. | Some observers believe that security is not very important and, therefore, does not have prestige. |

*Opportunities for Personal Growth*

| Advantage | Disadvantage |
|---|---|
| Many security positions include opportunities for attendance at seminars or conferences and professional association meetings. | Some managements see no reason for spending any more on security than is absolutely necessary. Security employees in these organizations will not be supported in their efforts to obtain additional training and experience. |

*Personal Risk*

| Advantage | Disadvantage |
|---|---|
| Despite contact with criminals and, occasionally violent persons, most security operatives do not experience much personal risk. | Each year, there are security people who die, or are handicapped, as a result of violent activities encountered on the job. |

*Addition to Profit Picture*

| Advantage | Disadvantage |
|---|---|
| The main purpose for having a security function in an organization is to save money, or to make money, in an operational sense. This adds to the "worth" of what security is; security can become a "profit center." | It is easier for security to show management how much it costs, than to document how much it contributes to profits. |

   dates the use of certain physical security measures, such as the installation of cameras and presence of bait money in the tellers' drawers.
3. Even small retail, transportation, and service organizations are likely to have a security manager today because of the high incidence of pilferage and employee crime in these industries.
4. In addition to the conventional and historical vulnerabilities to financial losses, the advent of computer crime has vastly increased the vulnerability in this area. A Government Accounting Office (GAO) report calls for a computer security officer at every computer facility. Computer security officers tend to have a background in data processing management, often with experience in programming. These officers have learned security principles in addition to computer processes.
5. The federal government has become in recent years an important employer of security personnel, separate from law enforcement officers.
6. Security guards are now appearing in surprising places. For example, fire departments may have a security guard watch the firehouse when the fire patrol is out on call. And some police chiefs have requested security guards to be placed in police stations so that the premises will be protected while the other police officers are sent into the field.

Getting the first position in security is not difficult if the individual is willing to start at the bottom, and meets the criteria discussed earlier in this chapter. Entry-level positions are plentiful in security work. Growing up through the ranks is related to a combination of factors, including seniority, ability, training and education, the growth of the organization itself, luck, and timing.

Security service opportunities can be found in private commerce and industry, public institutions (such as hospitals and educational establishments), private security organizations, state and local government, and the federal government.

While the competition for entry-level positions is not great, the competition for managerial and higher-paying positions remains keen. This is because of the large number of persons leaving government and the military who seek civilian employment. These people are frequently collecting a pension and therefore are willing to accept employment for less than the average managerial compensation. Their past experience permits them to bring to their new positions a dimension of experience that can be quite significant to the civilian sector.

## Positions in Federal Security Service

Several thousand security positions are available within the federal government each year. Almost every division of federal service has a security requirement that includes guarding, investigating, security planning, and administration. Some of these positions involve travel and offer worthwhile career opportunities.

The best starting point for investigating this type of employment is the Federal Job Information Center, which is located in federal buildings in most metropolitan cities. At the employment center, positions in security and law enforcement are described in the Civil Service Commission's publication BRE-38. Some additional specific federal employment suggestions follow.

**Department of Justice.** Persons interested in being considered for the position of narcotics agent, border patrol officer, deputy U.S. marshall, or immigration and naturalization inspector can ask for appropriate announcements. Applicants should expect to take "The Professional and Administrative Career Examination" to be considered for these positions.

Positions as special agents of the Federal Bureau of Investigation may be open to qualified college graduates, usually with graduate school education or other specialized experience or personal background the FBI may find valuable in its current investigative efforts. Request further information from the Department of Personnel, Federal Bureau of Investigation, J. Edgar Hoover Building, Washington, DC 20530.

**Department of the Treasury.** Special investigators with the Alcohol, Tobacco, and Firearms Bureau, internal security inspectors for the Internal Revenue Service, special agents for the Secret Service, border patrol agents, and intelligence division special agents are among the positions available, generally to persons with college training. Information on positions, including beginning compensation and availability, may be found at the Federal Job Information Center.

Information on positions within the Secret Service may be obtained by contacting the Personnel Division, U.S. Secret Service, Room 912, 1800 G Street NW, Washington, DC 20226.

**Department of Defense and Elsewhere.** Civilian security-related positions occur within Department of Defense operations, although a majority of the positions have a bias for persons with a military background.

Other opportunities for federal security service exist throughout government, for example, with the U.S. Fish and Wildlife Service (Interior

Department), the Forest Service (Agriculture), the National Park Service (Interior), the U.S. Postal Service, and the U.S. General Services Administration. These organizations have personnel concerned with physical and operational security, agents to enforce federal laws, and internal and external investigatory agents.

## SUMMARY

In recent years, the private security profession has grown in epidemic proportions. This growth may be attributed to many factors, including the ever-increasing crime rate and the growing inability of public law enforcement agencies to cope effectively with the problem. Without the aid of the private security sector, incidents of crime would overwhelm the public criminal justice spectrum.

The growth in the use of private security guards has been dramatic in the past generation. This rapid rate of growth will continue into the 1980s, assuming a plentiful supply of potential employees and the cost effectiveness of guard services relative to electronic security systems.

Until very recently, the contract guard and investigative business has had a high "ease of entry" rate; however this situation is changing. Some states now require a guard training program that the security company must finance. In addition, insurance companies are beginning to insist that guards be properly trained because of the large number of false arrest and other guard-related lawsuits they handle.

Private security may not convert the professional thief to more honest pursuits, but security systems and uniformed guards will unquestionably have an effect on the thief who acts only when opportunity arises. It stands to reason that a thief would rather enter unprotected premises than a fully alarmed room.

The private security sector is now turning its attention more and more to the elusive white-collar criminal. The growth of executive stealing, bribery, embezzlement, and computer manipulation has become a recognized part of the economy.

It is not possible to estimate with precision what the cost of crime to this nation actually is. In many cases, losses occur without management being aware of them, while in other cases administrators choose to bury evidence of crime, rather than have its existence serve as a reflection on their poor managerial ability or disturb the relationship of the firm with its insurers. In addition to the actual cost of crime are psychological factors, such as fear, distrust, and unwillingness to start certain projects.

It is into this environment that the private security sector supports and extends the efforts of public law enforcement and strives to protect the integrity of society as a whole through its efforts to reduce loss.

## NOTES

1.  Uniform Crime Report: *Crime in the United States, 1980,* U.S. Department of Justice, Federal Bureau of Investigations, 1981, U.S. Government Printing Office, Washington, DC.
2.  Private Security System Industry Study: E69, 1982, Predicasts Inc., Cleveland, OH.
3.  Lykken, D. T., "The GSR in the Detection of Guilt," *Journal of Applied Psychology.,* 1959, 43:385–388.
4.  Lykken, D. T., "The Validity of the Guilty Knowledge Technique: The Effects of Faking," *Journal of Applied Psychology,* 1960, 44:258–262.
5.  Marston, W. M., "Psychological Possibilities in the Deception Test," *Journal Criminal Law and Criminology.,* 1921, 11:551–570.
6.  Ellson, D. G., "A Report of Research on Detection of Deception," NONR 18011, Office of Naval Research Contr. No. 6, September 1952.
7.  Baesen, H., Chung, C., and Yang, L. Y., "A Lie Detector Experiment," *Journal of Criminal Law,* 1948, 39:532–537.
8.  Thackray, R. I., and Orne, M. T., "Effects of the Type of Stimulus Employed and the Level of Subject Awareness on the Detection of Deception," *Journal of Applied Psychology.,* 1965, 52:234–239.
9.  Kubis, J. F., "Studies in Lie Detection," RADC–TR–62–205, USAF, June 1962.
10. Ruckmick, C. A., "The Truth about the Lie Detector," *Journal of Applied Psychology,* 1938, 22:30–58.
11. Landia, C., and Wiley, L. E., "Changes of Blood Pressure and Respiration During Deception," *Journal of Comparative Psychology,* 1926, 6:1–19.
12. Gustafson, L. A., and Orne, M. R., "The Effects of Heightened Motivation in the Detection of Deception," *Journal of Applied Psychology,* 1963, 47:408–411.
13. Larson, J. A., "The Cardio-pneumo-psychogram and Its Use in the Study of Emotions with Practical Applications," *Journal of Experimental Psychology,* 1922, 5:323–328.
14. Bell, A. D., Jr., McQuiston, C. R., and Ford, W. H., The Official Gazette, Patent Number 3971032, July 20, 1976.
15. For a comprehensive guide to security consultants, see: *Security Letter Source Book* 1983, published by Butterworths, Woburn, MA.

# Chapter 6
# Physical Security Surveys and Specialized Security Subjects

Security systems must be designed to complement the individual characteristics of the situation, with particular emphasis on the type of annunciation and transmission as well as the policy of the local police department. Rarely can a combination of alarm devices — signal transmission and annunciation — be applied to more than one building or situation unless all the physical and environmental conditions are identical.

Generally, most attempts to "standardize" a security system have not been very successful. The approach of some alarm companies to simplify the system by limiting the protection system to a few magnetic door contacts and a light beam along the perimeter wall is often an admission that they cannot handle sophisticated volumetric intrusion alarms. Magnetic contacts and beams may eliminate the nuisance of false alarms, but they also eliminate the detection of the burglar. The alarm company does not want to answer frequent false alarms because it costs money, and thus there is an economic justification to keep false alarms to a minimum. But the overall cost could be expensive to the property owner. A balance must be achieved between economics and protection — a goal that has become very elusive in the past decade.

Another factor that must be considered in the design of an alarm system is selecting the particular alarm to fit a particular situation. A system designed for a small retail store cannot be indiscriminately expanded for use in a hospital or school building, which is the kind of policy being followed by many alarm companies. (Even if the situations in two buildings warrant an ultrasonic detector, the actual shape of the detector can affect the security. The unit installed in a retail store could be of any shape, but the unit in a school must be designed to keep the students from ripping it off the wall during the daytime.) Mismatching alarm equipment is a very common practice because of the inexperience of the alarm installer and the indifference of the user. Each situation requires a distinctive set of parameters and criteria, and of course the important economic factor of initial cost must be considered.

It is difficult to justify the cost of an alarm system if it exceeds the value of the property being protected. Yet sometimes value of the property cannot be the only criterion. A school district may find it economically justifiable to install $20,000 worth of special locks on exterior doors to keep out unauthorized intruders. Such an expense may be justified because the locks will have eliminated a single guard in the school whose salary was $15,000 a year (the salary is a recurring expense whereas the locks are a one-time capital expense).

Each element in a total alarm system must be balanced, carefully matched, and protected in every conceivable area of vulnerability. Consideration must be given not only to the economics involved, but also to the type of crime experienced in the neighborhood, the reliability of the local alarm bringing a response from the neighbors, and the integrity of the monitoring service or reporting agency. (Very few owners of protected premises bother to visit the central service even though they may take five days to investigate the background of a prospective employee and two days to purchase a typewriter.)

A security program must be an integrated whole — with each phase growing out of the actual requirements dictated by the unique circumstances affecting the facility to be protected. It must also consider the limitations placed upon it by the attitude of the employees who will control the system. Lastly, efforts must be made to avoid the tendency to create a fortresslike atmosphere, which may prevent unauthorized intrusion while ignoring the real possibility of internal theft. Emphasizing protection of the premises has frequently created a situation that permits employee theft to go undetected and may be a factor that has led to the increase in white-collar crime.

All too often the management of an organization will handle the growing loss from internal theft and external burglary by hiring a retired police officer only to find that this new security director does not understand "civilian" crime. Police work is not necessarily a good preparation for the security field and in fact is less related to it than a background in management. Furthermore, a significant percentage of inventory losses can be traced to the owners or directors of the enterprise being protected. For example, owners of burglarized premises often cover up their normal accounting inventory shrinkages by adding them onto the estimated loss claim when the burglary report is submitted to the insurance company. (To counteract this tendency, some insurance policies stipulate that all burglary losses must be computed after deducting the rate of the previous year's inventory shrinkage.)

When considering that only 20 years ago the only experts in the security field were the friendly neighborhood locksmiths, it becomes clear that building protection and security design comprise a relatively new field. The advances in alarm electronics and the increase in crime have created a new industry that has grown with very little control as to standards and ethics. There are now more private uniformed guards employed in the nation than policemen, and the number of alarms purchased each year far exceeds the growth rate of the general economy. Because security protection now constitutes a major industry, a more professional approach should be applied to the use of the equipment and a more careful analysis should be made before alarm systems are installed anywhere. This chapter deals with physical security and attempts to illustrate the need to customize a system even in the most basic situation.

## DESIGNING FOR SECURITY

Some of the most important considerations that must be analyzed before designing a protection system include the following factors:

1. Exterior Perimeter Protection
   a. Fencing (height and type)
   b. Walls and hedges
   c. Watchdogs
   d. Geese
   e. Guards (contract or in-house)
   f. Exterior lighting
2. Entrance Protection
   a. Doors (strength of door frame, etc.)
   b. Windows (grills vs. foiling)
   c. Miscellaneous entry (roof, basement, etc.)
3. Interior Protection
   a. Lighting
   b. Key control (types of locks)
   c. Special situations (number of hours of operation)
   d. Inventory control (computer safeguards)
   e. Safe and valuable areas

       f.  Alarms (sensors)
       g.  Local annunciation vs. central service
    4.  Environmental Considerations
       a.  Part of building to be protected
       b.  Insurance requirements (UL listed, etc.)
       c.  History of losses
       d.  Type and caliber of employees
       e.  Opening and closing procedures
       f.  Fire and safety regulations
       g.  Delivery and shipping policy
       h.  Situations peculiar to the building
    5.  Police Involvement
       a.  Transmission of alarm signal
       b.  Central service or direct connection to police station panel
       c.  Municipal ordinances
       d.  Police response time

### Exterior Perimeter Protection

The first objective in designing an effective security system is (if at all possible) to control the outer perimeter areas. Barriers should be selected in such a way that although they may deter a would-be burglar they in no way hinder police from responding to a break-in or intrusion signal. Most barriers often pose more of an obstacle to the police than they do to a burglar. It would be impractical to design a security system that anticipates that the police will overcome the barriers every time the alarm goes off (particularly since the rate of false alarms throughout the nation is well over 90 percent of all activations.) The owner of the premises, or a designated official of the organization, should be prepared to meet the police whenever an alarm is recorded — to lead them into and around the premises. Frequently, responding police, when they are unfamiliar with the premises, are hesitant to enter a building if the owner is not present, particularly if the "barriers" are difficult to overcome. There is a growing attitude that treats the police as if they were a private guard force, yet if the police do enter a burglarized premise without the owner being present they are accused of having stolen some of the merchandise after the burglar left.

**Fencing.**  A fence is often considered the first line of defense against intrusion and usually it functions as just that — an obstacle that discourages the would-be intruder. In most situations the fence is not impregnable, but it serves only as the first obstacle in a series of deterrents. Since the purpose of a fence is more symbolic than protective, it should be of the see-through type and no higher than 3 feet, unless unusual circumstances dictate the need for a higher structure. If a fence is to be used as the first line of defense, the mesh opening should be no wider than 2 inches square and the bottom should not be more than 2 inches above solid ground. The chain link fence is probably the most functional type and is appropriate in almost all situations. Barbed wire on the top of a fence typically obstructs only the amateur thief, since the professional burglar has means for circumventing the barrier. Only in rare situations (e.g., a nuclear power plant or storage area for vehicles and trucks) should sophisticated alarms be installed on the fence itself because so many environmental factors (wind, animals, etc.) are known to trigger false alarms. (The reason for limiting the height of the fence to 3 feet in nonindustrial situations is because this is the maximum height that can be seen over by police patroling in a car.)

Structural barriers rarely, if ever, prevent penetration by the determined thief. (After all, convicts continually escape from so-called impenetrable prisons.) Fences can be climbed, walls can be scaled, and locked doors and grilled windows can eventually be bypassed by forceful assaults.

**Walls and Hedges.**    Natural barriers can never be relied upon to function as a positive deterrent to intrusion. All barriers should be strengthened by structural barriers of some kind.

**Watchdogs.**    Watchdogs are more effective than guards in many situations. A watchdog is not only more loyal than the typical guard, but also has a better sense of smell and acute hearing ability. The three general categories of watchdogs include the alarm dog, the harassing dog, and of course the feared attack dog. Most burglars appear to avoid premises displaying a sign saying "Beware of Dog" on the gate or front door. In fact, some security experts claim that there are more buildings displaying this sign than there are trained watchdogs in the nation. The sign itself has proven to be an effective deterrent. If the sign is to be treated seriously, however, the owner should invest in a dog's feeding dish and doghouse to create a more convincing situation.

If watchdogs are to be employed outside or inside the premises, those involved in recommending such a protection technique should be aware of certain factors, such as the lawsuits that can occur if the dog bites an innocent person, the problem of "messes" during the night, and the cost of maintaining such a service. If properly used, watchdogs can be a highly effective system that in some circumstances can totally replace expensive alarms.

One of the first instances of protecting a large commercial establishment with watchdogs occurred in 1949 when a large department store in a metropolitan city decided to try this approach to protect the store at night.

This was a revolutionary idea since the store was located in the heart of the city and the possibility of dogs "smelling" or "messing up" the store was all too real. The results were astonishing. Night theft all but disappeared with the dogs in the store, while the department store across the street experienced an increase in crime in almost the same proportion that robberies decreased in the store with the dog patrol.[1] This is another classic case of controlling crime in one location by relocating it somewhere else.

**Geese.**    Some breeds of geese are formidable "watchdogs." They are sensitive to disturbances and will emit a high-pitched "doink" or "whee-haw" sound when strangers approach. They may even lower their heads and "charge," looking for a good place to bite. Like most animals, they quickly get used to their keepers and are vocal only to strangers. This fact helped the Romans protect themselves against the Gauls thousands of years ago.

Geese are effective in guarding against unauthorized intrusion and are used in many fenced-off sites to detect intruders. One of the world's largest distilleries (Ballantine in Scotland) uses geese to guard their storage areas while the liquor ages, and many missile sites also use geese to protect the interior of a fenced-off area. Usually, the area is wired with small microphones that detect and magnify the strange sounds made by the geese whenever someone approaches a secured area.

The two most popular "guard geese" are the Black African and the white Chinese, both of which are naturals for guard duty purposes. They also make excellent "lawnmowers" and "fertilizers," which are also self-perpetuating. In the event of overpopulation, they are the only security device that can be eaten. They make a fine fare on a Thanksgiving day and three eggs are a gourmet omelet for six persons.

Cracked corn or scratch feed plus a natural lawn is all that is needed. It costs approximately $10 per week for a gaggle of twelve geese. They are hearty in severe temperatures (0°) and adjust well to high temperatures (110°).

**Guards.**    (Guard protection is discussed in Chapter 5.)

**Exterior Lighting.**    Exterior lighting has always been a valuable device to deter nighttime intrusions. Proper use of lighting is such an effective weapon in crime control that many municipalities require business establishments to maintain acceptable levels of lighting at all times. Any light on the outside of a building is better than no light at all, but mercury vapor and high-pressure sodium lighting systems are superior to standard incandescent bulbs and give considerably more light per watt as well. The most energy-efficient kind of lighting is sodium vapor lighting since it consumes 50 percent less energy to produce the same amount of light as mercury vapor lighting. The exact choice of lighting fixtures and their location are determined by the specific dark areas around the building that must be eliminated.

The practice of adding extra lighting to combat a security problem has become almost a tradition in the industry. This policy has recently been questioned, and one government study has actually suggested that in certain situations interior lighting assists the intruder by giving him greater visibility by which to maraud the premises. Lighting, like every other aspect of security, should be carefully investigated before a decision is made on its use. There should be no assumption in developing a security plan or system.

---

Sodium vapor lamps were installed in a parking lot that had been experiencing a spell of vandalism and theft. These lamps give out a soft yellow glow that is perfectly suited for closed-circuit TV cameras used for surveillance. A short time after the lamps were installed, the staff complained because they could not find their cars in the lot since the lamps confused colors. As a result, the lamps were replaced by mercury lamps, but the closed-circuit TV system was thereby rendered less effective. Of course, after a rash of vandalism and car thefts, the lamps were changed back to sodium vapor. This is another case where security became important only after a crime wave occurred. Rarely is security installed before a crime is committed.

---

### Entrance Protection

**Doors.**   After exterior barriers, the first line of defense is the door or entrance into a building. The door is the most vulnerable area and the point where most illegal entries occur. According to the FBI, over 75 percent of all burglaries involve entry through the front or back door. Doors are often incorrectly fitted and have exposed hinges and weak frames. These weaknesses must be corrected before installing locks, since it would be foolish to have high-security locks installed on a door that could be pushed off its hinges.

As the cost of building materials has risen over the years, door security has diminished. The average door built today is of poor grade, often with cardboard filler and a thin covering of decorative soft wood. This hollow-core construction makes it possible to smash a hole through a door with a fist and reach in and unlock the door from the inside. Hollow-core doors are no protection against a determined burglar.

Most doors are delivered with the easy to compromise key-in-the-knob lock and require a second lock for adequate protection. A door should be equipped with a double-cylinder deadlock that unlocks from both the outside and the inside with a key. The lock should have a bolt throw (the distance the bolt travels into the receiver) of no less than an inch. If the door has nontempered glass panels within 40 inches of the doorknob, only a double cylinder deadlock that unlocks from both the inside and the outside with a key should be used. This is recommended in order to prevent an intruder from reaching in through the broken glass to unlock the door from the inside.

Key control is just as important as having secure locks since locks are only as good as the care shown the keys. All keys should be coded and changed periodically. (A stamp that designates "do not duplicate" offers very little assurance that the warning will be followed by the neighborhood locksmith.)

**Windows.**    Windows offer easy access to any building unless special precautions are taken to protect the window opening. Cutting or breaking a hole in window glass is a common practice used by many burglars. Burglary-resistant glazing can improve window security, and if appearance is not an important consideration wiremesh safety glass can be extremely useful.

Window locks have not proven very effective if the frame around the window is rotting or if the locks can be opened once the glass is broken. All windows should be equipped with key locks. Protective grills and grates, while not always aesthetically pleasing, do provide maximum security to all types of windows.

**Miscellaneous Entry.**    Other openings that must be protected are roof openings, transoms, and fire escapes. All these openings must be considered as vulnerable and potentially troublesome. Because human life is more valuable than any possible property loss, a fire escape may be a necessary weakness in any security system. It is possible to construct a fire escape that makes access difficult from the ground by keeping the lowest section off ground level, but no matter what precautions are undertaken the fire escape is a security hazard.

### Interior Protection

There is a growing trend away from barrier or perimeter protection to interior sensor alarms of the intrusion type. Intruders have become so adept at circumventing all types of fences, doors (locks), and walls that the most effective security designs ignore the perimeter of the premises and concentrate on detecting movement inside the premises. The selection of the sensor for a particular situation is extremely difficult and is the main object of most security surveys.

**Alarms (sensors).**   Popularly used devices like ultrasonic detectors provide excellent protection for most situations, but they could cause problems if used in a building totally enclosed with glass panels that tend to rattle when heavy trucks move by. Similarly, audio detectors continually have a high false alarm rate if used in noisy, crowded neighborhoods, while microwave units are troublesome if used in old wooden buildings (e.g., historic sites). As was previously stated, seldom are two situations or buildings so similar that they can use the same alarm configuration. When systems are installed using the size or shape of the room as the only criterion, results have proven less than satisfactory. Another problem area is created when security sensors are treated as just another piece of electrical equipment, which creates an "overkill" situation (too much security). In addition, many alarms are so sensitive that they continually trigger false alarms.

Criteria that must be explored before selecting an intrusion alarm system include:

1. Technical characteristics of the sensor
2. Skill of the installer and knowledge of the salesperson
3. Budget limitations
4. Value of property being protected
5. Reliability of the transmission link (local bells, telephone lines, etc.)
6. Reputation of the central station company
7. Maintenance required
8. Effort required to expand the system
9. Attitude of the local police

Fulfilling these basic considerations will not produce a perfect model but will certainly eliminate the "copycat" syndrome that has been so prevalent in the industry. In addition to all these considerations is the realization that the human element can greatly influence the effectiveness of any system. Some "human aspects" that have been known to shatter an effective system are as follows:

1. An installer who turns out to be dishonest
2. A central station that is not aware of a phone breakdown
3. A master key distributed to anyone who requests it

4.  The last person out of the building forgetting to turn on the alarm
5.  Neighbors who ignore the ringing bell or siren

Even if the system is functioning satisfactorily and every component within the system is in perfect working order, the possibility remains that the system may become obsolete within five years. This is because of rapid changes in the state of the art, the lack of proper maintenance, and the intelligence of the criminal. The only logical method to follow in establishing a total security system that will provide flexibility and adequate protection is to consider each area of vulnerability as equally important. The so-called ultimate system does not exist (or would be so sophisticated that no one would understand how to operate or repair it).

Oftentimes, the most important consideration in selecting any system is the cost of the alarm system in relation to the value of the property being protected. Frequently, jewelry vaults are protected by weak, ineffectual locks, while buildings in which there is no real justification to feel threatened by burglars are protected by systems and central stations that are better suited for nuclear power plants or military bases. This problem is complicated by the fact that architects are not likely to build security features into the building as part of the basic design. The percentage of incorrectly designed alarm systems is difficult to establish since few users of "bad" alarm systems will admit that they have made a mistake. (Ironically, the very individual who was responsible for purchasing the faulty system is usually the person queried about the effectiveness of the system.)

Despite the many incorrect uses of electronic intrusion and surveillance equipment, the growing popularity of sensory devices has had a decided effect in the apprehension of criminals. According to the National Burglar and Fire Alarm Association, premises protected by alarm systems are burglarized from one-half to one-sixth as often as those without alarms. The number of premises protected by alarms is over 4 million, with private residences accounting for 1.5 million of that total. Existing alarm systems have probably helped the police capture over 30,000 criminals annually. When used properly, alarms can significantly reduce the chance of burglary. Alarms — though far from the perfect solution — are still the most effective and economical crime prevention tool available.

Next are some examples of situations where internal and external protection controls and procedures were inadequate, owing to human error rather than a failure of the equipment, to perform their function.

A 12-inch thick steel door protects the front entrance of a world-famous New York City jewelry store. The main entrance is alarmed with every conceivable sensor and there is a direct connection to the police and to a central station.

It is Christmas Eve and the store closes early and dismisses its employees. An accountant from a nearby firm remembers on his way home that he needs to buy a gift for the holiday and rushes into the store at 4:15; upon entering the store he senses that something is amiss. Although he bumps into other holiday shoppers as he makes his way around the cases holding millions of dollars worth of jewels, there are no visible store personnel. After 15 minutes, a guard appears and requests the shoppers to leave since the store had already closed for business a half-hour ago.

Those last-minute shoppers were able to enter one of the most well-alarmed premises in the city without being challenged because someone had forgotten to lock the front door and turn on the alarm system. The central service had not been notified of the early closing and would not have noticed anything wrong until after 5:00 P.M., which would be 45 minutes after the accountant entered the store. Although nothing was stolen, the incident forced the store to immediately redesign the security system and change the lockup procedure.

A school building is constructed in an exclusive section of a Detroit suburb. Because of its circular shape, it wins numerous architectural awards. The rooms are brightly lit and the sun is always shining on 50 percent of the rooms, regardless of the time of the day. The building is an aesthetic masterpiece. After being reviewed in numerous professional journals, it is replicated by other cities, one of which is a school district in the ghetto of a large midwestern city.

The trouble with a round-shaped school in which discipline is a continuous problem is that no control is possible in the corridors. The round configuration prevents monitoring since visibility is limited to 30 feet before the curvature places the corridor out of sight. So while the sun continues to shine on all four sides of the suburban school, the ghetto school was vandalized to such an extent that a major renovation had to be made within 18 months.

City schools require complete surveillance of all corridors — not sunlight — to maintain order. This example is a typical situation in which a "copycat" procedure proved a security disaster.

An industrial plant installs an elaborate closed-circuit TV (CCTV) security surveillance system to monitor the critical areas of its large complex. The CCTV operator, a senior citizen seeking to supplement his retirement income, is paid only the minimum wage. He sleeps all night while sitting in front of the TV monitors. After a successful burglary goes undetected, he is fired and another senior citizen is hired to sleep in front of the TV monitors. (Security is often treated with less respect than a revenue-producing asset, but a breakdown in security can frequently put a company out of business.) This misapplication of priorities must be altered if industry is to overcome the enormous losses from burglary predicted for the 1980 decade.

A young security guard is hired to guard the entrance to a large trucking firm. He is responsible for checking all cargo going out of the building. He is a paroled convict whose background was never checked by the private guard service who hired him. The guard eventually steals more than he checks and the guard service contract is cancelled. A new guard service is given the contract and a new thief is hired to carry out the process again and again.

The supermarket installs an elaborate alarm system to control growing losses from shoplifting. Cameras and mirrors are placed all over the store so every corner of the store is under surveillance. The cashiers at the checkout counters are instructed to check the price labels on all merchandise carefully and are rewarded when they catch any alterations on the label. The management's efforts practically eliminate all shoplifting, yet shrinkage continues to remain at 5 percent of the sales level. Although shoplifters no longer patronize the store, the lowly paid young girls at the checkout counters continue to encourage their families and friends to push $80.00 worth of groceries through the checkout line while only $15.00 is rung up on the register. When all the attention is focused on external theft, it is difficult to monitor the cashiers. The retail establishment suffers more from employee theft than from shoplifting, burglary, and robbery combined.

A bank installs the alarm equipment specified by the federal government under the provisions of the Bank Protection Act of 1968. Cameras are monitored over the teller windows; the bank vaults are protected with audio detectors; and guards patrol the bank lobby. Although this system completely eliminates robbery, the bank vice-president continues to reprogram the computer so that funds can be withdrawn without detection or suspicion.

Losses caused by executive abuse of the computer are far greater than armed bank robbery of tellers. This problem is compounded by the fact that computer theft is very difficult to detect or prove and laws governing this type of crime are vague and difficult to prosecute. Not until 1979 was a federal statute against computer theft passed by Congress.

The stock brokerage firm installs a sophisticated card reader system to prevent employees from moving about in unauthorized areas. All stock certificates are carefully tabulated and recorded. No one can walk out with a negotiable stock certificate without being detected by the elite security force. Yet the lowest-paid employee (the mailroom clerk) continues to open the incoming mail and remove valuable incoming documents, immediately reinserting them in the outgoing mail envelopes addressed to himself. Not only is he using the facilities of the U.S. Post Office to become a rich man, but he doesn't have to pay any commission to the stockbrokers in his firm. And even the rise in the cost of a first-class stamp (from 18 to 20 cents) in 1981 was covered by his firm.

A hospital protects all its exterior exits, carefully monitors visitor and staff movement, locks up all narcotic drugs, and checks inventory regularly. Although this system eliminates thefts of sheets, towels, and toilet tissue, doctors and interns continue to walk out with expensive equipment. This is because the guards are intimidated by the medical professionals but feel confident to search the housekeeping staff. This is another typical case of the reluctance of management to place priority on security as an important function of operating procedures. (In early 1980, the style-conscious public became interested in the "scrub" shirts used by the medical staff in the operating room. As a result, millions of shirts disappeared from hospital storage rooms and laundry carts because the public was willing to pay more for a "real" hospital shirt than for a copy made by a garment manufacturer.)

A major cosmetic firm (with corporate headquarters in New York City) is experiencing difficulty in guarding corporate secrets describing new lipstick formulas and advertisement campaigns. Part of the blame is placed on easy access to executive offices since it is impossible to maintain a secure key control system. To overcome this weakness, all key locks on "important" doors are replaced with push button activated locks. It is believed that any weakness in door control can be overcome simply by changing the push button combination. The concept is logical but the practicability is far from successful. It turns out that most of the executives enjoy the luxury of long and fancy lunches punctuated by the consumption of at least a couple of cocktails. The immediate result of these midday "business meetings" is that the returning executive is unable to handle the complicated task of activating a series of five buttons to open his door. This inability to control the locking mechanism is known as the "martini syndrome," and it resulted in the reinstallation of the simple key lock. This is another example of a built-in reluctance to improve security if it causes inconvenience to the owner of the property.

Probably the most sophisticated and complex security system in existence today is that used to protect nuclear power plants. Because of numerous regulations dictated by the U.S. Department of Energy, as well as the recommendations of several other governmental and private organizations, the systems in use at most power plants create an almost impregnable fortress. There are times, however, when these systems are designed without regard for the environment. These lapses sometimes compromise the entire system. The classic illustration is the system used to guard a nuclear facility in the northern section of the country. The property is surrounded by a fence 10 feet high alarmed with every conceivable sensory device imaginable. It is therefore capable of distinguishing the impact of a leaf from an attempt to climb over the barrier by a human being. It has only one weakness, which was discovered during the first winter of use. When the snow drifts push up against the fence, rising 12 to 15 feet in height, they completely cover the fence and permit animals (or people) to walk "over" the barrier without being detected. If snowfalls are heavy the system is useless. When the snow thaws the alarm system becomes impregnable again. It is one of the best *seasonal* systems ever designed.

## PREMISES SURVEY AND SECURITY PLANNING

Performing a survey to determine the security needs is often limited to obtaining quotations from a few alarm installers or manufacturer salespersons. The results could prove very effective but also could result in poorly designed systems that are not reliable either technically or economically. Although there is no perfect alarm system, there are certain basic functions that all systems must contain in order to provide even a minimum amount of protection. A security survey involves a detailed analysis of the physical and environmental factors as well as the often overlooked attitude of the individual or firm requesting the alarm system.

In order to stress the need for an objective approach in the design of every alarm system, three situations are discussed to illustrate the complexity and uniqueness of each alarm system. The first situation is a single family home, the second is a retail store, and the third is a school building.

### Residential Home Security Survey

Even the basic one-family house can present a challenge when all the technical parameters are considered and all areas of vulnerability are analyzed. While there are several alternatives in the design of the protection system, some are superior to others and the more effective system may be less expensive to install. The size and location of the house are probably the most important and critical factors. A building in a remote location must be treated differently from a structure in a crowded neighborhood even if the buildings are almost identical in architectural design. Entrances should be protected with a high-security locking mechanism, and if any door has a large glass window it must be protected with a double cylinder so that a key is required to open the door from the inside. Protecting all windows with foil is usually aesthetically unacceptable but they can be secured by using magnetic switches or small vibration detectors.

Hidden pressure mats should be used in critical areas (entrances to master bedrooms or in front of all stairs). Panic buttons should be placed by the bed, smoke detectors installed throughout the house, basement windows protected with bars, and most important, neighbors should be notified that the house is alarmed so they will understand the significance of the loud siren or bell going off at any hour of the night.

All of these devices just described operate under mechanical movement and are less prone to false alarms than sophisticated intrusion alarms. Only in rare cases are space alarms (ultrasonic, microwave, audio, etc.) installed in a house because they are inherently susceptible to false triggering due to atmospheric changes and incorrect use and abuse by the homeowner. Of course, if the neighborhood or the value of the property justifies extreme measures, intrusion detectors may be incorporated into the alarm system, but they certainly should not be considered part of the basic system.

While all these conditions and techniques may appear to be quite simple and uncomplicated, in reality they are fairly complex. The choice of magnetic switches, the method of turning the system on and off, and the transmission of the alarm signal must be customized to the particular situation and the level of intelligence of the owner. Until 1970, most alarm systems (commercial and residential) were turned on and off with a key-operated switch mounted directly on the outside face of the front door. The owner would deactivate the alarm simply by turning the key switch into the off position (much like the ignition of a car) before entering the house. The key method was very convenient and a symbolic indication that the building was alarmed. It also indicated to the burglar that compromising the key switch (picking, shorting, etc.) would completely disarm the alarm system. Today, most residential systems have an on or off switch hidden in a closet, with no visible indication as to its exact location. Once the perimeter of the door (any door) is opened the system is activated, but only after a delay (approximately 30 seconds) does it send out an alarm signal. This delay allows the owner to reach the switch box to shut the system off before a signal is transmitted. The time delay sequence is repeated when turning the system on while leaving the house. The switch can be controlled with a key — or a push button panel or even a standard on and off light switch. The final selection must consider the convenience required by the owner as well as the owner's intelligence, since a significant number of false alarm signals result from the carelessness of the owner who forgets to turn the system off after entering the house.

In choosing the magnetic switch, the advantages of the hidden recessed type should be considered before a final selection is made. Most (probably 90 percent) of the magnetic switches in use today are the surface-mounted type only because they are cheaper than the recessed variety and because they are easier to install. They are totally inferior to the hidden (recessed) type. The final choice of magnetic contact switch is usually left up to the installer rather than the owner. (This is a misapplication of responsibility unique to the alarm industry. It is one of the few industries that leaves the selection of a purchased item entirely up to the salesperson without any input or suggestions from the customer other than the cost factor.)

One of the most important phases in the design of a total alarm system, and one that is often deemphasized, is the selection of signal transfer and annunciation of the alarm condition. Companies that possess a central monitoring service generally tend to recommend a direct connection (via telephone lines) to their control panel, where they can monitor the premises and summon the police if an alarm condition lights up their panel. The smaller, independent alarm installation companies usually rely on the use of a local bell or siren mounted directly on the building as the annunciator source. The actual choice of which device to use is determined by a number of factors, both technical and nontechnical. The advantages of local annunciation versus central monitoring has never been adequately addressed by any government regulation or laboratory standard. The ultimate choice must consider the amount of reliability required, the time duration between activation of the alarm signal and the arrival of the police, the cost factor, and the mandatory requirements of the insurance company. Generally, in residential connections the primary advantage of installing a "silent" alarm system and utilizing the services of a central service is that such a combination will assist the police in capturing the burglar. On the other hand, a local blast from a siren will scare the burglar out of the house and possibly get the neighbors to call the police. The final decision about which kind of alarm to use should rest with the homeowner.

Of course, the siren can be silenced by the burglar or ignored by the neighbors, which would completely incapacitate the alarm function. On the other hand, the use of a central system could be compromised if the phone line is cut or out of order, or if the police are too busy to respond within a reasonable time. In other words, there is no perfect system of annunciation, and each situation requires a different set of parameters to satisfy all the conditions for protecting the premises. In addition, no selection should be treated as final, for experience using the system is a very important factor in upgrading and modifying the system. Generally, an alarm system becomes obsolete whenever a burglary goes undetected (or after three years).

### Retail Store Security Survey

In actual square footage, the average retail store is not much larger than a house. Yet the amount of money spent to protect this type of commercial premises far exceeds the cost spent protecting homes. The obvious reason for this disproportionate expenditure is that a retail store advertises that they have valuables whereas a homeowner does not. In addition, in a store the valuables are in full view at all times. Many commercial establishments also are often in locations that are desolate at night and remote from pedestrian activity. This isolation provides the burglar with more time to enter and rob the premises than he would have in a residential neighborhood. As a result of these conditions, retail stores must be better protected than a home. Yet a retail establishment is often alarmed with the identical system used in a private home, owing to the lack of experience on the part of the owner and the alarm installer.

Insurance requirements have forced many retail stores to follow Underwriters Listed (UL) listed standards. Insurance firms sometimes offer reduced premiums when a store has installed an alarm system certified by a UL alarm company. The certificate usually signifies that the premises are monitored by a central service that has fulfilled a list of requirements relative to the physical structure of the building; a security officer or policeman will respond within a specific time (15 minutes for Grade A, 20 minutes for Grade B, and 30 minutes for Grade C); and the telephone line has some type of security protecting it against attack. The different levels of certification signify the extent of protection or response time or both. Certification, however, does not automatically signify that the premises are better protected than noncertified premises. Certification establishes a minimum level of protection that an issuance company has mandated. The homeowner is left totally to the reputation, integrity, and intelligence of the alarm installation firm with which he deals.

A security study on a retail store involves all the basic parameters examined for a private home but is not limited to windows and doors. Skylights, air-conditioning openings, and shipping docks all have to be protected. These areas are of particular importance to a retail store because the openings may be used by juveniles and young children and afterward the courts might interpret that they created an "attractive nuisance." Would-be thieves (under a certain age) have actually broken into stores through the skylight with the intent to steal, but they broke a leg in the fall. Sometimes they then sue the storeowner, who often pays a large settlement to the young thief under the doctrine of "attractive nuisance." In many cases the walls of the building are analyzed to determine the ease of forceful penetration, especially if it is a jewelry or appliance store or any building with a high concentration of valuables. Another factor that has to be considered is the number of employees that will be given the keys that activate and deactivate the alarm system. At a minimum, in actually choosing the alarm equipment the following questions must be answered:

1. Which type of magnetic switches will be used on doors?
2. Will foil be used on the windows versus protective grills inside the window area — or will roll-up doors on the exterior side of the windows be used?
3. What is the feasibility of using intrusion alarms within the ceiling and storage areas?
4. What is the location of the merchandise? (More valuable merchandise should be displayed away from the exit areas and small high-priced items under locked glass counters.)
5. What is the level of phone line security required by the insurance company?
6. What method is used to meet responding police whenever a break-in is reported?
7. What are the other factors as determined by the history of inventory shrinkage?
8. What are the internal auditing procedures, including the receiving and shipping procedures, processing of invoices, and the methods of entering and recording sales slips? (Salespeople can sell expensive items to their friends at low cost unless a method is devised to discourage this practice. Another popular practice is for a salesperson to use an unsuspecting customer's credit card to create two sales slips, returning only one to the customer. The second slip, already marked with the proper card digits, is then

processed later for a very expensive item, the signature is forged, and the salesperson quits. Or a customer purchases an item, like a can of paint, returning the next day with the salesslip, grabbing a can of paint off the selling floor, and requesting a refund on the item after producing a legitimate sales slip. Examples of employee and customer theft are so numerous and often so ingenious that detection is extremely difficult and time consuming.)

A record of every theft, burglary, robbery, and loss must be reported and reviewed, including the crime statistics on the neighborhood. Regular alarm system modifications should be expected in order to update the system. Consequently, each break-in should result in a less vulnerable premises. The ultimate decision as to location and extent of security protection should remain with the store management and not with the alarm company. A cost comparison should be presented by the alarm company to indicate comparable costs between the various transmission systems (McCulloh loop, multiplexing, lease line, or digital dialers) and the grade of line security provided. (It is even possible to have too much protection when the cost of maintaining the system far exceeds the cost of the merchandise being protected.)

No matter what other considerations are involved the retail store alarm system is designed to protect the merchandise from leaving the store at night in the hands of the burglar. In order to accomplish this an alarm device must detect the burglar, who is usually in a hurry. A clever burglar understands the operation of an alarm system and realizes that if he can accomplish his task in a few minutes he will get away with the theft even if the alarm system performed exactly as it was designed to perform. The ideal situation is for the police or security guard to arrive within 3 or 4 minutes, but in most communities this is impossible because of the distances involved and the priorities established by the police department. The most stringent requirement for a UL certificate is a 15-minute response time, but a great deal of damage can be done within this brief period (as proven by statistics). It appears that burglars are becoming more efficient and are performing their jobs within 4 or 5 minutes. Even the best alarm system cannot cope with the "hit and run" phantom thief. In these situations a method has to be applied that forces the burglar to flee without removing any merchandise. One solution that has proven effective is to mount a siren *inside* the store, and when the intrusion is detected, the signal is transmitted both to the central station and the siren. This particular siren creates a powerful noise that simulates the roar of a jet engine (between 125 and 130 decibels). At this level the siren is not functioning as an indicator or local alarm, but as a weapon against the eardrums of the burglar. The loud noise can actually cause damage to the eardrums or at least be so annoying that the burglar cannot function normally. It may never replace the need for a silent burglar alarm, but it is another example of an innovative approach to a situation that cannot be controlled with conventional methods or equipment.

## Public Schools and Specifications

The almost 100,000 schools in this country are under attack from the juvenile population. Never before have so many schools been destroyed as in the past decade. This destructive attitude toward the nation's school systems is a phenomenon shared by both urban and suburban districts. Some experts estimate that the school systems have purchased more alarms during the 1970s than any other industry, and the predictions for the 1980s indicate that this trend will continue to the end of the century. The choice of an alarm system for a school poses problems that are not shared by any other institution. Some of the unique considerations that occur in schools and cause problems with alarm system functions are as follows:

1.  The entire custodial staff is responsible for turning the system on or off and they often forget to activate the system because they have no vested rights in the property and its protection. Furthermore, whenever an alarm is received, a member of the custodial staff is usually required to respond to admit the police. If there are numerous false alarms, a lot of sleep is lost by both the custodial staff and the police for no justifiable reason.
2.  Installation of the system must go out for public bid since it involves a public agency. Preparation of these technical specifications usually falls within the purvue of the business manager who has little or no knowledge of the subject. Small school districts rely on the installer to prepare the specification, a situation that has caused a great number of problems in the system's operation.
3.  Even if the system detects an intruder, the buildings are so large that it is very difficult to find the vandal or thief despite a thorough search. This problem forces many schools to install a "zoned" system so that the exact section of the building in which the intrusion is taking place is clearly indicated.
4.  Maintenance is a huge problem because maintenance contracts involve very complicated bidding procedures, and additionally, most alarm installers are technically unqualified to test and repair the complex electronic components used in most alarm systems.
5.  There are so many windows in schools that perimeter protection is a practical impossibility.

6.  The alarm devices are exposed during the day to vandalism by the student population.
7.  The police usually place school security low in priority since the items taken are usually relatively inexpensive and the judicial system tends to be lenient when the youth or vandal is identified.

As a result of these and other special conditions, providing security in a school is a very difficult operation. One large school district (Newark, New Jersey) went through a procedure that can be assumed to be typical for large school districts everywhere. In 1972, the Newark (New Jersey) school system hired an engineering firm to draw up a set of alarm system specifications for protecting 68 of the 100 school buildings in the city. Using these specifications, an electrical contractor was awarded the contract to install the complex system that was to be monitored on an annunciator panel in the Newark Board of Education headquarters.

After four turbulent years of error, testing, redesigning, accusations, frustrations, and despair, the Newark school system became the owner of $500,000.00 worth of nonfunctioning electronic equipment. After many months of negotiations and a grand jury investigation, it was shown that the system appeared to fulfill all the requirements of the specifications except for one detail — it did not work.[2]

Everyone agreed that the concepts used in the original design indicated that if the components functioned as claimed in the manufacturer's literature, the system would have provided more than adequate protection. The reasons for its failure depended on the person being asked. The designer said it was a phone line problem; the installer blamed it on the mismatched combination of equipment; and the manufacturer was sorry he sold it to the installer.

The equipment consisted of an obsolete audio detector, a multiheaded ultrasonic sensor, and numerous surface-mounted magnetic door contact switches. The audio unit detected outside noises and was unable to operate "off" the speakers of the public address system. The ultrasonic heads broke down from misuse and the magnetic switches were constantly being vandalized. The school system had to go through a three-year period of redesign and testing before all the problems were corrected. Almost all school districts go through this learning experience in which they follow a predictable pattern:

• Phase I — Soliciting bids through local alarm vendors who often have little or no experience in the school environment.
• Phase II — Awarding the contract to a low bidder who uses whatever equipment he wants.
• Phase III — Making final payment to the alarm installer, who blames the failures on the equipment and the phone company.

- Phase IV — Abandoning the system, with the next business administrator hiring another alarm company to start the process over again.

Hopefully, personnel responsible for the selection of the alarm system will develop the confidence to become involved in the design of the system and recognize the difference between a good alarm system and a marginal system. While the original Newark experience was a disaster, the school system eventually developed the expertise to design one of the most effective systems in the nation. This learning experience was time consuming and costly, and only large urban cities can afford to participate in this procedure. What is really needed is some form of a clearinghouse where information can be exchanged between school districts. Up to now, each district has been at the mercy of the local alarm company.

One of the most innovative ideas that evolved out of the Newark experience was the fact that the alarm system was modified to monitor the energy systems in each school. The energy savings alone paid for the operational costs of the alarm system. Another concept that was developed was the use of electromagnetic locks on secondary exit doors. The use of this device was discouraged because of the potential fire hazard that it implied. However, when officials became aware that most secondary doors in schools were locked with chains, the use of electromagnetic hardware was approved and eventually the New Jersey State Department of Education sanctioned its use all over the state. (New Jersey accepted the electromagnetic door lock in 1982.) The locks are mounted on the top edge of each door, and when electric current flows through the unit, it holds the door shut, making the panic hardware useless. The power to the unit is supplied through the fire alarm system, which, when triggered, disconnects the power to the electromagnetic hardware, which then permits individuals to leave by operating the panic hardware. The system stopped unauthorized intrusion and did not compromise the safety of the students (see Figure 6-1).

Only a very few school districts have the necessary technical staff to institute innovative ideas or to prepare a detailed engineering specification and even fewer of them have the confidence to reject bids from unqualified bidders. To illustrate the details required for a thorough specification, the following excerpts are reprinted from a New York City alarm specification awarded in the spring of 1980 to a low bidder for a single school. The estimated cost schedule listed $9000 for material and $16,000 for labor. This amount covered only the ultrasonic equipment and labor to secure all corridors in a four-story building, protect 30 classrooms, and zone the system into five zones. It did not cover the method of annunciation or maintenance.

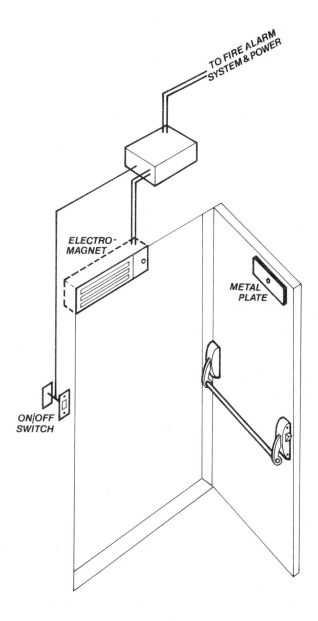

Figure 6-1. Electromagnetic lock system.

## TYPICAL ALARM SPECIFICATION

### Ultrasonic Intrusion Alarm System at P.S. 22, Borough of Manhattan

Bid Opening: April 15, 1980

Work Included

This contractor shall furnish all labor, materials, control panel, sensing devices, power and control wiring, alarm devices, and other necessary appurtenances to install a complete security system as described in the hereinafter schedule specification. Before starting work contractor shall arrange a job meeting with Board of Education inspector to review specification requirements.

2.1 *Description of New Equipment*
   A. *Relay Control Panel*
      1. *Type A relay control* panel shall be UL approved, complete with adjustable entry and exit delays, self-restoring alarm shutoff, two-zone protective circuit, fire alarm zone, remote control operations, and a 5AH battery chargeable from a power supply module with automatic transfer to a standby battery. Panel shall be modified as required to include the following:
         a. Automatic mechanical counter which shall register the number of times the system is triggered into alarm condition. The counter shall be nonresettable, have a minimum of three digits, and be visible when the panel door is closed.
         b. N.O. dry contacts for connection to central station transmitter in a separate junction box adjacent to panel.
         c. 12-volt power supply for operation of alarm devices.
         d. Three spare keys for control panel.
      2. *Type B relay control* panel shall be a multiple-zone panel for up to 22 zones consisting of main control unit with two zones plus a 24-hour panic circuit, built-in entry or exit delay, bell shutoff and restore, ac-power LED indicator plus alarm memory and bell or battery test switch. Entry or exit delay zone shall be fixed at 45 seconds; 24-hour panic zone shall operate with any latching-type holdup device. Each of these zones shall have its individual LED indicator. Automatic bell shutoff and restore shall be set at 12 minutes.
         The remaining zones (up to twenty) shall consist of four zone expansion modules. Each zone shall be *independent* and capa-

ble *of connection to and activating a digital communicator* regardless of the status of the other zones. Expansion modules shall be powered from a power source of main control unit. Two of the four zones in each module shall be field convertible to 24-hour supervised zones. Each zone shall be equipped with a zone LED which will light and stay lit, when a loop is disturbed, until the system is disarmed. Above each zone LED shall be a switch which can be used to shut out individual zones if it is desired to partially arm the system. Any attempt to shunt out a zone once the system is armed shall trigger an alarm for that zone. Zone switches may be turned on at any time. Type B relay panel shall be 1024 main control with 1034 four-zone expansion modules or equal to provide number of zones specified. Type B relay panel shall be modified as specified for Type A relay panel.

B. *Ultrasonic Control Panel*
  1. Type A ultrasonic control panel shall be a master transceiver unit and have capacity for an additional eighteen transmitters and receivers or nine transceivers and 1000 feet of cable. Control transceiver shall be equipped with lead acid standby battery with 35-hour capacity, phantom walk test light, and on-off test switch. Ultrasonic control transceiver shall be as per Sontrix No. 1508, complete with transformer and battery, or approved equal.
  2. Type B Ultrasonic control panel shall be as follows:
    a. Capacity for up to 200 transmitters and receivers.
    b. Capacity for 100,000 feet of cable with up to 2000 feet on each run.
    c. Equipped with lead acid standby battery and charger. Battery shall have 35 hours capacity.
    d. Provided with Sonalert.
    e. Provided with double pole, double throw output relay which is activated when panel goes into alarm.
    f. Derive power from 16-volt secondary of a 120/16 volt transformer. Suitable transformer with primary and secondary leads shall be provided with panel.
    g. Provided with "on," "off," and "test" switch.
    h. Provided with transmitter circuit to which all transmitters are connected and derive power.
    i. Provided with receiver circuit to which all receivers are connected.
    j. Provided with receiver sensitivity control.
    k. Provided with three spare keys for panel.
  Type B ultrasonic control panel shall be Sontrix No. ASP2001, complete with transformer and battery, or approved equal.

3.  Type C Ultrasonic control panel shall have same characteristics specified for Type B ultrasonic control panel and in addition be complete with main control and additional four zones, for connection of sensing equipment, through auxiliary modules. Each zone shall have a separate double pole, double throw relay which is activated when its respective zone is triggered into alarm. Master control panel shall have main control and four processing boards within a single cabinet having an "instant information" window all as per product or approved equal with suitable transformer.

C.  *Zone Switches* (for Type B ultrasonic panel)
Zone switches shall be military-type toggle switches (5 amp. rating) mounted on cover of 515B hinged cabinet. Switches shall be double pole, single throw for disconnecting receiver circuits or transmitter circuits, or both, as specified. Engraved nameplate shall be mounted over each switch to designate area it controls as specified elsewhere in this specification.

D.  *Alarm Device Switches*
Alarm device switches shall be military-type toggle switches (5 amp. rating) single pole, single throw. Switches shall be mounted on cover of an Ademco 515B hinged cabinet. Alarm device switches and zone switches (where used) may be mounted on one 515B cabinet. Engraved nameplate shall be mounted over each switch to indicate alarm device it controls as specified elsewhere in this specification.

E.  *Transformers*
Transformers and power supplies for relay control panel, ultrasonic panel, digital communicators, and alarm devices shall be installed in a hinged metal box at location specified. Unless otherwise specified, transformer for ultrasonic panel shall be 120V/16VAC, 20 VA, and transformer for digital communicator shall be 120V/16VAC, 20VA. All other transformers and power supplies shall be as specified elsewhere in this specification. Contractor may at his option install multivoltage transformer of sufficient rating complete with fused terminal strip for power to each panel and alarm device.

F.  *Ultrasonic Sensing Devices*
1.  *Transmitters and Receivers*
*Omnidirectional receivers and transmitters* shall be compatible with ultrasonic master control panel and capable of being recessed in hung ceilings. Receivers shall be provided with variable sensitivity control. In locations without hung ceilings, contractor shall provide surface-mounted box. Omnidirectional trans-

mitters and receivers shall be respective. *Semidirectional receivers and transmitters* shall be compatible with ultrasonic master control panel and mounted in a deep surface metal raceway box with stainless steel cover with opening for transducer head. Semidirectional transmitters and receivers shall be respective. Where transmitters and receivers are specified as combined units (transceivers will not be accepted), transmitters and receivers shall be alternately spaced in the specified area. Spacing between transmitters and receivers shall not exceed 25 feet; exact locations shall be adjusted to provide maximum coverage without false alarms. Proximity to bells, air vents, or shafts shall be avoided without exceeding the 25-foot spacing limitation.

2. *Ultrasonic General Use Transceivers shall be as follows:*
   a. Compatible with ultrasonic master control panel.
   b. Adjustable transducers.
   c. Approximately 700 square feet of coverage.
   d. Phantom LED walk test light shall be disconnected internally as per manufacturer's recommendations.
   e. Each transceiver shall be provided with a separate formed metal screen guard.
   Ultrasonic general use transceivers shall be Sontrix TR-2 with PS-8 formed metal screen, or approved equal.

3. *Ultrasonic Long-range Transceivers shall be as follows:*
   a. Compatible with ultrasonic master control panel.
   b. Provides 60 to 90 feet of narrow coverage, 6 feet wide and 60-foot distance in free space.
   c. Each transceiver shall be provided with a separate formed metal screen guard.
   Ultrasonic long-range transceivers shall be Sontrix TR60 with PS60 formed metal screen, or approved equal.

4. *Audible Remote Sonalert shall be as follows:*
   a. Surface mounted on ceiling.
   b. Shall be used for test purposes to determine if transmitters and receivers are operating.
   c. Shall produce an audible signal when master control is in walk–test position and receivers are triggered into alarm.
   d. Shall be wired into receiver circuit and derive power from master control.
   Audible remote sonalert units shall be Sontrix RS-1 or approved equal.

G. *Magnetic Contact Switches*
Each magnetic contact switch shall consist of two separate parts, completely concealed in a dust-free casing and capable of being

recess mounted in door or window. When the two parts are installed adjacent to each other, the magnetic switch is held in the closed position. The contact switch shall be recess mounted in upper frame of door and approximately in center of opening. Frame and door shall be drilled to receive switch parts. Magnetic contact switches shall be of the *wide-gap type*.

H. *Roll-up Door Contacts*

Roll-up door contacts shall be suitable for mounting at the base of garage and roll-up doors. The switch portion shall be contained in a low-profile cast aluminum housing and anchored directly to the floor. Contact shall be designed so vehicles can pass over it without causing damage and water-front compound shall protect switch mechanism from water and shock protection. Contact shall be mounted in a weatherproof cast aluminum housing and switch shall be a single pole, double throw magnetic reed with insulated sleeves coming from the reed switch. Roll-up door contacts shall be equal complete with 18-inch aluminum tubing to protect wires and No. 58 junction box.

I. *Photocell Detectors*

Photocell detector units shall be pulsed infrared type with transmitter and receiver in same enclosure. Units shall be suitable for surface mounting, have NO/NC relay contacts, operate on 12VAC, and be equipped with standby battery. Units shall produce infrared beam that is completely invisible to the eye and be equipped with gating circuit so the receiver responds only to its respective transmitter. Any interruption in the amplitude of the reflected beam caused by an object in its path shall cause the unit to trip.

The specification continues for 15 pages more listing in technical detail the description of each component, the size of the connecting wire, the method of installation, and the exact location of each intrusion detector. (The estimated cost was $25,000.) Very few organizations (especially small school districts) have the staff or capability to prepare a specification in such minute detail. As a result, most large installations are designed by the installer or equipment manufacturer. In reality, any complex system should reflect the needs and talents of the user rather than the whim of the installer. Until security is given more priority by the nation's school systems it will continue to baffle school officials and their staffs. This situation is shared by most large organizations (governmental as well as private). The problems associated with preparing specifications are compounded by the fact that even the most sophisticated organizations are not only limited in their ability to design a security system but are also incapable of monitoring the installation to determine if it conforms to the specification requirements.

## ELECTRONIC EAVESDROPPING AND COUNTERMEASURES

No one knows how much bugging, wire tapping, or industrial espionage occurs each year, or what this theft of information costs businesses in dollars. Although electronic surveillance is illegal in the United States and Canada, such practices continue to grow because the rewards are great, the risks are few, and the technology is readily available.

Most corporate information is "given away" by employees who wittingly or unwittingly "leak" information about their workplace. Whether or not these employees are being paid for the information they give out, they are expensive security risks to business.

The potential information thief may be a disgruntled employee; a "spy" planted by a competitor; or a freelance operator posing as a contract guard, repairperson, or cleaning service employee. The modus operandi used include tape recordings, radio transmissions, telephone lines, photographs, xerography, paperwork disposed of in the garbage, and word of mouth.

Electronic surveillance crimes are covered under Title III of the Omnibus Crime Control and Safe Streets Act of 1968 (18 U.S.C. — 2500–20). This law provides penalties for anyone who intercepts or discloses the contents of any oral or wire communications to which they are not an invited party, by use of any electronic or mechanical means. It also prohibits the manufacture, sale, advertising, or possession of eavesdropping devices. This crime is considered a felony, with a punishment of up to five years in prison, a fine of not more than $10,000, or both.

Although the laws against electronic surveillance are stringent, it is a very difficult crime to detect. For this reason, management has been consistently resistant to admitting the problem of information theft. Often, its effects are attributed to coincidence or a competitor's superior abilities or both. Unlike other segments of the assets protection program, the need for information protection is difficult to document. Although the potential savings are high, the concept of loss is a nebulous one.

Information protection must become a vital component of the overall security program. The cost of protecting corporate information is small when compared to the value of lost proprietary information. The two most important elements in designing an information protection and electronic countermeasure program are the selection of proper personnel and equipment.

### Proper Personnel

The overall quality and effectiveness of the information protection program will be directly proportionate to the knowledge and enthusiasm of the person selected to carry it out. The candidate chosen should have the following qualifications:

1. An electronics background with an emphasis on information transmission systems, and some knowledge of basic physics.
2. State-of-the-art knowledge of security technology and a continuing quest to learn more.
3. The ability to teach and supervise.
4. The flexibility to work unusual hours and travel to other company locations on a regular basis.
5. The ability to communicate with corporate management in a clear, convincing way through direct oral and written communications.

Protection of company secrets requires the cooperation of all employees. The ability of the information security specialist (ISS) to mesh with and move the rest of the corporate community smoothly is vital to the overall effectiveness of the effort. This person must be able to communicate to others the need for information safeguards and to supervise assistants when conducting periodic audio surveillance detection sweeps. Out of necessity, much of this work will be done after normal business hours. This is when much can be learned about the general lack of information within corporations, and eavesdropping detection sweeps can be made without alerting the rest of the employees or disrupting the daily routine.

### Equipment

Once the right person has been employed as the information security specialist, the next step is to equip the department with the proper instrumentation to aid in eavesdropping detection. Following is a typical "shopping list" that might be proposed:

1. *Nonlinear Junction Detector* (approximate cost: $18,000) — The nonlinear junction detector is a microwave transceiver that detects the existence of semiconductors within its operational range and alerts the operators to that fact. This unit has become the ideal instrument to detect hidden transmitters, tape recorders, amplified microphones, voice-activated switches, and other electronic circuits. Detection of these semiconductors will occur even if the circuit they are in is turned off or is broken at the time of the

sweep. The unit is highly portable, thus lending itself for use in corporate limousines and aircraft. Depending upon the medium, the unit can "see" from 3 to 6 inches into an object. (This unit is only available from Microlab/FXR, Livingston, N.J. 07039.)

2. *Telephone Analyzer* (approximate cost: $4500 to $8000) — The telephone analyzer, available from at least five major manufacturers, is comprised of several common electrical test instruments. A complete system should be able to perform the following tests and measurements: (a) resistance measurements, (b) capacitance measurements, (c) inductance measurements, (d) hi-gain amplification testing, (e) pulsed high voltage tests, (f) testing for single and multiple tone activation, (g) current measurements, (h) voltage measurements, and (i) a method of testing for audio leakage on all combinations of wires leading to the phone unit.

Additional, but nonessential, options that can be considered include a *cathode ray vector scope*. With this device, the Lissajous figures of the wires being tested can be observed. This aids in determining the electrical characteristics of an "unknown" in a circuit, giving a clue to its identity. Adaptor cables and complete instructions for use on the major phone systems should be included.

Another option for telephone testing is the *time domain reflectometer*. This is an excellent piece of test gear designed to locate major faults along the length of a cable. This device will show how far away the wires have been cut by vandals or shorted out by a watermain break, and the location of some taps. This device, however, has limitations as a telephone surveillance countermeasure because a well-placed bug may easily slip by it.

Because of the nature of telecommunication transmissions, absolute telephone privacy should never be assumed. This is especially true in international traffic, much of which is routinely monitored by governments. In any community, one must also keep in mind that company employees may have relatives, friends, or "union brothers" who work for the local company, thus further compromising security. Since certain types of bugs or taps do not change the electrical characteristics of the telephone lines, detection by instrumentation is not totally reliable, and a physical search of the lines is necessary.

3. *Digital Volt-Ohm Meter* (approximate cost: $125 to $180) — The digital volt-ohm meter (DVOM) is very helpful when obtaining voltage and current readings at telephone terminations and checking to see if the mysterious wires in the ceiling are "hot."

Although the telephone analyzer is capable of taking the same measurements as the DVOM, the latter unit is smaller and much more portable, allowing the assisting technician to check wiring in tight spots while the ISS is working with the telephone system.

4. *High Gain Audio Amplifier* (approximate cost: $200 to $350) — The high gain audio amplifier is used to determine if audio information is being transmitted over a pair of wires. Cheaper units are even more readily available, but they do not meet the desired specifications for this type of work. Things to look for when making this purchase include:

   a. At least 100db gain at 1kHz/600 ohm load
   b. Several inputs with impedances of approximately 90,000, 10,000, and 700 ohms (protected to more than 250 VDC)
   c. A line driver with a 600-ohm input impedance, supplying several milliamps of current within a range of 12 to 24 volts d.c.
   d. *Options:* Tone output that can be used for line tracing, low-pass filter (reduces high-frequency line noise), low battery indicator, and type of headphones desired

5. *Radio Receiver* — At one time, a good quality receiver was the heart of a complete countermeasures kit. With the advent of the nonlinear junction detector, however, the radio receiver has become only a backup tool. Unless sophisticated transmission techniques are used, radio emissions are fairly easy to detect, and "wireless microphones" are used only by amateur eavesdroppers.

6. *Tool Kit* (approximate cost: $100 to $350) — It is possible to purchase either a prepackaged set of tools or a custom kit assembled to suit specific needs. Essential items include screwdrivers (all types), flashlight, soldering iron and solder, electrical tape, set of wrenches (ratchet or box), hammer and assortment of nails, extra batteries, telephone lineman's handset, pliers (various types), and simple first-aid items.

7. *Forms* (approximate cost: under $50) — Preprinted forms facilitate the sweep effort. Records to be kept include an account of all telephone lines and instruments checked, tests performed and measurements taken, an account of all rooms and areas scanned with the nonlinear junction detector (with results and abnormalities noted), and a master file of areas swept more than once, showing all readings in a side-by-side format for easy comparison.

The forms should be custom designed to suit company needs, easy to read and fill out, and should act as a checklist for the persons conducting the sweep.

### Wiretapping

By far the most common method of information theft is wiretapping. Each year the American Telephone and Telegraph Company receives over 5200 customer requests for wiretap checks.

A typical wiretap check request to the local phone company office is referred to the security department, which is responsible for conducting an investigation. The investigation is conducted by a special agent and two repairpersons. The first repairperson is responsible for physically inspecting the customer's equipment, wiring, and pole connections; meanwhile, the second person tests the suspect lines from the central office frameroom. Only 3.75 percent of all telephone company searches turn up evidence of wiretapping or other tampering for eavesdropping purposes. What is usually discovered during a normal telephone company search tends to be the work of a rank amateur.

Telephone company policy on reporting the existence of wiretaps found on customer lines is generally restrictive. Federal law prohibits the disclosure of a legal device to the subscriber. The phone company will not answer subscribers' questions about the existence or nonexistence of a court order to wiretap their line. If an illegal device is found, both law enforcement officials and the subscriber are notified, and the device is usually removed within 48 hours.

### Consultants

There are few competent professional consultants available in the field of information protection. If a company opts for this form of protection, care should be taken in selecting the proper consultant. Following is a list of questions that should be considered:

1.  Is there a rate sheet? Are rates standard for all clients?
2.  Does the consultant's contract specifically protect your confidentiality?
3.  What is the "expert's" background and training? What instrumentation will be used?
4.  Does the individual have sample reports and recommendations? Ask to see them.
5.  Are scare tactics being used to "sell" you? Make sure your consultant is not a vendor in disguise. You should not have to pay someone to give you a sales pitch.

Consultant services should include a survey that analyzes the generation, flow, and storage of the corporation's information from a security standpoint; an unbiased analysis of security equipment the company proposes to use for information security; and the ability to research information protection topics.

## ALARM EQUIPMENT: THE TECHNICAL ASPECTS OF SECURITY

There has been a great deal of resistance on the part of practitioners in the field of private security to involve themselves in the hardware and electronic area of physical security controls. The whole concept of alarm and perimeter protection has somehow developed into a mysterious subject known only to a few manufacturers and consultants. This situation has made it difficult for the security professional or security student to obtain a working knowledge of one of the most important aspects of private security. No longer can the design of the security system be left solely to the salesperson. The security professional must get involved, and in order to do so he must develop some understanding of the basic principles behind locking devices and electronic sensors.

The following chapters deal with the theory of physical security and cover every conceivable aspect of the subject in a manner that can be understood by a nontechnically educated person.

- Chapter 7 explains the different types of locks in use and attempts to analyze the application and limitation of each type. The discussion includes the history of the lock, the newest innovations in the field, and a description of lock picking.
- Chapter 8 includes a description of the conventional mechanical protection devices. This category includes traps, switches, and single-point detectors.
- Chapter 9 introduces electronic alarms that control and monitor interiors of rooms rather than entrance areas. Such devices as ultrasonic and microwave detectors are described along with passive infrared and audio detectors. The subject is presented in a manner that enables the reader to understand the basic operational characteristics of the newest sensors on the market and how they can best be used.
- Chapter 10 deals with the important subject of communication and the transfer of an alarm signal to a remote location. Subjects covered include tape and digital dialers, leased line connections, and the recently developed multiplexing equipment.

## NOTES

1. Story related to the author by Frank Fay, Security Director at R. H. Macy in New York City for 40 years.
2. Frazier, Osborne, "Salvaging a School Alarm System," *American School and University,* October 1979, pp. 64–65.

# Chapter 7
# Locking and Door Protection

Most entrance doors and locks in use today serve as protective barriers and are effective against accidental entry, but are generally inadequate against deliberate intrusions like burglary. Nevertheless, the door lock remains as the primary source of protection.

Burglary is often a crime of opportunity in which the criminal seeks out conditions of vulnerability. While a simple lock can discourage an amateur, even a good lock will not stop the experienced burglar. However, it can slow him down to the point where the potential risk of discovery is enough to discourage the attempt.

Sophisticated locking hardware is available to protect all types of buildings in all types of neighborhoods from most attempted break-ins, but since there are few municipal codes governing security (as compared to fire detection equipment), many locking techniques are insufficient or become outdated. As a result, many buildings remain relatively easy prey for the determined criminal, even though some security professionals estimate that 90 percent of all "convenient" break-ins could be eliminated if the proper lock or door protection device were intelligently selected.

This chapter explores all aspects of lock technology, from its simple beginnings in prehistoric times to the complex industry into which it has grown today. It demonstrates that there is no such thing as a "universal" lock, explaining why two locksmiths may render two different solutions for a single door protection problem. A wide range of locks, cylinders, and access control devices are defined and examined from the standpoint of effectiveness and economy. The ultimate aim of this chapter is to provide the information and knowledge necessary to effectively select and utilize locks and protective devices in the design of a total security program.

## LOCK TECHNOLOGY: CAVEMAN TO YALE

The very first lock was probably created when Neanderthal man decided to roll a boulder in front of his cave to protect himself against animal attack. This may have offered some protection toward that end, but it was ineffective against shielding him from other cavemen. From the boulder, prehistoric man moved on to develop a barlike piece of wood that was installed on the inside and across the cave entrance. For a time this method succeeded in keeping out intruders, but only as long as someone remained inside the cave to lift the heavy bar.

The first recorded use of a lock that could be opened from the outside was in Egypt. Excavations in Egyptian tombs have disclosed locks that utilized a massive key to move the locking device from the outside. This device functioned with a series of tumblers and keys. Although the unique key shape developed by the Egyptians has undergone many changes throughout the centuries, the "silhouette" is retained in what is referred to as a warded or skeleton key. The Greeks and Romans replaced this locking device with the padlock, which at first was thought to be an improvement over the warded keyway. Soon, however, it was learned that the key could be easily duplicated by making a wax impression (see Figure 7-1).

It was not until the early 1700s, when the lever tumbler type of lock was produced, that significant improvements were made to the warded lock. The lever tumbler mechanism introduced a very complicated system of combining levers and wards. This lock proved much more difficult to pick and became the standard of the lock industry for over a century.

The main problem with all locks used up to the end of the eighteenth century was that they were handmade, relatively expensive, and they required a large, cumbersome key. Very little was done to improve upon lock technology until the nineteenth century when Linus Yale devised a system to standardize components. Using the ancient pin-tumbler principle, he developed a mechanism that made manufacturing easier and permitted some interchangeability. This was a revolutionary concept since masterkeying was possible for the first time (see Figure 7-2).

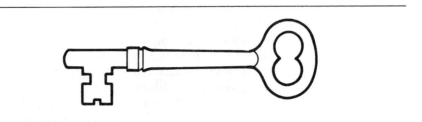

Figure 7-1.  Skeleton key.

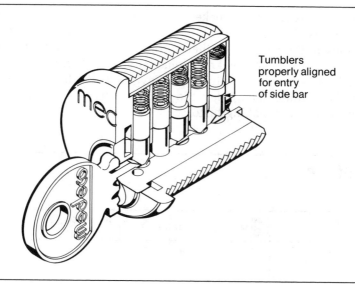

Tumblers
properly aligned
for entry
of side bar

Figure 7-2.   A cut-away of a pin tumbler lock showing the springs and tumblers. When the correct key is inserted into the lock, it will align all of the tumblers in a straight line to allow the plug to turn and operate the locking mechanism. (Courtesy of Medeco Security Locks, Inc.)

Several years later Yale's son, Linus Yale, Jr., developed the first practical pin-tumbler cylinder, which eliminated the drawbacks of his father's invention. In 1860 he patented a lock that used thin keys. Up until that time, the thicker the door, the longer the key had to be to reach the lock. Under this new design, the key-activated mechanism was placed close to the outer face of the door and the length of the key remained the same, whether the door was 1 inch or 1 foot thick. This lock revolutionized the industry because it could be mass produced, consequently making it less expensive.

Another device invented by Yale was the mortise cylinder. This device proved to be one of the most important development in lockmaking history. It created an easily installed threaded cylinder that was completely interchangeable and separate from the locking mechanism.

In the century and a half since the Yale family modernized the door lock, only slight improvements to the original patent design have been made. Today, the pin-tumbler mechanism remains one of the most popular locks on the market. While the Yale lock has provided more than adequate security for over a century, it is now becoming easier to compromise. In the United States a burglary is committed every 13 seconds, and most of these illegal entries are made through doors with traditional pin-tumbler locks and cylinders. Although the cylinder is not always the item compromised, it still represents one of the weakest links in providing door protection. The recent increase in criminal activity has encouraged more changes in lock technology in the last decade than in the preceding hundred years.

The history of lockmaking demonstrates that improvements have been sudden rather than gradual. The Egyptians developed the key; Yale, the mortise cylinder; and today, the high-security pick-resistant cylinder and card reader are making history.

# Functions

| TYPE OF LOCK | KNOB OUTSIDE | LOCK SILHOUETTE | KNOB INSIDE | OPERATION |
|---|---|---|---|---|
| PASSAGE DOOR LATCHSET | | | | Latch bolt by knob from either side. Both knobs always free. |
| STORE DOOR LOCK | | | | Latch bolt by knob from either side, except when both knobs are locked by key in either cylinder. Cylinder in either knob locks or unlocks both knobs. |
| COMMUNICATING DOOR LOCK | | | | Latch bolt by knob from either side, except when knobs are locked by key in either cylinder. Each cylinder locks or unlocks its own knob. |
| COMMUNICATING DOOR KEYLESS LOCK | | | | Latch bolt by knob from either side, except when locked by turn button in either knob. Each turn button locks both knobs. Both turn buttons must be manually returned to unlocked position to release knobs. |
| HOTEL AND MOTEL GUEST ROOM DOOR LOCK | | | | Latch bolt by inside knob at all times. Outside knob always rigid. Latch bolt by guest key and master key in outside knob, except when locking button in inside knob is depressed (use end of key to push), thus shutting out all keys except emergency key. Depressing the locking button operates visual indicator on the face of the outside knob, thus showing that room is occupied. Turning inside knob automatically releases indicator and shutout feature. Latch bolt by emergency key in outside knob at all times. |
| ENTRANCE OR OFFICE DOOR LOCK | | | | Latch bolt by knob from either side, except when outside knob is locked by turn button in inside knob. Inside knob always free. When outside knob is locked, latch bolt may be retracted by turning key or rotating inside knob. Turn button must be manually returned to unlocked position to release outside knob. |
| ENTRANCE OR OFFICE DOOR LOCK | | | | Latch bolt by knob from either side, except when both knobs are locked by turn button in inside knob. Turning key or manually returning turn button to unlocked position releases both knobs. |
| CLASSROOM DOOR LOCK | | | | Latch bolt by knob from either side, except when outside knob is locked by key in cylinder of outside knob. Inside knob is always free. |
| STOREROOM OR EXIT DOOR LOCK | | | | Latch bolt by key from outside and by knob inside. Outside knob always rigid. Inside knob is always free. |

Figure 7-3.   Functions overview.

## TYPICAL LOCKING MECHANISMS

There is a certain amount of confusion surrounding most locking mechanisms. The average consumer treats a lock and its key cylinder as one inseparable unit. This is understandable since the customary purchase of a lock almost always includes the cylinder. In actuality, the lock and cylinder are two distinct entities. The *lock* protects the door against forceable entry. The *cylinder* is the portion of the mechanism that accepts the key and activates the linkage that moves the lock in and out of the door frame.

Figure 7-3 is a brief overview of selected locks currently available including their typical applications.

### Key-in-the-Knob Lock

Key-in-the-knob lock is the most commonly used type of lock. It is found on many inner room doors in commercial and institutional buildings. It incorporates all the features that often invite crime. These units are relatively simple to install, and are also simple to open by picking, smashing, or "loiding" (sliding a celluloid credit card between the frame and the door). There is usually a locking button on the inside knob and a cylinder on the outside. It can be made more resistant to attack by adding a deadlatch that interlocks with the main latch bolt when the door is shut (see Figure 7-4).

Key-in-the-knob locks are frequently specified by architects because they come in many decorative shapes and colors, are easy to install, and are relatively low in cost. In addition, in emergency situations they can be opened from the inside, whereas other types of locks may become stuck in a locked position. If a key-in-the-knob lock is used, it should include the trigger deadlatch feature.

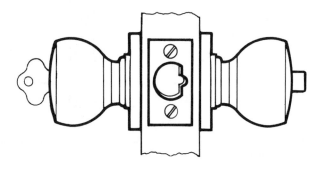

Figure 7-4.   Key-in-the-knob.

A disadvantage of the key-in-the-knob lock is that, because the knob includes the cylinder, the lock is destroyed if the knob is broken off. Once the knob is removed, the opening mechanism is exposed and can be operated with the index finger or a screwdriver. This lock provides minimal security protection.

### Mortise Lock

The mortise lock provides more security than other locks generally provided by the builder. The basic design of this lock has undergone very few alterations since Yale, Jr., introduced it in 1860. Since it is "mortised" into the door body it is not exposed to crude attack, and it often utilizes a deadbolt.

Almost all mortise locks have both the convenient latching (privacy) feature and the deadbolt security feature. Even if the knob is broken off, the burglar still cannot open the door since the knob is not part of the locking mechanism. The bolt cannot be opened by loiding. Additionally, if the bolt throw is at least an inch into the door frame, jimmying and prying are almost impossible (see Figure 7-5).

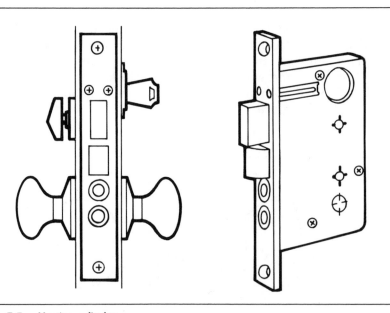

Figure 7-5.   Mortise cylinder.

One of the weaknesses of this lock is that the key cylinder is held in place with a single set screw. If this screw is removed by a thief during the day, he can easily return, remove the cylinder from the outside, and operate the bolt and latch with his fingers. Covering this screw with a protective plate or a little wood putty or nail polish has proven effective in preventing removal, not because it actually prevents tampering, but because it makes the screw readily apparent. Use of aluminum cement or other substances that would prevent future removal of the cylinder by authorized individuals should be avoided. Since this lock is recessed it can weaken the door, and therefore it should be used only in thick wood or steel doors and never in hollow-core doors.

### Rim Locks

The rim lock category includes any lock mounted on the surface area of a door rather than installed through, or mortised into, the side. This lock is usually added after the door is in place, and therefore is not considered a primary lock. The rim lock offers added strength and resistance to normal attack.

Rim locks offer varying levels of security. Many factors should be considered in choosing them. For example, if a door has a glass panel, the lock should have key cylinders on both sides of the door and one-way screws for installation. If someone broke the panel, he could not then reach in and open the door from the inside.

Several rim locks are considered next.

**Vertical Drop Bolt (Segal Lock).**   This is the most popularly used rim lock that interlocks the drop bolt with the door frame stride. It was developed by Samuel Segal in 1912 and is often referred to as a Segalock. This lock ranks in importance along side the invention of the pin-tumbler cylinder in its effect on the locking industry. The lock provides the mechanical advantage of attaching itself to the door frame, which overcomes the vulnerable aspects of a deadbolt that simply slides into (but is unattached) the door frame. This "grabbing" effect prevents loiding, prying, smashing, and, most important, the spreading of the door frame (see Figure 7-6).

**Deadbolt.**   This lock is considered an excellent device for maximum security because it provides adequate protection against most burglary attacks. The better deadbolt locks have at least a 1-inch throw whether they are used on mortise or rim locks.

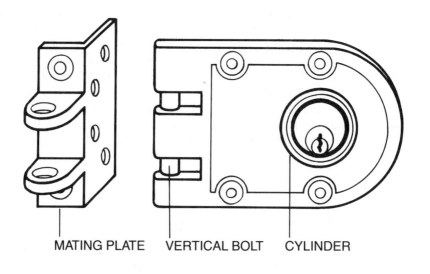

MATING PLATE    VERTICAL BOLT    CYLINDER

Figure 7-6.   Vertical drop bolt.

**Spring Latch.**   It is typically found on the back door of older houses, and offers very little security. This type of lock can be forced or loided with very little difficulty. The spring latch is not a security device, but a "door closer." Its use should be limited to closets and bathrooms, and to prevent the wind from blowing the door open. It should never be used as the primary lock on a front door (see Figure 7-7).

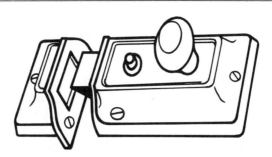

Figure 7-7.   Spring latch.

### Bar Lock and Brace Lock

These devices were introduced to the market by the Fox Police Lock Company and both of them are still sometimes referred to as "police locks." They share a common function of protecting the door by transferring the stress to either the jamb or the floor.

**Bar Lock (horizontal).**   This device is generally used on doors that swing outward (factories, etc.). They are mounted across the center part of the door with the ends resting against the door jamb. The bar gives added strength to the door if the jamb is in good shape. In addition, even if the outside hinge pins are removed, the door cannot be lifted out of place (see Figure 7-8).

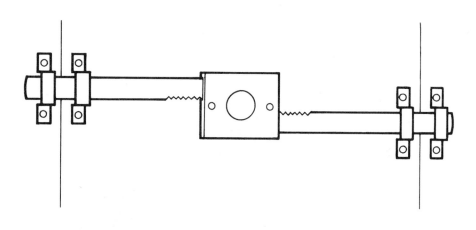

Figure 7-8.   Bar lock.

**Brace Lock (vertical).**   This lock is in the form of a long metal tube that is "braced" against the center section of the door and connected to the floor. It is not an attractive device, but it serves the protective function of transferring the weight placed against the door directly to the floor. It is mostly used with doors that swing inward and is primarily intended for premises to be guarded in the owner's absence (see Figure 7-9).

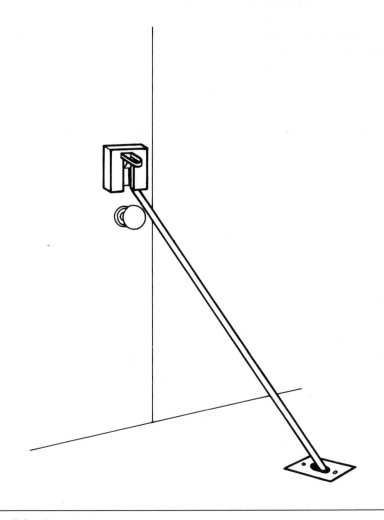

Figure 7-9.   Brace lock.

### Chain Lock

The chain lock is not an effective barrier. Any experienced burglar can reach in and unhook, cut, or snap the chain out of its socket. Although models have been made that sound an alarm if the chain is pulled taut, people tend to ignore the noise (see Figure 7-10).

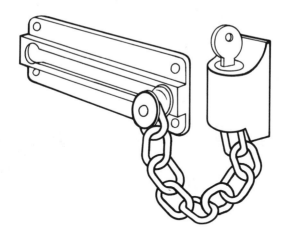

Figure 7-10.    Chain lock.

### Electric Solenoid Lock

The electric solenoid lock is commonly used in apartment houses and banks. This lock is more a convenience device than a security mechanism. The "locking" is accomplished by remotely switching the power on or off, thereby releasing or trapping the latch in the strike. In some instances, loiding is possible against solenoid locks, a weakness that can be minimized by welding a plate over the exposed bolt mechanism. Although they are rarely used, deadlatches further enhance the effectiveness of this type of lock.

### Electromagnetic Lock

The electromagnetic lock represents a new application of an old principle: several electromagnets are used to "bond" the door to its frame. These locks have no moving parts or bolts, and locking and unlocking are positive and instantaneous. This device requires electrical power to operate and can be attached to circuitry controlled by a key, switch, or push button. The holding power of certain commercial units can withstand the pushing of four men. Furthermore, the power can be interconnected to the fire alarm system, which cuts off the power, releasing the "bonding" effect in case of fire. The electromagnetic lock is very practical if a high rate of vandalism makes panic bars and other rim locks impractical. Of course, if the wire is cut the door is no longer in a locked condition (see Figure 7-11).

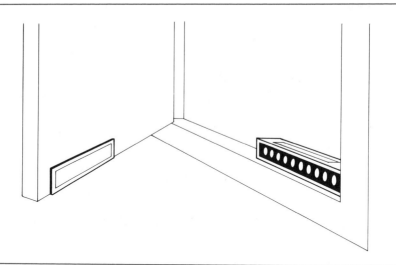

Figure 7-11.   Electro-magnetic lock.

### Panic Bar

The panic bar spans the inside of most public exits — theaters, schools, municipal buildings, etc. This device prevents people from entering the premises, but it opens freely to anyone on the inside. Most are installed because of fire code requirements, not because of any security advantage.

There are some models on the market that, when pushed, activate a switch that sends an electrical signal to a central panel. This mechanism alerts authorities to the opening. The government is now working on a panic bar that will not open until 30 seconds have elapsed. This would permit authorities to investigate the action before the door is opened. This device will not be available until it satisfies fire codes (see Figure 7-12).

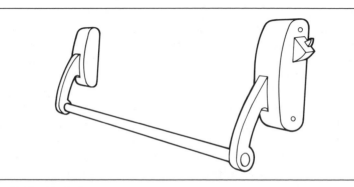

Figure 7-12.   Panic bar.

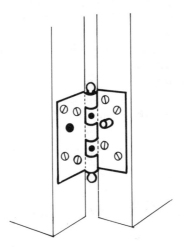

Figure 7-13.   Hinge bolt.

### Hinge Bolt

Hinges are sometimes installed on the wrong side of doors making the hinge pins visible from the outside. They can be removed and the door pivoted on the hinge side right off the frame. The hinge bolt prevents this because even if the hinges are removed, the protruding bolt mounted below the hinges sticks out (into) the door frame (see Figure 7-13).

### CYLINDERS AND KEYS

The old cliché that a chain is only as strong as its weakest link holds true when designing security hardware for a door. A lock may have the strength required to withstand forceable entry, but security is lost if the cylinder is easy to compromise. The average lockset usually comes with a cylinder that is relatively easy to pick. Since picking tools are not difficult to obtain, the situation is a cause of concern to the nation's law enforcement agencies. At the present time, more research and development work is being done in the field of cylinder design than in lock design. This reevaluation of priorities is a recent trend, which was probably encouraged by the fact that sophisticated burglars are concentrating more effort on compromising the cylinder than in forcing the lock mechanism. This new research has produced many high-security cylinders, some of which can resist practically all types of attacks ranging from sensitive picking to smashing by brute force. The choice of cylinder design and key shape should involve as much consideration as the selection of the lock mechanism.

The illustrations indicate how the key (the cuts) actually moves the pins into different positions. If the proper key is used, the pins rest in a position that permits turning of the key, moving of the arm, and unlocking of the door. If the wrong key is set in place, the pins will not fall into the required shear line, preventing the turning of the key. By placing pins on top of other pins, additional shear lines are created that permit the use of master keys. Changing the pin length automatically prevents the old key from functioning (see Figure 7-14).

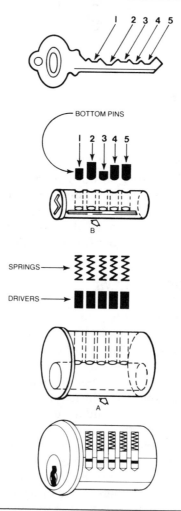

Figure 7-14. Components of a pin-tumbler cylinder.

### Straight Pin-Tumbler Key Cylinder

Since the time Linus Yale perfected its design, the pin-tumbler cylinder has been the most popular key cylinder in use. This device is easily manufactured, and it is a relatively simple task to cut a key to match the pin heights. By placing pins on top of other pins more than one key (shape) can be used to open the same cylinder. This capability of adding second and third levels of pins has created the masterkeying system.

The pin-tumbler cylinder can be made more secure by designing it so that the key blank (before cutting) is unique and unavailable from the local hardware store. Large distributors usually specify a special and restricted key blank, but in general any pin-tumbler lock can be compromised with picking tools.

### Twisting Pin-Tumbler Key Cylinder

One of the most popular cylinders in the high-security category is a system that relies on a basic pin-tumbler principle with pins whose tips are cut on an angle. The key cuts are also on an angle so that the movement of the pins is in a twisting motion as well as up and down. This type of cylinder is almost impossible to pick. The company that designed this twist pin movement did not make locks until very recently, which demonstrates the importance of combining different manufacturers for locks and cylinders (see Figure 7-15).

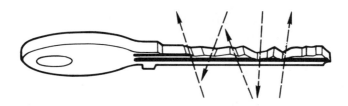

Figure 7-15.    Twisting pin-tumbler key.

### Dimpled Key

The dimpled key is a relatively new key and cylinder design that uses a unique variation of the pin-tumbler concept. It offers far more security than the standard straight up-and-down pin tumbler, and yet it can be master-

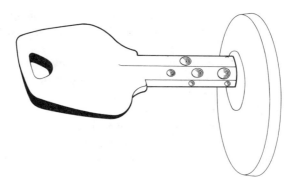

Figure 7-16.    Dimpled key.

keyed with the same flexibility. The unique advantage of using dimples instead of vertical cuts in the key is that the small indentations (dimples) can have various depths. Additionally, this key requires a special machine for duplication because instead of using five-pin configurations like the standard cut key, the dimpled key has four indentations on each side of the key and two on the top.

Not only is the dimpled key difficult to pick, but also it is almost impossible to make wax impressions of it. Each key has a serial number that is recorded by the manufacturer and an authorized signature must be provided in order to obtain a duplicate key. Nationwide, there are few machines available that are capable of duplicating this type of key, which provides the dimpled key with a unique control feature not available with the standard key (see Figure 7-16).

### Round Keyway

Round keyways are usually used on vending machines and alarm panels. They are more secure than the simple pin-tumbler cylinder because the pins are located in the rear of the cylinder instead of on top of the unit. Consequently, they cannot be picked with the standard set of lock picks. When this mechanism was first introduced, it appeared to be a major advance in cylinder design. However, soon an inexpensive tool was developed that simulated almost every round key (see Figure 7-17 and Figure 7-18).

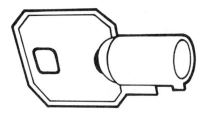

Figure 7-17.   Round key.

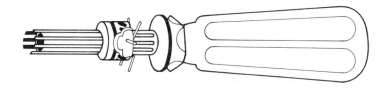

Figure 7-18.   Pick for round keyway.

### Other Cylinders

While there are a few other speciality cylinders, the major choices in pin-tumbler cylinders fall within the units described. With all their limitations, they successfully protect millions of doors. There is no recommendation to use only high-security cylinders since pick resistance is not always the criterion that is important. For example, it would be senseless to install a high-security cylinder on a glass door, since the simple act of breaking the glass and reaching in overcomes all the design advantages of a high-security cylinder. On the other hand, there are many situations in which protection requirements warrant higher security cylinders than the poorly designed ones now protecting many doors. Balancing the cost against the vulnerability factor is a task that the architect and builder should seriously consider.

### SPECIAL LOCKS

There are many specialty locks that cannot be adequately covered in a book of this type. They range from telephone dial locks to computer room locks. It has been a tradition in the locksmithing industry to develop a unique lock for every situation. Some locks become obsolete even before they are manufactured, while others disappear soon after they are introduced.

One recent lock cylinder that reached the consumer market required the complete capture of the key before the cylinder could turn. A string was used to remove the disappearing key, but if the string broke it became extremely difficult to recover the key.

Another experimental cylinder permitted two keys of different shapes to operate the cylinder while only one key could be removed after insertion. This captive key was designed for the one-time user, who lost the use of the key upon each entrance. The owner, returning later, had the other key that removed the captured key while opening the door. It was an excellent idea, but people got the similar looking keys mixed up and the device soon disappeared from the market.

While these two examples describe failures, there are numerous special locks and cylinders that are highly successful and fill a real need.

### The Typewriter Lock

The typewriter lock is an example of a locking device that is more complex than most people realize. The most common typewriter lock bolts the typewriter to the desk. There are at least twenty-five versions of this lock currently on the market. All of them operate in basically the same way: a bolt is screwed through a hole in the desk and directly into the bottom of the typewriter. The bolt head is protected by use of a round lock that has to be removed before the bolt can be turned with a screwdriver. This technique not only mars the desk, but also has proven ineffective since the normal vibration of the typewriter causes the bolt to vibrate out of position. Burg-

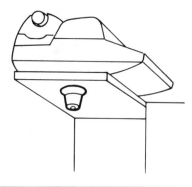

Figure 7-19.   Conventional typewriter bolt.

lars have learned that the bolt can be "ripped" out by applying a pipe over the lock and bending it out of position (see Figure 7-19).

A more effective typewriter lock that uses a totally innovative concept was introduced to the market in 1982. This new lock uses an adhesive plate to attach the typewriter to the desk. The holding strength of the "glued pad" is greater than the bolt and it doesn't mar the desk with holes. In this technique, the typewriter (or calculator or computer, etc.), is "glued" to a plate with four protruding bolt-shaped devices sticking out of the unit. A second adhesive pad is mounted on the desk top with a maze that captures the upper plate bolts. Once the upper plate is inserted into the bottom maze, the units are locked in place and only someone with a knowledge of the maze can separate the two units. No locks are involved and no tools are required to install the system. This unique approach is an example of the need to be innovative even when dealing with the conventional locking sector of the security industry. More and more specialized locks are entering the market to fulfill requirements that did not exist a decade ago (see Figure 7-20).

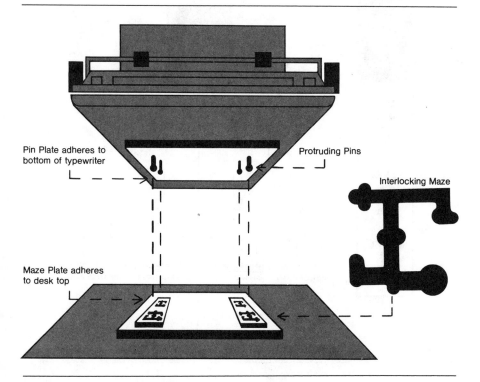

Figure 7-20. Adhesive typewriter lock.

### Other Special Locks

Other special locks include vault locks, padlocks, combination locks, car locks, luggage locks, and phone locks. Some padlocks on the market are "shackless," which means that there is practically no neck area for a metal cutter to grab. Combination locks available include locks that allow the owner to set his own combination rather than accept a preset series. This is a definite advantage to the consumer since locksmith code lists are readily available to anyone who requests them.

There are numerous other locking devices of which very few people are aware. All too often door openings are designed around available locking hardware instead of vice versa. Choosing a lock is a complex task, but with proper education the consumer can be assisted in making an effective choice.

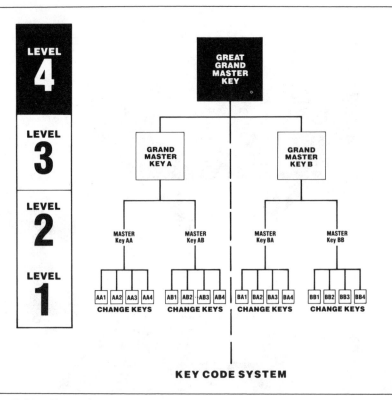

Figure 7-21.   Key code system.

## MASTERKEYING

A master key is a key that opens more than one type of cylinder. Masterkeying should not be confused with cylinders that are "keyed alike." For example, some homeowners have the same cylinder installed on the back door as on the front door. They can then open both doors with one key. This is not masterkeying because both doors have identical cylinders.

A key that can open one cylinder and no other in a large building complex is referred to as "keyed different." A master key is a key that can open doors that are keyed differently (i.e., doors with different pin configurations). If an employer wishes to have one key that opens the front door and all interior office doors, he would obtain a master key. The building custodian might be granted access to these areas in addition to offices on other floors by means of a grand master key. This system of masterkeying becomes more complicated as the number of different combinations and uses increases. Figures 7-21 and 7-22 indicate some of the typical keying systems for various large installations. In addition, Table 7-1 lists locksmith schools, which are a good source of basic information about locks.

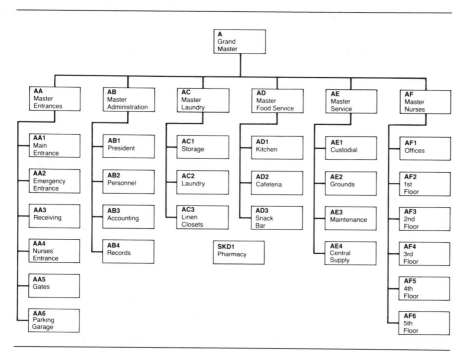

Figure 7-22.   Key control.

**Table 7-1.  Locksmith Schools**

The locksmith schools are a good source of basic information on the operation and maintenance of existing locks. Most provide published lesson books for correspondence courses or concentrated classes. School personnel can provide practical assistance in the development of new locking devices.

Belsaw Institute
315 Westport Rd.
Kansas City, MO 64111
(816) 561-9255

National Crime Prevention Institute
University of Louisville, Shelby Campus
Louisville, KY 41222
(502) 588-6987

California Institute of Locksmithing
14425 Sherman Way
Van Nuys, CA 91405
(213) 944-7425

National School of Locksmithing
    and Alarms
600 W. Jackson Blvd.
Chicago, IL 60606
(312) 930-1999

Central City Occupational Center
c/o William J. Hornbeck
1646 S. Olive St.
Los Angeles, CA 90015
(213) 625-5579

New York School of Locksmithing
152 W. 42nd St.
New York, NY 10036
(212) 354-8777, (800) 223-6466

Golden Gate School of Lock Technology
3722 San Pablo Ave.
Oakland, CA 94608
(415) 654-2622

North Bennett St. Industrial School
39 N. Bennett St.
Boston, MA 02113
(617) 227-0155

Locksmith Business Management School
P.O. Box 8525
Emeryville, CA 94608
(415) 654-2622

Security Systems Management School
1500 Cardinal Dr.
Little Falls, NJ 07424
(201) 265-4512

Lockmasters
476 North A1A
Satellite Beach, FL 32937
(305) 777-2175

Universal School of Masterlocksmithing,
    Inc.
P.O. Box 254868
Sacramento, CA 95825
(916) 645-8593

Locksmithing Institute
1500 Cardinal Dr.
Little Falls, NJ 07424
(201) 256-4512

Wisconsin Institute of Locksmithing
8050 N. Port Washington Rd.
Milwaukee, WI 53217
(414) 352-0330

*Source:* High Security Locking Devices: A State-of-the-Art Report #PB82-165499, U.S. National Bureau of Standards, January 1982.

Regardless of the lock system, if the master key is lost or if too many duplicate keys are in circulation, the system is useless as a protective device.

The best key system is one in which there are no master keys. Since it would be impractical, however, for a custodian or security officer to carry 200 different keys for 200 different doors, it is often necessary to establish some type of masterkeying system. Key control is actually more important than the selection of the lock. If at all possible, only one key should be used, and it should remain in the possession of one authorized individual. Preferably, the key blank should be of a type that is difficult to obtain. There are blanks in circulation that are available only through the manufacturer, and the only way to obtain a duplicate is to inform the manufacturer (using a code word) that another key is needed. It is then sent via registered mail. This procedure may cause a problem in emergency situations, however.

## LOCK PICKING

It is estimated by various sources that over half of all illegal entries are accomplished by amateurs who know very little about sophisticated lock picking. There are few sources of information available in the lock technology field, and often the criminal is more adept than the locksmith at keeping up with new developments in the state of the art.

The skillful locksmith is gradually being replaced by the "key maker" whose technical knowledge has often been obtained solely from a thirty-lesson correspondence course. These courses are open to anyone who can pay the nominal fee. They train hundreds of so-called students each year in the specialized art of lock picking and related subjects.

There is enough information readily available to the determined individual to enable him to open most of the locks in the country. Locksmith supply houses carry a full line of lock picks and "how-to" books that can be ordered through the mail. Code books are also available that list, by serial number, the numbers of many combinations made. The auto industry, too, encodes keys so that it is a simple matter to obtain the key shape for virtually every car on the road today. In easy-to-read tables, the car model, make, and year are listed along with the exact key cuts. This information permits the duplication of any key with the use of a key blank and file. The depths of the key cuts are translated from the serial number on the car ignition (older cars). Although these published lists were developed for the locksmith, they are available to anyone requesting copies.

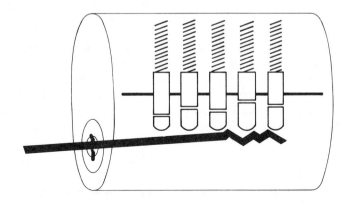

Figure 7-23.   Pick in cylinder.

## Composition of the Pin-Tumbler Cylinder

The majority of all cylinders manufactured contain five pins. Some have six; a few have seven; and some have as little as three or four pins. It is logical to assume that the more pins there are in a cylinder, the more difficult it will be to pick it. While this is true, the combination of the pins (the staggered arrangement of pins of varying lengths) is much more significant than their number.

The quality of a cylinder, in terms of its pick-resistance potential, is determined mainly by the "tolerance" of its component parts. A tolerance measures the degree of precision to which the parts fit together within the cylinder. Every pin-tumbler cylinder, as well as any other mass-produced mechanical apparatus, possesses some degree of tolerance to imperfection (these tolerances become progressively more imperfect as they are used).

While the number of pins and their combination are the elements that resist the picking procedure, the tolerances of the cylinder enable a picking tool to open the lock (see Figure 7-23).

## Operation of the Pin-Tumbler Cylinder

The primary parts of the pin tumbler are the (1) housing, (2) plug (core of the cylinder), (3) bottom pins, (4) drivers, and (5) springs.

It should be noted that the drivers are very similar to the pins and are sometimes called "top pins." In the majority of cylinders, the drivers are of uniform length. The most visible difference between the drivers and the pins is that the drivers are flat on both ends.

A cylinder would be assembled by inserting the springs into the individual (driver) chambers of the housing and then loading the drivers on top of them. Next the pin chambers of the plug are loaded with the pins (in the sequence that corresponds with the key bittings for the proper combination), and the plug is then slipped into the housing. When the chambers of both the housing and plug become vertically aligned, the driver springs press the drivers downward, projecting them into the plug chambers by transmitting spring-loaded pressure onto the pins.

An important item to note in pin-tumbler cylinder operation is the operation level or shear line of the assembled cylinder. This is an imaginary line that bisects the point at which the inner surface of the housing contacts the outer surface of the plug in the immediate area of the upper and lower chamber apertures. When the pins are raised, they in turn propel the drivers, forcing them upward into the housing in opposition to the pressure of the driver springs. At exactly the point when the lower surface of the individual driver in each separate chamber rises above the level of the shear line, the plug is free to rotate within the housing. This is the unlocked position that must be duplicated by picking.

### Picking Tools

Lock picks are usually constructed of tempered spring steel, and are always thinner than the key. The pick is used to probe inside the keyway, elevating each pin to the shear line — much in the manner askewed by the "cuts" in a key.

A second tool, called a tension wrench, is used to apply a regulated amount to inertial tension to the mechanism of the cylinder. This tool is inserted into the lower section of the keyway, and is used to take up the slack or the loose, side-to-side movement of the plug. Both tools must be used in picking (see Figure 7-24).

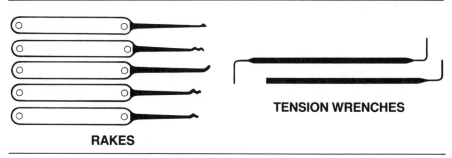

**RAKES**                                    **TENSION WRENCHES**

Figure 7-24.  Picking tool.

### How to Pick a Lock

Insert the pick into the keyway. One at a time, slowly and carefully, locate each pin with the tip of the pick, and gently elevate them. At this time, you are applying a very slight degree of tension, and are testing for an indicating degree of resistance to the upward pressure. Some of the pins will respond very freely as you apply this vertical pressure to them. As the pressure of the pick is relaxed, you will feel the reciprocal pressure of the spring forcing the pin (via the driver) back downward to its original position. The "loose," uncontrolled response will occur until the widest, most "tension-bound" driver is located.

By gradually increasing and relaxing tension and probing each pin one at a time, you will quickly discover that one pin will present a significantly greater degree of resistance to your pick. When you finally feel the "inertia" of the tension-bound driver as it is being pushed up into its chamber in the housing, and thus over the shear line, apply very gentle pressure. If you push it too hard, or too fast, you will force the pin itself over the shear line where the effect of tension will hold it suspended between the housing and the plug. Just raise the pin carefully until you sense a solid, distinct resistance to the applied lifting motion. This will indicate that the driver has been raised above the shear line, and into its chamber in the housing. This solid resistance is caused by the top edge of the pin contacting the misaligned bottom surface of the housing.

When you release pressure at this time, the pin will descend freely into its chamber in the plug, leaving the driver trapped up in its chamber where it can no longer impede rotation of the plug. That pin and driver have been separated at their shear line. It is now important that an even and

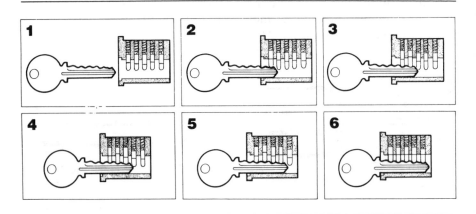

Figure 7-25.   Pin movement.

sensitive degree of tension be maintained. If you significantly relax tension at this time, the misalignment of the plug and housing will decrease. The driver, responding to the compression of the spring, will "escape" and drop back down into the plug. When this occurs, it is normally detectable by a very soft "clicking" that is easily recognizable (see Figure 7-25).

A successful method used in picking is the raking technique. In this procedure, a pick tool is placed at the furthest depth inside the keyway and a forward-and-backward movement is applied (like the raking of leaves). At one point in this movement, the "bouncing" pins will line up correctly for a split second, permitting the turning of the cylinder. The more tolerance, the more likely the rate of success. In addition, the greater the masterkeying, the greater the chances of bouncing into a shear line. If only one key opens the door, there is only one shear line. If the key is mastered, there would be more than one way to create the shear line or there could be additional shear lines.

## THE KEYLESS LOCK: LOCK OF THE FUTURE

Manufacturers have endeavored to devise more pick-resistant lock cylinders, and they have achieved notable success. At the same time, a new category of locking devices has grown in popularity in business and industry; they are known as the "keyless lock." Several of them are considered next.

### Push Button Locks

There are two basic types of push button locks: the mechanical unit, which is mounted directly onto the locking mechanism, and the electrical unit, which can control the lock from a remote location. Both types utilize the same coded push button principle. They are usually available in four- and seven-digit combinations (it would take 41,660 consecutive working days to press all the possible combinations in an attempt to find the correct seven-digit system).

There are, of course, certain advantages to using push button activated locks rather than the standard key type. The most important is that they are pickproof, and have proven practical on most safes and vaults. In addition, there is no key control problem. (Of course, the combination should not be kept in an obvious location or provided to others.)

There are significant disadvantages to using push button locks on the door of an office or private home, however. The combination can be forgotten or read over someone's shoulder, and in addition, criminals have

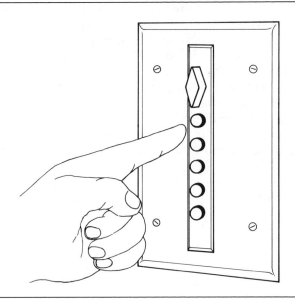

Figure 7-26.   Push button lock.

discovered that the digits in use always show more wear than the unused numbers (see Figure 7-26).

Theoretically, there may be 10,000 possible combinations of three digits on a ten-button lock, but by reading the worn condition on the three most used buttons, a limited number of combinations are possible. If the combination were (1-2-3) and these numbers were identifiable by observing the worn finish, the possible combinations would be limited to (1-3-2), (2-3-1), (2-1-3), (3-1-2), (3-2-1), and finally (1-2-3).

Electric keyless locks operate in much the same manner as mechanical locks, except that the keyboard (buttons) can be located at a place that is remote from the controlled door. The circuitry can be designed to lock out certain sequences, or react to more than one combination of numbers, which permits masterkeying possibilities. Other advantages include a lock-out and alarm signal that responds if combinations are not completed within a specified period of time, or when any button is pushed out of proper sequence.

With recent advances in the technology of microprocessors, the push button device can be expanded to control numerous functions. With a simple six-button panel, six functions can be programmed on the processor. For example:

| Combination | Controls |
|---|---|
| 1236 | Zone 1 |
| 2354 | Zone 2 |
| 3165 | Zone 3 |
| 4621 | Zone 4 |
| 5421 | Zone 5 |
| 6231 | Zone 6 |

Thus, if the security officer wished to enter a six-story building that is completely alarmed, he could disconnect the alarm system from the first floor by pressing (1-2-3-6). This will allow free access to the first floor, but not to the other floors. This same design approach can be used to monitor six doors or six locations.

Another very important advantage of all types of push buttons is that they allow temporary admittance through a door without compromising security. If the conventional key cylinder were used, the only way to delegate admittance would be to give away the key. With combination locks, the holder of the combination need give away only the last digit. For example, if the combination were (1-2-3-4-5), the owner would push (1-2-3-4) and tell the temporary user to push (5) for admittance for one time only. Once (5) is pushed, the only way to activate the lock again is to press the entire series of numbers.

Of the two types of keyless push button locks available, the mechanical lock enjoys wider usage. This is because it is less expensive and may be installed by a locksmith or maintenance employee. The electrical unit, on the other hand, is a more complex mechanism and requires an electrician for installation.

### Magnetic Keyless Locks

Magnetic keyless locks are a new innovation. This device should not be confused with keys that utilize a magnet within the keyway. There are no keyways in this unit. The key is replaced with a small round disc about the size of a half-dollar, coded by various arrangements of small magnets. The small magnetic disc must be aligned with the magnetic field incorporated in the door knob. If everything matches, the handle will turn. This device has not yet achieved wide acceptance.

## ACCESS CONTROL AND IDENTITY VERIFICATION SYSTEMS

The locking mechanisms mentioned possess a potential weakness — they have no intelligence and cannot determine if someone inserting a key into a keyway is authorized to do so, and they cannot prevent a single key from operating the lock without stopping all keys by changing the lock code. Since even the most complex key control procedures cannot prevent duplication and transfer of keys, these shortcomings limit the use of mechanical locks and keys to conventional situations. Consequently, many businesses — especially sensitive government installations, nuclear power plants, and computer complexes — are turning to means beyond locking mechanisms to achieve maximum security protection. This extension of the lock industry is called "access control."

Mechanical keys and cylinders and door locks differ from "access control" systems in many ways. A key tells you only *where* you can enter while access control devices not only tell you where you can enter, but can also identify the user of the "key" and can deny or permit access individually to an unlimited number of persons through hundreds of doors at various times without issuing them different keys. This is a far more sophisticated technique than even the most expensive mechanical lock can offer.

When someone attempts unsuccessfully to gain entry to a traditional lock or cylinder protected doorway, this attempt goes undetected. If an entry attempt is made upon access controlled premises, this foiled attempt can be detected, recorded, and an alarm actuated. When a single key is lost or stolen, some access control systems can void that individual key without affecting any of the other keys that are capable of opening the door. If the lost key is found, it can be made operational again. Groups of keys can be voided and certain keys can be "programmed" to work only on weekends, holidays, or on certain work shifts. This is called "time zoning." It can

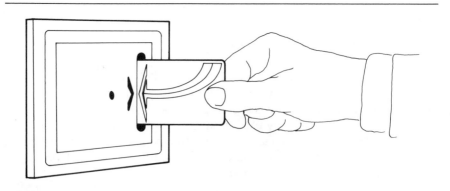

Figure 7-27.   Card reader.

electronically masterkey a system so that any key can be programmed to open any number of doors, and these "special" keys can be automatically or manually changed in the equipment (reprogrammed) without the expense of issuing new keys. It can monitor the status of doors to report if a door is open or closed, locked or unlocked, or if the bolt or latch is actually in its strike. (The lock bolt in the door at Watergate was taped back into an unlocked position.) Access control systems are as far away from keys and locks as the train is from a guided missile (see Figure 7-27).

### History and Development

Just before the turn of the century, Herman Hollerith devised a method of storing data used for taking the census on punched paper cards and sorting them mechanically, an idea that was developed in programming complex patterns used on weaving looms. This "Hollerith" card became the familiar "IBM" card, which became popular during World War II as an identification device. Along with a magnetic "cardkey" (patented in 1941), the IBM card ushered in the era of using a card instead of a key to gain access to a locked area. The cardkey system was easily adaptable to the computerized energy control systems that automatically monitored office lighting, air conditioning, and heating (and monitored alarms). These systems, installed primarily for energy conservation reasons, were modified to incorporate a badge reader and a plastic card with magnetic stripe to store the identification card number. The public acceptance of access control systems really began during this period.

With advancements in electronic circuitry, there are now methods available that not only control the door, but also print out the names of the individuals passing through. Not all the identification devices must be inserted into a slot; some can be read without being removed from a wallet or purse. In addition, there are techniques either available or under development that translate characteristics that, in conjunction with coded cards, are unique to the individual and cannot be duplicated, for example, fingerprints and voice patterns. The cards themselves reflect every conceivable physical process: magnetism, capacitance, inductance, infrared, ultraviolet, translucency, color, magnetic wire, fiber optics, embossing, debossing, precious metal inserts, holography, and even the original punched holes. In fact, the punched hold cards regained popularity during the 1980s because of their use as a disposable hotel key. (Hotels use more locks and keys than any other single industry, and until the increase in court judgments against hotels caused by unauthorized entry into guest rooms in the 1970s, key control was almost nonexistent.)

Just as the space program generated new communications technology, so did the needs of hotels spawn a new lock technology. Hotels also need to void keys that are not returned at checkout, but hotel lock inventors, realizing that connecting all room card readers to a central computer is too costly, have approached the problem differently. They make the *lock code* easily changed. In some systems the change is made automatically when a new guest inserts his key for the first time (Uniqey, Ellissonlok, Yaletronic, Schlage). This requires a microprocessor and electric battery-operated locks to be installed in the door. Other mechanical locks offer manual quick code changing (Corkey, TrioVing, Winfield). These novel systems are sure to find larger commercial acceptance in the coming years.

Specific advantages and disadvantages of manual systems depend on the criteria used for determining access approval. If the entrance is used by a large number of people, either more guards have to be deployed or the movement slowed up to permit visual identification. The manual system is expensive and extremely vulnerable since it relies completely on the abilities of low-salaried, and often uneducated, guards.

**The Machine-Aided Manual Entry Control System.** This system utilizes entry control equipment to assist guards in determining the authenticity of the individual's credentials. This system is slightly more reliable than the purely manual system since it provides the guard with more decision-making information than a familiar face, and it allows a single guard to monitor many entry points.

Machine-aided manual systems normally use closed-circuit television (CCTV) and either a stored image or a picture stored in a badge for comparison with the CCTV image of the individual requesting entry. The badge may contain coded data to further identify the person, but a guard is still required to verify the individual's visual identity, as badges could be exchanged. However, the use of videotape equipment allows the electronic storage of the image.

**The Automated Entry Control System.** This system allows personnel to enter and exit without a guard present until an alarm situation is indicated. There are a great many advantages to an automated system because the electronics used to control the entrance are more reliable and impartial than a guard. In addition, this system is flexible and can be altered at any time. This type of system is usually based on some type of badge identification possessing the required information for the electronic surveillance system. The badge is issued to individuals to certify authority for access to controlled entrances or areas. Often a keyboard "password" or number is required with the badge to prevent entry by someone using another person's card.

The ultimate goal of automated systems is to possess the capability of using some type of positive personnel identity verification technique to grant or deny access to a controlled area. This technique utilizes some unique personal characteristics that are part of the individual's biological makeup. Prototype equipment has been developed that utilizes finger-prints, speech, handwriting, eye retina patterns, and various other individual physical characteristics. One system now produced compares hand and finger geometry.

## The Card Reader Systems

Card readers, in effect, substitute the mechanical key function with plastic cards similar to a credit card. The basic unit usually consists of a small box containing the card reading mechanism or electronics or both. This is installed inside the room with a faceplate containing a narrow slot mounted on the outer surface of the wall near the door. The card that is inserted into the slot is fabricated with a distinct and usually invisible code number so that each employee can be individually identified whenever he uses the door entrance. The card reader is connected to a central control box some distance away.

Card reader systems possess the capability of authorizing entry to specific door(s) to designated individuals at mandated times. For example, if there are twenty employees and five doors, the key card system can be programmed to admit everyone to one door between 9:00 A.M. and 5:00 P.M., seven individuals to three doors between 6:00 A.M. and 8:00 P.M., and two individuals to all five doors on a 24-hour basis. The combinations are infinite and are limited only by program requirements. This capability is referred to as multilevel time zone access control.

Upon demand, the system can supply a printed list of all individuals who passed through a control point during a specific period of time. If at 10:00 A.M. it is desired to tabulate a list of those individuals who are absent, the processor will print out all cards that did not pass through the entry area. The printout of each individual's movement is often used for payroll purposes. A nuclear facility lists the names of the persons on the premises periodically in the event of an alarm condition requiring evacuation.

Another important function of a card reader system is its ability to prevent the same card from being used consecutively by two individuals. This is called anti-passback. An employee cannot (after he is inside the building) use his badge to gain entry for someone else, or admit a second vehicle into a controlled parking area. This requires a card reader at both the entry and exit locations. The card must be recorded in/out and never in/in or out/out, or an alarm will be sounded and access denied.

The card controller can also accomplish instant access change. This function is used whenever a coded credential is lost or stolen, or when an individual's access authority has changed or terminated. The controller can be reprogrammed to instantly void the continued use of any card without the necessity of actually recovering it.

Card reader systems can read various types of credentials to determine if an individual attempting to gain access to the premises is authorized to do so. The final selection of an appropriate credential system is determined to a large extent by cost, reliability of the manufacturer, availability of service, and site-specific characteristics such as the number of entry control points, the number of badges in the system, the number of levels of access that need to be accommodated, and the administrative procedures that are used to issue badges. Considered next are some card reader credential systems.

**Photo Identification (ID) Card.**    This is the most common credential used for access control. This is an easily recognizable color-coded card worn as a badge, containing a facial photograph. It can be visually checked by a guard. A significant disadvantage of using this type of badge is that it can be easily falsified, or an individual can make up his face to match a stolen badge or exchange his photo for the photo in the badge in an effort to gain unauthorized access. Employees known to guards have worn badges with photos of gorillas for months without being questioned.

A badge exchange system minimizes the possibility of the badge being counterfeited, lost, or stolen. Under this system, duplicated badges are held at each entry control and exchanged for another badge that admits the individual to the inner area. The individual's badge is held at the entry control point until the employee leaves the area, at which time the badges are again exchanged. In this way, the exchange badge worn within the controlled area is never allowed to leave the area. Usually the internal badge is not coded to enter the main facility and therefore someone stealing it cannot use it to reenter the building.

**Optically Coded Badge.**    This type of badge contains a geometric array of spots printed on an insert laminated into the badge. Photo detectors in the badge reader detect the optical transmission of the spots, and hence the code. Usually the pattern of spots is concealed by making the badge opaque to visible light and transparent to infrared light.

**Electric Circuit Coded Badge.**    This is one of the older and now rarely used techniques for card reader systems. Inside the plastic laminated badge is a flat printed circuit pattern that selectively closes electrical circuits when inserted into a badge reader. For this credential, the badge reader is simply a card-edge connector normally used for a printed circuit board. This can be decoded with a simple electrical continuity tester. Consequently, counterfeit badges can be easily fabricated.

**Magnetic Coded Badge.**   This is the most widely used of all cards. It contains a sheet of flexible, permanent magnetic material on which a pattern of magnetic spots has been magnetized. The code is determined by the polarity and location of the magnetized spots. A typical reader unit is mounted on the wall, and when the card is inserted into the unit, a series of small magnetic sensors are activated that "read" the code. A great deal of information can be placed in this card, but the magnetic spots can be decoded. This ease of decoding could encourage the fabricating of a false credential or the alteration of the code.

**Magnetic Stripe Coded Badge.**   This is the type that is used in commercial credit card systems. A stripe of magnetic material located along one edge of the badge is encoded with badge data. These bits of information are then read as the magnetic stripe is moved past a magnetic head. Forgery is possible, but attacking the code card to gain entry into a controlled area is seldom attempted because of the risk that the forged card will be detected or set off an alarm. Illegal entry by use of a stolen card before it is voided is a common occurrence.

**Passive Electronic Coded Badge.**   This is the most unusual and unique of all the badges described. While all the other card badges require insertion of the card into a "slot" for the reader unit to function, this passive system requires only that the badge pass near the reader unit (within about four inches). In other words, the card can remain in a wallet (in a pants pocket) and the unit will read it if it is positioned correctly.

This badge is laminated with a small, flat electrically tuned circuit, but there are no electrical components or batteries in the card. In order for the code to be read, a swept-radio frequency(RF) field is generated and then the frequencies at which significant energy is absorbed by the card are detected. If the absorbed frequency corresponds to the tuned circuit within the reader, the reader reacts positively. If the card frequency and the reader unit tuned frequency are different, then the system sends an alarm. Commercial units are available that can distinguish up to 10,000 different frequencies and can be read by a single system.

**Active Electronic Badge.**   This type consists of a portable, electrically coded badge and a stationary interrogation unit. The interrogation unit supplies power to the badge components by magnetic induction and receives and decodes the credential number transmitted from the badge. The individual carrying the badge is not required to take any action to accomplish the badge reading since the badge is read automatically when it passes through the radio frequency field generated by the interrogation unit.

### Identity Verification Systems

There has been a slow but steady progression away from the traditional lock and cylinder concept in the field of access control. The card reader is certainly a significant advancement over the key cylinder since it permits not only door control, but also personnel identification. According to some security professionals, the access control system of the future is the personnel identity verification system. The concept of credit card use is now universally accepted and very little education would be required to have individuals add another card to their wallet in place of the conventional and easy-to-compromise key. A great deal has already been accomplished in this area, but new breakthroughs and further sophistication of existing devices are expected in the next few years. Table 7-2 lists the types of cards in use from 1890 until today.

Fingerprinting has been used for more than a hundred years and is still considered one of the most reliable means of distinguishing one individual from another. The use of fingerprints as an identity verification technique is relatively new (1972), but it is gaining wide acceptance. These systems rely on pattern recognition and computerized data processing. All automatic identification systems using fingerprints rely on accurate finger positioning and pattern measurement for reliable identification. However, they are very slow systems, acceptable only at maximum security locations.

**Speech Verification.** This system is still in the development stages, but at least one system is commercially available. The basic procedure with this type of technique is to repeat a four-word phrase selected at random by a computer from a file of 32 phrases constructed from 16 monosyllable words. The repeated phrase is processed and compared with data previously stored on the disc files at the time that the individual was enrolled in the system. If the four-word phrase is verified, the individual is permitted access and the data in the file are updated to reflect minor changes in the individual's voice. The concept is excellent in that it is difficult to duplicate a human voice, but it is also very slow.

**Handwriting Signature.** This system usually consists of a pressure-sensitive tablet or pen and a microcomputer that compares the written word (usually a signature) with handwriting digitally stored in the computer. The system measures the pen pressure as a function of time to distinguish one signature from another.

**Hand Geometry.** The operating principle in this system is that an individual's hand characteristics (length of fingers and their dimensional relationship to each other, as well as the translucency of the skin between the fingers), are as unique as fingerprints. This complex device encodes the hand geometry data on a card that is carried by the employee. To enter the area, the card holder inserts the identity card into the machine, places his full hand on top of the reading unit, and allows the unit to compare the data on the card to the hand dimensions. If they match, entry is permitted. This system has proved highly reliable and difficult to compromise. These verification systems are of the esoteric type; however, the trend in designing security systems for sensitive areas is to rely more on positive personal verification rather than on devices that can be passed from one individual to another.

## SUMMARY

Lock technology has developed tremendously from its simple beginnings to the complex industry it is today. Although the technology has reached a high level of sophistication, lock picking and key duplication techniques have advanced at a comparable speed. This conclusion is supported by the significant number of break-ins and illegal entries reported each year. (Most locks are compromised by use of a stolen key or a duplicate key. Picking accounts for a very small percentage of illegal entry.)

The increase cannot be attributed solely to poorly designed locks, since there are many locking mechanisms and access control devices available that are virtually burglarproof. The vulnerability of most entrance doors, whether on banks or private homes, is sometimes due to a lack of knowledge by the individuals who selected the protective mechanism during the design stages of construction or by improper installation of the proper lock, door strike, or hardware.

In some cases, high-security locks are mounted on thick doors that protect valuable premises, but the cylinder chosen to operate the lock can be easily manipulated. More often, the strike supplied by the manufacturer is not anchored well into the door frame and a well-placed kick can open the door. Key control is another problem, especially in facilities where everyone on the staff has a key.

This chapter has enumerated typical door protection devices currently available as well as innovative access control approaches scheduled for release in the near future. Every effort has been made to acquaint the student with the many changes and complexities of what is far too often considered a "simple device," and to emphasize the fact that door protection problems do not end after the installation of the lock. It is hoped that this information will assist the concerned individual in the proper selection and utilization of locking and door protection hardware.

**Table 7-2.   Types of Cards**

| Number | Date | Manufacturer | Type of Card Used |
|---|---|---|---|
| 1<br>1a | 1890-on | IBM | "Hollerith" punched card<br>(later smaller badge size used) |
| 2 | 1941-on | Card Key Systems | Paper card containing metal shims—magnetic |
| 3 | 1965-on | Oil Companies | Plastic embossed credit cards; notches in edge to operate card lock (later bar codes used) |
| 4 | 1966 | A.V.I.D. Enterprises (patents sold to Card Key Systems in 1966) | Plastic cards containing barium ferrite magnetic rubber |
| 5 | 1966 | Toye Photo Plastics | Hollerith and magnetic insert cards |
| 6 | 1967 | Rushell Industries (Rusco in 1970) | Barium ferrite discs set into plastic card |
| 7 | 1968 | Industrial Instrumentation Inc. (became Notifier in 1970) | Copper etched circles in card, inductive reader |
| 8 | 1969 | Identi-Logic (later division of Eaton Yale & Towne) | Printed circuit card |
| 9 | 1970 | Detex | Plastic card containing metal sheet with punched holes |
| 10 | 1972 | Mohawk Data Sciences | Hollerith badge |
| 11 | 1972 | Cincinnatti | Hollerith and embossed card |
| 12 | 1972 | Panasonic | Punched-hole card, optical reader |
|  | 1972 | IBM | Magnetic stripe card |
| 13 | 1972 | RCA | Hololock card, laser holograph reader |
|  | 1972 | Litton Poly-Scientific | Piezoelectric ceramic crystal card |
|  | 1972 | KMS | Holographic fingerprint verification using card containing small holograph picture of print |
| 13a | 1972 | Identimation | Hand geometry plus magnetic stripe card |
| 14 | 1973 | Schlage Electronics | Radio frequency sensing of card code |

**Table 7-2.  (continued)**

| Number | Date | Manufacturer | Type of Card Used |
|--------|------|--------------|-------------------|
| 15 | 1973 | Sentracon | Capacitance reading of metallic pattern |
| 16 | 1973 | Toye Photo Plastics | "Differential optics" plastic cards |
| 17 | 1973 | Mosler | Magnetic stripe |
| 18 | 1973 | Diebold | Rusco magnetic card |
| 19 | 1974 | MIL, Australia (now Del Norte) | Key-shaped card with barium ferrite insert |
| 19a | 1974 | CorKey Control Systems, Inc. | Steel-encased magnetic key |
| 20 | 1974 | ADT | Punched hole plastic hotel key card |
| 21 | 1974 | AB-ID-KORT (Sweden) | Optical pattern printed on card |
| 22 | 1974 | Automatic Parking Devices | Magnetic insert and differential optics card |
| 23 | 1974 | Continental Instruments | Plastic key with notches for card code |
| 24 | 1974 | Juki—Japan Hell—Germany | Photo engraved on Hollerith plastic card |
| 25 | 1975 | Wiegand (Patents licensed to Echlin marketed "Sensor" | Magnetic wires in plastic card |
| 26 | 1975 | Uniqey | Paper hotel key containing punched hole foil sheet |
| 27 | 1977 | Ellissonlok | Hollerith punched plastic hotel key |
| 28 | 1979 | Alpha—Japan | Punched hole paper hotel key |
| 29 | 1978 | Trio Ving | Punched hole plastic hotel key |
| 30 | 1979 | Omron—Japan | Magnetic stripe hotel key |
|  | 1979 | Continental Instruments | Infrared card data |
| 31 | 1980 | Tann—England | Watermark plastic card reader |
| 32 | 1981 | Enigma | "Field absorption" reader |
|  | 1981 | Yaletronic | Punched hole hotel key |

## GLOSSARY

### Locking Terms

*Access Control.*    Method used to identify traffic (individuals or vehicles) as it/they pass through a "controlled" entrance or exit of a protected area. The term signifies that anyone entering the area must be identified and possibly recorded at a central location. Most often it refers to a card reader system, but it can also refer to a guarded entrance or one monitored by closed-circuit TV, etc. The more elaborate systems can be programmed to automatically admit single individuals — or groups — of employees between specified hours. Certain "cards" will allow entrance between 8 A.M. and 4:30 P.M. and deny entrance to the same cards at other times. Other sets of cards would be admitted only between 4:30 P.M. and midnight, etc. By adding a computer to the system, each individual could be identified by name, time of entering or leaving, and location of door used. This data-gathering technique is used to develop payroll and attendance records. Individuals could be "locked out" simply by removing their names from the computer circuit. Furthermore, the access control system often identifies the use of unauthorized cards whenever an attempt is made to use a rejected card to enter a secure area. This provides superior security to a key and lock since there is no way to determine if an illegal attempt to use an old key in a new cylinder has been made. Modern systems now include alarm monitoring and CCTV in the same controller.

*Change Key.*    A key that will operate only one lock in a series, as distinguished from a master key that will operate all locks in a series.

*Cylinder.*    The part of a lock mechanism that contains the tumblers (pins) and the keyway.

*Deadbolt.*    The unit that is usually rectangular in shape and is activated by a key or knob and becomes locked against end pressure when projected into a door strike.

*Dead Latch.*    The lock with a beveled, latch-type bolt that can be automatically or manually locked against end pressure when projected with the door closed.

*Double Bitted Key.*    A key having bittings, or cuts, on two sides, to activate the tumblers of the lock.

*Jamb.*    The inside vertical face of a door or window frame.

*Key Way.*   The opening in a lock cylinder into which the key is inserted.

*Latch.*   A door fastening device, usually with a sliding or spring bolt, but usually having no locking function.

*Master Key.*   A key designed to operate two or more locks of different changes in a group, each lock capable of being operated by its own individual or change key.

*Mortise.*   An opening made to receive a lock or other hardware, usually in the thin edge of a door.

*Pin Tumblers.*   Small sliding pins in a lock cylinder, working against coil springs and preventing the cylinder from rotating until a key is inserted to raise the pins to the exact height that creates a shear line.

*Strike.*   The part, pierced or recessed to receive the bolts of locks or latches, and applied to the door frame.

# Chapter 8
# Conventional Electromechanical Alarm Devices

This chapter and the following two chapters describe the operational theory of sensory devices that are designed to detect unauthorized entry. Conventional electromechanical devices are discussed in this chapter and refer to the kind of alarm device that usually always requires a physical action of an intruder to activate a "sensor" (i.e., opening a door, stepping on a floor mat, etc.). Chapter 9 concentrates on the theory of the more sophisticated volumetric space detectors (ultrasonic microwave, etc.), and Chapter 10 deals with the various methods of transmitting the alarm signal within a building and from a protected premises to the central monitoring service. The material in these three chapters covers every conceivable sensory device and transmission medium used in modern-day security alarm systems.

Until the mid-1960s most premises limited their protection to a door lock, and if more protection was desired, a dog was purchased. Gradually, more and more alarm devices were added to supplement the perimeter lock until practically all highly valued premises, regardless of the location, had some type of sensor installed to protect the interior space. This evolution began with simple devices designed to protect vulnerable perimeter openings — windows or skylights — and proceeded to the development of motion detectors, which have revolutionalized the old concepts of security protection. The growing popularity of motion detectors reduced the need to rely on the more conventional electromechanical devices and sensors.

Motion detectors did not, however, completely replace conventional devices even though it significantly lessened the need for them. Conventional devices still have a valued place in any protection system, and it is important to understand their operation since they still are in popular use. These electromechanical units are usually more reliable, easier to install, and less expensive than motion detectors. Conventional devices include magnetic door switches, window foil, floor mats, traps, and light beams, among others.

The magnetic door switch was developed 30 years ago and is still the most popular alarm device in use today. From a reliability standpoint, it is superior to any other security device because it operates millions of times without breaking down. This characteristic is important since this kind of switch often is mounted on the entrance to busy commercial establishments where it must operate thousands of times a day due to normal customer traffic. When a commonly used door is secured at night and opened by an intruder, this small inexpensive device must operate effectively the first time it is challenged. Conversely, the unit must protect emergency exits that are very seldom opened. In comparison to more sophisticated devices, conventional electromechanical security devices are limited since they generally protect a single position or location. They do not detect penetration through or around the protected area. This obvious shortcoming was the motivating factor that encouraged the development of the more sophisticated motion detectors that are discussed in the next chapter.

## MODERN TECHNOLOGY

The change of emphasis from mechanical alarms to electronic devices occurred when the demand for better protection encouraged manufacturers to adapt, for the private sector, techniques originally developed for national defense. Except for the minor influence of Underwriters Laboratories, this rapid growth in electronic alarms was not accompanied by the development of universally enforceable performance standards or practical guidelines. As a result, the market became innundated with electronic devices that were often poorly made, incorrectly installed, and difficult to operate by the user, thus helping the "old" and more reliable conventional devices maintain their importance in the security field.

### False Alarms

The major technological shortcoming of all alarm systems still is their proneness to false alarm and the public's resulting lack of faith in their value. It is estimated that between 90 and 98 percent of all alarms transmitted are false. This has prompted a negative response on the part of police who often are hampered in responding to genuine emergencies by faulty alarm systems. Consequently, police tend to give alarms a low priority.

In addition to the problem of faulty equipment, more than half of all false alarms are directly the result of user error or negligence. Alarm systems are commonly set off when doors and windows are left unlocked or when the secured area is entered by mistake.

### Alarm Installation

Other major factors leading to false alarms are improper device application and poor installation and servicing. Most alarm installers have little or no training in the field of electronics. At the present time, the lack of codes, guidelines, or standards to insure competence in the trade has created a situation where any person, with or without knowledge, ability, or credentials, can open up an alarm business. Some states have licensing statutes, but in general the industry is mostly unregulated in the residential field. Commercial firms almost always use the UL standards as a basic guideline.

Typically, the installation industry has been comprised of small entrepreneurs who enter the business simply because it is easy to enter. Electricians usually shun the electronics, and since all alarms are powered by less than 30 volts, there are often no licensing requirements. Most alarm panels come with small transformers that plug into the nearest power outlet, instantly lowering the voltage below the level that requires a licensed electrician. This is not to suggest that all alarm installers are incompetent, but something is wrong if an industry can tolerate such a high false alarm rate. There is a great deal of self-policing to be done before the alarm industry can be taken seriously by the public (and the criminal). Understanding the operating function of mechanical–electrical devices and motion detectors will do much to restore confidence in alarm systems.

## COMPOSITION OF A TYPICAL ALARM SYSTEM

Numerous alarm systems are available, but not all of them offer the reliability needed in a system that may lay dormant for years before it is finally challenged. There are three tests that must be met by every alarm system if it is to act as an effective protection device: (1) it must work the first time it is challenged no matter how long it has remained inactive; (2) it cannot continue to produce false or nuisance alarms; and (3) it should not be easily defeated by burglars.

Every alarm system has several essential components: sensor–control, communication path, and annunciator. When these elements are combined, they form an alarm system that is not only capable of detecting intrusion, but also of transmitting and articulating a message for help.

### The Sensor—Control

The heart of any alarm system is the *sensor* and its method of detection. This functional device detects or "senses" an existing condition and notes any changes in status. Analogous to the way fire detectors respond to fire signatures, anti-intrusion sensors operate by indicating the presence or absence of changes in certain physical phenomena such as electric currents, mechanical vibrations, magnetic and electromagnetic fields, electrical fields, acoustic waves, and optical and thermal rays.

All security alarm sensors, in effect, are only switches activated by human movement that changes the switch/sensor from an "OFF" to an "ON" position. They have no means of distinguishing authorized entry from unauthorized entry. Sensors do not ring bells or dial the police. They simply close a contact between two pieces of metal or cause a component to move from one position to another and change an electrical circuit condition.

To expand this sensor to a total intrusion detection system requires a *control* device that is responsible for initiating a reaction to the closing or opening of the switch/sensor. The role of the control device is analogous to that of the brain, which controls the nervous and circulatory systems in the human body. The nervous system collects and evaluates information from various sources and transmits signals to the muscles for appropriate action, while the circulatory system provides the power source to maintain the ability of the system (sensor) to function. Similarly, the control unit provides the power to receive information from the sensor, evaluates the information, and transmits it over the second part, which is the communication path to the final part of the alarm system — the annunciator.

### The Communication Path

In a local bell ringing system, the communication path is simply the wiring to the bell. In a central station system, it may be the leased telephone line connecting the protected premises to the central station, and in a proprietary system, it is the in-house wiring connecting the sensor or control to a central annunciator location.

### The Annunciator

The *annunciator* is the part of the detection system that causes the system to go into "alarm," thus alerting someone to the fact that there has been a

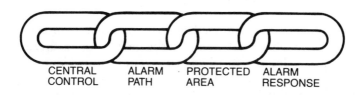

| CENTRAL | ALARM | PROTECTED | ALARM |
| CONTROL | PATH | AREA | RESPONSE |

Figure 8-1.   The protection chain.

All alarms are constructed to operate at low d.c. voltages and current (usually 6 or 12 volts). Such power requirements were selected by the manufacturers to make it safer to install the equipment while at the same time avoiding conforming to local electrical codes in many cities. Nonlicensed and unskilled individuals can install practically all alarm devices from the door switch to closed-circuit television without the need of an electrical certificate. The low-power operation also permits the equipment to operate from batteries and allows the use of small guage wires for installation. Some newer devices permit the use of either house current or batteries without any alteration to the device. All circuits are generally protected by a continuous flow of current since the easiest way to attack an alarm system is to attack the wiring. By providing the continuous flow of current, the system becomes "supervised," which means that the cutting or shorting of the wire at any location within the system will change or stop the "flow" of current that causes an alarm condition.

change in the sensor environment. The annunciator could be a bell, siren, buzzer, flashing light on a panel in a police department, or a ringing phone many miles away in a remote central station (see Figure 8-1).

## TYPICAL CONTACT DEVICES

Contact devices rely on a direct physical action to the unit to activate the mechanism. This group of sensors is referred to as *electromechanical devices* because a direct physical action must occur in order for the device to be activated. They are the simplest and most widely used protection devices in the alarm industry. Since statistics illustrate that most illegal entries are made through doors, it is evident that emphasis should be placed on supervising the opening of a door or any other perimeter opening.

### Mechanical Switches

*Mechanical switches* are generally constructed with spring-loaded levers or plungers that operate when a door, window, or cabinet cover is removed or opened. They come in many forms, but the most popular is the "door jamb button." Even though it is one of the oldest devices on the market, it is still an excellent device, particularly since it is usually completely hidden when the door is in a closed position.

### Magnetic Switches

*Magnetic switches* are comprised of two components: a self-contained magnetically operated switch and a magnet. This configuration has changed from the device described in a patent obtained by Edwin Holmes in 1857, but the operating principle remains basically the same. The magnet is mounted on the door directly beneath the frame-mounted switch so that it is forced away from the switch when the door is opened, stopping and/or increasing the flow of current that is detected by the control unit. When the door is closed, the near proximity of the magnetic field causes a closing movement in the flexible metal in the switch. There are probably 30 million magnetic contact switches in operation today with one large manufacturing company responsible for the sale of over 20 million units. A well-designed magnetic contact switch incorporates design features such as:

1. Shows very little wear, regardless of the number of openings (most switches have a life span of more than 5 million operations)
2. A sealed housing in which the switch is encapsulated
3. Concealed terminals to prevent tampering
4. Has more security against compromise than a mechanical switch if it is installed properly

Contact switches are available in numerous shapes, each of which is made for a specific application. While the wooden door-mounted switch is

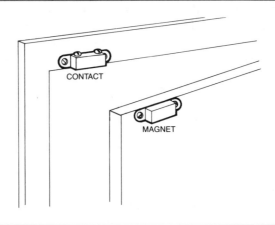

Figure 8-2.  Surface mounted magnetic switch.

the most popular, other units are designed for sliding doors, windows, overhead doors, etc. (see Figure 8-2).

**Surface-mounted Magnetic Switches.**    This type of switch is easy to install. While mounting them inside the room offers some protection against tampering, the exposed housing and terminals lessen their value as a high-security device. Simply placing a wire across the exposed terminals makes the switch useless, in effect, since the current continues to flow across the terminals even if the door magnet is moved away from the switch (a technique that is known to many criminals and delinquents). However, some switches are wired to open one circuit and close another, which makes them a little more difficult to bypass.

**Recessed Magnetic Switches.**    These devices are far superior to surface-mounted devices. The function of these switches is identical to that of surface-mounted switches, but because the entire unit is hidden within the door frame the terminals are completely protected from attack. While these switches are a step forward, they are still vulnerable to attack by use of a foreign magnet that, when held near the switch, can "fool" the switch into thinking that the magnet is nearby even if the door is opened. (This can be done only on doors made of wood or other nonmagnetic material and that also open "in." If the door opens "out," the foreign magnet cannot be placed properly. If the door is made of steel, it will short-circuit the "flux" of the foreign magnet. In addition, the polarity of the foreign magnet must agree with that of the real one) (see Figures 8-3 and 8-4).

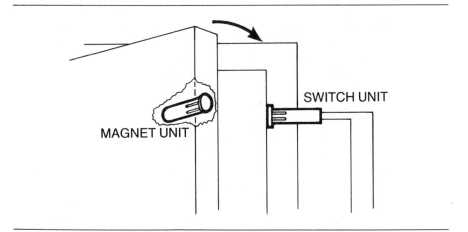

Figure 8-3.   Recessed magnetic switch.

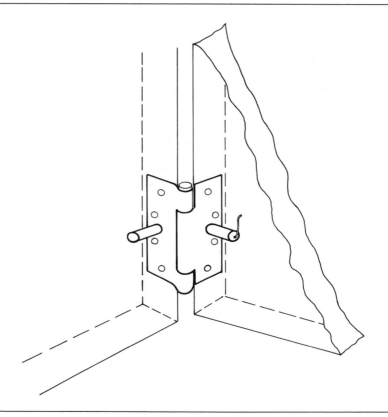

Figure 8-4.   Magnetic hinge switch.

**Balanced Magnetic Switches.**   These switches are defined in certain government documents as "a device that will go into an alarm state upon sensing a magnetic field larger or smaller than that which maintains the switch in its secure state." The typical magnetic switch consists of two units: (1) a magnetic reed switch with a small (bias) magnet in one housing and (2) a bar magnet similar to the one described for the common magnetic contact switch. Separation of the reed switch from the magnet (mounted on the door) causes the reed to relax and shift from one set of contacts to another, thereby initiating an alarm. The reed is balanced against the biasing magnet in such a way that any attempt to capture the reed by use of extraneous magnets causes the reed to shift contacts, again generating an alarm signal. The balanced magnetic switch has proven to be the solution to the potential defeat of the standard magnetic switch, but it is more expensive than the standard magnetic switch.

## Foiled Windows

For many years, the most popular method of window protection was to tape large plate glass windows with foil. The material used in *foiling* is a lead alloy that is so thin and flexible that it possesses very little tensile strength. This built-in weakness causes the foil to break when the glass surface to which it adheres is broken or cracked. The installed foil is covered with a coating of varnish to electrically insulate it and give it physical protection by covering it with a hard protective coating. To place the foil into an alarm system requires electrical current to continually pass through it. If the glass is broken, the foil breaks causing an interruption in the current flow and the activation of an alarm signal. (When plate glass is supported on four sides, it has a property characteristic of developing at least one crack that will travel to an edge whenever and wherever the glass is broken. To protect a glass surface it is necessary only to apply foil around the edge rather than all over the surface.)

When foiling is used so that it is an effective technique, so much foil is required that it is not always aesthetically appealing. In the last decade, changing attitudes toward security protection have altered the notion that security has to be visible in order to be effective. As a result, "Beware of Dog" sign tactics have been replaced with devices that are subtle, unobtrusive, and, if possible, completely hidden.

Today, foiling is no longer the first measure chosen for window protection. Although it is still used in situations where appearances are unimportant and where large window areas completely cover the first floor of the protected premises, windows now are either ignored or are being protected by small silver-dollar–shaped vibration (impact) detectors that are able to "read" the frequency vibration of cracking or breaking glass.

## Alarm Screens

*Burglar alarm screens* are another example of changing concepts in the alarm field. At one time, these screens were used to protect difficult-to-alarm openings, by placing many small wooden dowels across the opening with a thin wire (26 gauge hard-drawn wire) running through the center. When the dowel (and the wire) was broken, the current flow was interrupted and the system went "into alarm."

Dowelled screens are still used for roof openings (such as skylights). For window protectors, however, in many residential applications they have been replaced by the popular aluminum framed screens. The mesh of these screens is nonmetallic but a thin strand of metallic wire is woven into the mesh in such a way that it is almost invisible. When the screen is cut, this woven strand is also cut sending the unit into an alarm condition. Under normal conditions, the screen provides the same ventilation as any "fly screen."

### Floor Traps

The *floor trap* (or trip wire) is a crude technique that relies on the intruder blundering into a thin wire strung across an opening 12 to 18 inches above the floor. The wire is spring loaded and connected to a switch or contact points. When the wire is broken or if it is moved in either direction (stretched or retracted without breaking), the wire moves the switch into an alarm position. The protection circuit current is designed to flow through the wire itself so that, if the wire is cut, an alarm still results. This crude device is often used by the amateur alarm installer and possesses little value in most situations. It must be set and removed each day and is therefore subject to damage that may cause false alarms.

### Pressure on Floor Mats

*Pressure* or *floor mats* are very popular, relatively inexpensive, and difficult to avoid if properly placed. The typical mat is constructed of two layers of copper screening separated by a soft sponge rubber insulation with large holes in it. After wire leads are brought out from each layer of screening, the various layers of copper, sponge, and so forth, are sealed in an outside rubber jacket. When someone steps on any part of the mat surface, the two layers of screens are pressed together through the holes in the insulation, making contact and closing the electrical circuit.

Pressure mats are generally concealed under rugs and carpeting so that they can be placed over a wide area without detection. The mats are produced in various lengths and shapes, and they can be cut and replaced easily. They do tend to wear out if used in a high-traffic area (especially when used to automatically open doors to buildings, such as supermarkets, or in homes with big dogs and small children).

### VIBRATION DETECTORS

*Vibration detectors* have many applications, but the electromechanical type is becoming a rarely used device. They are made in both electromechanical and electronic forms, and are mounted to a wall or ceiling so that they can sense the mechanical vibration caused by chopping, sawing, drilling, and other attempts to enter the structure. They are generally used in areas like vaults. They are of little use in private dwellings, since a false alarm situation could be produced by a vibration as commonplace as the passing of a truck. Electronic vibration detectors can selectively screen out these unwanted vibrations by sensitivity and "count" adjustments, and they are fast replacing audio detection as the primary way to protect vaults.

**The Use of Vibration Detection Systems in Fence Protection.** The use of detection systems mounted on fences is growing in popularity, especially around military establishments and nuclear power plants. One of the early systems used for outdoor perimeter protection was known as the *accoustical fence*. Microphones were attached to the chain link fence at intervals of 50 feet. The output of these microphones was processed through an audio amplifier. Theoretically, the noise generated by someone climbing over the fence was supposed to be distinguishable from normal fence noises. On windy nights, this "normal" noise was extremely high, which made it difficult to determine climbing noises from the sound of blowing wind. It was obvious that there were problems with this system that made it ineffective as a fence protection device.

The *taut wire detector* is probably one of the most false-alarm-free systems ever devised for outdoor fence protection. It consists of a wire or series of wires under tension installed on top of or next to a chain link fence terminating in a switch-type mechanism. Either pulling or releasing the wire causes switch action. It is rendered false-alarm-free by a system that compensates for temperature changes that would normally alter the length of the wire to such an extent that it would create an alarm. Nevertheless, the system is easy to compromise by cutting parts of the chain link fence away from the wire or tunneling under it.

The high incidence of sabotage and terroism in recent times has prompted new developments in the field of outer perimeter protection. One of the most popular techniques to emerge is the mounting of vibration detectors, spaced every 10 feet apart (usually on fence posts), along a tight wire mesh fence. These detectors react much like the units described previously in that they "hear" sudden impacts against the fence caused by climbing humans or the clinking and cutting of the fence. Vibration detectors are generally in the form of mercury switches, pendulum switches, or the newer type of detector called ceramic diodes. When a certain movement causes the diode to generate a voltage or the mercury or pendulum to make "contact," an alarm condition is created. The control panel is supposed to be programmed to ignore random movements such as the wind, passing traffic, and so forth. (It is semieffective toward this end.)

**E-Field.**    These are sophisticated fence protection systems that do not rely on impact motion directly on the fence to record an alarm condition. They utilize an E-field sensor to generate an alternating current around a wire (called a field wire) that is mounted on cross arms attached to the chain link fence or the freestanding posts installed parallel to the fence. This field wire transmits an omnidirectional E-field to the ground. In nontechnical terms, this means that when a large body approaches the system, a change in the E-field pattern takes place and a second or third wire (called a sensing wire), placed at different locations within the transmitted E-field pattern, picks up any change in that pattern. Only changes that fall within the band of human movement are programmed to set off an alarm. This system is growing in popularity because of the need for fence protection around buildings like nuclear power plants. However, there are certain inherent shortcomings. The wires (both the field and sensing types) usu-ally act as antennae, and they can be susceptible to external electrical interference called EMI (e.g., lighting or electromagnetic or radio fre-quency interference). Additionally, the wires must be under a high degree of spring tension so that a high-frequency vibration will be produced when they are struck by small foreign objects or blown by the wind. With a tight wire, these frequencies are outside the band of frequencies of the receiving circuitry. Birds tend to land on the wire one by one and roost there. The system compensates for the small change created by this kind of distur-bance. However, if something frightens the birds and they leave all at once in a large body, a false alarm is created.

### Buried Cable Sensors

The buried cable sensor is difficult to use but it has found an application in highly secure areas, primarily military installations. It has the advantage of being completely covered and can function without the need of a fence to support the sensing cable. The cable is buried in the ground, and when it is subjected to disturbances by either an intruder's footsteps or the metal (e.g., a gun, belt buckle, or the nails in shoes) etc. on an intruder's person, a small, detectable change in characteristic is generated, amplified, and processed.

Installation of the buried cable sensor can be fast and easy if proper trenching machines are used. The fact that it is covert rather than on a fence, which would make it possible to be bridged or tunneled under, is an advantage in outside application. There are basically three types of buried cable in use, each offering certain advantages and disadvantages:

**Seismic-Magnetic Buried-Line Sensor.**    This type generates a small voltage when metal or footsteps are detected. It is still in the experimental stage and probably will take some time before it is available.

**Seismic-Buried-Line Sensor.** This category is comprised of several devices. One utilizes a series of devices called *geophones* to sense the seismic disturbances caused by an intruder. Another type consists of two parallel oil-filled hoses with sensitive pressure switches on the ends of the tubing runs. These, also, are buried in the ground and detect pressure changes in the soil caused by an intruder's footsteps. This approach to outer perimeter protection has not been very successful, since the system loses sensitivity as the ground freezes.

**Magnetic-Buried-Line Sensor.** This type is a passive wire loop system that is sensitive to disturbances in the local magnetic field caused by nearby movement of ferromagnetic material (e.g., iron or steel). This system was primarily used by the military for the purpose of detecting a person carrying a weapon. Supposedly, the system is sensitive to seismic activity, since the weight of a man walking in the line will shift the buried loop of wire with respect to the earth's magnetic field and will generate a detectable current in the loop. This device is not, and probably never will be, used commercially in the United States since the presence of metal on the intruder is mandatory for it to detect a person. It is useful in protecting a nation's borders from enemy raiding parties.

## CAPACITANCE RELAY

Capacitance detectors, or proximity alarms, are used on metal safes and cabinets and record changes in capacitance whenever someone touches or comes near the metal enclosure. This device takes advantage of the fact that whenever someone comes near the safe, it creates a change in the safe's capacitance to ground. The safe must be mounted on rubber discs (or other nonmetallic insulated material) to isolate it from the ground. The device operates upon the principle that the individual approaching the safe changes the capacitance of a "tuned circuit." It is somewhat the same principle as the disturbance in the picture of a TV set caused by the nearness of a human body.

## LIGHT BEAMS

These extremely popular devices utilize narrow beams of infrared light to protect openings or a long wall surface. The two components consist of a light source (transmitter) and a photocell (receiver). The receiver goes into alarm if the light source is momentarily cut off by someone moving in between the two units. The receiver must be sensitive to even a small amount of the projected light or else it would go into alarm if the beam were blocked by fog or dirt, or even furniture. The better designed systems (called photoelectric) possess reserve power so that an alarm is created only after 75 (indoor) to 95 percent (outdoor) of the light is cut off. On the other hand, the beam width must not be so narrow as to cause the system to go into an alarm condition from the airborne interruptions caused by insects, birds, and leaves.

The system should be designed so as to avoid being "fooled" by a substitute light source. Beam bypass threats are easily handled by designing the system so that the photocell acceptance angle inside the receiver unit is limited. This would require that a substitute light source be placed at an exact angle in order to be successful.

Early photoelectric beam devices relied on incandescent lamps as a transmitting source and a photocell as the receiver device. As the technology developed, the transmitter lamp was filtered to block visible light and allow only infrared "light." The receivers were also filtered to allow only IR. This prevented normal white light from affecting (fooling) the system. Various methods were tried to modulate the "beam," such as placing shutters (choppers) that rotated in front of the transmitting lamp. Because of the high power consumption, the incandescent lamp was replaced in the early 1970s with "red" LED (light-emitting diodes). (This "red light" unit is called an *active* infrared device and should not be confused with the "body heat" motion detector called *passive* infrared.)

The most sophisticated beam systems use modulated light to further protect the system from bypass threats. Pulsating or modulated light is not steady like that emitted from a flashlight or the sun, but is "chopped light" so that it goes on and off at a preset frequency. These pulses of light are the only ones the receiver will accept. Steady light sources (or other frequency patterns) are rejected. Modern solid-state devices are particularly fast and can capture the change in intensity caused by a running intruder. Modulated systems have the further advantage of not always being disabled by sunlight, automobile headlights, or other steady light source that are accidentally imposed upon them. Of course, beams can be avoided if the beam path can be determined. Mirrors can be used, however, to conceal the true beam path by zigzagging the beam around the area at various heights. The mirrors are placed so as to reflect the beam into various criss-cross patterns. This permits the use of a single light source to cover unusual patterns against which other devices cannot protect without the use of multiple units. About 10 percent of the light beams now being sold contain both the transmitter and receiver in a single unit, bouncing the lights off the opposite wall by use of a mirror.

Almost all the photoelectric light beams in use today utilize a miniature LED that requires little power to send a light source across a room. The small LED can be optically focused to flood an area so that various receivers can be used with one transmitter. This system has important advantages over the conventional straight–narrow beam units. In time, this LED technique should replace the ordinary incandescent lights found in conventional photoelectric beams, since LEDs contain no filament to burn out the light source. LEDs are rated at millions of hours of life.

A rarely used device in the beam category is the *laser beam* system, which is capable of transmitting a narrow beam more than 10,000 feet. It can also be effectively used at shorter and more practical distances associated with the concentrated or modulated beam units.

## FIRE AND SMOKE DETECTORS

Although sensors that react to the heat and smoke of fires do not fall into the category of typical contact devices, they do warrant consideration in this chapter since they are almost always made a part of the total premise protection plan. Municipal ordinances and state building codes mandate their installation more frequently than they require intrusion alarm systems. The fact that smoke detectors have become so available and inexpensive in the last few years is another important reason for their inclusion in this text.

There are several types of fire detection systems, each relying on its specific method of detection. Some react to heat, some to light, and others to radiation (infrared, ultraviolet, alpha particles, etc.). Some detectors react to wisps of smoke while others measure water flow through a sprinkler system. Each type possesses some unique advantages as well as accompanying drawbacks. Generally, the sensors are not interchangeable, nor are they able to function in all situations. The major categories are as follows:

1. *Heat-sensitive units* — react to high (fixed-temperature type) or rapidly changing temperatures (rate-of-rise type).
2. *Smoke detectors* — sense the products of combustion (invisible gases) and/or the visible smoke given off before the flame is visible.
3. *Flame or gas sensors* — "see" the special light emitted by a flame or detect the flammable gases. Gas sensors are rarely used as a fire detector since their primary function is to detect "explosive" situations.

### Heat-Sensitive (Thermal) Detectors

*Heat-sensitive (thermal) detectors* have been commercially available for more than 60 years, and for most of that time they were the only devices manufactured in the field. Thermal-sensitive devices are of two basic types: *fixed-temperature* and *rate-of-rise*.

**Fixed-Temperature Devices.**   Fixed-temperature devices use bimetallic materials that warp or melt at preset temperature points. (A sprinkler head is a fixed-temperature device.) Critical temperatures can be selected over a wide range. Generally, devices responding at 135°F are the most versatile. In locations that maintain consistently high temperatures (e.g., boiler rooms, lofts, or kitchens), 190°F detectors are used. The metals used in the sensor have different heat expansion coefficients, and as the area temperature rises the bimetallic strip warps. At the critical temperature a contact is closed, triggering the alarm. This is similar to the operation of a room thermostat that controls the heat in a house.

There are many variations on this technique of detection. One type of unit has a bimetallic disc that actually snaps, like a "cricket" noisemaker, at the premeasured temperature. Most bimetallic devices reset automatically as the temperature cools; some, however, are intended only for a single operation and must be replaced, much like a blown fuse.

Another unusual device in this category is a long cable laced across a protected area. Inside the cable are two current-carrying wires twisted and under tension but held apart by a thermal-sensitive plastic coating. At the critical temperature the plastic melts and the wires make electrical contact, thus activating the alarm.

Still another device is the *eutectic fuse*. This is sometimes used in sprinkler heads in addition to fixed-temperature devices because the melting point can be controlled better than the wax that was formerly used. When the fuse melts, a spring snaps over to close the alarm contacts. Some firms have developed a fragile bulb for sprinkler heads that breaks at the preset temperature, turning on the sprinkler. The sudden water flow is sensed by a vane-in-pipe device that closes a contact. One company manufactures a fixed-temperature unit with a small bit of solder that melts at the given temperature, and drips down to complete a circuit between two alarm contacts.

**Rate-of-Rise Devices.**   Rate-of-rise devices react when the temperature shoots up rapidly. They are generally faster in reacting to a fire than the fixed-temperature type. Such detectors are effective over a wide temperature span and will detect a fire even in an igloo, while the fixed-temperature device probably would not. There are two basic types of rate-of-rise detectors: *electric* and *pneumatic*.

The electric units depend on the differing expansion rates of dissimilar metals, while the pneumatic units act upon the principle that air expands when heated. In this second system, heat causes a change in an air chamber that includes a flexible diaphragm. During normal expansion and contraction of the air in the chamber, the unit "breathes" through a small hole (or vent). When a fire occurs, the air temperature rise is so rapid that the air in the chamber cannot vent fast enough and the chamber "bulges." This disturbs the diaphragm and makes an electrical contact, causing an alarm. Usually, a 15°F per minute rise will cause a reaction. Sometimes, these unique devices respond to a fast heat not caused by a fire, such as the opening of an oven door in a bakery. They may not trigger an alarm if the heat buildup from fire is gradual, which occurs when a smoldering fire generates a gradual heat buildup at the ceiling level.

**Combination Detectors.** Combination detectors are the most popular thermal detectors, having the advantage of both fixed-temperature and rate-of-rise devices. This unit actually combines both types of thermal detectors in one unit so that when the temperature rises too fast or goes above a preset point, the alarm is activated. While fixed-temperature units are sold as self-contained detectors, the rate-of-rise device is most often a part of a combination unit, and only in rare situations does it function by itself.

### Smoke or Product of Combustion Detectors

There are two types of smoke detectors in use today: *ionization detectors* and *photocell detectors.* They are relatively new to the consumer field, but millions of them are now sold annually. Competition has brought prices down so low that they are now affordable by most households.

There is a great deal of confusion surrounding the claims and test data being circulated by the manufacturers of these devices in their attempt to prove that one is better than the other. The ionization producers claim that their units can detect smoke that is invisible, while the photocell advocates make the counterclaim that their units are superior in the detection of smoldering fires. Since both units have proven effective in detecting smoke before a flame is visible, the choice between the two remains difficult, although by no means critical. Both of them react so fast that they have revolutionized the entire area of fire detection, making thermal detectors obsolete in most situations. While the two smoke detectors are constructed under different technical principles, both rely, to a great extent, on the weight of material burned in a given interval of time.

Combustible materials, when heated by fire, tend to travel upward because they are lighter in weight than the surrounding cooler air. These particles (both visible and invisible) spread out when they encounter obstructions (such as ceilings) in the same manner as water does when poured upon a floor. The majority of deaths caused by fire each year are the result of inhaling these products of combustion (smoke) as well as the toxic gases given off by burning material. Some synthetic materials give off particularly lethal gases when they burn. A significant number of fire-related deaths occur long before the flame actually reaches the victim. In fact, the fire may never reach the victim. The use of smoke detectors has significantly reduced fire-related deaths and injuries.

**Ionization Detectors.** The basic ionization principle and first operating unit were developed in Nazi Germany around 1940, and later perfected in Switzerland before being imported to the United States. The typical unit is constructed of a detecting chamber containing a minute quantity of a radiation source of alpha particles (the most widely used material is Americium 241). These particles "ionize" the air molecules between two plates with the positive molecules attaching themselves to the negative plate and the negative molecules (or ions) being attracted to the positive plate. The radioactive material continuously bombards the air particles in

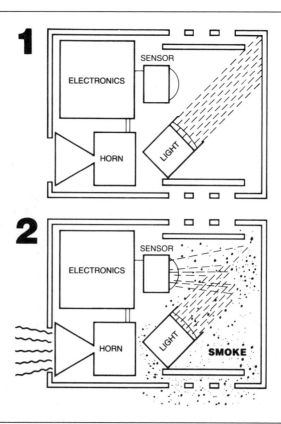

Figure 8-5. Ionization smoke detector.

the chamber, creating charged ions that now allow passage of an electric current. The current flow is so minimal that a simple battery can operate for well over a year without failing. This slow current drain is one of the outstanding features of the ionization detector, and it permits the use of battery-operated units in ceilings because a battery change is required only once a year. (Around 1980 the photocell unit was redesigned to also permit battery operation. Up to that time the need for a constant light source required house current to operate the unit. At the same time, however, ionization units that operated with house current were introduced into the marketplace in order to meet local fire codes.)

When the incoming smoke particles attach themselves to the charged ions, they, in effect, add weight to the ions and slow down their movement. This causes the current to decrease, which can be detected and recorded as an alarm condition. The actual design of the units varies by manufacturer, and usually cost considerations are the most obvious distinctions. The most expensive units, but also the most stable, are the dual chamber units. The added chamber compensates for the effects of temperature, humidity, and pressure on the sensing (primary) chamber. Smoke has a hard time getting into this reference chamber but flows easily into the detecting chamber. Slow atmospheric changes, temperature, humidity, and pressure, affect both chambers equally and a balance is thus obtained (see Figure 8-5).

**Photocell Detectors.**    Early photocell detectors operate on the same principle used in the early 1930s for light beam intrusion detectors. (They were called "projected beam" detectors.) This theory maintains that smoke can "block" a light beam just as a human blocks the light beam on the intrusion device, except the system was adjusted to detect a 4 to 20 percent reduction in light due to smoke intercepting the beam. The need for a steady light source usually requires a connection into the house current, but newer units use a pulsed LED that can function on batteries for a year or more.

The photoelectric principle allows detection of visible smoke, and it is more effective in areas where there is a high concentration of combustible products (e.g., garages, furnace rooms, or welding areas). These areas could prompt a false alarm with an ionization detector.

The modern photocell detectors (refractory or tyndall effect type) can also be used in most locations in which ionization detectors are normally installed. The operational principle is similar to that of a miniature movie theater. If the theater were smoke and dust free, it would be very difficult to see the beam of light between the projection booth and the screen. The beam actually "lights up" the smoke particles along its length. In the photocell detector, the projection booth is replaced by a light bulb, or LED, and when smoke particles enter the chamber, they are illuminated and

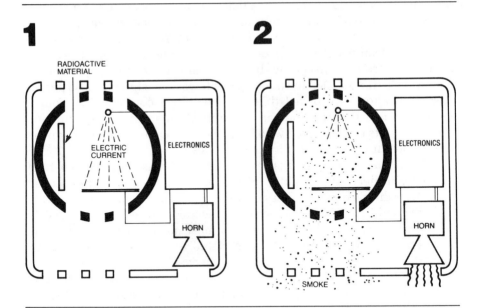

Figure 8-6.   Photocell smoke detector.

immediately detected by a sensitive photocell (see Figure 8-6). This generates a small output voltage that is amplified by a transistor circuit. If the
voltage is high enough, an alarm condition is generated (by using a flashing
light source and proper calibration, the photocell will detect only those
particles that are visible for at least 5 to 10 seconds and eliminate temporary
harmless smoke concentrations). These devices are also available in
battery-powered versions for the residential market.

The majority of home smoke detectors purchased up to 1980 are of the
ionization type (estimates made by the National Electrical Manufacturers
Association indicate that the percentage could be as high as 90 percent).
The ionization unit is extremely sensitive to the invisible particles of
combustion emitted by highly dangerous and fast burning smokeless fires.
The photoelectric type of detectors are sensitive to the larger, more visible
particles of combustion usually emitted by slow burning, smoldering fires.
(Currently, both types are available in battery-operated or hard-wire
housed models.) Neither ionization or photoelectric detectors are "perfect"
but both have had a significant effect in preventing injury from fire and
have revolutionized the science of early warning fire control.

While ionization smoke detectors respond somewhat slower than
photoelectric detectors to slow, smoldering fires, photoelectric smoke detectors respond somewhat slower than ionization detectors to fast burning

fires. Because of the inherent characteristics of each detector, it would appear that the ideal situation would consist of two smoke detectors — one a plug-in photoelectric detector and the other a battery-operated ionization detector. If only one detector is to be used, the type usually selected is the ionization type because of its sensitivity to products of combustion. The fact that radioactive material is used in this type of unit has led to a great deal of controversy in the industry.

### Radioactivity Safety

According to the report published by the Ionization Smoke Information Bureau, the amount of Americium 241 used in almost all smoke detectors is virtually undetectable with standard radiation measuring devices. It is considered negligible and is less than 1/1000th of the exposure received from natural background radiation sources, such as cosmic rays from the sun. Tests indicate that the radiation material is harmless while in the detector, or if released when involved in a fire, and that the risks in handling Americium 241 are negligible (even if the unit is treated as trash and burned or incinerated). Nevertheless, there is opposition to the use of ionization smoke detectors, relating to the overall increase of background radiation that people are exposed to today, for many consider a very slight increase of low-level radiation as harmful.

### Flame and Gas Detectors

**Flame Detectors.** Flame detectors are used only commercially since they are specifically designed to react to the light emitted by a flame or explosion. They react instantly, setting them apart from all other fire detectors, which are activated only after an accumulation of heat and smoke. They function in a manner similar to a light meter reacting to changes in light intensity caused by a flame. Rather than being sensitive to normal light, they are constructed to be sensitive to either ultraviolet rays or the infrared light present in all flames. Both units try to ignore flare light (e.g., sunlight, light bulbs, or heating coils). Generally, they are used to monitor refining or other gasoline storage facilities (e.g., airport hangars).

Although infrared detectors sometimes can be fooled by incandescent lights or someone lighting a cigarette, the better quality units respond only to a certain flame flicker (usually around 13 cycles per second). The ultraviolet detector cannot be fooled by heating elements or lamps since only an actual flame gives off ultraviolet radiation; hot glowing material does not. It is possible that these detectors could be fooled by the ultraviolet light contained in florescent lamps, but special filters eliminate this weakness.

**Gas Sensors.** The primary gas detector produced uses a small piece of porous metal. This metal is heated to several hundred degrees. Oxygen molecules attach themselves to the porous surface of the metal. This sets up a resistance on the surface of the metal that stops the current flow. As a flammable, gas flows across the surface of the metal; the oxygen molecules attach themselves to the newly introduced oxidizable gas. This lowers the electrical resistance, allowing the current to flow across the metal surface and setting off the alarm. It has one unique advantage over all the smoke detectors in that it is sensitive to oxidizable gas such as propane and carbon monoxide. Photocells and ionization detectors will not react to the exhaust of a running automobile in a closed garage, but the TAGUCHI gas sensor will. It will also react to smoke, but not as fast as the units called "smoke detectors."

The gas sensor is of foreign manufacture, and it was considered a very promising device until 1974 when the National Bureau of Standards rejected it as an early warning device. That decision destroyed its market potential as a smoke detector. It does have a unique value to the fire and gas detection field, but as yet it does not compete with the two previously discussed smoke detectors.

## SUMMARY

Motion detection devices have advanced in sophistication throughout history from very simple devices, like chimes, all the way up to laser beams, which have the capability of traveling thousands of feet. In earlier times, the emphasis of security was upon protection of the national welfare, while in the last two centuries, this emphasis also includes the protection of private and commercial property.

It is evident that this shift has been caused by the rising crime rate. It is estimated that two persons out of every hundred are victimized by burglaries each year, and the rate is still increasing. Commensurate with this increase in crime has been a growth in the use of security alarms and central alarm services.

This chapter has provided an overview of the basic concepts and methods used in conventional security alarm detection. It has examined some of the problems confronting the field, such as false alarms and poor alarm installation. Typical contact devices from mechanical switches to smoke detectors have been defined and explained. The one area of sensor detection that remains to be considered is volumetric alarm systems — the fastest growing segment of the alarm industry. This subject is covered in the next chapter.

## GLOSSARY

### Alarm Terms

*Actuator.*  A manual or automatic switch or sensor such as a holdup button, magnetic switch, or thermostat that causes a system to transmit an alarm.

*Air Gap.*  The distance between two magnetic elements in a magnetic or electromagnetic circuit, such as between the core and the armature of a relay or the space between the door and frame separating the two parts of a magnetic switch.

*Alarm Device.*  A device that signals a warning in response to an alarm condition such as a bell, siren, or other annunciator. In the fire alarm industry, it is sometimes called an indicating device.

*Alarm Discrimination.*  The ability of an alarm system to distinguish between stimuli caused by an intrusion and stimuli that are a part of the environment. Sometimes it is the name of the "count" control in a audio or vibration detection system.

*Alarm Station.*  (1) A manually actuated device installed at a fixed location to transmit an alarm signal in response to an alarm condition such as a concealed holdup button in a bank teller's cage. (2) A well-marked emergency control unit, installed in fixed locations usually accessible to the public, used to summon help in response to an alarm condition. The control unit contains either a manually actuated switch or a telephone connected to a source of help.

*Alarm System.*  An assembly of equipment and devices designated and arranged to signal the presence of an alarm condition requiring urgent attention such as unauthorized entry, fire, temperature rise, etc. The system may be local, proprietary, police connected, or central station.

*Annunciator.*  An alarm-monitoring device that consists of a number of visible or audible signals such as "flags" or lamps indicating the status of the detectors in an alarm system or systems. Each device is usually labeled to identify the location and/or condition being monitored.

*Area Sensor.*  A sensor with a detection zone that approximates an area, such as a wall surface or the exterior of a safe. Volumetric sensors, such as motion detectors, are sometimes called area sensors.

*Audible Alarm Device.*   A noise-making device such as a siren, bell, or horn used as part of a system to indicate an alarm condition.

*Authorized Access Switch.*   A device, often a key-operated switch, used to make an alarm system or portion of a system inoperative in order to permit authorized access through a protected doorway.

*Beam Divergence.*   In a photoelectric alarm system, the angular spread of the light beam.

*Burglar Alarm (B.A.) Screen or Pad.*   A supporting frame laced with fine wire (screen) or a fragile panel located with foil or fine wire (PAD) and installed so as to cover an exterior opening or surface in a building, such as a door, wall, or skylight. Penetration through the protected surface or opening breaks the wire or foil and initiates an alarm signal.

*Capacitance.*   The property of two or more metal (conducting) objects that enables them to store energy in an electric field between them. Earth ground is usually one of the objects.

*Capacitance Alarm System.*   An alarm system in which a protected object is electrically connected as a capacitance sensor. Earth ground is the surface to which the system is referenced. The approach of an intruder causes sufficient change in capacitance between object and ground to upset the balance of the system and initiate an alarm signal. Also called a proximity alarm system.

*Closed-Circuit System.*   A system in which the sensors of each zone are connected in series so that the same current flows in each sensor. When any activated sensor breaks the circuit or the connecting wire is cut, an alarm is transmitted for that zone.

*Coded-Alarm System.*   An alarm system in which the source of each signal is identifiable. This is usually accomplished by means of a series of current pulses that operate audible or visible annunciators and/or recorders to yield a recognizable signal. This is usually used to allow the transmission of multiple signals on a common circuit.

*Combination Sensor Alarm System.*   An alarm system that requires the simultaneous activation of two or more sensors to initiate an alarm signal. This is known as the "and" configuration. Some combination systems will alarm if either sensor is activated, which is known as an "or" hookup.

*Contact.*   (1) Each of the pair of metallic parts of a switch or relay, which by touching or separating makes or breaks the electrical current path. (2) A switch-type sensor.

*Contact Microphone.*   A microphone designed for attachment directly to a surface of a protected area or object, usually to detect surface vibrations.

*Control Unit.*   A device, usually electronic, that provides the interface between the alarm system and the human operator or the alarm system and its signaling circuit. It produces an alarm signal when its programmed response indicates an alarm condition. Some or all of the following may be provided for: power for sensors, sensitivity adjustments, means to select and indicate (access mode or secure mode), monitoring for line supervision and tamper devices, timing circuits, for entrance and exit delays, transmission of an alarm signal, etc.

*Detection Range.*   The greatest distance at which a sensor will consistently detect an intruder under a standard set of conditions.

*Door Trip Switch.*   A mechanical switch mounted so that movement of the door will operate the switch.

*Duress Alarm Device.*   A device that produces either a silent alarm or local alarm under a condition of personal stress such as holdup, fire, illness, or other panic or emergency. The device is normally manually operated and may be fixed or portable.

*E-Field Sensor.*   A sensor that detects changes in the electric field of a wire caused by the nearby movement of an intruder.

*False Alarm.*   An alarm signal transmitted in the absence of a real alarm stimulus. These may be classified according to causes: *environmental*, e.g., rain, fog, wind, hail, lightning, or temperature; *animals*, e.g., rats, dogs, cats, or insects; *man-made disturbances*, e.g., sonic booms, EMI, or vehicles; *equipment malfunction*, e.g., transmission errors or component failure; *operator error*; and unknown causes. If the reason for the alarm is obvious, it is called a nuisance alarm.

*Fence Alarm.*   Any of several types of sensors used to detect the presence of an intruder near a fence or any attempt by him to climb over, tunnel under, or cut through the fence.

*Floor Trap.*   A trap installed to detect the movement of a person across a floor space, such as a trip wire switch or mat switch. Photoelectric beams are sometimes called traps.

*Foil.*   Thin metallic strips that are cemented to a protected surface (usually glass in a window or door) and connected to a closed electrical circuit. If the foil is broken the circuit opens, initiating an alarm signal. Also called tape. A window, door, or other surface to which foil has been applied is said to be taped or foiled.

*Glassbreak Vibration Detector.*   A vibration detection system that employs a contact microphone attached to a glass window to detect cutting or breakage of the glass.

*Holdup Alarm System, Automatic.*   An alarm system that employs a holdup alarm device, in which the signal transmission is initiated without the knowledge of the intruder, such as a teller removing money from a money clip in a cash drawer.

*Holdup Alarm System, Manual.*   A holdup alarm system in which the signal transmission is initiated by the direct action of the person attacked or an observer of the attack, such as operation of a hand button or foot rail.

*Intrusion Alarm System.*   An alarm system for signaling the entry or attempted entry of a person or an object into the area or volume protected by the system.

*Line Sensor (detector).*   A sensor with a detection zone that approximates a line or series of lines, such as a photoelectric sensor that senses the blocking of a direct or reflected light beam.

*Line Supervision.*   Electronic protection of an alarm line accomplished by sending a continuous or coded signal through the circuit. A change in the circuit characteristics, such as a change in its electrical characteristic because the circuit was tampered with, will be detected by a monitor. The monitor initiates an alarm if the change exceeds a predetermined amount.

*Local Alarm System.*   An alarm system that, when activated, produces an audible and/or visible signal in the immediate vicinity of the protected premises or object. This term usually applies to systems designed to provide only a local warning of intrusion and not transmission to a remote monitoring station. However, local alarm systems are sometimes used in conjunction with a police station connection known as a "direct connect."

*Magnetic Alarm System.*   An alarm system that will initiate an alarm when it detects changes in the local magnetic field. The changes could be caused by motion of ferrous objects such as guns or tools near the magnetic sensor.

*Magnetic Switch.*   A switch that consists of two separate units: a magnetically actuated switch and a magnet. The switch is usually mounted in a fixed position (door jamb or window frame) opposing the magnet, which is fastened to a hinged or sliding door, window, etc. When the movable section is opened, the magnet moves away from the switch, allowing it to operate.

*Mat Switch.*   A flat area switch used on open floors or under carpeting. It may be sensitive over an area of a few square feet or several square yards.

*Mercury Switch.*   A switch operated by tilting or vibrating that causes an enclosed pool of mercury to move, making or breaking physical and electrical contact with conductors. These switches are used on tilting doors and windows, and fences.

*Normally Closed (NC) Switch.*   A switch in which the contacts are closed when no external forces act upon the switch.

*Open Circuit System.*   A system in which the sensors are connected in parallel. When a sensor is activated, the circuit is closed, permitting a current to flow that activates an alarm signal.

*Photoelectric Alarm System.*   An alarm system that employs a light beam and photoelectric sensor to provide a line of protection. Any interruption of the beam by an intruder is sensed by the sensor. Mirrors may be used to change the direction of the beam. The maximum beam length is limited by many factors, some of which are the light source intensity, number of mirror reflections, detector sensitivity, beam divergence, fog, and haze.

*Pressure Alarm System.*   An alarm system that protects a vault or other enclosed space by maintaining and monitoring a predetermined air pressure differential between the inside and outside of the space. Equalization of pressure resulting from opening the vault or cutting through the enclosure will be sensed and will initiate an alarm signal.

*Proprietary Alarm System.*   An alarm system that is similar to a central station alarm system except that the annunciator is located in a constantly manned guard room maintained by the owner for his own internal security operations. These guards monitor the system and respond to all alarm signals, alert local low enforcement agencies, or both.

*Proximity Alarm System.*   See Capacitance Alarm System.

*Secure Mode.*   The condition of an alarm system in which all sensors and control units are ready to respond to an intrusion.

*Seismic Sensor.*   A sensor, usually a "geophone," generally buried under the surface of the ground for perimeter protection, that responds to minute vibrations of the earth generated as an intruder walks or drives within its detection range.

*Shunt.*   (1) A deliberate shorting out of a portion of an electric circuit. (2) A key-operated switch that removes some portion of an alarm system from operation, allowing entry into a protected area without initiating an alarm signal. A type of authorized access switch.

*Silent Alarm.*   A remote alarm without an obvious local indication that an alarm has been transmitted.

*Standby Power Supply.*   Equipment that supplies power to a system in the event the primary power is lost. It may consist of batteries, charging circuits, auxiliary motor generators, or a combination of these devices.

*Strain Gauge Alarm System.*   An alarm system that detects the stress caused by the weight of an intruder as he moves about a building. Typical uses include placement of the strain gauge sensor under a floor joist or under a stairway tread.

*Supervised Lines.*   Interconnecting lines in an alarm system that are electrically supervised against faults or tampering. See also Line Supervision.

*Tamper Switch.*   A switch that is installed so as to detect attempts to remove the enclosure of alarm system components, such as control box doors, switch covers, junction box covers, or bell housings. The alarm component is then often described as being "tampered."

*Trap.*   (1) A device, usually a switch, installed within a protected area, which serves as secondary protection in the event a perimeter alarm system is successfully penetrated. Examples are a trip wire switch, photoelectric beam placed across a likely path for an intruder, or a mat switch mounted by an inner door. (2) A volumetric sensor installed so as to detect an intruder in a likely traveled corridor or pathway within a security area. Photoelectric beams are sometimes called "traps."

*Trip Wire Switch.*     A switch that is actuated by breaking or moving a wire or cord installed across a floor space.

*Vibration Sensor.*     A sensor that responds to vibrations of the surface on which it is mounted. One type has a normally closed switch that will momentarily open when it is subjected to a sufficiently large vibration. Its sensitivity is adjustable to allow for the different levels of normal vibration, to which the sensor should not respond, at different locations. A second version is an electronic contact microphone that generates a small voltage when subjected to vibration. It is similar to contact microphones used on musical instruments.

## NOTE

1. "The Facts Concerning Ionization Smoke Detectors," National Manufacturers Association, 197.

# Chapter 9
# Volumetric Intrusion Detection Systems

Volumetric detection alarm systems constitute the fastest growing segment of the alarm industry in the 1980s. Volumetric alarms differ from the mechanical devices described in Chapter 8 in that mechanical sensors generally protect only a single point, individual openings, or a narrow beam area, while volumetric systems are capable of flooding an entire room in all three dimensions with a protective screen. For this reason, these devices are also referred to as *space alarms*. Some of these volumetric devices are designed for small areas as short as 8 feet square while others can be used to detect movement as far as 200 feet from the sensor. The actual shape of the protective screen can be varied by changing the power, the antenna, or the optics of the space alarm. In general, the longer the protection coverage, the narrower the beam. Some of these space alarms are designed so the selection of the antenna or optics can alter the protective pattern from 30 feet by 30 feet to 100 feet by 6 feet. The electronics for both units are identical and in fact the volume coverage is also identical — only the shape of the pattern is altered.

Although some volumetric systems have been in existence for over 25 years, it is only since the late 1970s that they have begun to have a significant impact on the security industry. While most of the initial engineering theory relating to space technology was created in English laboratories (microwave) and in the United States (ultrasonic), in the 1980s there has been a tremendous growth of the Japanese influence in this area of "three-dimensional" intrusion detection. In the mid-1960s, when these detectors were introduced to the security marketplace, only a few firms produced the devices. These pioneering manufacturers had a great deal of difficulty in selling a new concept to an industry that is generally reluctant to adapt to changes in technology. The acceptance rate has been slow, but it is estimated that the space detection market constitutes the fastest growing segment of the alarm market.

There are still some technology problems associated with space detectors (ultrasonic range is affected by humidity, passive IR is suseptible to RF radiation, etc.), but in general, both the workmanship and reliability are improving each year. Problems still remain because there is now an acceptable method of comparing one device to another and there are no standards that have any effect on the area of coverage. The only effective method that can be used to determine which device is best suited for a particular situation is by trial and error. The lack of technical information has also adversely affected the market. This chapter was developed with the intent of clarifying much of the mystery surrounding the subject of space alarms. A basic description of these detectors include the following devices:

1.  *Ultrasonic and ultrasound* — sends high-frequency (above the normal human hearing range) sound waves into an area the size of an average classroom. Detection is in response to changes in the sound waves caused by movement within the protected area. The shape of the protection pattern is generally limited to room size.

2.  *Microwave* — operates on the same general theory of ultrasonic detection with an important difference in the frequency of the transmitter and receiver. It operates in extremely high radio frequency ranges, and can penetrate some kinds of wall material and be directed to protect areas as long as 400 feet. (Radar detectors are identical in operational performance.)

3.  *Audio* — highly sophisticated amplifier that is critically tuned to "listen" to sounds in specific bandwidths. This discriminating feature eliminates reaction to outside noise and detects sounds made by human movement. This is the primary distinction between a detector and a simple *amplifier.*

4.  *Passive infrared* — usually confused with the light beam detector that uses an infrared colored filter to disguise the beam. There is absolutely no relationship between the two. The light beam device simply records any interruption in the narrow beam of light. It requires both an active "sending" source of energy and a receiver. A passive IR system operates on an entirely different physical principle. It is "passive" in the sense that it does not require both a sender and a receiver. The sender is the infrared energy of the human body, which can be detected as long as the

temperature is different from the room temperature. Therefore a "passive" IR consists only of a receiver.

These four devices, in addition to motion detectors used as a component of a closed-circuit television system, are further delineated and discussed in this chapter.

## THE EARLY DEVICES

Intrusion technology, as described in the previous section, had its beginnings in the discovery of electricity in the eighteenth century along with the industry's attempt to find in this advancement a more sophisticated application of mechanical detection principles. Among the early demonstrations of this theory were the photoelectric light beam and the "wired" magnetic switch manufactured around 1850. Many of the companies that pioneered in the adaptation of mechanical equipment to electrical devices are still in existence today (e.g., Holmes Protective, Electric Signal, ADT, Potter, Western Union, and Gamewell).

By 1930 the alarm industry had reached a new level of sophistication that was concentrated in magnetic switches and light beams, with the entire industry controlled by a few large central alarm stations. The birth of electronics in the succeeding decades introduced transistors, printed circuit boards, and computers, effecting the almost total replacement of electromechanical concepts with new electronic techniques.

The greatest impact upon the industry occurred in 1952, when the first volumetric motion detection system was patented by Sam Bagno.[1] The invention made use of the application of the principle that the change (or echo) of a sound wave can be measured whenever it is disturbed by an intruder. Although this device was relatively effective, the security industry, comfortable with more traditional mechanical devices, was slow in accepting this electronic newcomer to the field.

Ultrasonic alarms were introduced to the market before the public understood their limitations, and well before the alarm installer was prepared to accept a replacement for mechanical alarms. New manufacturing companies entered this new market during the late 1960s, often without any knowledge of the security industry, and frequently eliminated the "luxury" of laboratory testing their products. By 1970 the rising false alarm rate of the ultrasonic devices, as well as other inherent deficiencies, forced the industry to develop more stable equipment. As a result, the ultrasonic manufacturers practically redesigned their product, while the alarm installer returned to the more reliable mechanical devices until about 1975.

By the mid-1970s, however, there was a resurgence in ultrasonic technology, and the marginal manufacturers gradually dropped out of the industry. Research and development efforts by a few companies produced a product far superior to the item introduced prematurely in the 1960s. This new acceptance of volumetric alarms encouraged the development of the more sophisticated passive infrared and microwave detectors. This technological competition did not hurt the ultrasonic market, but instead helped to publicize the unique advantages of volumetric systems in general and actually assisted in increasing ultrasonic sales. In turn, this produced wider acceptance of volumetric techniques. Today volumetrics are the primary system used to augment a perimeter system.

## ULTRASONIC AND ULTRASOUND DETECTORS

As previously stated, the oldest and most widely used volumetric device on the security market today is the ultrasonic detector. This device sends out high-frequency sound waves and responds to changes in those waves caused by movement within the protected area.

### Theory of Ultrasonic Detection

Sound is the mechanical phenomenon of air in vibration. It travels through the air in a wave-type motion. Without air, sound cannot be transmitted from one point to another (only radio waves or light or microwave signals can be detected in a vacuum). Sound can be generated by a vibrating object, a loudspeaker cone, the movement of a tuning fork, and so on, but it needs air to carry the signal from one point to another (see Figure 9-1).

The "pitch" of the sound is the frequency of the wave motion traveling toward the eardrum at a speed measured in waves per second. The

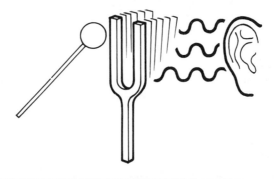

Figure 9-1.  Tuning fork.

higher the frequency, the higher the pitch. If only one wave travels through the air every second, it has a frequency of 1 Hertz (HZ).

Sound may also be defined as the range frequencies between 30 HZ and approximately 18,000 HZ that can be heard by most people. Any sound below or above this range of frequencies cannot be heard by the average human ear. Sound above this "normal" range of human hearing is called "ultrasound" or "ultrasonic." (Hearing does not stop abruptly at 18,000 HZ, particularly if the sound is strong enough and the listener has good hearing. Frequencies up to 22,000 HZ can be heard by some people (for some unexplained reason women have most of these sensitive ears). Animals are very sensitive to extremely high frequencies, particularly dogs who respond to dog whistles that are undetected by most humans.)

The manufacturers of ultrasonic alarms usually select frequencies slightly above human hearing for their ultrasonic alarms. The most popular frequencies fall in the range of 19,000 HZ, 21,000 HZ, 26,000 HZ, and as high as 40,000 HZ. The exact selection of frequency is based on various technical factors and practical considerations.

There is no single "perfect" frequency, since each frequency offers some advantages as well as disadvantages. The final choice is a balance of the many technical considerations that define sound waves. The industry generally tries to stay as close to the audible range as possible, but high enough so that the ultrasound does not penetrate the room barriers or be confused by common noises like hissing radiators or telephone bells ringing.

---

If someone were asleep in a room next to an apartment that had its stereo record player adjusted to maximum volume, the following would occur: The sleeper would be awakened by the sound of the drums and the low notes of the guitar, but would have difficulty hearing the high "brassey" sounds of the horns. Those high-frequency sounds remain confined to the inside walls of the apartment where the stereo is being played.

---

The sound should be above 20,000 HZ so that a burglar would be unaware of the detector's presence and location. However, it should be lower than 50,000 HZ since frequencies at higher ranges are easily absorbed by the air (any absorption significantly reduces the distance a detector can cover). Higher frequencies offer certain advantages since barriers (walls, ceilings, floors, and windows) cannot vibrate at higher frequencies. This means that more ultrasonic energy is forced back into the protected area. Very low frequencies (falling within the audible range) are not absorbed by the air, but can lose some of their overall effectiveness by vibrating the walls and windows. This lowers the important "bounce" or reflex characteristic. There are products on the market that are called *sonic* detectors because they operate in the audible range in a deliberate attempt to scare away, rather than capture, intruders.

The two most popular ultrasonic frequencies in use today by manufacturers are 20,000 HZ and 26,000 HZ.

### Doppler Effect

All ultrasonic systems use the principle of *doppler shift* as their basis for operation. The *doppler effect* is best described by using the classical example of a moving train. If a person were standing near the track watching a speeding train approach, he would hear a changing sound caused by the train whistle. As the train came closer, the pitch or frequency would rise. After the train passed, the whistle would appear to be reduced to a lower pitch.

Actually, anyone sitting on the train would hear exactly the same pitch sound during the entire trip. The man standing near the tracks was experiencing the basic effects of a doppler shift. As the train approached, its forward movement forced more sound waves per second to hit the man's

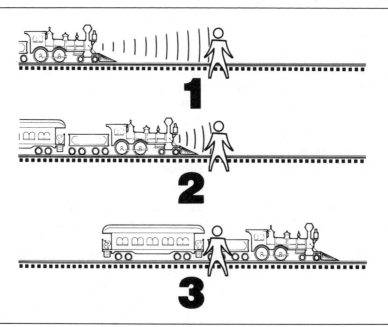

Figure 9-2.  Doppler effect.

eardrum, causing a sensation simulating a higher frequency or pitch. In any situation, as a person moves toward a sound source he intercepts sound waves. The faster he moves, the greater and higher the pitch change. Reversing the direction causes fewer sound waves to strike the eardrum. Ultrasonic detectors use this principle (i.e., movement causes changes in pitch) as their basis for operation (see Figure 9-2).

### Transducers, Receivers, and Piezoelectric Crystals

A *transducer* is an electronic component that converts energy from one form to another. All ultrasonic devices, regardless of their particular design or operating frequency, use two transducers, one to produce a sound (or ultrasound) wave and the other to receive sound. In the case of motion detectors, these are called *transmitting transducers* and *receiving transducers*.

- *Transmitting transducer* — converts electronic impulses into sound waves (like a loud speaker)
- *Receiving transducer* — captures incoming sound waves from the transmitter and converts them back into electronic impulses (like a microphone)

The first ultrasonic devices proved unstable and difficult to maintain with temperature and humidity changes. False alarms occurred as a result of the receiver reacting to "noises" that were not emitted by the transmitter. Many common noises (e.g., telephone bells, leaking steam, or squealing brakes) can produce ultrasonic frequencies that fall close enough to the tuned frequency to "fool" the system into signaling an intrusion alarm.

This limitation was overcome with the development of the *piezoelectric crystal*. This element enables the ultrasonic detector to maintain an exact frequency while ignoring extraneous and ambient noises. When an electrical signal is applied to the crystal, it vibrates at a predesigned frequency, sending a signal out and into the room. When this sound is "heard" by the receiving crystal and converted back into an electrical signal at exactly the same frequency that was originally transmitted, no alarm is recorded.

An alarm condition would occur if someone walked into the area covered by the detector, thus altering the sound wave pattern. The better ultrasonic detectors are designed to ignore very small changes. This capability is needed to keep the system from reacting to air in motion (drafts) and the movement of drapes or curtains. If the intruder moved very, very slowly, he could possibly defeat the system, but it would require a long time to move across a 30-foot room to steal the jewelery. But, of course, sometimes the reward is worth the effort.

An intruder moving at a normal pace in an area controlled by an ultrasonic transmitter and receiver would create a predictable change in frequency that would be measured as a doppler shift. The amount of shift is dependent on the speed of the intruder. This requires that careful design be incorporated into the detector to eliminate such distractions as air movement. This is easily accomplished by filtering out low doppler shifts without losing the sensitivity to a moving human.

For example, an ultrasonic device could be perfectly tuned to detect human movement at 100 HZ. This means that if the transmitted frequency were 20,000 HZ, a normal human movement toward the receiver would change the frequency to 20,100 HZ. A movement away from the receiver would lower the frequency to 19,900 HZ. A change of exactly 100 HZ in either direction would trigger an alarm. A change less or greater than the 100 HZ frequency caused by a draft would register as such by the system, and it would not generate an alarm.

### Single Units vs. Multihead Units

There are basically two types of ultrasonic devices in use today: the *transceiver* (or monostatic) detector and the multihead (or bistatic) detector.

The transceiver is a single station unit that encloses both the transmitter and the receiver. All electronics are encased within a single housing, and in effect the device functions as a complete alarm system.

The multihead unit separates the transmitter from the receiver for distances generally up to 30 feet. All power and signal processing is done in the master panel with the ultrasonic "heads" posessing only sending and receiving crystals. These small units can be mounted inconspicuously in separate locations and can cover greater areas at lower cost than transceivers. Some control panels can process and power up to 100 pairs of heads, which in a multiroomed building like a school is a great advantage over the conventional and bulkier transceivers.

The first units placed on the market were multiheaded (bistatic) but were soon replaced by single-headed transceivers. While transceivers still make up a significant portion of the market today, they are gradually being replaced by multiheaded units (A sort of reverse of its original history.) There is some debate in the industry as to the efficiency of single station versus multihead units. Generally speaking, both are highly reliable, with the multihead unit possibly more economically acceptable in multiroom areas.

## MICROWAVE DETECTION

The microwave detection field grew out of the need for a sophisticated device that would effectively detect motion without being distracted by external environmental stimuli (e.g., air currents or insects). The first microwave devices were introduced around 1968, which was at a time when the industry was just beginning to understand the advantages of ultrasonic technology. Initially, sales representatives for the one company that manufactured microwave alarm units spent more time educating the alarm installer about microwave theory than "selling" the device. Because of the unfamiliarity of the industry with microwave theory, the device was frequently misapplied and misinstalled, with the result that many components failed and false alarms occurred far more often than the industry could economically tolerate.

### Theory of Microwave Detection

Over the years, microwave detection has been identified by several different (and sometimes confusing) names: RF (radio frequency), radar detection, radiation resistance detection, and, finally, microwave.

The earliest versions of microwave detectors did not use the frequency shift effect to detect motion. They operated in the lower radio frequency range, and although sometimes referred to as microwave frequencies, they really were not high enough to be considered microwave. Those first units utilized a simple pole-shaped antenna that radiated RF energy in every direction surrounding the antenna. Any movement within its range reflected energy back into the antenna, changing the pattern of the antenna radiation. Not until the late 1960s when the government permitted operation at extremely high frequencies did microwave come into its own. Another important factor that helped promote microwave detectors was the availability of cost-effective microwave sources (oscillators).

### Ultrasonic vs. Microwave

Ultrasonic units operate in the 20,000 HZ to 40,000 HZ range. AM broadcast frequencies are around 1,000,000 HZ and microwave systems generally operate at the 10,525,000,000 HZ range, which is also called the 10.5 GIGA HERTZ range. It is included in what is called the "X" band.

In accordance with FCC regulations, microwave detectors are permitted to operate only within a limited power and range, and at only five

THEORETICALLY, MICROWAVE ENERGY
CAN REACH THE MOON—BUT
THE MICROWAVE DETECTOR WOULD
NEVER "SEE" THE ENERGY COMING BACK
BECAUSE IT WOULD BE SO WEAK.

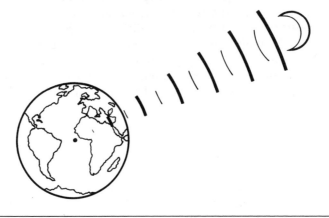

Figure 9-3.   Microwave energy.

specific frequencies. Techniques were developed to take advantage of these high band frequencies, which introduced a new technology into the motion detection field. The 10.525 GHZ frequency is the most popular frequency used, and almost all commercial microwave systems are manufactured to operate on this frequency. Although microwave techniques have not replaced ultrasonic devices, they offer a new approach to large area monitoring by one transceiver that could not be achieved with any other motion detection system (see Figure 9-3).

### Method of Operation

High-frequency microwave signals are generated by a solid-state device called a *Gunn diode*. These diodes consume relatively small amounts of power in order to remain within the limits mandated by the FCC. The power generated is less than 10 millivolts or 1/100 of a watt. This low power is sufficient to drive a signal up to 400 feet, but cannot (as some microwave critics claim) affect the operation of a pacemaker or cause other physical damage to humans.

In order for the Gunn diode to radiate the required microwave energy, the transmitter and receiver must be installed in a metal box with one side open. This enclosure is called a *microwave cavity*. The same "cavity" can cover different areas simply by changing the antenna shape. The overall volume of coverage remains constant, but the coverage pattern can be altered from a narrow path of 300 feet × 2 feet × 1 foot (600 cubic feet) to cover a room that is 10 feet × 10 feet × 6 feet (also 600 cubic feet).

This shape-changing ability is a favorable feature since a basic shortcoming of other devices is that they are difficult to modify for different situations. Each microwave unit transmits the "wave" into a protected area, striking stationary objects in the room. These waves are reflected back to the receiver. The receivers are adjusted to ignore the signals from stationary objects because they do not create a doppler shift. They are sensitive, however, to anyone moving within this field of coverage. This is similar to the operational theory of ultrasonic devices, but there are several characteristics that make microwave units unique and, in many situations, superior to other volumetric alarm devices. They are virtually immune to false alarms caused by changes in temperature, humidity, or higher frequency *noise* created by bells, sirens, or air conditioners. They are also immune to *air current* movement associated with heaters and air conditioners. As a result of this ability to "ignore" random air disturbances, microwave units are ideally suited for large open areas and extremely long hallways. To be more competitive with ultrasonic systems, units are now on the market that have a relatively limited range of 30 feet, which is far shorter than the original designers intended.

## Microwave Power

The energy (or power) generated by a microwave detector is a small fraction of the amount used in microwave ovens or radar systems that can reach the moon. As a motion detection device, the microwave unit is usually restricted to transmissions of less than 400 feet. Although this is insignificant compared to transmissions generated by large units at airports, it is much stronger than the average ultrasonic or passive IR system.

The circuitry in the microwave is designed to "read" the doppler shift between 20 HZ and 120 HZ. Any movement falling within this range would be detected. The amount of sensitivity depends on six conditions: (1) amount of radiated energy, (2) size of the object, (3) distance of the object from the microwave cavity, (4) speed of the object, (5) direction of movement, and (6) reflection and absorption of waves by room material.

One microwave detector can protect an area as large as a football field, and even further, if the object is larger. If a person is detected at 300 feet, it is conceivable that the same system could detect a truck at 400 feet, a jet aircraft at 500 feet, and so on.

A bird at close range may be detected by the unit; however, since it moves faster than an intruder and causes a doppler shift greater than 120 HZ, which is higher than the detection range, it will generally be ignored. On the other hand, a moth would not be detected no matter how close it flies to the cavity because of its small size. The speed of a bird approximates that of an intruder when it slows down to take off or land. To compensate for this, the microwave system can be designed to ignore the bird's presence by rejecting any movement that does not last three seconds or longer.

While this technical immunity to normal ambient disturbances has given microwave units certain inherent advantages over other volumetric devices, there are four distinct precautions that must be followed before designing a security system that relys on microwave techniques.

Microwave ability to penetrate into undesired areas and detect movement outside a protected area can cause false signaling. The actual amount of unwanted penetration is easily determined because the security industry has over 10 years experience in dealing with this characteristic (see Figure 9-4).

| Material | Penetration |
|---|---|
| Glass | 100$U$ |
| Dry wall | 50$U$ |
| Cinder block | 10$U$ |
| Metal | 0$U$ |

While penetration is unwanted in most cases, it can be used to an advantage. By placing a long-range microwave in the attic, the signal pattern can be directed to cover an entire house because of the ability of the "waves" to travel through the wooden ceiling. On the other hand, it can cause trouble when the pattern travels through windows and detects movement outside the premises.

A second and very common characteristic is the unit's ability to be reflected off stationary metal objects when microwave energy is aimed at the surface. Sometimes this "bounce" effect can increase the intensity of the coverage in a given area.

A third characteristic is that the *size* and *movement* of the target can be a cause of false triggering. If, for example, a 100-foot microwave detector were aimed at an overhead door located 150 feet away and even though it is outside the area that is being protected, any rattling of the door (from wind or other causes) will probably trigger the microwave detector. This problem occurs because a 100-foot detector is designed to "sense" a man taking three steps at 100 feet. The intruder (man) is composed predominantly of

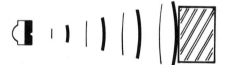

STEEL OR METALLIC SURFACES ARE NEAR PERFECT REFLECTORS.

CONCRETE FLOORS AND WALL ALSO ARE GOOD REFLECTORS,
WITH ONLY SLIGHT PENETRATION.

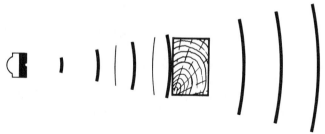

SOLID WOOD REFLECTS SOME OF THE MICROWAVE ENERGY
BUT PENETRATION WILL OCCUR.

GLASS READILY TRANSMITS THE MICROWAVE ENERGY.

Figure 9-4.   Transmission of microwave.

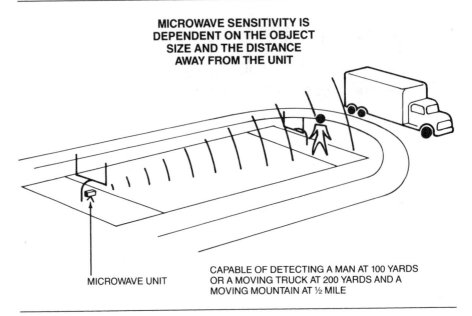

**MICROWAVE SENSITIVITY IS
DEPENDENT ON THE OBJECT
SIZE AND THE DISTANCE
AWAY FROM THE UNIT**

MICROWAVE UNIT

CAPABLE OF DETECTING A MAN AT 100 YARDS
OR A MOVING TRUCK AT 200 YARDS AND A
MOVING MOUNTAIN AT ½ MILE

Figure 9-5.   Microwave sensitivity.

water, a poor reflector of microwave energy, while the rattling door, because of its size and reflectivity, may be sensed at distances greater than the
range that the detector is supposedly protecting (see Figure 9-5).

Another factor that must be considered before designing a security
system using microwave detectors is the amount of vibration of the surface
that the unit is mounted on. Passing trains, compressors, and so forth can be
interpreted by the detector as the movement of a large object and result in
false alarming.

## AUDIO DETECTION

One of the most familiar concepts in the field of electronics is the function
of the microphone and its sensitivity to even the slightest sound levels. The
microphone (or speakers that function exactly like microphones) operate
by converting sound into an electrical impulse that can be amplified. In a
similar manner, this cycle of sound–electrical impulse–sound is the basis
of operation for the *audio detection system.*

Audio detection systems are designed to "read" the signatures of
sounds picked up by strategically located microphones. If the detected
sound is loud or continuous enough, or at a specific frequency, it will cause
the system to go into alarm.

The principle of audio detection is based upon the theory that intruders will create a noise of known frequency and volume as they move around a room. Almost every movement creates a detectable noise even before the creator of the noise enters the protected premises. The audio detector can often "sense" intrusion before it occurs (e.g., a key being placed in an outside lock or physical attack against a building). Ultrasonic and microwave units do not have this capacity.

---

Audio and vibration detection is the only acceptable technique approved by insurance companies to be used inside bank vaults. In the quiet atmosphere of the small vault area, the audio detection microphone can sense the burring and drilling into concrete and steel, or the hammering or shoveling around the outside vault area. It "sees" what is not there!

---

Even a low-level noise can be detected by an inexpensive microphone mounted high on a wall or ceiling, amplified and analyzed for frequency patterns. When used in a bank vault, no frequency discrimination is necessary, since all detectable sounds in this normally quiet environment are suspicious. A great deal of ambient noise is present, however, when used in a building in a residential or commercial area. In this environment, special electronic circuitry is required to distinguish intrusion sounds from recurring common sounds.

### Theory of Audio Detection

The primary difference between ultrasonic and audio detection units is that ultrasonic units are active; they transmit their own sound patterns and actually control their operating frequency. Audio units, on the other hand, are passive since they do not transmit signals. They are only receivers and must be accurately programmed to detect the frequencies of sound created by human movement. The one significant advantage of audio detection becomes apparent when it is used with a remote central station. The signal is annunciated on a control panel like all other alarm signals. The operator, alerted to the alarm condition, must take responsible action to record this alarm condition and alert responsible individuals to take corrective action. The only way to determine the reason for the alarm is to send someone to survey the building where the alarm condition occurred. This often proves to be a time-consuming and frustrating process, since alarms transmitted are frequently false. The audio detector possesses the special advantage of allowing the central station operator to actually "listen in" to the source of the alarm condition. With a little practice, any operator can identify the familiar sounds of banging pipes, airplanes, traffic noise, or can even monitor and record the actual conversation of burglers. The audio detector is the one method currently available to analyze false alarms, thus avoiding false responses without resorting to desensitizing the alarm system.

**Frequency Selection.** Sounds are generally broken down into measurements of cycles per second (HZ), with most sounds falling in a range between 1500 HZ and 6000 HZ. Sounds below 1500 HZ are considered low frequency, and can cause a problem when picked up as a "street noise" by sensitive audio detectors. For this reason, sophisticated audio detectors are designed to capture all sound between 1500 HZ and 6000 HZ and filter out frequencies below 1500 HZ. In this way, the detector is able to discriminate outside noises that may occur inside the building. There are special situations in which the detector is tuned to a specific frequency range, for example, when used in bank vaults, attack noises on concrete are rich in 200 HZ, and when used at schools to detect vandalism, breaking glass is around 4,700 HZ.

**Accumulation and Pulse Count.** Even though audio detection electronics are designed to function within a narrow bandwidth (1500 HZ to 6000 HZ), confusion may still be created by interior ambient noises, such as clocks, bells, furnaces, water, or steam hammer effects. To compensate for this problem, a technique was developed to introduce circuits that accumulate the noise and count the number of pulses within a specific period of time.

---

If a detector were adjusted to react only to noises repeated three or four times within a predetermined period, it would not react to an explosion or a jet breaking the sound barrier (even though the loudness of these sounds is extreme). It would, however, sound an alarm if a person repeated a sound four times (foot steps) within a protected area. This capability is referred to as *pulse count.*

---

The reason why the low sounds of a person walking are able to set off an alarm is not due to pulse count alone. The sophisticated audio detector also possesses an *accumulation circuit* that is capable of adding sounds together if they are similar and occur within a preselected time frame.

Since burglers and vandals have been known to move hurriedly, the accumulation circuit is an important feature. Another asset of the accumulation circuit is that it will discriminate between noises, such as the steady ring of the phone or the hourly ringing of a bell.

## Use of Audio Detectors in Special Situations

There are numerous self-contained audio detection units designed for home use only. These portable units are made to look like hi-fi speaker cabinets and contain sirens as well as detector circuits. This type of detector has a low-grade (or none) discrimination circuit and reacts to lightning, thunder, animals, and other external stimuli. Hopefully, it would also go into alarm if a would-be intruder tried to force open a window. Although its siren might frighten the intruder away, it probably would not bring the police (or even the neighbors) since its proneness to false alarms has caused others to disregard it. When this self-contained unit is used in commercial establishments, it has produced less than satisfactory results, and is sometimes stolen along with the merchandise.

There are many situations in which audio detection can be superior to other alarm devices. One example is in buildings that possess a public address system (P.A.) with speakers installed throughout the entire structure. This existing network of speakers can be easily converted into an audio detection system when the speakers are utilized as microphones.

A large number of schools in the United States are alarmed with audio detector systems. This system operates by means of placing an audio detection unit adjacent to the public address control panel and connecting it to the P.A. speaker wiring. During the day, the P.A. system is used normally. At night, however, the P.A. amplifier is turned off and the audio detector switched on by the last person to leave the building. This action utilizes (electronically converts) all the speakers to microphones, and allows a panel operator to "listen in" to all areas throughout the building equipped with P.A. speakers. This is possible even though the only wiring connecting the detector to the speaker cable harness is behind the P.A. rack.

Generally, the results of using the P.A. systems for audio detection have been disappointing. In most cases, audio detectors are poorly matched for this application. Although electrical circuits can be designed for proper matching, most manufacturers have not undertaken the research and testing necessary to produce an effective device. There are a few acceptable systems available, however, but they are generally disregarded because of the poor reputation created by companies who prematurely introduced an inefficient product. One of the largest manufacturers in the audio detection field sells its audio vault alarm (no discrimination) as an audio detector for use in buildings that experience steady outside noises. The company actually repackages the existing system and mounts two identical vault alarms in a single enclosure. The first unit monitors noises inside the building, and the second unit is connected to a microphone (speaker) mounted outside the building. Since the system does not have any frequency discrimination, both units can "hear" outside noises at the same time. The unit monitoring the outside area will disconnect the system temporarily if it detects sound — a crude method of applying a cancellation circuit to a system designed specifically for a quiet bank vault.

The primary advantage of audio detection systems is their ability to transmit sounds over a phone line for determination of the source or type of sound being detected. This capability is becoming more and more important in an industry that produces equipment that is frequently activated by false signals. This ability has given audio detection a potential to recapture a significant portion of the credibility it has lost in the last decade to other alarm detectors.

### Audio Detectors: Primary Characteristics

1. Discriminates all sounds that fall outside the 1500 HZ to 6000 HZ range.
2. Counts pulses of sounds while disregarding single disturbances.
3. Has an effective sensitivity control.
4. May be matched electronically to public address speakers or remote microphones.
5. Possesses a cancellation circuit to eliminate persistant outside noises.
6. Provides for supervised protection of the cable between the main panel and the microphones.
7. Incorporates hi-fidelity amplification to permit "listening in" from a central station.

## PASSIVE INFRARED DETECTORS

During the Vietnam war, the federal government perfected, as a surveillance device, a technique to detect ground movement at night from low flying reconnaissance aircraft. This system was different from the existing methods of photography and radar and possessed the following unique characteristics:

1. It did not require visible light, as did camera surveillance techniques.
2. It did not (like radar, microwave, and ultrasonic) require a transmitted (active) signal to measure movement.
3. Its detection (unlike audio systems) was totally unrelated to noise or sound.

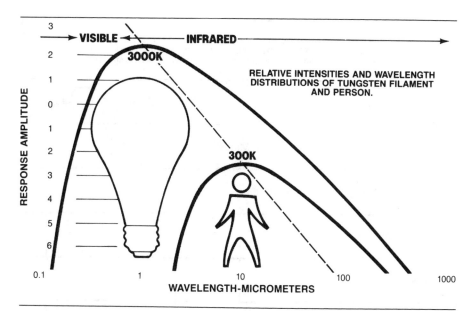

Figure 9-6. IR phenomenon.

The system utilized the physical phenomena found in certain materials that experienced a change in their electrical characteristic when bombarded with infrared energy. The passive IR motion detection system became a practical addition to the detection field due to the development during the 1960s by the Department of Defense. Prior to that period, the only practical application of this technology was its use in medical laboratories, where it was discovered that carcinogenic tissues projected more IR energy because of a higher oxidation rate than healthy tissues. Although there are major differences between the IR equipment developed for the detection of malignant tumors and that used in aircraft surveillance, the basic concept remains the same (see Figure 9-6).

The theory of passive infrared technology had its origin over 23 centuries ago when the Greeks observed the changes that took place when a certain crystal (tourmaline) was placed in hot ashes. The material attracted and then repelled the ashes as it heated up. This was the first recorded incidence of the operation of a pyroelectric sensor ("pyro" for fire and "electric" for the change in polarity). The obvious advantage of any passive technology is that it uses what is already there — it is completely natural and harmless. It utilizes the invisible glow of objects and people as a source of energy (see Figure 9-7).

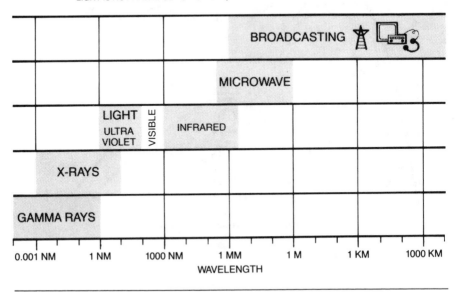

THE NATURE OF RADIANT ENERGY DEPENDS ON ITS WAVELENGTH, RANGING FROM GAMMA RAYS, LEFT, TO EXTREMELY LOW FREFQUENCIES, RIGHT. VISIBLE LIGHT IS NOT HARMFUL TO HUMANS, BUT OTHER WAVELENGTHS MAY BE.

Figure 9-7.   Electromagnetic spectrum.

### IR Radiation: Primary Characteristics

1. Infrared is a form of transmittable energy normally emitted by every object because of its temperature.
2. Infrared energy is transmitted without physical contact between the emitting and receiving surfaces.
3. Infrared energy warms the receiving surfaces and can be detected by any device capable of sensing a change in temperature.
4. Infrared energy is invisible and completely silent.

### Operational Characteristics

The passive IR detector is basically an optical device that utilizes a simple lens system to focus IR radiation onto a small piece of material called a thermal sensor. The industry has experimented with three different types of sensors over the last two decades: (1) thermocouple, (2) thermistor, and (3) pyroelectric. Almost all manufacturers today use the ceramic pyroelectric type. (Some firms are experimenting with a plastic type that is less expensive than ceramic, but it does not offer any superior technical characteristic.)

In a pyroelectric device, a change in temperature creates a change in polarization, which is just another way of describing an electric change. Thus a pyroelectric device is capable of producing current only when it experiences a temperature change. When the element is at a constant temperature, no current is produced.

The passive infrared detection system consists of three major elements:

1. The *window* restricts the incoming light by functioning as an optical filter for the wavelength band of interest (blocks the wavelength of no interest), and it also protects the sensing element and internal electronics from physical damage and moisture. Different materials are available and the particle selection is based on what one is looking at and what might interfere.

2. A *sensing element* responds to the light energy and produces a signal that can be amplified. The material has names like lithium tantalate. In recent years, these "sensors" have been made with two identical elements encapsulated in one cavity called a dual element sensor.

3. *Integral electronics* assist in mating the signal with other components. If the power of incident light were great enough, no additional electronics would be needed to detect the change in the electrical characteristic of the sensing element. However, this is seldom the case because the input light energy is usually low in power and some signal amplification is necessary. The integral electronics element is usually mounted within the detector package rather than external to it (see Figure 9-8).

The focusing of IR energy on the sensing element (transducer) is accomplished by "bouncing" the energy waves off a lens and focusing it onto the element, somewhat like a camera lens does to the film surface. The major difference in handling IR energy from visible light is that IR energy cannot go through glass material. Consequently, two techniques had to be developed that focus the energy without obstructing the movement: (1) reflective focusing, which bounces the energy off a concave mirror, and (2) the Fresnel lens, which allows the energy to travel directly to the sensing element.

Both techniques are readily available with the reflective design the more popular of the two. In order to detect human movement at various distances, the optics have to be changed, which is more expensive in the reflective type. Changing optics in the Fresnel type only requires a replacement of an inexpensive plastic cover "lens." Of course, the reflective type is more efficient since it gathers 100 percent of the incoming energy while the Fresnel lens, by its very characteristic, absorbs some of the

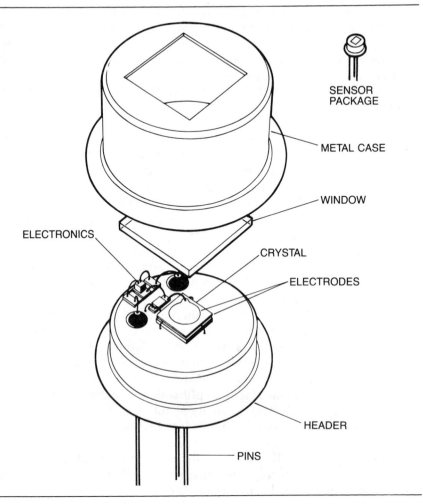

Figure 9-8.   Sensor package.

energy. To compensate for this loss, the lens is made larger. Both techniques seem to produce equal results and the industry will probably continue to produce both types for the foreseeable future (see Figures 9-9 and 9-10).

### Sensitivity

Passive IR detectors are so sensitive to heat that there are some devices being made that can distinguish between temperatures that are within a fraction of one another, and they can accomplish this feat at distances over

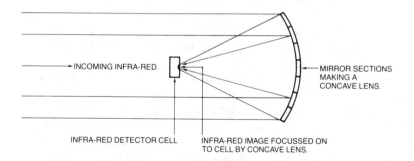

INCOMING INFRA-RED.

MIRROR SECTIONS
MAKING A
CONCAVE LENS.

INFRA-RED DETECTOR CELL

INFRA-RED IMAGE FOCUSSED ON
TO CELL BY CONCAVE LENS.

AN IMAGE OF THE HEAT RADIATED BY AN INTRUDER IS CAST
ON THE LENS, AND FOCUSSED ON THE CELL. HIS MOVEMENT
WILL CAUSE A CHOPPED SIGNAL DUE TO THE SECTIONED LENS.

Figure 9-9.   Reflective type IR optics.

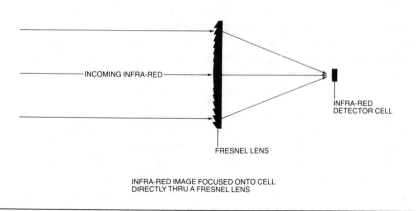

INCOMING INFRA-RED

INFRA-RED
DETECTOR CELL

FRESNEL LENS

INFRA-RED IMAGE FOCUSED ONTO CELL
DIRECTLY THRU A FRESNEL LENS

Figure 9-10.   Frensnel lens (direct focus).

2000 feet. These sophisticated sensors require supercooled temperatures that would be technically and economically impractical for the alarm industry accustomed to paying $100 for a sensor. On the other hand, the military purchases units that cost $50,000 or more for use as a surveillance device rather than as a detector.

All objects emit IR radiation, but they do so at different levels that are dependent on temperature. Figure 9-6 points out the visible region within the narrow band between 0.45 and 0.75 micron (units of light energy are measured in microns: 1 micron = 1/1000 of 1 millimeter). The infrared region lies below the frequency of light and at a bandwidth of 0.75 to 1000 microns. The peak energy of the sun is in the visible region, yet most of its radiant energy is in the infrared band. Even objects as cold as dry ice and liquid air transmit infrared radiation. Since a human body radiates IR energy in the region of 7 to 14 microns, the motion detector is designed to concentrate on this narrow band.

Once the optical IR detector adjusts to the amount of IR radiation being emitted from the surrounding environment, it is sensitive to any sudden changes in emitted IR radiation. Small movements in the environment are usually ignored, but whenever a body that has more than a 2°F temperature differential moves between the detector and the background upon which it is focused, it will be detected. Since every solid object in a room emits different amounts of IR energy, it is almost impossible to build a shield at one ambient temperature that could hide a moving intruder. When the room temperature reaches 80° to 85°F, the sensitivity of the system is greatly reduced because skin temperature of humans falls into this range.

IR motion detectors do not measure actual temperature, but instead react to the difference in the radiated heat of the objects captured by the lens system. Although heat is not an actual measurement of temperature, radiated infrared energy bears a close relation to temperature. The higher the temperature, the greater the infrared radiation. IR energy does not travel slowly, like heat waves, but moves rapidly through space at the speed of light. Consequently, infrared detectors are infinitely more sensitive to changes in temperature than thermometers.

The mercury tilt switch in a wall-mounted thermostat automatically controls the heat given off by the furnace and radiators when a bimetallic strip tilts the switch. The mercury moves back and forth, making and breaking the contact, depending on the fluctuating temperature. Infrared-sensitive elements (transducers) also react to temperature change — only at a much faster rate — and can be focused on a small spot in a room rather than having to sense the ambient temperature surrounding the device.

### Passive IR Detector as a Surveillance Device

As previously mentioned, passive IR detectors were used as surveillance devices during the Vietnam war. This was accomplished by installing the unit in low flying reconnaissance aircraft. Liquid nitrogen was added to the atmosphere around the transducer enabling the unit to respond to changes in IR radiation. The plane was thus able to spot nighttime enemy encampments by detecting the temperature difference between the "body heat" or IR energy of the enemy and the slightly cooler temperature of the ground surface.

This particular system was so effective that it was used to record the encampment of the enemy even after they had gone. This was possible since, during a normal encampment period the enemy equipment would shade the ground surface beneath the equipment, leaving it cooler than ground struck by sunlight. When the convoy left the area, the cool "silhouettes" of its equipment were left on the ground. Since it took some time for the cooler surface to warm up, it was possible for the IR surveillance equipment to detect the cooler surfaces and actually record a clear impression of the equipment even though it had been removed hours before. Of course, as time passed, the entire area would reach thermal equalibrium and detection would no longer be possible.

### Use of Passive IR Detectors

When passive IR devices were first introduced onto the market, they were limited to a 30-foot range and competed with ultrasonic units. Now units are available to cover various distances by changing the optics and many manufacturers make their devices in two modules. One contains the necessary electronics and relays and power supply and the other encloses the optics and the sensing element (in the reflective type systems). Fresnel lens devices require only a lens change. Simply inserting the desired optical unit can change the field of protected view from 30 feet × 30 feet to 7 feet × 150 feet and even to 300 feet. (Ultrasonic systems are limited to a maximum of 40 feet since it would require too much power to force a soundwave signal to a greater distance.) It must be pointed out that the long-range units are extremely difficult to operate since "telephoto" distance magnifies all movement (see Figure 9-11).

Once again, it must be pointed out that there is a great deal of confusion in the security protection field regarding the use of the photoelectric light beam (which often uses an infrared color filter) and the passive infrared motion detector. *The two are alike in nomenclature only.*

The photoelectric light beam device requires a transmitter and is, therefore, like ultrasonic and microwave units, considered an ACTIVE alarm device. The passive IR unit does not require both a sender and a receiver. The infrared energy of the human body acts as a sender, and the device is therefore considered a PASSIVE system.

Although they are not the panacea to all protection situations, passive IR sensors are immune to many environmental conditions, such as humidity, air currents, and soundwave disturbances. They can be a little trouble-

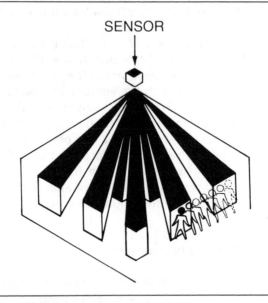

SENSOR

Figure 9-11.    Passive IR detection pattern.

some if pointed directly at rapidly rising heat sources. Windows are not normally a problem, but if covered by loose blinds or curtains that may be moved by air turbulance, the unit will detect a net temperature change between a bare window and the blind or curtain that covers the window. Space heaters and ovens are a particular problem because they heat rapidly on their exterior. Incandescent light bulbs can also cause problems because their glass shell heats rapidly when turned on. Yet with these minor limitations, the advantages appear to overcome the disadvantages and passive IR has become the fastest growing segment of the volumetric alarm industry.

## CLOSED-CIRCUIT TELEVISION (CCTV)

The use of CCTV as a security device is growing in popularity and flexibility. (Figures 9-12 and 9-13 illustrate various CCTV systems and optional equipment.) CCTV is used in almost every type of industrial and commercial situation from high-security environments (nuclear plants) to the controlling of movement in a public school. The use of TV systems for security purposes closely followed the same growth pattern followed by the home unit that displayed radio frequency transmitted signals. Most security

## ONE CAMERA WITH ONE MONITOR

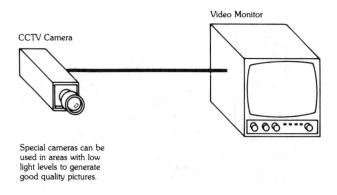

Video Monitor

CCTV Camera

Special cameras can be
used in areas with low
light levels to generate
good quality pictures.

## ONE CAMERA WITH MANY MONITORS

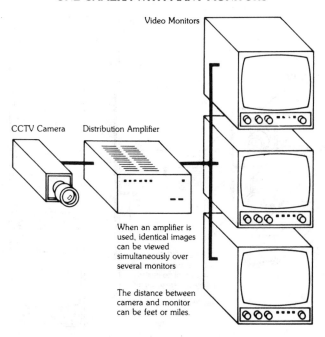

Video Monitors

CCTV Camera    Distribution Amplifier

When an amplifier is
used, identical images
can be viewed
simultaneously over
several monitors

The distance between
camera and monitor
can be feet or miles.

Figure 9-12.   CCTV systems. (Courtesy of Chubb Security)

## MANY CAMERAS WITH ONE MONITOR

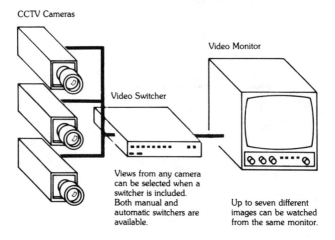

CCTV Cameras

Video Monitor

Video Switcher

Views from any camera can be selected when a switcher is included. Both manual and automatic switchers are available.

Up to seven different images can be watched from the same monitor.

## MANY CAMERAS WITH MANY MONITORS

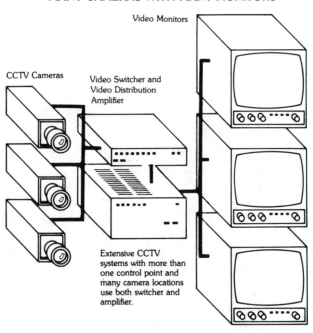

Video Monitors

CCTV Cameras

Video Switcher and Video Distribution Amplifier

Extensive CCTV systems with more than one control point and many camera locations use both switcher and amplifier.

Figure 9-12.    (continued)

systems use a far less expensive lens, since resolution is not as important as on the home units. Also, CCTV systems utilize black and white tubes rather than color because of cost considerations. The most important technical difference between CCTV systems and the conventional 13-channel home sets is that the 13-channel system utilizes a tuner and a roof-type antenna to "capture" a radio frequency signal that is displayed on the monitor. Because CCTV monitors are not as mass produced as commercial units, and have to operate reliably 24 hours a day, they are more expensive than the "home" unit. These factors of low production and high reliability overcome the economic fact that there are less components in a CCTV system.

In CCTV systems, each camera is wired directly into an individual monitor. In situations where CCTV is connected into a conventional home unit (to display the entrance area to an apartment complex on an empty channel), the CCTV camera has to "feed" the picture image through a device called a modulator into the master antenna, where it is tuned along with the channels that transmit radio frequency signals. (There is no practical method to view commercial TV channels on a basic CCTV security system.)

The only limit on the numbers of cameras and monitors that can be used as part of a security surveillance system is the ability of the monitor to follow the action on the various screens. Too many screens could confuse

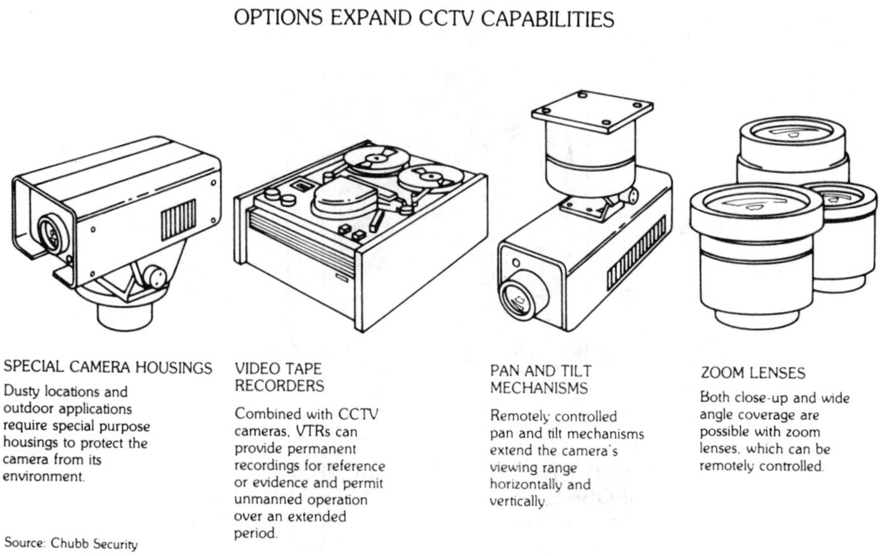

OPTIONS EXPAND CCTV CAPABILITIES

SPECIAL CAMERA HOUSINGS
Dusty locations and outdoor applications require special purpose housings to protect the camera from its environment.

Source: Chubb Security

VIDEO TAPE RECORDERS
Combined with CCTV cameras, VTRs can provide permanent recordings for reference or evidence and permit unmanned operation over an extended period.

PAN AND TILT MECHANISMS
Remotely controlled pan and tilt mechanisms extend the camera's viewing range horizontally and vertically.

ZOOM LENSES
Both close-up and wide angle coverage are possible with zoom lenses, which can be remotely controlled.

Figure 9-13.   Options that expand CCTV capabilities.

an operator, cause fatigue, or possibly make him drowsy. Often, several cameras are "sequenced" onto a single screen, with each camera projecting its image on an automatic time-share basis. Even by combining cameras, the strain for an operator to keep alert can be overwhelming. Most multi-screened surveillance systems interconnect intrusion detection devices (or magnetic door switches) with individual monitors. The intrusion sensor is used to alert the panel operator to a particular screen. A more sophisticated method of combining intrusion detection with CCTV monitoring is by incorporating a motion detection type of sensor directly into the CCTV monitor circuit. This need for constant concentration can be eliminated if a CCTV system is modified to incorporate a motion detector device into the conventional circuitry.

### CCTV Motion Detection

A light-activated motion detector, when used in conjunction with a CCTV system, can actually perform the same function as the operator (and in many situations is more sensitive to movement than an operator). Further-more, the use of motion detectors expands the application of CCTV to situations where detection is possible even if no one is in the building, a situation that competes with other volumetric sensors.

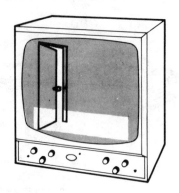

THE MOTION DETECTOR REMEMBERS THE
COMPOSITE VIDEO SIGNAL OF THE NORMAL
SCENE AND IS CAPABLE OF ELECTRONICALLY
COMPARING RAPID LIGHT CHANGES
CAUSED BY MOVEMENT.

Figure 9-14.   Motion detector CCTV.

The motion detector generally functions as an electronic "storage" unit that is coupled to a conventional CCTV system. It is designed to respond to changes in the grey contrast from one sweep of the picture (called a raster) to the next.

Each scene on the TV monitor possesses a certain amount of light intensity. The motion detector is capable of measuring and storing this level of light (to be used as a reference level). If the scene remains the same, no change is recorded by the detection system. If a door is opened, or a man walks down the hallway under the TV camera, the amount of light projected on the monitor (TV tube) is increased or decreased (see Figure 9-14). This is instantly detected as a change from the reference level by the detector unit. It is almost like reading a light meter continually focused on the CCTV.

> The earliest use of motion detectors for CCTV application was actually a light meter with the light-sensitive element mounted inside a rubber suction cup. This cup was "popped" onto a small spot on the TV tube. The spot could be a doorway, a window, or even a display case. When someone entered the scene, the light meter sensed the change in light intensity and activated an alarm or some device to alert the operator that something was moving within the surveillance area. It was a simple application of the CCTV principle. Problems arose with this technique due to light changes caused by conditions other than intrusion (e.g., flickering of the scene or light bouncing into the area being observed). The device did serve a useful purpose, however, by demonstrating the value of the automatic light sensing technique and assisting in encouraging the development of a more sophisticated system.

Perfected CCTV systems record scenes in such a way that they program out many of the false light signals experienced with this device. Furthermore, this new technique can concentrate on specific areas on the screen, while ignoring less important areas. In other words, if a scene contained ten doorways leading into a long hallway, the motion detector could be set to monitor only two critical doorways. Movement from the other eight doorways would not affect the sensory circuit. (CCTV monitor detection systems should never be used outdoors.)

### Cameras

Basically, CCTV cameras rely on five types of image detection techniques each of which is constructed for a particular advantage and sensitivity. They are as follows:

1. Separate mesh vidicon tube.
2. Newvicon tube.
3. Silicon diode tube.
4. Intensified target (starlight) tube.
5. Solid state imaging device. (SID or CID)

The *vidicon* is the most popular of the CCTV tubes and the least expensive. It is adaptable to both indoor and outdoor application when used under fairly bright light conditions. In situations where less light is available (dark parking lots, dimly lit warehouse, etc.), the Newvicon tube is probably more suitable. The *silicon diode* tube is often used under artificial lighting (preferably when the light source is sodium vapor bulbs).

*Solid state imaging devices* utilize a "checkerboard" type of matrix chip. This device permits much smaller camera dimensions than the tube-types and are practically maintenance free which offers great advantage when used in security situations. However, they suffer lower resolution (300 lines vs. 650 lines for the commercial tube-type), and the cost is 5-10 times more than the tube-type. With new advancements in this technology the solid state device may eventually out perform the conventional tube-type vidicons.

In situations where the light is extremely poor (starlight), the need to amplify the signal requires the use of an *intensified target tube* a very expensive but highly important tube in many security situations.

While the CCTV motion detector is extremely useful and flexible, it remains prone to false alarms, and is best used only as an aid to the CCTV monitor. When used in this manner, it can alert the operator to whether a situation needing attention is present. This is enough reason to warrant the installation of the monitor detector in many CCTV systems. The CCTV motion detector is only slowly being accepted by the security industry, but with the tremendous growth of CCTV, it will become a major component in the near future. However, a cost-effective analysis is sometimes used to justify the motion detector device over the less complex magnetic contact switch mat or other simple sensors that can be externally connected to the annunciator to attract the operator's attention to view the affected monitor.

### SUMMARY

This chapter has explored the major volumetric alarm systems currently available and described their various applications to the security field. Unlike mechanical alarms, which almost always detect only direct, physical attack, volumetric systems are capable of protecting an entire three-dimensional area without physical contact.

Volumetric alarm systems fall into four major categories: (1) ultrasonic alarms (which react to motion sound waves and can be contained within walls); (2) microwave alarms (which react to microwave frequencies and can "see" through walls; (3) audio alarms (which react to "noise" and allow monitors to "listen in" to the alarmed area; and (4) passive infrared alarms (which react to the infrared energy created by "body heat"). (Table 9-1 lists the applications of these systems.) Although closed-circuit TV systems are not a major volumetric category, when modified to function as motion detectors, they can be grouped along with audio detectors and passive infrared systems since no signal is transmitted by the CCTV cameras.

Volumetric systems are not immune from the problems that plague other areas of the security field. Devices arrive on the market without adequate testing and are frequently prone to malfunction and false alarms. As a result, many alarm installers are baffled and frightened by volumetric systems.

Police and other authorities are rapidly losing faith in automatic alarms and electronic sensors. Some municipalities have a policy of refusing to respond to automatic alarms, while others fine the property owner for each false alarm and require the removal of the device if more than a specified number of false alarms are reported in a set period.

There is no such thing as a security system that is foolproof against false alarms. All detection systems will generate some false alarms if they are to remain sensitive enough to report unauthorized entry in a genuine intrusion situation.

Some volumetric systems are overly sensitive to external stimuli. Ultrasonics may be triggered by air currents or large insects; audio detectors by ambient noises; and CCTV systems may react to light changes caused by conditions other than intrusion.

Ultrasonic and microwave units detect motion even if the intruder is silent — a situation that cannot be detected by the "noise responsive" audio detector. The audio detector, on the other hand, can "sense" intrusion before it occurs by "hearing" a physical attack against the building perimeter.

It is difficult to determine the best volumetric system for a given situation. Each has its own unique set of attributes and shortcomings, but for a given situation, one may be more suitable than another.

**Table 9-1. Intrusion Alarm Application**

| Environmental and Other Variables | Ultrasonic | Passive Infrared | Microwave |
|---|---|---|---|
| Vibration | Can balance to reduce | Minimum | Can create problem |
| Reduction of range by drapes, carpets | Can change | None | None |
| Sensitivity to movement of overhead doors | Careful placement | Minimum | Can create problem |
| Effect of humidity change on range | Can change | None | None |
| Water noise from faulty valves | Can create problem | None | None |
| Sensitivity to small animals | Problem if animals close | Problem if animals close but can be aimed so beams are well above floor | Problem if animals close |
| Ultrasonic noise | Bells, hissing, some inaudible noises can cause problems | None | None |
| Heaters | Careful placement | Minimum | Can cause problem |
| Radio interference, AC line | Can cause problem transients | Minimum | Can cause problem |
| "Piping" of detection field to unexpected areas by AC | None | None | Can cause problem |

| | | | |
|---|---|---|---|
| Radar interference | Can cause problem | None | Minimum |
| Effect of temperature change on range | None | Will change | Small change |
| Movement through thin walls or glass | Careful placement | None | None |
| Reflection-metal objects changing area coverage | Will create problem | None (unless mirror like surface) | Minimum |
| Drafts, air movement | None | None (unless directed at unit) | Can create problem |
| Sun, moving headlights, through windows | None | Careful placement | None |
| Heaters | None | Careful placement | Can cause problem |
| Current consumption (size of battery required for extended standby power) | Highest | Minimum | In between |
| Moving machinery, fan blades | Careful placement | Minimum | Careful placement |
| Radio interference, AC line transients | Can cause problem | Minimum | Can cause problem |
| Range adjustment required | Yes | No | Yes |
| Interference between two or more sensors | Can cause problem if not different frequency | None | Can cause problem if not crystal controlled |
| Cost per square ft., large open areas | Least expensive | Most expensive | In between |
| Cost per square ft., divided areas or multiple rooms | In between | Most expensive | Least expensive |

## GLOSSARY

### Motion Detection Terms

*Accumulator.*   Usually part of the circuit of an audio detector that is designed to "add" the amplitudes of a series of pulses and trigger an alarm condition whenever these pulses become larger than a preset threshold level. Sometimes referred to as an integrator, counter, or discriminator.

*Active Intrusion Sensor.*   Detects the presence of an intruder within the range of the sensor because of a disturbance in the transmitted (or radiated) field. Examples include ultrasonic motion detectors, microwave motion detectors, and photocell beam detectors. A designation given to any protection device that possesses both a transmitter and receiver component. (If it is in the same housing, it is called a transceiver.)

*Area Protection.*   Protection of the inner space or volume of a secured area. A method of detecting an intruder's presence anywhere within a specifically defined protected area, as opposed to detection at a specific point such as an entrance (door or window).

*Audio Frequency.*   Sound frequencies within the range of human hearing, approximately 15 to 20,000 Hz.

*Audio Detection.*   An amplifier type of device that detects noises made by an intruder. Usually used with a series of widely scattered microphones or can be made to use the speaker section of a public address system as the microphones. Single speaker units (used as microphones) are used inside bank vaults and can detect attacks against the vault barrier prior to actual intrusion.

*Doppler Effect (Shift).*   An apparent change in frequency of sound or radio waves when reflected from or originating from a moving object. This is the basic principle involved with most of the active volumetric sensors.

*Infrared Motion Detection (Passive IR).*   A volumetric sensor capable of detecting slight changes in the infrared heat radiating from objects in a protected area. The presence of an intruder introduces a different level of infrared energy and would be detected as an alarm condition by the IR sensor.

*Microwave Detection.*   The method of detecting the presence of an intruder through the use of extremely high radio frequency generating and receiving equipment. It uses the doppler shift principle to protect an area and is an active motion detection system.

*Motion Detection.*   A sensor that responds to the movement in a protected area by an intruder.

*Sonic Motion Detector.*   A sensor that detects the motion of an intruder by his disturbance of an audible sound pattern generated within the protected area. Usually refers to frequencies below 20,000 Hz, above which is considered the ultrasonic range.

*Ultrasonic Detection.*   A sensor that operates above the frequency range of human hearing. The inaudible sound waves using the doppler effect principle to detect any shifting of frequency due to movement of an intruder.

## CCTV Terms

*Automatic Iris.*   A device that automatically self-adjusts optically to light level changes via the video signal from the television camera. They are used on newvicon, silicon, SIT, and ISIT cameras.

*Camera Tube.*   An electron tube that converts an optical image into an electrical current by a scanning process. Also called a pickup tube and a television camera tube.

*Mount.*   An industry standard for lens mounting. The c-mount has a 1-inch barrel diameter with 32 threads per inch.

*Coaxial Cable.*   A cable capable of carrying a wide range of frequencies with very low signal loss. Coaxial cable usually consists of a narrow metallic shield with a single wire accurately placed along the center of the shield and isolated from the shield.

*Depth of Field.*   For a lens the area along the line of sight in which objects are in reasonable focus. Depth of field increases with smaller lens apertures (higher f-stop numbers), shorter focal lengths, and greater distances from the lens.

*Field of View.*   The field of view is the width and height of a scene to be monitored and is determined by the lens focal length and the lens-to-subject distances.

*F Number (F#).*    The speed of a lens is determined by the amount of light it transmits. This is the relationship between the lens opening (controlled by the iris) and the focal length and is expressed as a fraction referred to as the f-number. Example: an f/4.0 lens is one with an aperture ¼ of the focal length. The markings (f/stops) on lenses are arbitrarily chosen ratios of aperture to focal length, such as f/1.0, 1.4, 2.0, 2.8, 4.0, 5.6, 8, 11, 16, 22, etc. The smaller the f/stop number, the faster the lens speed.

*Focal Length (FL).*    The distance from the lens center to the focal plane (vidicon faceplate) is the lens focal length and is expressed in inches or in millimeters.

*Frame.*    The total picture area that is scanned while the picture signal is not blanked. One thirteenth of a second (525 lines) is standard for NTSC CCTV systems.

*Horizontal Resolution.*    The maximum number of individual picture elements that can be distinguished in a single horizontal scan line. Also called horizontal definition. Typical resolution is 500 lines with 4 MHz bandwidth.

*Impedance.*    The input or output characteristic of a system component that determines the type of transmission cable to be used. The cable used must have the same characteristic impedance as the component. Expressed in ohms. Video distributors have standardized on 75-ohm coaxial and 124-ohm balanced cable.

*Iris Diaphragm.*    A device for mechanically opening or closing the lens aperture, to control the amount of light transmitted through a lens. In this way, the iris adjusts the f-stop of a lens.

*Newvicon Tube.*    A camera tube with a cadmium and zinc telluride target, which provides sensitivity about 20 times that of a sulfide target. Spectral response is somewhat narrower than a silicone diode tube, 470 to 850 nm. The Newvicon operates like a silicon tube, in that it uses a fixed target voltage and must use an auto iris lens system.

*NTSC Standard Format.*    National Television Systems Committee. A committee that worked with the FCC in formulating standards for the present-day U.S. color television system, which has 525 horizontal scan lines, 30 frames per second. Commonly used in the United States and Japan.

*Pinhole Lens.*    A special lens designed with a small (0.1 to 0.25 inch) front lens diameter to permit its use in covert (hidden) camera applications.

*Silicon Tube.* The silicon target is made up of a mosaic of light-sensitive silicon material, and depending on the light source is between 10 and 100 times as sensitive as a sulfide vidicon. Other advantages are very broad spectral responses, 380–1100 nm, and high resistance to vidicon burn. The silicon tube does not permit automatic sensitivity control by means of signal electrode voltage regulation; therefore an automatic iris must be used.

*Vertical Resolution.* The number of horizontal lines that can be seen in the reproduced image of a television pattern. 350 lines maximum with the 525 NTSC system.

*Video Tape Recorder.* A device that accepts signals from a video camera and a microphone, and records images and sound on video tape reels, cassettes, or cartridges. It can then play back the recorded program for viewing on a television monitor or receiver.

*Vidicon.* An electron tube used to convert light into an electrical signal. The standard vidicon tube utilizes an antimony trisulfide ($Sb^2 s^3$) target and is the most widely used image tube for closed-circuit surveillance. The spectral response covers most of the visible light range and most closely approximates the human eye. A useful feature of the vidicon is the ability to control the target voltage and to be controlled to permit variation of sensitivity. The tube has a spectral sensitivity from 300 to 800 nm.

*Zoom Lens.* A zoom lens is a variable focal length lens. The lens components in these assemblies are moved to change their relative physical positions, thereby varying the focal length and angle of view through a specified range of magnifications.

## NOTE

1. Patent awarded to Sam Bagno of Alertronic Corporation of America, Clifton, New Jersey.

# Chapter 10
# Transmitting the Sensor Signal

Understanding the technical characteristics of the sophisticated intrusion detection devices such as ultrasonic, microwave, and passive infrared does not equip someone with all the knowledge necessary to effectively design a complete protection system. Manufacturers and users often put too much emphasis on the selection of the sensor when the applicability of any security system actually depends upon four operational elements: *detection, transmission, annunciation,* and *response.* The proper combination of these elements for a particular application is most important. Placing too much emphasis on one element at the expense of the other three can compromise any security system.

As indicated in Chapter 7, the *sensor* is an electronic switch that detects an existing condition or change in status. It cannot always distinguish authorized changes from unauthorized changes. The *control* device, used to separate authorized entry from unauthorized entry, accepts and stores information from the sensor. It may be programmed to evaluate the information furnished to it. For purposes of this chapter, the sensor and control unit are considered as a single element. The *annunciator* is the part of the alarm system that alerts someone (via bell, siren, buzzer, etc.) that there has been a change in the sensor environment.

While it is a common practice to place most of the design effort on the selection of an appropriate sensor, many of the problems associated with security systems can be traced to an improperly selected transmission media. All too often, the sensor may be the only component functioning in an alarm system. Bells may ring on store fronts, but be ignored by passersby, or sirens may wail all night in a deserted warehouse while central station services fail to detect that the system was never turned on or that a connecting phone line has been out of order for three months. Often, the only person aware of these deficiencies is the burglar.

Installing a sophisticated type of sensor is a waste of money unless it is accompanied by a transmission system that is just as reliable. Although transmission is as important as the other elements that comprise a complete alarm system, it is too often selected with a minimal amount of forethought or investigation.

The most popular means of transmission is a pair of wires that connect the sensor–control units to a nearby annunciator. It could also be a complex multiplexing system sent over phone lines, or a radio signal sent from the sensor location to a police station panel many miles away. The transmission media is often the weakest link in an alarm system because of its exposure and potential vulnerability to attack. It is often the phase causing most of the problems affecting the alarm system (see Figure 10-1).

Reliability may well be the most important characteristic of any alarm system. A transmission may be termed reliable if it possesses four essential requirements:

1.  It must have a proper annunciation *every time* the sensor is activated.
2.  The communication must be prompt.

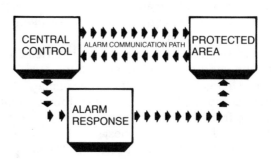

- THE CENTRAL CONTROL
- THE ALARM COMMUNICATION PATH
- THE PROTECTED AREA
- THE ALARM RESPONSE

Figure 10-1.   Four facets of an alarm.

3.   Interpretation of the alarm signal must be easily understood.
4.   It must be stable and not react to ambient or external influences.

The process of bringing the technology developed in a laboratory to the commercial marketplace usually involves a gap of 3 to 5 years. Sophisticated and effective security systems are available, but because of the lack of understanding of security systems and their functions, much of the equipment in use today can become obsolete unless it is upgraded periodically. Alarms, like other aspects of the electronic industry, can be obsolete in a relatively short time, yet they are rarely replaced with new technology.

## TRANSFERRING THE SENSOR SIGNAL

### Wire Connections

By far the most popular form of transmitting the alarm signal from the sensor–control panel to the annunciator is a pair of wires. They carry the electrical impulse (current) each time the circuit is activated by the alarm sensor (whether it be a mechanical switch, window foil, or ultrasonic motion detectors). (The sensor and control panel function very much like a wall-mounted light switch. Activation of the sensor is an automatic simulation of the manual operation of the light switch. Each detected intrusion would cause the light to go on, visibly signaling to alert someone to the intrusion.)

The above example demonstrates how an alarm sensor functions. If someone cuts the wire between the switch and the light bulb, the sensor is no longer able to operate the light when intrusion is detected. The industry refers to this basic wire transmission system as an *unsupervised open circuit*. The word *unsupervised* refers to any situation where the wiring system permits electrical current to flow only after the sensor is activated. This open circuit system provides very little transmission security because the wiring is vulnerable to faults, accidental breaks, or compromise by criminal or malicious attacks.

A superior transmission system is a slightly modified version that requires the current to flow at all times, except when the sensor is activated. In other words, the activation of the sensor opens the wire connection, causing the current to stop flowing. The obvious advantage of this modification is that if the wire were cut, it would stop the current flow, causing an alarm condition. This superior transmission circuit is termed *supervised* since the wiring itself is monitored at all times. Another form of supervised circuitry goes one step beyond the simple closed loop configuration. In situations where a high degree of security is required, supervision is made so sensitive that any change in the amount of current level is detected. Without this extra sensitivity, the circuit can be compromised simply by inserting a false or external source of current that keeps flowing after the line is cut. The cut is not noticed as long as the foreign source of current continues to flow through the line. High-security systems incorporate a method that permits the system to monitor not only current flow but also the amount of current. Any significant deviation above or below the established current level will be detected as an attack on the line. In order to compromise this type of circuit, the external source of current must match the normal electrical characteristic of the original current level. By monitoring and detecting any rise or fall of current beyond the established limits makes any compromise attempt extremely difficult. Direct wire connections constitute over 95 percent of the installations in the United States. Until recently, direct or hard wire was the only way to connect a sensor to the annunciating indicator.

**Low-Voltage Hard Wire Connections.**    Practically all of the wire connections with security equipment are of the low-voltage type (similar to the telephone line used inside a house). These relatively thin wires are not generally placed in protective pipes or jackets and are usually stapled or fastened directly to the wall, unless some electrical code specifies otherwise. The current that flows through the wire is very low, and all voltage choices are below 30 volts (the average system panel operates at 6 to 24 volts). The primary reasons for these low operating voltages are as follows:

1.    Systems are capable of operating with low-cost or commercial power, allowing the equipment to function in cases of power failures. Some systems are designed to operate from battery power only.

2.    Low-voltage, low-current equipment allows the use of thin, inexpensive wires and the stapling of exposed wires to the wall. Since the voltage is below the 30-volt level, such wiring techniques are covered by less stringent sections of local electrical codes. Therefore an alarm installer does not need to have an electrical license. Even if the alarm equipment operates at the common power of 110 volts, it can be arranged to be wired with low-voltage wiring to avoid all the stringent rules governing high-voltage, high-current equipment.

3.    Low-voltage wiring is often handled by less skilled grades in the electrical unions. Therefore the cost of installation is significantly lower.

A large metropolitan hospital specified an elaborate closed-circuit TV monitoring system throughout its five main buildings. The distance from the monitoring panel to the furthest TV camera was over 2000 feet. All total systems require 20,000 feet of interconnecting cable. Rather than using low-voltage cameras, the engineers drew up specifications that required 110-volt cameras powered by low-voltage wiring. This feat was accomplished simply by "stepping down" the voltage at the central panel to 48 volts. This meant that thin, exposed wires were run to all the cameras, and the voltage within the camera enclosure was stepped up to 110 volts. This approach avoided all licensing requirements and accomplished a cost savings of 70 percent over the price of a high-voltage system, and yet the hospital was able to use standard 110-volt TV cameras.

### Wireless Connections

Another method of signal transmission, appropriately termed *wireless connection*, avoids wires altogether. In this system, each sensor is connected to a battery-operated radio transmitter. The transmitter is a small transistorized, low-powered unit (like a small transistor radio). When a sensor is activated, it triggers the transmitter — sending a brief coded radio frequency signal that is detected by the receiver. This indicates that an alarm condition exists somewhere on the premises. Encoded frequencies are used so that the transmitter will not affect a neighbor's system operating at the same frequency. Brevity of message is a requirement of the FCC. The frequencies chosen are allowed in the communication radio band, but the power transmitted is so low that it would not affect a radio receiver located over 300 feet away (even if it were on the same frequency).

The specially designed radio receivers are tuned to listen only to the frequency and encoding of the sensor transmitters. A centrally located receiver can "hear" an unlimited number of sensors within the 150- to 200-foot range.

Some sites using wireless transmission systems use a single encoded frequency for every sensor, since the primary purpose of the system is to detect entry into the building regardless of the specific point. More sophisticated wireless systems are designed to assign each sensor a different coded signal on one frequency, enabling the receiver to record the specific location of the activated sensor. This "zoning" configuration is similar in operation to a CB receiver programmed to constantly scan all the channels and stop at the one that is transmitting.

Wireless systems do not provide as high a degree of security as direct hard wire connections since there is no way to determine if the sensor–transmitter is in working order other than by repeated and frequent testing. Nevertheless, they are growing in popularity because they are easy to install and avoid unsightly wires. They also have an inherent advantage in that the sensor can be moved from one location to another without disturbing or requiring any changes in the overall system design or wiring. The whole concept of wireless transmission was developed after the introduction of remote control garage door openers. With only slight changes, the garage door transmitter–receiver system was converted to a security device. This is another example of how the development of many alarm devices has evolved from the technology of another industry. (In 1980 transmitters were placed on the market that sent a signal when the battery was so low that it had to be replaced. This feature significantly enhanced the security of security wireless transmitters.)

## Multiplexing Interior Wiring

*Multiplexing* is an electronic technique that places a second signal "on top of" or "along side of" another signal. These multiple signals are capable of being transmitted on a common pair of wires without interfering with each other. There are several commercially available approaches for achieving this sharing of wiring. One is to use existing high-voltage wires that are in all buildings and superimpose a coded signal on the 110-volt circuit. Another method is to run new wiring throughout the building just to carry the signals. There are other more complex arrangements possible, but they are not covered in this text. The decision whether or not to use multiplexing transmission is a function of the number of signals to be transmitted versus the higher costs of multiplexing equipment as compared to the lower cost of individual wires. The cost to install either type of technology must also be considered.

When the existing house wiring is used, a transmitter is plugged into any convenient wall socket, thus sending a low-frequency signal over the house wiring. Since all the wires in the house are interconnected to the incoming pair of wires provided by the electric company, all electrical outlet boxes are capable of receiving the multiplex signal transmitted from any other outlet. A special receiver is plugged into another outlet, and whenever the transmitting module sends a pulsed signal, it is instantly detected at the receiver. This sending–receiving procedure is completely independent of the 110 volts of current, even though it is run on the same wires. Of course, the power to transmit the coded signal relys on the 110 volts and if there is a power failure the signaling system would fail along with everything else in the building. The transmitter or receiver modules can be plugged into any house outlet so that the location of the sensor can be chosen without worrying about connecting wires between the sensor and the receiver.

The main advantages of this system are the low cost, which is due to the elimination of wiring labor, and the fact that sensor location can be changed (or added) without disturbing the overall system configuration. Intercom systems are available that can send speech back and forth over the 110-volt circuit using a similar technique.

Most major commercial buildings have experimented with multiplexing over existing wires, but as the building gets larger (i.e., has more than one incoming electrical service or power transformer), the transfer of the signal from the transmitting sensor to the receiver becomes technically more difficult and may require additional equipment and wiring interconnections.

There are various techniques of multiplexing that differ in the method of sharing the common wire. Each, however, has some inherent advantages and limitations over the other. All techniques do offer a potential cost effectiveness over conventional point-to-point wiring (especially in high-rise buildings, which sometimes contain more than 1000 sensor locations). The selection of direct point-to-point wiring methods against multiplexing wiring lies in the total installed cost of both methods. In some situations the customer may dictate one method against another regardless of cost.

One popular and simple method of multiplexing is to connect all sensors in series. In this system, the communication link serves as a party line that carries no signal as long as none of the sensors has an alarm to transmit. When an alarm condition occurs, the affected sensor immediately transmits a signal over the single party line. The advantage of all party line systems is that any sensor can transmit an alarm signal at any time. In the simplest party line systems (the previously described house wiring multiplexing unit is a good example), the sensors are connected in series and the receiver indicates only that an alarm has occurred at one of the sensors. The obvious disadvantages of a series line are that it is not possible to determine the exact location of the sensor that transmitted the alarm signal and it is not always possible to supervise the circuits; a blown fuse on a branch power circuit, for example, can cause trouble.

A somewhat more advanced technique is the *McCulloh Loop System* in which each sensor is able to transmit a unique identification signal so that the receiver can determine which sensor is in alarm. The disadvantage of McCulloh multiplexing systems is that if two or more alarms occur simultaneously, all the alarm sensors attempt to send a signal over the line at the same time. The resulting signal is referred to as a "clash," and it is as garbled as when two people talk at once over a party line. The problem is usually inconsequential if alarms occur so infrequently that the clashes are unlikely. In addition, when clashes do occur, the beginning of one signal and the end of another can usually be read by an experienced operator.

---

A typical situation in which multiplexing is preferred over special wiring is in a high-rise building with numerous fire detectors, alarm pull boxes, and burglar alarms. Each sensor point on one particular floor is connected to a single, centrally located (on the same floor) encoding box. Each "floor box" is encoded with a different multiplexing signal. The vertical pair of wires connecting these floor boxes is terminated in the main panel on the main floor where the signals are decoded.

When a sensor is activated, the floor location is indicated on the main panel. For installations in which the exact sensor is required, it is necessary to encode each sensor separately. Each floor is also encoded. This might be represented by a symbol "8–16," indicating the eighth sensor on the sixteenth floor; "8–15," indicating the eighth sensor on the fifteenth floor, etc.

If the building had 10 floors with 10 sensors per floor, it would not mean that 100 different sensor encoders would be required. Each set of sensors on the floor might have the same encoders as the set of sensors on the other floors; however, each of the 10 floors would have a different code to identify the particular floor.

---

## SIGNALING TECHNIQUES

The techniques described thus far have been limited to the transmission of the sensor signal to an annunciator located in the same building or property. These systems, as you will recall from Chapter 8, are referred to as *local alarm systems*. Major techniques for both on-premise and off-premise monitoring are reviewed below:

1. *Local alarm* — This is a simple device, installed directly in the building, that detects and records intrusion, activating a visual and/or audio signal whose main function is to frighten the intruder and also call the attention of the neighbors or the police to the scene.

2. *Local–direct connect system* — In this system the equipment is designed to transmit an alarm signal to a municipal center, such as a police station, as well as sound the local alarm.

3. *Combination local–central station* — An arrangement where alarm signals are sounded locally and are also transmitted to an independent central station.

4. *Proprietary alarm* — Alarms and all signals are monitored on the premises by a guard or other employee who is in constant attendance at a panel that controls all the sensors in a building. Proprietary systems are used by a single owner or user, usually for a single premises, but can be used for noncontiguous properties such as multilocation store chains, nuclear facilities, large commercial buildings, large hospitals, colleges, museums, or prisons. Signals in proprietary systems are often transmitted by one or more methods, hard wire or multiplexing.

5. *Central alarm station* — This alarm signal is received at a remote facility located away from the protected premises where the signal is monitored by an independently owned alarm agency. Police are then notified of the active alarm. An initial installation fee is charged, and a monthly service charge is collected for the monitoring service and the rental of the phone line.

6. *Police direct connect* — There are two methods by which messages may be sent directly to police headquarters. In one method the alarm is connected to a signal panel at the station. The other method allows an automatic telephone dialer to call the police (via existing phone lines) and play a prerecorded message. Generally, police departments charge no fee for alarm connections; however, some panels in police headquarters are owned by independent alarm system operators who charge a fee even though the panel is monitored by the police. Police departments throughout the country are beginning to resist the use of automatic telephone messages because of the high incidence of false alarms and are issuing summonses if the false alarm rate exceeds a certain maximum.

## Local Alarms

This technique is popular because it is easy to install and inexpensive to operate. It relies completely on the cooperation of local citizens who voluntarily call the police when they hear (or see) the alarm activated. Even if no one reacts to the indicated alarm, the noise may scare away the intruder. In a society of growing indifference to a neighbor's problems, this technique is rapidly becoming unreliable. In fact, some of these noise-making devices are destroyed by the very neighbors they were designed to summon. In general, the major advantage of a local alarm in residential service is in awakening sleeping inhabitants. As a burglary preventive device, its use is limited, but it may be the only resource available in certain areas, such as in small towns with no staffed police station at night. In those situations the local populace "still cares."

If a local alarm must be used, it should be selected with some under-standing of its function. As limited as they are in general, some local alarms are superior to others. The primary types are described below.

**The Bell.**   The only practical bell unit for security purposes is one that is housed within a protective enclosure. If tampering is attempted, a special circuitry triggers the bell. Of course, if the entire enclosure is ripped off the wall, and the wires cut, the bell may no longer be part of the system.

Some security systems include very elaborate protective enclosures that are difficult to remove, but leave the connecting wires completely exposed so that cutting of the wires transforms the bell into a hanging ornament compromising the rest of the system. In some types of local alarm systems, notably bank systems, the bell power is contained within the bell housing, and the bell will continue to ring even if it is pulled off the wall.

**The Siren.**   The siren alarm annunciator is a popularly used alternative to the bell. While the sound of a bell in large cities has become so common that it is often ignored, the siren provides a sound that better typifies an emergency situation. In addition, the siren is much louder than a bell, and can be made to "warble." Bells and sirens must be as high as possible, but not higher than four stories (a height that can be reached by a ladder but not by a vandal).

Table 10-1.

| Physical Reaction | Decibel Level (db) at 10 feet | Example |
| --- | --- | --- |
| Hurts eardrum | 150 db or higher | Concorde jet |
| Uncomfortable | 100– 150 db | Thunder |
| Loud | 60 db | Busy retail store |
| Quiet | Less than 40 db | Hospital |
| Very quiet | 20 db | Whispering |

Table 10-1 indicates the various categories of sound levels: The db levels listed in Table 10-1 are for comparison purposes only. The actual decibel level is not a pure number since each manufacturer arrives at the db level using nonstandardizing testing procedures. This problem of non-standardization of sound levels is more pronounced today because sirens are no longer limited as a device to annunciate an alarm (mounted on the roof of a building). Sirens are now being placed inside a building (store, warehouse, etc.). If four 40-watt sirens are concentrated within a relatively small area, the sound could force the burglar out of the premises — even causing eardrum trauma. Some manufacturers state that their device was measured with a db meter at 10 feet, a distance that has somehow become a voluntary standard. The only practical method that should be used is to establish the amount of power developed by the siren, rather than db output. A 40-watt siren (fully powered) is louder than a 30-watt siren, and so on, regardless of how it is tested. Until some standard is accepted by the security industry, comparing one siren againt another is still a very unscientific procedure.

Manufacturers have used their imagination in designing sound levels for their equipment. Standards are vague or nonexistent, and therefore comparing one siren to another is simply accomplished by placing two units near each other in the same environment. Claims of astronomical db levels by manufacturers are the result of wishful thinking rather than effectively being able to drive a burglar out of the premises. Sirens have become another weapon against intrusion.

**The Light.**    At one time, a flashing red light on a building was an attention getter. Now, however, this device has become so widely used that it no longer looks out of place, or indicates an emergency situation. If a flashing light is to be used, it should be enclosed in unbreakable glass and mounted inside a wire mesh cage. The bulb should be of the strobe light type (like those used at airports), which flicker at high speed and intensity and clearly indicate the alarm condition. Not all strobe lights are the same, even though most manufacturers claim 1,000,000 candle power. Light intensity is a function of both candle power and power output, not just candle power alone.

Another advantage of light is that it can attract the attention of citizens outside the building without the intruder being aware of the signaling source. The police can then be summoned while the thief is still inside the building.

**The Combined Approach.**    Unusual situations often call for special devices. In crowded ghetto areas where crime statistics indicate a high incidence of break-ins, the use of both a siren and a strobe light might be required. If used separately, the strobe or the siren would "bounce" off the surrounding high-rise tenements, confusing the police as to the exact location of the break-in. This problem can be avoided by timing the burst of light in the strobe to "peak" at the instant the siren hits its highest pitch. In this way, the authorities will be able to determine the correct building within the shortest amount of time.

The above application indicates that there are situations in which standard alarm equipment cannot provide adequate protection. Standard equipment is designed for the "average" situation — not for all situations. THERE IS NO SUCH THING AS A UNIVERSAL SECURITY SYSTEM OR DEVICE. And, unfortunately, the use of custom designed systems is a relatively new concept that has not been readily accepted by some sectors of the alarm industry. As a result, the customer generally purchases whatever is available, rather than what is needed, unless he is able to discover a true security professional.

## Central Station Service

From a security standpoint, the transmission of an alarm signal to a location remote from the protected premises is infinitely more desirable than any kind of local alarm system. Alarm devices such as sirens and strobe lights, and the local system that uses them, are rapidly being replaced by central station systems. This is largely because local alarms are too often ignored, and are even criticized by the very community that the devices rely upon to summon help.

The local alarm has some value as a deterrent, but its value is questionable even in this area. Intruders have learned that a siren indicates that the security system is not connected to a central station, and that once the local alarm is disabled, there is nothing left on the premises to detect his movements. In fact, the constant activation of local alarm systems by false alarms has become so annoying that a growing number of municipalities have begun to establish "noise abatement ordinances" controlling the use of local alarms (the maximum duration of an alarm must be 15 minutes, the volume level of the sounding device must be severely limited, etc.).

A silent alarm transmitted to a location that is sometimes miles away is generally superior to most local alarms for a multitude of reasons. The use of the phone line not only enables the alarm signal to be transmitted over long distances, but also in some situations it can be designed to permit the remote operator to actually "listen in" to the sounds originating at the protected premises to determine the cause of the alarm. Thus the operator can decide if it is an intrusion or nonintrusion disturbance. This "listening-in" technique is the only effective method for minimizing false alarms since it may provide the intelligence needed to identify or verify the actual event that activated the alarm signal.

There are numerous methods for transmitting the alarm signal to a remote monitoring system. Some of these techniques even require elaborate computerized panels at central control stations; others require only a standard phone line in police headquarters. Most popular systems in use today require the services and cooperation of the phone company.

The use of leased telephone lines to carry the alarm signal has become such a convenience that almost all systems rely upon this transmission media. If the alarm industry loses this easy and relatively inexpensive communication link, most existing equipment may have to be replaced. This possibility is now threatening many central station companies, whose future to a significant extent is controlled by the FCC and telephone company policies and tariffs. Until some radical changes are made, however, the alarm industry will continue to rely on the telephone line as the principal connecting link between the monitoring service and the protected premises.

There are five primary communication–transmission systems in use today, four of which require telephone links. They are as follows:

1. Tape dialers
2. Digital communicators (dialers)
3. Leased/dedicated direct wire phone lines
4. McCulloh loop and multiplexing networks
5. Radio transmission (FM)

**The Tape Dialer.** Tape dialers are another transmission device. Although tape dialers are inexpensive, easy to install, and somewhat reliable, many police departments have refused to respond to them and their use has been banned in some municipalities.

The first dialer was introduced in the early 1940s. It had a wind-up motor coupled to a metal finger that was used to dial a standard telephone. When triggered, the device would dial a preset number and play a recorded message (e.g., This is 15 Park Avenue, Hoboken, N.J. Suspected burglary in progress. Send help) (see Figure 10-2).

Early dialers employed record discs (especially the 45 RPM) to transmit their message. As technology advanced, however, these discs were rapidly replaced by tapes, which were easier to produce than records. They also eliminated the problem of unintelligible messages recorded by individuals possessing unfamiliar regional accents. Tape recorded messages were so easy to produce that the installer himself could prerecord the message. He generally possessed a dialect compatible with the region in which he was working.

Figure 10-2.   Tape dialer.

The tape dialer filled a need during a period when there was no other choice in self-contained and portable communication equipment. The machine, once activated, sends a message over the existing phone to any phone number preprogrammed on the tape. Once the proper series of numbers are dialed, there is a delay (blank tape), which is built in to allow for a time duration of about three rings, after which the programmed message is transmitted. The tape continues to play until all the messages are given. Then, a simulated signal, in effect, hangs up the receiver. The tape dialer is capable of transmitting two or three additional numbers and repeating the message on one run of the tape. At the end of the tape, the machine is ready to send the same series of messages if activated again.

Tape dialers can be made to dial anywhere in the United States, and messages can specify situations other than intrusion. If, for example, the dialer were connected to the fire alarm, the preset number would be that of the fire department, and the message would explain that a fire emergency existed. The tape dialer could also be connected to a thermostat, and it could be programmed to start when the temperature on the premises went below freezing (or go off when the refrigerator went above freezing).

The major advantages of this "blind" obedience to a preprogrammed tape are also the reasons for most of its shortcomings. The tape machine has no control over the sensor or communication link to the answering phone. If the intrusion alarm sensors are prone to false alarms, the dialer will continually go off.

There are other factors that have limited the acceptance of the tape dialer. Since there is no way to test the system from a remote location, its use as a high-security device is questionable. For example, the sensor could be broken or the phone line cut (or out of order). If the sensor were broken, the dialer would not operate. Similarly, if the phone line were cut, the dialer would operate but would deliver its message to a dead phone line. Perhaps, its most critical limitation is the fact that even when the sensor and phone are in perfect working order, the dialer has no way of determining if anyone is actually listening to the message. It can, and often does, deliver an emergency message to a busy signal.

Even though the popular attitude is to blame tape dialers for false alarm messages, it is usually the activating sensor that is at fault. Nevertheless, the trend has been to prohibit or control the use of tape dialers by municipal ordinances. A growing number of municipalities have restricted their use to individual installations approved by the police. In these situations, only approved dialers are given a "secret" police number. If there are too many false alarms by any user, that person is either fined or the use of the special number is rescinded. In this way, the police can establish some control over the tape dialer problem.

Only the better-made dialers have their mechanism constructed in such a manner that even if not used for years, they will operate when called upon to do so. Most dialers, like any electromechanical device, tend to "stick" or break down after lying dormant for two or three years. The most common complaint received about telephone dialers from the industry itself is the fact that the programmed tape must be made at the factory or by the installer. This necessitates a dangerous delay when the tape message and/or phone number has to be changed. While all manufacturers sell a *programmer* capable of making tapes, there are so many different and noninterchangeable models that the cost of purchasing programmers becomes exorbitant. There are now products on the market that come with built-in programmers including microphone, tape, and dialing device. This solves the problem of inconvenience, but not the problem of potential faulty equipment.

**The Digital Dialer (Communicator).** The widespread acceptance of the automatic tape dialer has encouraged the development of a more sophisticated device — the *digital dialer*. In order to differentiate this device from the tape unit, the industry has been attempting to change the nomenclature to "digital communicator."

Aside from the fact that tape and digital devices both rely upon existing phone lines, there are virtually no similarities between them. Unlike the tape dialer, the digital communicator does not send an audible voice message; instead it transmits tone-coded signals that are then decoded by a special digital receiver. While the tape dialer is comprised of a single sending unit, digital communicator systems require two components: the transmitter (at the sensor location) and the receiver (at the monitoring station). The tape dialer, as previously explained, has no interconnection with the number being called. The digital communicator, on the other hand, relies upon communication with a programmed receiver at one particular location.

Digital communicators cannot send messages to a phone location anywhere as tape dialers can. A digital communicator can transmit only to a special digital receiver that possesses the capability of decoding the message(s) sent. Although the digital transmitter unit can be programmed to dial any number, that number must be at a location where the phone line is connected to a special receiver. One receiver can monitor hundreds (usually up to 1000) communicators.

The programming of some communicators is stored in a small electronic component called a "memory chip." Since all chips look alike, it is not possible to decipher anything about the coded message by mere appearance. In lieu of chips, some units use plug-in cards, and others have "switches" mounted directly on the digital transmitter. These units are more vulnerable to deciphering than those that utilize memory chips. The most advanced communicators now incorporate microprocessors within their circuitry. Programming (or changing codes) is accomplished by plugging a small programmer the size of a calculator into the communicator and simply "instructing" the transmitter to operate in whatever mode desired.

The memory chip, along with the other circuitry in the digital communicator (or transmitter), electronically simulates the dialing of a phone. This number can be addressed to any phone, anywhere in the country, equipped with the special receiver.

---

One of the largest communication monitoring systems in the United States is located in a city on the East Coast where it controls alarm systems in 48 states. If a call comes in that the temperature in a chicken coop in Kansas has dropped below a certain temperature, the receiving unit immediately records the situation. An operator then dials the owner of the chicken farm to alert him to the problem.

---

The transmitting communicator will continue to dial until it gets a special signal back from the receiver (similar to hearing the phone picked up at the other end). This "handshake" signal then initiates the electronic conversation, but serves only to verify that a connection to a "live" receiver has been made. At this point, the only useful knowledge communicated is that the receiver has been placed into the system and is awaiting further communication to identify the sender.

Next, a series of coded numbers appear in the receiver to identify the caller. The Kansas farmer might be designated 067; while a factory in New York City may be 939. If more than 999 locations are required, a second receiver would be connected to a second incoming phone line, and so on. The information given must be repeated twice, one behind the other, to satisfy the receiver and to overcome jamming by a third party.

After the receiver properly identifies the sender's location, the transmitter is alerted to send still another type of coded signal. This last signal indicates the type of problem by listing "04" to indicate a burglary, "02" for a fire, and so forth. When all this information is displayed on the receiver panel, a signal is sent back to the transmitter to reset (hang up), thus becoming ready for future intrusion. Some types will send a full message up to four times. Typical receiver codes are established by the central station. Generally, the lower the number, the more threatening the situation is to human life. For example:

| | |
|---|---|
| 01 — Medical emergency | 06 — Test |
| 02 — Fire | 07 — Extra |
| 03 — Hold-up | 08 — Battery low |
| 04 — Burglary | 09 — Extra |
| 05 — Reset | |

There are many features that cannot be accomplished with tape dialers that can expand the system. For instance, the digital dialer can be programmed to dial a second receiver if there is line trouble at the first location. Since the communication link can create a situation where two phones are electronically connected, a microphone can be connected to the transmitter, permitting the receiver to actually "listen in" to the protected premises. This feature is usually free since the price schedule generally used covers a full 3 minutes of time, and the coded signals establishing location and trouble rarely take longer than 15 seconds. This leaves 2 minutes and 45 seconds for listening in without additional phone charges.

Digital communicators are the fastest growing devices in use for transmitting the alarm signal to the central station. They are infinitely more reliable than the tape dialer and provide almost as much information as a human conversation. Their primary drawback as a high-security device is that they rely on existing switched phone circuits to transmit their messages. While it may be inexpensive to use this type of telephonic transmission, phone lines are vulnerable to cutting. Since the connection between the transmitter and the receiver utilizes normal switched telephone circuits, there is no way to "supervise" the line between the protected premises and the central station. Some of this weakness can be overcome by using two separate incoming phone lines at the protected premises. Using this method, the digital transmitter would be connected in such a way that if one line were cut, it would send notification of this event via the second phone line (of course, this method would be ineffective if both lines were cut simultaneously). There is another device available that reads the phone line voltage on the outgoing line. If the voltage goes to zero (cut wire), a local bell or siren is activated in the protected building to alert someone to the defective phone line. This device, of course, relies on someone being in the area to notice the alarm.

Because it offers a reasonable alternative to equipment requiring the rental of special phone lines, the digital communicator is a technological advancement exercising a profound effect on the entire industry. In 1982 digital communication systems were upgraded to a Grade B rating by Underwriters Laboratories with certain restrictions. This rating is equivalent to the classification given to the direct wire McCollough loop circuits. Among the special conditions that must be met by digital users is a "test" at least once every 24 hours. This stipulation can be achieved simply by requiring the user to send a closing signal every evening. (The central station cannot determine if the telephone connection is cut, but the 24-hour test does eliminate many of the shortcomings.)

**The Leased or Dedicated Direct Wire Phone Line.**   Tape dialers and digital communicators function more or less as telephone extensions that connect into existing phone lines but require special or extra interface equipment from the phone company, other than an interface jack. *Leased (or dedicated) phone lines,* on the other hand, require special connections between the protected premises and communication centers (e.g., central service stations or police departments). Alarm companies are no longer permitted the convenience of running wires over roof tops to their customers' properties as they did 60 years ago; they are now forced to lease lines from phone companies.

Leased lines can be run into any building that can have telephone wire running into it. Leased lines represent the most practical transmission method since they make use of an existing pair of cable wires running between the protected premises and the central station by "dedicating" them to alarm service. This method involves no switching at phone company terminals and no change in phone instruments. A single pair of wires is selected out of a cable and run from the protected premises to the phone exchange. There it is connected to another pair of wires that runs from the phone exchange to the central station.

Many leased line systems employ indicator lamps and audible devices, which are activated upon an alarm in the system being received or when there is some type of phone line trouble. Typically, these are the fully supervised types with the power source, backed up by batteries, at the central station. The transmission system can sense some changes in current level as well as open or shorted lines. The degree of resistance to compromise for this transmission method is a function of how close the alarm limits are set to the normal current level. Underwriters Laboratories has set a change of 50 percent as one of its criteria for this capability, although some systems in use sense a change as small as 5 percent from normal current. Furthermore, increased compromise resistance can be gained by adding additional supervising signals or tones to the transmission to further confuse the criminal. The most sophisticated type in use today incorporates random coding of certain tones with a repetition rate so long and unpredictable to the outsider that the chance of compromise is, for all practical purposes, about zero. (The tone sequences can be made so that they will not be repeated for 10 years or longer.)

Another problem with leased lines is their high rental cost. There have been runs made of over 100 miles, but generally the cost factor defeats the advantages if the distance between the central station and the protected premises exceeds 10 miles (see Figure 10-3).

Leased lines have not proven a profitable venture for the phone company. They bring in less revenue than regular phone lines since rental

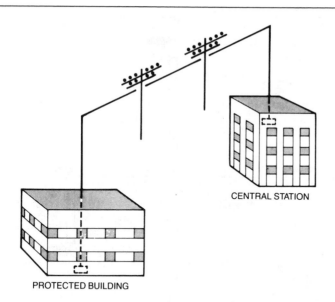

CENTRAL STATION

PROTECTED BUILDING

POINT-TO-POINT TRANSMISSION WITH D.C. GRADE TELEPHONE LINE. NO PHONE PIECE IS INVOLVED SINCE THERE IS NO REQUIREMENT FOR VOICE COMMUNICATION. THIS "LEASED LINE" IS SIMPLE. A PAIR OF WIRES THAT RUN FROM THE PROTECTED PREMISES TO THE CENTRAL STATION AND IS RENTED FROM THE PHONE COMPANY AT A FIXED RATE DEPENDENT ON DISTANCE ONLY.

Figure 10-3.   Direct wire.

fees are based only on distance and do not include "add-ons" such as long-distance calls or overtime. The phone company would rather use the leased line for regular phone service than lease it to an alarm company. For what is now one customer's use, the phone company could place hundreds of phone conversations on that pair of wires — and collect much more than they would with a fixed rate lease line. In addition, alarm lines (which must be in perfect working order at all times) require close attention from the phone company.

**The McCulloh Loop.**     The McCulloh loop is another system of transmission universally used by central stations to overcome the cost factor of leased lines. This system of connecting several locations into one incoming line connected to the central station has been in use for almost a hundred years. The McCulloh circuit is, essentially, a form of "party line," through which several protected premises share a single loop or circuit and are wired in series from the phone company terminal (see Figure 10-4). A single pair of

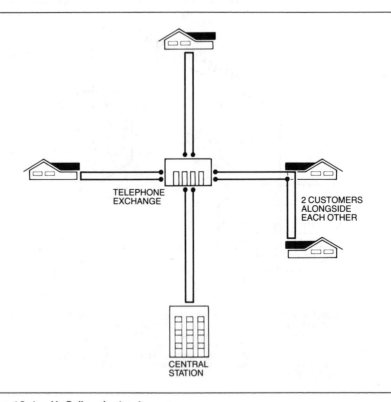

Figure 10-4.   McCullough circuit.

wires is then run from the terminal to the central station. Identification is accomplished by programming each sensor on the circuit to transmit a unique signal so that the receiver can determine which sensor is alarming. The code is usually presented in the form of a gearlike apparatus that, when activated, hits a series of contacts that transmit the code set by the spacing of the gear teeth. The system is wired in such a way that if there is a break in the phone line, there is a way for the phone company to determine immediately the exact location of the problem.

**Multiplexing Networks.**   Underwriters Laboratories defines multiplexing as a "method of signaling characterized by the simultaneous and/or sequential transmission and reception of multiple signals over a communication channel for the purpose of positively identifying each signal." Multiplexing systems were developed because of the potential unavailability of copper wire and the fact that they can carry more information than the McCulloh system of transmission. In multiplexing, the central station

There are two opposing methods of placing multiple signals on a common line: *time division multiplexing* (TDM) and *frequency division multiplexing* (FDM). Both of them can communicate information back and forth between the subscriber and the central station location. Each approach offers some advantages and disadvantages over the other.

**Frequency Division Multiplexing.**   Frequency division multiplexing (FDM) divides the frequency of the bandwidth of the telephone communication channel into a number of subchannels (or tone channels). FDM enables many different transmitters to simultaneously transmit from various locations without interfering with one another. A receiver tuned to the appropriate transmitted frequency can pick up its signal out of thousands of transmitted signals at any time.

When applied to an alarm and telephone system, this means that each location sharing a single telephone network has a tone transmitter falling within the bandwidth of the telephone channel. Some of these channels can be broken into almost a hundred subchannels, with each assigned a specific "tone." At the central station receiving location, the tones are sometimes is required to install a transmitter–receiver instead of just a receiver, and the subscriber uses a unit called a *transponder* rather than a transmitter. This creates a system permitting communication in both directions along a channel capable of carrying a voice. (The lease line carried only d.c. current.) By using the more flexible voice grade circuit, the distance limitations applied to the d.c. grade (and McCulloh Loop) are no longer a factor in system operation since the circuits are treated like regular phone lines and the phone company maintains signal levels and integrity (see Figure 10-5).

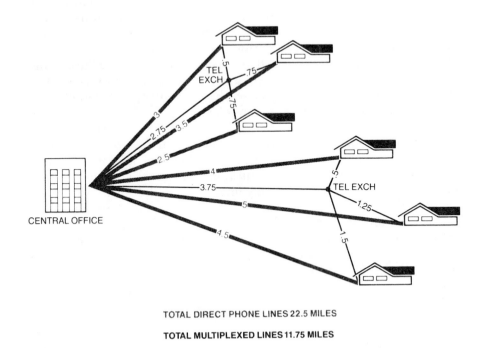

TOTAL DIRECT PHONE LINES 22.5 MILES

**TOTAL MULTIPLEXED LINES 11.75 MILES**

Figure 10-5.   Cost comparison.

"demultiplexed" using a simple electronic circuit called a bandwidth filter. Each filter is tuned to cover a subchannel or tone frequency. Information can be continually heard on all channels with no interference between them (even though all of them are transmitting on the air at the same time). This procedure would be analogous to sitting in a room with ten radio receivers — each tuned to a different radio station.

The FDM technique (or tone multiplexing) has been used in industrial process control for over 50 years because it is easily adaptable to telephone technology and possesses excellent signaling reliability (touch tone dialing is an example of its flexibility). The primary factor inhibiting this technique's widespread acceptance is cost. Another limiting factor is that FDM components are sensitive to telephone line noises and susceptible to false signaling caused by mechanical shock and vibration. These shortcomings have kept the tone multiplex from becoming a widely popular device.

Frequency division multiplexing has seen a rebirth in the last few years with the introduction of better components capable of controlling and defining a single tone within a very narrow bandwidth. This new design relies on a mechanical tone filter that is so stable that it is able to separate a phone line channel into 100 easily distinguishable subchannels. Of course, the use of tone generation is useful only in situations where only one signal is required and where only one directional transmission satisfies the situation. In other words, it can signal only those conditions per subchannel. When used only as an alarm indicator, the FDM provides adequate information making it a superior system to the McCulloh loop. In addition, it requires far less wiring than the dedicated lease line configuration.

---

A typical operation of the frequency (tone) division multiplexer would have 60 buildings (subscribers) all connected through bridging circuits at the phone company terminal. A pair of connecting wires would be run from the last terminal to the central office. Each of the 60 locations would constantly send a special tone through the system. The tones would be decoded at the central station. As long as the tones were "heard" by the main receiving panel, everything would remain normal, but if the signal were to pulse, the decoder could read this signal as an alarm condition. If the signal stopped altogether, the decoder would interpret this silence as a phone line break or an intrusion signal (see Figure 10-6)

This is a simple method for obtaining a great deal of information over a minimum number of wires. One of the drawbacks is that the main panel may not have provisions for distinguishing an alarm condition from a broken line since both will light up on the main panel. The operator then has to use equipment to determine if the alarm is indicating a pulsating signal or a dead signal.

---

**Time Division Multiplexing (TDM).** Time division multiplexing (or digital multiplexing) has more flexibility than frequency division multiplexing. This system depends on having all events occurring in the network reported to the central station in time sequence. Subscribers are required to continuously report their status, one after the other, in a prescribed sequence. This one-at-a-time condition is a fundamental difference between TDM and the previously discussed FDM.

No two remote subscribers (transmitting from different sensor locations) can be actively signaling at any one time. If such a situation occurred, it would create a "clash" such as that described for the McCulloh transmission system. This possibility is prevented by the fact that the sequence of each reporting subscriber's equipment is controlled by the equipment at the central station. The central station sends an interrogate signal (one at a time) to each subscriber's premises commanding it to transmit (respond) its security status. Such a system is known in the alarm industry as an "inter-

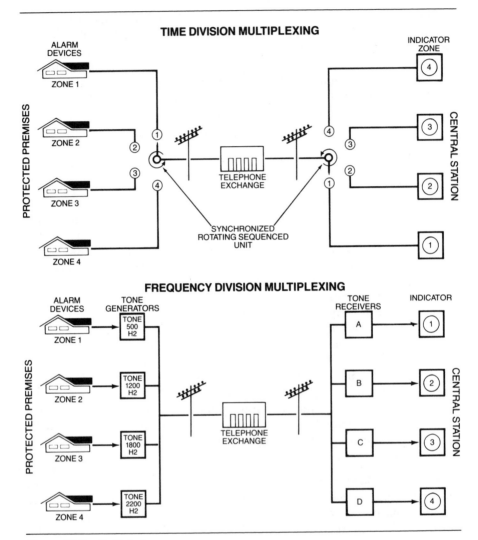

Figure 10-6. Multiplexing.

rogate response." To maintain the proper sequence to each subscriber, the telephone network must be bidirectional. Signals not only come from the protected premises, but command signals must also go from the central station to the subscriber.

The need for an action–reaction procedure requires that the phone company provide extra equipment to accomplish this feat (interrogation and response). Since the requirements are somewhat different from normal telephone systems, there has been some difficulty in implementation. With the rapid growth of computer time sharing based on a phone line connection, however, this technique is becoming more readily available.

It should be noted that the need for two-way communication can become a distinct advantage if the alarm system is connected to various environmental controls within the building. Since TDM sends a digital signal when interrogated, the signal can be coded to indicate any number of conditions. For example, if the temperature drops below 40, the transponder will send a digit "8"; if the temperature rises above 75, the digit sent would be "20." The central station can activate switches and controls at the subscriber site to raise or lower the temperature. It is capable of operating in two directions, permitting the central station operator to turn on the lights or air conditioner at the subscriber's location. TDM is, indeed, a very important addition to the technology of phone line transmission. Further advances in signal transmission technology have been made that dramatically reduce the impact of noise on the telephone lines from affecting the signal integrity.

### Radio Transmission (FM)

The obvious need for an alternate method to phone line transmission has encouraged a rapid advancement in low-powered radio transmission technology. The result of these efforts is a system of transponders capable of communication between the protected premises and the central control station. Multiplexed FM coded signals can reliably send messages up to 30 miles in flat, unobstructed terrain, and 10 to 15 miles in the commercial centers of large cities. This distance directly competes with phone line communication links because almost all subscribers to central station services lie within a 15-mile radius. Distances greater than that become economically inefficient since phone line rental costs become greater at long distances.

The initial application of electronics to automatically identify a specific transmitter occurred after World War II when the need for such a device became critical. Radar systems, though able to detect flying objects, could not distinguish one object from another (or one "blip" from another on a radar screen). The use of transponders was successfully demonstrated during World War II under the system known as "Identification: Friend or Foe (IFF)." Since many aircraft were operating within the radar range, it was essential to identify a friendly blip from an enemy blip. The IFF system consisted of a transceiver at the ground radar station and a transponder on all friendly aircraft. The radar station would continually transmit a radio signal to the aircraft within the radar surveillance area each time the radar antenna pointed to the specific aircraft during a 360-degree cycle. The aircraft would translate the radar station "impulse" or interrogation and automatically transmit back the proper code of the day (or mission). As the radar antenna continued to sweep the sky, it would continue to receive coded signals from all friendly aircraft. If no signal were received or if the code were incorrect, the aircraft would be considered unfriendly.

This system is now in use in all military and commercial aircraft and in most private aircraft. A modified version is in use as a security device. The transponder identifies the protected premises after being interrogated by a central monitoring station.

The system used by the military was very powerful. It utilized large ground antenna and required a room full of computerized electronics. The security systems that function on the same concept use low-powered (about 1 to 1½ watts), small, integrated circuits and omnidirectional antennae. The identifying code is preset before the transponders are installed in the subscriber's building. The power and frequency assignment of the equipment is dedicated by FCC regulations, which allocate frequency and power according to need and in order to avoid interference with other radio communication equipment in the area (the same frequency can be assigned to several stations as long as they are separated by hundreds of miles). The use of very high frequency (VHF) or ultra high frequencies (UHF) may limit the useful distance to 30 miles, but it also eliminates the "skip" problems often associated with low-frequency AM radio (CB band, etc.).

There are two basic types of radio signals — AM (amplitude modulation), where a transmitted sound causes the amplitude, or height of the radio wave to vary. FM (frequency modulation), where the frequency rather than the height is varied to carry the sound. All radio waves may pick up electrical disturbances during transmission but they have a much greater effect on the amplitude than on the frequency. These interference signals remain a part of the AM reception but are mainly ignored by the FM transmission systems. Because AM sound is based on wave amplitude, it is not possible to filter out the electrical static without removing a significant portion of the sound as well. AM reception is susceptable to common disruptions created by lighting, power lines, and neon signs. On the other hand, FM systems are able to filter out the amplitude variations, leaving the reception relatively clear, which is the reason for the popularity of FM systems. AM broadcast waves can actually bend around obstructions and tend to follow the curvature of the earth. The upper atmosphere (ionosphere) reflects AM signals back to earth, which is why some stations can be heard at fairly long distances after dark when the ionosphere layer rises. While FM signals are capable of bending like the AM signal, they can be controlled as a line of sight device, and since they pass through the ionosphere, they do not skip and confuse one signal for another. This advantage also limits their range to 30 miles or less over flat terrain (see Figure 10-7).

**Technical Operation.**    Each set of protected premises require a transponder that, when triggered by the activation of a sensor, notifies the central service of the event. If instead of a transponder (which is basically a combination of a receiver and transmitter), the protected premises has only a transmitter, the system would function in one direction only. This would mean that when an alarm device were activated, the transmitter would send an encoded signal to the controlling central service receiver. If two or more alarms come in simultaneously, the encoding allows for separating the multiple signals. The problem with this system is that there is no way of telling if the transmitter is in working order. It functions as an unsupervised system, and therefore is unacceptable for high-security situations.

The more sophisticated transponder system receives signals from the central station every few seconds and reports back that there is no intrusion. This reaction also indicates that the transmitter is in working order. The time-sharing technique permits the typical radio transmission central service to monitor 500 subscribers over a single transmitter–receiver net-

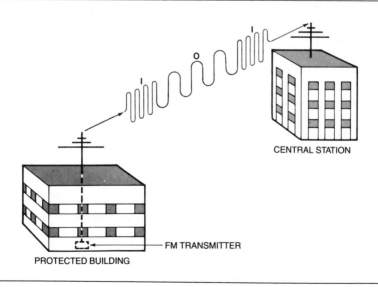

Figure 10-7.   FM transmission.

work. The central service sends 500 identical signals over the omnidirectional antennae one at a time to all subscribers. The returning signal from the protected premises is different for each subscriber, enabling the central station to know whose premises it is interrogating at any particular instant. When the protected premises receive the proper code, they immediately retransmit a condition code back to the central station. Up to eight conditions may be transmitted from each location with most commercially available systems. After this condition code is recorded, the central station goes on to interrogate other premises. The 500 subscribers can transmit special codes, but since the transponder is programmed to do this only when interrogated on a sequential time-sharing basis, the central station knows its exact status because of its position on the sequence cycle. It takes only a few seconds to interrogate all 500 subscribers.

The primary reasons for the slow acceptance of FM radio transmission are the high cost of reliable equipment, the stability of frequency assignments by the FCC, and the fact that the run of the mill alarm installer is unfamiliar with radio transmission. Radio transmission should grow significantly in the 1980s as the equipment becomes less costlier and fixed and permanent frequency assignments and dedicated phone lines become more difficult to obtain.

## CABLE TV

It is predicted by many practitioners in the field that by the 1990s, close to 50 percent of America's households will subscribe to cable TV (a growth rate from 23.5 million homes in 1982 to 52.8 million homes in 1992).[1] With a cable directly linked to a house from a central transmitting station, the homeowner would then have a choice between the telephone connection and a cable connection to monitor the security system.

A two-way interactive cable TV system, via the coaxial cable, would transmit entertainment and other programming signals from the cable headend (downstream communication) and receive signals from the home on the same cable (upstream communication). Information such as intrusion alarm, banking function, etc. may be sent without subscriber action. Two-way CATV works by means of a small home terminal connected to the TV set in the cable subscriber's home that receives data downstream and transmits upstream to the cable headend. The terminals may be equipped to monitor the household's burglar alarm, fire alarm, medical alert, and to provide readings of electric and gas meters. It can then send this information upstream to the cable headend.

The cable system headend computer can be programmed to "sweep over" the cable system every few seconds. In doing so, it can perform a variety of functions, including making a record of which sets are turned on for pay-perviewing, monitoring of system performance, and continuously rolling of interrogating subscribers' security system for the presence of an alarm alert condition. Systems are available that transmit outgoing signals and incoming signals on different bands so that the outgoing alarm signal does not interfere with the incoming TV signal.

The cable security system is in direct competition with the traditional telephone line communication signal with the cable connect offering many advantages over most of the techniques used over phone lines. CATV is a far better communication system than conventional McCulloh Loop circuits and digital dialing concepts, and it is cheaper than the telephone dedicated line. When AT&T is free to enter unregulated markets, it will probably enter the alarm service market but it will have to actively compete with the CATV techniques. With both AT&T and CATV companies entering the field, significant changing should result in security communication technology during the later half of the 1980s.


### SUMMARY

Transmission of the alarm signal is and will continue to be one of the most important phases in the alarm system. Faulty transmission is a major contributing factor to the high false alarm rate that has caused many police departments to ignore, and even ban, certain alarm devices. The customary use of wire to interconnect sensors, control panels, and annunciators provides the most effective transmission technique; however, the world's supply of copper is diminishing and the easy accessibility of phone company connections is slowly disappearing. The constant threat of the phone company to curtail use of dedicated copper wires for alarm use has led to a great many techniques that allow "shared" lines. Time division multiplexing and frequency division multiplexing are slowly growing in popularity, and this shift in technique is being encouraged by the phone company. The growth of radio transmission as an alternative to all types of phone line connections indicates that ingenuity and innovative approaches to security controls are still a major part of the industry. New techniques will be developed as the need arises, and it is predicted that with the growing use of cable television, both phone line connections and radio transmission will be replaced in a few years with this new communication method.

## GLOSSARY

### Multiplexing Terms

*Alarm Hold.* A means of holding an alarm once sensed. The typical magnetic contact does not hold or "latch" and thus the reclosing of a trapped door resets the typical magnetic contact. A hold circuit applied to such a device indicates the door has been opened and continues to until it is reset.

*Balanced Telephone Line.* A telephone line that is floated with respect to ground so that the impedance measured from either side of the line to ground is equal to that of the other side to ground.

*Bandwidth.* The difference between the upper and lower frequency response of a communication channel.

*Bridge.* A means of isolating one transmitter from another so that a failure of one does not affect the others, which is necessary in multiplex systems because transponders are in parallel.

*Carrier.* High-frequency energy that can be modulated by voice or signaling impulses.

*Carrier on Microwave.* A means of transmitting many voice messages on one microwave radio channel. Transmission is point to point by microwave antennae mounted on towers or tall buildings.

*Carrier on Wire.* A means widely used by the telephone company to transmit many voice messages on a single pair of wires. Circuits involving one or more carrier links never evidence d.c. continuity.

*Carrier System.* A means of conveying a number of channels over a single path by modulating each channel on a different carrier frequency and demodulating at the receiving point to restore the signals to their original form.

*Channel.* A path for electrical transmission between two or more stations or channel terminations. A channel can consist of wire, radio waves, or both.

*Code.* In multiplexing, the number identifying a location.

*Communication Channel.* A signaling channel having two or more terminal locations and a suitable information handling capacity depending on characteristics of the system used. One terminal location is the central station and the other terminal location or locations are sources from which are transmitted alarm signals, supervisory signals, trouble signals, and such other signals as the central station is prepared to receive and interpret.

*Control.* Any mechanism that sequences the interrogation of protected site units, resets latched alarms, and performs similar functions.

*Decoder.* The companion device to an encoder (see Encoder).

*D.C. Continuity.* A circuit in which an impressed d.c. voltage induces a d.c. current — a reading on a conventional ohmeter applied across the terminals of a circuit with d.c. continuity will result in a deflection of the meter.

*Demultiplexing.* The process of separating multiplex signals that have been changed in form for the purpose of transmission back to their original form (also known as decoding or demodulating).

*Digital.* Characteristic of data in the form of electrical impulses as applied to representation, storage, or manipulation of data in the form of digital quantities, thus, a digital computer or a digital memory device. Digital refers to discrete, noncontinuous quantities (usually multiples of some elementary unit) as contrasted with continuous quantities.

*Digital Communication.* The transmission of intelligence by the use of encoded numbers — usually uses binary rather than decimal number system.

*Encoder.* The device that provides coding of a signal in response to some input.

*Filter.* An electronic circuit element that reduces interference and unwanted signals, or allows certain desirable signals to pass through.

*Frequency Division.* A means of splitting a channel into subchannels for more efficient use of the channel.

*Frequency Division Multiplexing.* A signaling method characterized by the simultaneous transmission of more than one signal in a communication channel. Signals from one or multiple terminal locations are distinguished from one another by virtue of each signal being assigned to a separate frequency or combination of frequencies.

*Full Duplex.*    A multiplex system that can simultaneously transmit in both directions on a transmission line.

*Half Duplex.*    A multiplex system that can transmit in both directions on a transmission line but not at the same time.

*Hard Wire.*    A colloquialism meaning a circuit with electrical continuity. It is a full copper pair of wires from point A to point B.

*Laser Communication Link.*    Same as a microwave link except that the basic channel is provided by a laser beam rather than a microwave beam.

*Latching.*    A technique for storing an event such as the momentary breaking of a perimeter circuit. The fact that the event has occurred will be indicated until the latched circuit has been reset.

*Line Fault Protection.*    A means of eliminating or reducing the effect of faults that occur on a transmission line such as a telephone circuit. Such faults include momentary losses of transmission due to outages or high noise levels.

*Line Supervision.*    A continuous means of determining that a transmission line is functional.

*McCulloh Loop.*    The original multiplex circuit used in the security business — consists of a series connection of many subscribers via telephone lines. Analogous to party line operation for ordinary telephone service.

*Multiplexing.*    A signaling method using wire path, cable carrier, radio carrier, or combinations of these facilities characterized by the simultaneous and/or sequential transmission and reception of multiple signals in a communication channel including means for positively identifying each such signal.

*Readout.*    A means of displaying an electronically transmitted message in a form meaningful to human intelligence.

*Receiver.*    Any device capable of accepting a message. Examples of messages include the transmission of an alarm from a remote sensor or an "all's well" signal from an unstimulated sensor as well as ordinary voice messages.

*Satellite Station.*   A satellite station is a normally unattended location remote from the central station and linked by communication channel(s) to the central station. Interconnection of signal receiving equipment or communication channel(s) from protected premises with channel(s) to the central station is accomplished at this location. If the link between the satellite station and central station is lost, the satellite station can be operated manually to continue to provide service.

*Sequencer.*   All multifunction terminals have a sequencer. The sequencer will select in sequence the data for each of the functions at the terminal. This includes both data to and from the channel.

*Signal Encoding Device.*   A system component located at the protected premises that will initiate the transmission of an alarm signal, supervisory signal, trouble signal, or other signals the central station is prepared to receive and interpret.

*Simplex.*   A multiplex system that can transmit in only one direction on a transmission line.

*Simultaneous Transmission.*   A full duplex system where transceivers communicate with each other simultaneously.

*Time Division Multiplexing.*   A signaling method characterized by the sequential and noninterfering transmission of more than one signal in a communication channel. Signals from all terminal locations are distinguished from one another by each signal occupying a different position in time with reference to synchronizing signals.

*Time Division Multiplex Channel.*   A path established for a segment of time during which the central station equipment obtains a signal indicating the status of a signal encoding device.

*Time Sharing.*   A means of making more efficient use of a facility by allowing more than one using activity access to the facility on a sequential basis.

*Transmission Medium.*   Essentially the same as a transmission channel when the latter is fully described. Various mediums include telephone, radio, and laser transmissions.

*Transmit-on-Alarm.*   A security device that activates only when triggered. Most security devices are of this nature — however, in one-way multiplexed systems, it is usually impossible to determine whether or not transmit-on-alarm devices are actuated or whether the transmitter has failed or the communication channel is inoperative.

*Transmit-on-Interrogation.*   The response of a security device that stores an alarm until it is interrogated in an appropriate manner. Used in multiplexed systems to avoid the problem of two simultaneous transmissions of alarm by two or more different stations.

*Transmitter–Receiver.*   A device capable of maintaining two-way communication between subscriber premises and the central station.

*Transponder.*   A multiplex alarm transmission system functional assembly located at the protected premises. This assembly is capable of receiving interrogation signals from another location by way of a communication channel and then supplying response signals indicative of the status of the signal encoding devices connected to it.

*Trunk Facility.*   That part of a communication channel connecting two or more leg facilities to a central or satellite station.

*Two-way Radio.*   A radio channel wherein both terminals are equipped with both transmitting and receiving equipments to permit two-way message traffic or conversations.

*Uncompensated Telephone Lines.*   Typically, a standard hard wire pair. Compensation of such a pair involves the addition of electronic components to improve the frequency response of the line and hence its quality of transmission.

*Voice Grade.*   A telephone circuit suitable for transmitting band pass from 300 to 2700 HZ or greater with certain standards of signal level, noise, and interference such that intelligible speech can be transmitted.

## NOTE

1.  "Home-Security — The Impact of Cable TV," published by International Resource Development, Inc., 1982, as quoted in Security Letter, Vol. xii, No. 15, Part II, August 2, 1982.

# APPENDIX

## A DIRECTORY OF SECURITY AND SECURITY RELATED ORGANIZATIONS

Security and security related organizations are growing in numbers and size. Fifteen of the forty-eight organizations listed in this directory are less than 15 years old.

Year of founding is given in parentheses following the organization's name. Membership is approximate as stated. For those wishing further information on any of these groups, write or call the name provided:

*Academy of Security Educators and Trainers*, Inc. Dr. Norman Bottom, President. Indiana University of PA. Dept. of Criminology, 62 9th St., Lucern Mines, PA 15754 (412) 357-2720

*Airport Security Council* (1968) 97045 Queens Blvd., Forest Hills, NY 11374. (212)275-9300. Edward J. McGowan, Executive Director, deals mostly with cargo and related crime losses in the NY/NJ Port Authority area

*American Bankers Association.* John C. Wolff, Associate Director, Insurance and Protection, 1120 Connecticut Ave. NW, Washington, DC 20036. (202)467-4000

*American Polygraph Assn.* (1966) Suite 106, Central Office Park, 5805 Lee Hwy., Chattanooga, TN 37421. (625)894-7358. William L. Bennett, Secretary. Members, 1800

*American Recovery Assn.* (1965) Box 52076, New Orleans, LA 70152. (504)367-0711. Huey Maryonne, Executive Director. Members, 375, repossession companies

*American Society for Amusement Park Security.* Ronald Fussner, Secretary, c/o Cedar Point Amusement Park, Security Office, Sandusky, OH 44870. (419)626-0830

*American Society for Industrial Security* (1955) Suite 651, 2000 K St. NW, Washington, DC 20006. (202)331-7887. Ernest J. Criscouli, Jr., Executive Director. Members, 17,000

*American Society for Safety Engineers.* Judy T. Neel, E.A.E., Executive Director, 850 Busse Hwy., Park Ridge, IL 60068. (312)692-4121

*American Trucking Assn. Security Council.* Clark Martin, Director of Safety and Security, 1616 P St. NW, Washington, DC 20036

*Associated Locksmiths of America.* (1956) 3003 Live Oak St., Dallas, TX 75204. (214)827-1701. Joyce A. Laurie, Executive Director. Members, 6500

*Association of Federal Investigators* (1957) Suite 824, 815 15th Street NW, Washington, DC 20005. (202)347-5500. Ms. M. J. O'Connell, Administrator. Members, 750. Active and retired federal investigators, especially those in preemployment screening

*Association of Former Agents of the U.S. Secret Service* (1970) Box 31073, Washington, DC 20031. (301)894-2115. Floyd M. Boring, Executive Secretary. Members, 300

*Association of Former Intelligence Officers* (1975) Suite 303A, 6723 Whittier Ave., McLean, VA 22101. (703)970-0320. John E. Greaney, Executive Director. Members, 2600

*Aviation Security Assn. of America-International* (1981) Box 17082, Washington, DC 20041. (703)256-7541. James Parker. Members, 50. Composed of FAA security officers and others with an interest in aviation security.

*Bank Administrators Institute.* Keith C. Marshall, 303 South NW Highway, Park Ridge, IL 60068. (312)693-7300

*Committee of National Security Companies.* John J. Horan, Executive Director, 33 N. Fullerton, Mountclair, NJ 07042. (201)783-3838

*Computer Security Institute* (1974) 43 Boston Post Road, Northboro, MA 01532. (617)393-3663. John C. O'Mara, Executive Director. Members, 2200. Not so much an institute, rather a for-profit company that puts on a superior annual meeting on computer security.

*Council of International Investigators.* Richard S. Goldberg, Board Member. c/o Goldberg Detections, Inc., 6427 Roswell Rd., Atlanta, GA 30328. (404)256-2500

*EDP Auditors Assn.* (1969) 373 Schmale Rd., Carol Stream, IL 60187. (312)682-1200. Frederick J. Archer, President. Members, 5500

*Fire Equipment Manufacturers Assn.* (1925) 1230 Keith Bldg., Cleveland, OH 44115. (216)241-7333. Thomas Associates, Inc. Members, 20.

*Independent Armored Car Operators Assn.* (1973) c/o Security Armored Car Service, 1022 South 9th St., St. Louis, MO 32104. (314)231-4030. Ronald Bray, Secretary-Treasurer. Members, 35 companies

*Institute of Internal Auditors, Inc.* Stanley Gross, President, 249 Maitland Ave., Altamonte Springs, FL 32701. (305)830-7600

*International Assn. of Arson Investigators.* Robert May, Executive Secretary, P. O. Box 600, Marlboro, MA 01752. (617) 481-5977

*International Assn. of Campus Law Enforcement Administrators* (1958). Box 98127 Atlanta, GA 30359. (404) 261-8136. James L. McGovern, Executive Director. Members, 700 institutions. College and university security administrators.

*International Assn. of Credit Card Investigators* (1968) 1620 Grant Ave., Novato, CA 94947. (415) 897-8800. D. D. Drummond, Executive Director. Members, 1700 individuals

*International Assn. of Chiefs of Police* (1893) 11 Firstfield Rd., Gaithersburg, MD 20878. (301) 948-0922. Norman Darwick, Executive Director. Members, 12,000. Active and former law enforcement and some members in private security.

*International Assn. of Fire Chiefs.* Donald D. Flin, General Manager, 1329 18th St. NW, Washington, DC 20036. (202) 833-3420

*International Assn. for Hospital Security.* (1968) Box 3776 Merchandise Mart Station, Chicago, IL 60654. Thomas C. Seals, President. Members, 1500

*International Assn. for Identification.* (1915) Box 139 Utica, NY 13503. (315) 732-2897. Walter G. Hoetzer, Secretary-Treasurer. Members, 2500. They are interested in the examination and identification of physical evidence.

*International Aviation Theft Bureau* (1974). 7315 Wisconsin Ave., Bethesda, MD 20014. (301) 951-3866. Robert J. Collins, Executive Director. Acts as a clearinghouse in the identification and recovery of stolen private aircraft and equipment.

*International Assn. of Security Services* (1973) 466 Central St., Northfield, IL 60093. (312) 441-8950. Howard W. Ross, Executive Director. Members, 1000 companies, some direct — others through state associations.

*International Assn. for Shopping Center Security.* Anthony N. Potter, J., CPP, Executive Director, P. O. Box 370247, Miami, FL 33137. (305) 573-3616

*International Educational Security Personnel Assn.* Sylvia Bate, Secretary. P.O. Box 11077, San Diego, CA 92111 or Joe Norwood, President, c/o University of Houston Downtown College, One Main St., Suite 354, Houston, TX 77002. (713) 749-3066

*International Retail Security Assn.* Paul V. Brothers, 946 Sibley Tower, 25 North St., Rochester, NY 14604. (716) 454-3953

*Jewelers Security Alliance of the U.S.* (1883) 6 East 45th St., NY 10017. (212) 687-0328. James B. White, President. Members, 4000

*National Armored Car Carriers Division* (1930) Box 1776, Ramsey, NJ 07446. (201) 825-1655. Jack Taffe, Executive Director. Members, 20 companies. A division of the Contract Carriers Conference-American Trucking Assns.

*National Assn. of Chiefs of Police.* Colonel Fred Pearson, Executive Director, 1000 Connecticut Ave. NW, Suite 9, Washington, DC 20036. (202)293-9088

*National Automobile Theft Bureau* (1912) 10330 S. Roberts Rd., Palos Hills, IL 60482. (312)430-2430. Paul W. Gilliland, President. Members, 425 insurance companies

*National Burglar and Fire Alarm Assn.* (1948) 1101 Connecticut Ave., Washington, DC 20036. (202)857-1120. Michael Brown, Executive Director. Members, 550

*National Council of Investigative and Security Services* (1975) 515 Benfield Rd., Servena Park, MD 21146 (301) 342-6733. Charles Dennis, Executive Director. Members 120 companies

*National Council of School Security Administrators.* (1976) 2 Cedar Street, Newark, NJ 07102. (201)733-8307. Osborne Frazier, Executive Director. Members, 450

*National Crime Prevention Institute* (1976). School of Justice Admn., Shelby Campus, Louisville, KY 40292. (502)588-6987. Richard Mellard, Director. Members, 350, 60 companies. Formerly LEAA sponsored; provides technical exchange

*National Fire Protection Assn.* (1896) Suite 217, 2665 30th St., Santa Monica, CA 90405. (213)450-4141. Members, 100 companies.

*National Safety Council.* Charles Vance, Public Relations Director, 444 N. Michigan Ave., Chicago, IL 60611. (312)527-4800 ext. 510

*Risk and Management Society, Inc.* Ron Judd, Executive Director. 205 East 42nd St., Suite 1504 New York, NY 10017. (212) 286-9292

*Security Equipment Industry Assn.* (1971) Suite 217, 2665 30th St., Santa Monica, CA 90405. (213)450-4141. Members, 100 companies

*Society of Professional Investigators* (1955). 8504 Queens Midtown Expressway, Elmhurst, NY 11373. (212)-335-3257. William Rowland, Secretary. Members, 375. NYC area members

*World Assn. of Detectives.* Norman J. Sloan, Executive Director, P. O. Box 36174, Cincinnati, OH 45236. (513)-554-0500.

# Index